Kaiulani Of Hawaii And The Fall Of Her Kingdom

Kaiulani Of Hawaii And The Fall Of Her Kingdom

Peter W. Noonan

MAGISTRALIS

Ottawa, Canada

"Hawaii is ours. As I look back upon the first steps in this miserable business, and as I contemplate the means used to complete the outrage, I am ashamed of the whole affair."

Former US President Grover Cleveland

". . . we have a saying here – Pau. It means that a thing is finished, that there is no hope for it, that it is dead, that the end has come. It means a great deal for such a little word. Well, do you know when I think of it all, of my country, my flag, my people, my kingdom, that is the word that I must say to myself – PAU."

Princess Kaiulani

Contents

Cast of Characters

Princess Kaiulani, born Victoria Kawekiu Kaiulani Lunalilo Kalaninuiahilapalapa Cleghorn

Crown Princess of Hawaii from 1891

Princess Miriam Likelike, born Miriam Likelike Kekauluohi Keahelapalapa Kapili

Mother of Princess Kaiulani and wife of Archibald Cleghorn

Archibald Scott Cleghorn

Father of Princess Kaiulani and husband of Princess Likelike

Princess Ruth Keelikolani, born Ruth Keelikolani Keanolani Kanahoahoa

Half-sister of King Kamehamha IV and King Kamehameha V, hanai mother to Prince William Pitt Leleiohoku II, and godmother to Princess Kaiulani

King Kalakaua, born David Laamea Kamanakapuu Mahinulani Naloiaehuokalani Lumialani Kalakaua

Monarch of the Hawaiian Islands; brother of Prince Leleiohoku, Princess Likelike, and Princess Liliuokalani, and uncle to Princess Kaiulani

Prince William Pitt Leleiohoku II

Brother of King Kalakaua, Princess Likelike, and Princess Liliuokalani, and uncle to Princess Kaiulani; Crown Prince of Hawaii from 1874 – 1877

Queen Kapiolani, born Julia Kapiolani Napelakapuokakae

Wife of King Kalakaua and Queen Consort of the Hawaiian Islands; aunt to Princess Kaiulani

Queen Liliuokalani born Lydia Liliu Loloku Walania Kamakaeha

Monarch of the Hawaiian Islands and aunt to Princess Kaiulani

John Owen Dominis

Husband of Queen Liliuokalani and uncle to Princess Kaiulani; Lieutenant General of the Hawaiian army, and Governor of Oahu Island

Princess Kekaulike, born Victoria Kuhio Kinoiki Kekaulike
Sister of Queen Kapiolani and mother of Prince David Kawananakoa, Prince Edward Abnel Keliiahonui, and Prince Jonah Kuhio Kalanianaole

Princess Poomaikelani, born Virginia Kapooloku Poomaikelani

Sister of Queen Kapiolani and hanai mother to Prince Edward Abnel Keliiahonui

Prince David, born David Laamea Kahalepouli Kinoiki Kawananakoa

Eldest son of Princess Kekaulike and hanai son of Queen Kapiolani; a member of Queen Liliuokalani's Privy Council, and a reputed suitor of Princess Kaiulani

Prince Edward, born Edward Abnel Keliiahonui

Middle son of Princess Victoria Kinoiki Kekaulike and the hanai son of Princess Poomaikelani

Prince Kuhio, born Jonah Kuhio Kalanianaole

Youngest son of Princess Kekaulike and the hanai son of Queen Kapiolani

Princess Elizabeth, born Elizabeth Kahanu Kaauwai

Wife of Prince Kuhio

Dowager Queen Emma, born Emma Kalanikaumakaamano Kaleleonalani Naea Rooke

Queen Consort of King Kamehameha IV, and electoral opponent of David Kalakau during the 1874 election of a new monarch for the Hawaiian Islands following the death of King Lunalilo

Princess Bernice Pauahi Bishop, born Bernice Pauahi Paki

Wife of prominent banker Charles Reed Bishop and the last of the Kamehameha royal dynasty

Prince Higashifushimi Yorihito, styled earlier Prince Yamashina Yorihito

The head of a cadet branch of the Imperial Family of Japan mooted as a prospective husband for Princess Kaiulani

Elizabeth Lepeka Kahalaunani

Former common law spouse of Archibald Cleghorn and the mother of Princess Kaiulani's half sisters, Helen Cleghorn, Rose Cleghorn, and Annie Cleghorn

Helen Cleghorn

Half-sister of Princess Kaiulani

Rose Cleghorn

Half-sister of Princess Kaiulani

Annie Cleghorn

Half-sister of Princess Kaiulani; she accompanied Princess Kaiulani to Great Britain

Marion Barnes

Princess Kaiulani's first governess; a native of Australia

Gertrude Gardinier

Princess Kaiulani's subsequent governess; a native of the United States

Theophilus (Theo) Harris Davies

Prominent British investor in the Hawaiian sugar industry and the legal guardian of Princess Kaiulani during her education in Great Britain; political advisor to the Princess

Clive Davies

Eldest son of Theo Davies and sometimes mooted as a potential suitor of Princess Kaiulani

George Davies

Youngest son of Theo Davies and sometimes mooted as a potential suitor of Princess Kaiulani

Alice Davies

Daughter of Theo Davies and a friend and travelling companion to Princess Kaiulani

Phebe Rooke

A distant relative of Dowager Queen Emma and governess of Princess Kaiulani during her stay in Brighton, England

Caroline Sharp

Headmistress of the Great Harrowden Hall School for Girls in England attended by Princess Kaiulani

Annie Whartoff

Friend and confident of Kaiulani's in Great Britain; her temporary lady-in-waiting during Kaiulani's trip to America in 1893

Robert Louis Stevenson

The teller of tales and one of the most prominent novelists of the nineteenth century; a sojourner in Hawaii, and a friend of Princess Kaiulani

May Atkinson

A childhood friend of Princess Kaiulani

Maude Wright

A friend and schoolmate of Princess Kaiulani at the Great Harrowden Hall School for Girls

Fiona Jones

A friend of Princess Kaiulani who corresponded with her after the overthrow of the monarchy

Kate de Vida

A childhood friend of Princess Kaiulani

Eva Parker

A childhood friend of Princess Kaiulani; the Princess became ill after attending Eva's wedding on Hawaii Island

Helen Parker

A childhood friend of Princess Kaiulani

Rear Admiral Sir William Wiseman and Lady Wiseman

Friends of Princess Kaiulani in Great Britain

Nevinson William (Toby) de Courcy

Princess Kaiulani's close friend and male confident during her years in Europe

Andrew Adams

A suitor of the Princess after her return to Honolulu

Mr. And Mrs. Bailie Darsie

Friends of Princess Kaiulani and of her father, Archibald Cleghorn, in Scotland

Mrs. Thomas Rain Walker

Wife of the British consul in Honolulu; Princess Kaiulani's guardian during her voyage from Hawaii to Great Britain in 1889

Alice Rix and Miriam Michelson

Reporters for the San Francisco Call who interviewed Princess Kaiulani in San Francisco and Waikiki

Samuel Parker

Father of Princess Kaiulani's friends Eva and Helen Parker; Owner of the Parker Ranch on Hawaii Island where Princess Kaiulani became ill; Foreign Minister in Queen Liliuokalani's last cabinet

Edward C Macfarlane

The Queen's Envoy to the United States following the overthrow of the monarchy in 1893; he held briefs to represent the interests of the Queen and Princess Kaiulani

Colonel George Macfarlane

Hawaiian military officer and a royal household official

Captain Julius Palmer

New England sea captain who served as private secretary to Queen Liliuokalani during her trip to the United States in 1897

Charles B Wilson

Marshal of the Kingdom under Queen Liliuokalani

Colonel Curtis Iaukea
Hawaiian diplomat and a royal household official

Major Sam Nowlein

Commander of Queen Liliuokalani's Royal Guard; advisor to Queen Liliuokalani on the drafting of the new constitution

Captain Henry Berger

Bandmaster of the Royal Hawaiian Band

Dr. John Mott Smith

Hawaiian Minister to the United States

Abraham Hoffnung

Hawaiian Minister to Great Britain

Paul Neumann

Hawaiian attorney and the Queen's Envoy to the United States following the overthrow of the monarchy in 1893

Walter Murray Gibson

King Kalakaua's favoured Premier and Cabinet Minister

Claus Spreckels

American businessman whose interests in Hawaii gave him a predominant political position within the Kingdom during the reign of King Kalakaua

Robert W Wilcox

Hawaiian politician, insurrectionist, and rabble-rouser

John E Bush

Hawaiian politician and journalist

Joseph Nawahi

Hawaiian politician; advisor to Queen Liliuokalani on the drafting of the new constitution

William White

Hawaiian politician; advisor to Queen Liliuokalani on the drafting of the new constitution

Lorrin Thurston

Hawaiian lawyer and conspirator; the architect of the overthrow of the monarchy and the leader of the Hawaiian annexationists

Sandford B Dole

Hawaiian politician and jurist; President of the Provisional Government of

Hawaii established after the overthrow of the monarchy and President of the Republic of Hawaii

Samuel M Damon

Hawaiian businessman and politician

John L Stevens

Controversial American Minister to Hawaii; a key figure in the overthrow of the Hawaiian monarchy who authorized the landing of US troops in Honolulu, recognized the Provisional Government, and proclaimed an American protectorate over Hawaii

James G Blaine

Secretary of State of the United States; he changed US foreign policy from benign support of the Kingdom of Hawaii to active cooperation with local forces seeking the US annexation of Hawaii

Benjamin Harrison

The twenty-third President of the United States 1889-1893; he signalled US support to Lorrin Thurston if he succeeded in the overthrow of the Hawaiian monarchy and then sought the annexation of Hawaii by the United States

Captain Gilbert C Wiltse

The commanding officer of the USS Boston; in command of the US marines and sailors that were were landed in Honolulu during the insurrection in January, 1893

Grover Cleveland

The twenty-second and twenty-fourth President of the United States; an anti-expansionist who received Princess Kaiulani at the White House

James H Blount

Former US Congressman; Special Representative of President Cleveland sent to Hawaii to investigate and report on the causes and circumstances of the overthrow of the monarchy

Albert S Willis

The American Minister to Hawaii during the Cleveland Administration

Henry Cabot Lodge

Republican Senator from Massachusetts and an American imperialist; he sought the annexation of Hawaii by the United States

Captain Alfred Thayer Mahan

The leading American naval theorist of the nineteenth century Captain Mahan strongly favoured the annexation of Hawaii by the United States

Theodore Roosevelt

Assistant Secretary of the Navy during the period preceding the annexation of Hawaii; a strong supporter of the US annexation of Hawaii

William McKinley

The twenty-fifth President of the United States; a supporter of Hawaiian annexation

Harold M Sewall

American Minister to Hawaii; he presided over the ceremony by which the sovereignty of Hawaii was surrendered to the United States in 1898

James H Wodehouse

Longtime resident British Minister to Hawaii; he worked to sustain Hawaiian independence as far as diplomatic neutrality would allow

Hay Wodehouse

Son of the British Minister to Hawaii and brother-in-law to Princess Kaiulani through his marriage to Kaiulani's half-sister Annie Cleghorn

Glossary

The Hawaiian language consists of five vowels and eight consonants for a total of thirteen letters. The written language employs diacritics, such as macrons and glottal stops but for the purposes of this work the Hawaiian words that I have borrowed have been anglicized, and the diacritics have not been used. Thus, when written in Hawaiian the Hawaiian words in this work may appear different. Some Hawaiians did not readily employ diacritics. For instance, Princess Kaiulani did not use the diacritics that are present in the Hawaiian spelling of her name. For the purposes of this work therefore, these are the meanings of the Hawaiian words as used in this text:

alii – a member of the noble class of the Hawaiian Islands

haawi ke aloha – the respectful recognition of other Hawaiians by an *alii*

hanai an informal adoption mechanism practised in Hawaiian society

haole – a foreigner, particularly a white person

hapa-haole – half-foreign; a term applied to Hawaiians of mixed descent

Hawaii Nei – This Hawaii; a term of endearment by Hawaiians for their country

heiau – a Hawaiian temple in the pre-Christian religion of Hawaii

Hee nalu – wave sliding, the Hawaiian expression for surfing

holuku – a popular long one-piece gown worn by women in Hawaii

Hookupu – a gifting ceremony in which Hawaiians presented a gift to an *alii*

Hooulu Lahui – increase the nation; a political slogan used by King Kalakaua

hula – a form of Hawaiian dance

kahili – a feathered standard used by Hawaiian royalty as a mark of distinction

kahuna – a member of the priestly class of the Hawaiian Islands

kapu, (tabu) – a ban or prohibition in the traditional Hawaiian religious beliefs

kipi – a rebel

Kuhina Nui – the vice sovereign of Hawaii between 1819 and 1864; sometimes rendered as Premier

Kukui – *(Aleurites moluccanus)*, the candlenut plant

lanai – a covered porch or verandah

lei – a garland or wreath. An *ilima lei* is one made from the hibiscus plant found in Hawaii (*sida fallax*)

Lei Niho Palaoa a whale tooth pendant

luau – a party, feast

mahele – part or section; the *Great Mahele* was the King's division of Hawaiian lands

mahiole – a helmet crown with an elevated crest that was worn by the higher *alii* at public events, and during wars.

maile – a fragrant vine

Mama Nui – Princess Kaiulani's name for her Hawaiian godmother, Princess Ruth

mana – a spiritual or supernatural force

mele – a chant that is sung

mele inoa – a name chant

makaainana – the class of the common people of the Hawaiian Islands

Onipa – steadfast

paa – topless wrap worn by females in pre-Christian Hawaii

Papa Moi – an expression used by Princess Kaiulani to refer to King Kalakaua

pau, finished, ended, over

pikake – jasmine, a favoured scent of Princess Kaiulani; also a peacock

poni – literally purple but also the religious anointment ceremony of a sovereign in pre-Christian Hawaii

puela, – a triangular device borne as a symbol by ancient Hawaiian chiefs when at sea

puloulou – Hawaiian royal staffs

The Sun-Blessed Kingdom

The Hawaiian Islands lie in the north Pacific Ocean between latitude 18°55' N and 28°27' N and longitude 154°48' W and 178°22' W, and are blessed with a tropical climate moderated by easterly trade winds that give the islands a uniformly pleasant temperature throughout the year, although the topography of the islands often gives rise to micro-climatic differences. The island chain is volcanic, and the process of volcanic island-building can be measured by the tectonic progress of the islands from the south-east to the north-west, with the active volcanic islands lying in the south-east, especially on the island of Hawaii (or the Big Island as it is called by the resident population) and the ancient islands to the north-west, which are now eroded to the point where they are but a shadow of the grand islands they must once have been. The principal islands are clustered towards the south-east, and consist of Niihau, Kauai, Oahu, Molokai, Lanai, Kahoolawe, Maui, and Hawaii. Because of its geographical position the Hawaiian Islands are the most remote land area on the surface of the Earth, and were among the last inhabitable parts of the planet to be occupied by humans.

The total land area of the Hawaiian Islands is approximately 6,423 square miles, and on the island of Hawaii, the largest in the chain, is the tallest mountain on earth measured from its base on the ocean floor. Mauna Kea is 33,482 feet in height, exceeding the height of Mount Everest in the Himalayas, although Mauna Kea only reaches a height above sea level of 13,796 feet – the rest of it is hidden beneath the waves. Hawaii Island is also the centre of the current volcanic activity within the Hawaiian Island chain. The Hualalai, Mauna Loa, and Kilauea volcanoes remain active, and the Big Island continues to grow through volcanic activity to the current day.

Due to its isolation, flora and fauna only gradually accreted to Hawaii over many centuries by drifting across the seas, or by being forced onto Hawaii by storms. However, once established, new flora and fauna evolved in the climate of Hawaii to form many new species of plants, birds, and insects (but only two mammals are native to Hawaii). Lush tropical vegetation became established, and was later supplemented by flora transported to the islands by the original Polynesian settlers.

At first, there were no humans in Hawaii but between the years 200 – 500 AD the first of several waves of settlers arrived in the islands. The original colonists came from the Marquesas, according to the archaeological record, and were later supplemented by settlers from elsewhere in Polynesia, principally from Tahiti. These later migrants proved to be culturally, and perhaps politically dominant over the original Marquesans, and it is Tahitian culture that proved formative in the development of the unique Hawaiian culture. Over time, the Hawaiians developed a hierarchical and feudalistic society of three classes ranging downwards from the *alii*, or noble class, which included kings who controlled parts of the islands, or even entire islands. Below the *alii* were the *kahuna*, or priestly caste. Both the *alii* class and the *kahuna* class were supported by the common people, the *makaainana*, consisting of both tradesmen and craftsmen and including fishers, dancers, carvers, and boat builders, as well as the peasantry, who laboured in agricultural pursuits. Below these three social classes were slaves, who also provided the *kahunas* with their supply of victims for human sacrifice.

All Hawaiians were constrained by the system of *kapu*, or taboo, which regulated the social conduct of each and every class of Hawaiian. The *kapu* system prescribed acceptable conduct in social relations and reinforced the hierarchy of Hawaiian society. Those who violated *kapu* faced severe penalties, often death, even for very minor transgressions. However, a wrongdoer could be absolved of the sin of their transgression by reaching a recognized sanctuary before the penalties of a *kapu* transgression could be enforced upon them. Despite the limitations imposed by the *kapu* system, the Hawaiians developed a sophisticated culture that embraced fine art, dance, and theatre, as well as competitive games and recreational activities. In both numbers, and the level of societal sophistication, the Hawaiians were the greatest of the Polynesian peoples.

Into this verdant paradise in January, 1778, a strange sight appeared to the residents of Oahu Island. The white sails of two ships appeared on the horizon. They were *HMS Discovery* and *HMS Resolution* under the command of Captain James Cook of the Royal Navy of Great Britain on a voyage of exploration. Cook and his ships eventually made a landfall on the island of Kauai where they were welcomed by the local population. Cook's expedition was the first confirmed European contact with the Hawaiian Islands, although there is speculation that Spanish mariners may have had some earlier contact with the inhabitants of Hawaii on one of their regular passages between Mexico and Manila, in the Philippines.[1] Cook was well received on his first visit to Hawaii but on a later visit to Hawaii Island he encountered difficulties over the theft of a boat belonging to his ship, and when he tried to retrieve it by force Cook was killed by the Hawaiians. Hawaii was now firmly on the world map however, and soon other visitors came from Europe, and from the new United States of America, to a place that was beginning to be called the paradise of the Pacific.

During the early period of western contact visitors to Hawaii discovered that there was no overarching political structure in the islands. Rather, one island, or sometimes a group of islands, would be under the control of a local king, which necessitated negotiations by westerners with more than one political entity within the islands. Eventually, four competing island kingdoms were established within the Hawaiian Islands chain. Hitherto, it had not been possible for one king to conquer the entire island chain, or even most of it, but western technology held out the promise of a decisive military advantage and a man of impressive capabilities, Kamehameha, of Hawaii Island, quickly perceived the utility of the new western technology. Through a series of wars marked by his ability to perceive and take advantage of the military weakness of his rivals, and with guile, treachery, and bluff, Kamehameha consolidated his control over most of the Hawaiian Islands by 1795, the year in which he established the Kingdom of Hawaii. By 1810 he had obtained control of the remaining islands and was the master of Hawaii, as King Kamehameha I, often referred to as Kamehameha the Great, the first King of a united Hawaiian Kingdom.

The constitutional structure of the new kingdom that was created in

1795, maintained the feudal structure of Hawaiian society, although a sort of Privy Council was created to advise the King, and it was filled with five chiefs who had long aided Kamehameha in his wars of conquest. Those Councillors were routinely consulted with respect to all major state decisions taken by King Kamehameha.[2] A younger man, also a chief, was appointed as an executive to assist the King in the administration of the kingdom. Another influential person who was always at the side of the king was the King's favourite consort Kaahumanu. To maintain his control over the neighbouring islands governors were appointed by the King on each of the populated Hawaiian islands. The public law of the kingdom remained the *kapu* system, anchored in the constellation of Hawaiian gods that formed the religious cosmology of the Hawaiians.[3] Thus, the *kapu* system continued to be the glue that held together Hawaiian society. At the apex of the Hawaiian kingdom, Kamehameha I ruled as an absolute monarch, reinforced by the *kapu* system, as there was no constitutional restriction on his powers. The constitution of Hawaii at the time, such as it was, was entirely of an oral construction, and the King had a great latitude both with respect to the interpretation of his powers, and for the creation of any necessary constitutional innovations.

Preserving the sovereignty of the Kingdom was the overarching public issue for the King and the *alii* of Hawaii. To protect their sovereignty the Hawaiians adopted a policy of westernization, with hopes of obtaining foreign recognition for their Kingdom. King Kamehameha is credited with authorizing the Hawaiian national flag, which incorporated the British Union flag in the canton, and alternating red, white, and blue stripes in the fly (the original nine stripes were later reduced to eight in 1845 – one stripe for each of the eight principal islands in the chain). Kamehameha the Great closely aligned his foreign policy with Great Britain and even purported to cede the islands to a later British explorer, Captain Vancouver, a cession that the British Government never ratified, preferring that the islands remain separate.

Upon Kamehameha's death in May, 1819, his favourite consort, Kaahumanu, took advantage of the flexibility provided by an oral constitution to create a place for herself in the continuing administration of the kingdom by presiding over the accession ceremony for Kamehameha's heir, Prince Liholiho, and stating in the accession proclamation that ". . . we two [i.e., Kaahumanu and Liholiho] shall share in the rule over the land" a declaration to which the new King acquiesced. At the age of 22, Liholiho was ill-equipped to suddenly take the place of the absolute monarch that had sired him, and Kaahumanu, an intelligent and ambitious woman, saw an opportunity to provide a new role for herself as the first occupant of a new political office in the Kingdom, the *Kuhina Nui*. The role of the *Kuhina Nui* is sometimes equated with the role of the Premier in the King's cabinet but it should be more accurately described as the vice-sovereign, a subordinate but powerful position in the government of the Kingdom. Although Kaahumanu purported to honour the express wishes of the late King in establishing the office of *Kuhina Nui*, there was no independent verification of Kamehameha's wishes before his death concerning the future constitutional arrangements in the Kingdom.

Liholiho took the regnal name of Kamehameha II, beginning a naming tradition that would be followed by his successors to the Hawaiian throne during the Kamehameha dynasty. King Kamehameha II had a very sheltered upbringing as a child, and he was unsure of his ability to govern the kingdom so he relied on

Kaahumanu, for political guidance. Kaahumanu had one important policy goal for Hawaii from the outset of Kamehameha II's reign, and that was to abolish the ancient *kapu* system. With the assistance of Keopuolani, who was Kamehameha II's mother, Kaahumanu pressed the King to make this significant policy change. It is unclear why Kaahumanu desired to overthrow the *kapu* system but western contact had produced a great culture shock to the Hawaiian cosmology and the clear superiority of western technology, and the evident imperviousness of westerners to punishment by the Hawaiian gods for breaches of *kapu*, no doubt undermined the traditional belief structure amongst perceptive Hawaiians. Nevertheless, the abolition of the *kapu* system carried with it a significant risk to the Kingdom because the *kapu* system supported the constitutional structure of the state.

King Kamehameha II was hesitant to abolish the *kapu* system[4] but Kaahumanu was insistent and, reluctantly, the King agreed to do as she wished. In November, 1819, at a great feast the King publicly broke *kapu* by dining with women, and afterwards the *Kuhina Nui*, Kaahumanu, consigned the temples and statuary of the traditional Hawaiian cosmology to destruction.[5] The abolition of the traditional Hawaiian cosmology, which had been consistently upheld by King Kamehameha the Great, caused consternation and a brief rebellion in the Kingdom but the royal government was able to suppress the revolt and to restore order. Nevertheless, there was now a vacuum in Hawaiian life that raised the threat of chaotic social disorder in the future.

Coincidentally, however, while Kaahumanu was abolishing the *kapu* system a society of New England protestant missionaries were sailing from the United States to Hawaii to proselytise the Christian faith to the inhabitants of the islands. On March 20, 1820, they arrived at Hawaii Island, the first of twelve companies of missionaries that would arrive in Hawaii between 1820 and 1848, to begin a ministry that would shape the culture and politics of the Hawaiian Islands throughout the remainder of the nineteenth century. The missionaries who preached to the indigenous people of Hawaii were initially sponsored and associated with the American Board of Commissioners for Foreign Missions, and their intimate involvement with the indigenous population, and the local government, led to their obtaining positions in the cabinets and departments of the early Hawaiian state. A separate missionary group, the American Seamen's Friends Society, also sent missionaries to Hawaii, among them Samuel C Damon, whose family would become prominent in the later days of the Kingdom. However, the latter missionary group only ministered to the religious needs of western mariners whose ships called at the Hawaiian Islands, and they played no substantial role in the early Hawaiian Government.[6]

The missionaries obtained an important ally in their cause to convert the Hawaiian people when Kaahumanu fell ill and was attended by the wife of one of the missionaries. The superior western medicines, and the immunity to disease that many people from the west displayed contributed to the significant cultural shock experienced by Hawaiian society, and encouraged the abandonment of the old beliefs that had long sustained Hawaiians. As Kaahumanu gradually warmed to Christianity, other *alii* began to accept the new religion, and subsequently so did other Hawaiians, until eventually the kingdom became Christian in its religious practices. For the ensuing twenty-five years the missionaries would supply the predominant Caucasian influence in Hawaiian affairs. The missionaries also brought other benefits to Hawaii, most importantly, the creation of a written version of the Hawaiian language based on an alphabet of twelve (originally seventeen) letters, and Hawaiians developed a near universal literacy.[7] The Hawaiians assimilated the moral values of the west from the missionaries, and became wiser in their commercial transactions with visiting western ships to the point where they could no longer be taken advantage of in commercial transactions with sailors. However, the missionaries, with their austere and chastened outlook on life, also took away many of the activities that brought joy to the Hawaiian people, and in that way they significantly damaged the vibrancy of the indigenous culture.

Both King Kamehameha the Great and King Kamehameha II followed a foreign policy of maintaining close relations with Great Britain. As he gained greater exposure to the arts of government King Kamehameha II evinced a desire to visit London, and to meet King George IV of Great Britain. Accordingly, he embarked on a voyage to Great Britain with his Queen and left the government in the hands of the *Kuhina Nui*, Kaahumanu, and the King's Chief Minister Kalanimoku, or Billy Pitt, as he liked to be called. While King Kamehameha II was at sea Kaahumanu and Kalanimoku issued proclamations establishing a Hawaiian legal code modelled on the Christian teachings of the missionaries. In this way, a new religious-based legal system following Christian theology was put in place to replace the discredited *kapu* system, and the new western system provided the underlying values for the future constitutional evolution of the island kingdom.

On his voyage to England, King Kamehameha II stopped briefly at Rio de Janeiro, the capital of the Empire of Brazil, where the Hawaiian ship was received with a 21 gun salute, and the King of Hawaii was hosted and entertained by the Emperor of Brazil, Dom

Pedro I. This was the first meeting of a Hawaiian monarch with the sovereign of another state, and it was an important event in the international recognition of Hawaii as an independent country. The two monarchs exchanged gifts, King Kamehameha II giving his host a Hawaiian feather cloak, and receiving from Dom Pedro a fine sword in return.[8]

While the King was away, trouble occurred at home when a rebellion broke out on the island of Kauai, and *Kuhina Nui* Kaahumanu was compelled to suppress the rebellion by force. Afterwards, Kauai was treated as a conquered province of the Kingdom, and the special status that the island had previously enjoyed, as a result of the peaceful merger of the former Kingdom of Kauai with the Kingdom of Hawaii, disappeared.[9]

Arriving, rather unexpectedly, in Great Britain in the spring of 1824, the Hawaiian royal party was treated with courtesy and respect by the British government, and the King and his retainers toured the capital and were hosted at receptions in their honour. Unfortunately, in a harbinger of a tragedy that would fall upon the Hawaiian people as a whole throughout the nineteenth century, a number of the party, including the King and Queen, contracted measles and the royal party did not have any immunity to such western diseases. The disease took a terrible toll, killing both the Queen and her bereaved King, who succumbed to the disease on May 14, 1824. The rest of the Hawaiian party recovered from the illness and the ranking chief within the remaining party subsequently met with King George IV on behalf of the Hawaiian government. The King assured the Hawaiians that Britain would aid the Kingdom of Hawaii if other countries sought to take the islands but that Britain itself would not take forcible possession of Hawaii.[10] Furthermore, the British government agreed to appoint a consul to Hawaii and so for the first time, the Kingdom of Hawaii established a formal diplomatic relationship with a western power.

The bodies of the King and Queen, together with the surviving members of the Hawaiian delegation returned to Honolulu in May, 1825, following which the royal couple received a Christian funeral service. On June 6, 1825, an Accession Council convened and proclaimed the accession to the throne of Kauikeaouli, the younger brother of the late King, who took the regnal name of King Kamehameha III. However, as the new King was only nine years old, the *Kuhina Nui*, Kaahumanu, became the Regent of Hawaii, and the Chief Minister, Kalanimoku, was appointed as the personal guardian of the young King.

The early years of King Kamehameha III's reign were tension-filled as Honolulu and Lahaina became important provisioning ports in the Pacific whaling trade, and an influx of rabble-rousing sailors conflicted with the insistent moral standards propagated by the missionaries, leaving Hawaiian officials in an unenviable middle position between them. There were also port calls by the fast clipper ships that engaged in the China trade, including the *Sovereign of the Seas*, which was especially noted for making a record-breaking passage between Honolulu and New York. Between the missionaries, and the whaling industry, Hawaii of the 1830's became culturally influenced in a profound way by New England.

Kaahumanu continued to administer the kingdom as Regent for King Kamehameha III until her death in 1832. She was followed in the offices of *Kuhina Nui* and Regent by Kinau, a half-sister to the King. The Council of Chiefs, first established by King Kamehameha

11

the Great continued to function as an advisory body to the executive officers of the kingdom, an early form of the Privy Council of Hawaii. The missionary influence remained strong, and many younger Hawaiians became well educated by the standards of the day.

As with Kaahumanu and King Kamehameha II, the *Kuhina Nui* continued to act as a check on the unbridled powers of the King, and there were some heated policy disputes between Kinau and King Kamehameha III as he grew into manhood. Hawaii was a country much different than the Anglo-Saxon countries in one particular respect, the degree to which political space existed for women to participate in the public life of their country. In Hawaii, female *alii* were as highly respected as the male *alii* and the leading women in society often possessed a higher *mana* (i.e., spiritual force) than their male compatriots, giving them both a spiritual and a political base of power.[11] As such, there was an acceptance of women in significant political roles in the Kingdom of Hawaii. Several of the Chiefesses were appointed to the House of Nobles, the upper house of Parliament that was created by King Kamehameha III, during the reigns of the monarchs of the Kamehameha dynasty, among them Laura Konia, the *hanai* (i.e., adoptive) mother of the future Queen Liliuokalani.[12] Four women, Kaahumanu, Kinau, Kekauluohi, and Victoria Kamamalu served as *Kuhina Nui*, the most powerful post in the Hawaiian Government next to the Sovereign. Female *alii* possessed of great *mana* and who coupled that with intelligence, willpower, and competence, could rise high in the government of the early Hawaiian state.

Women were also appointed to the Privy Council of Hawaii, as advisors to the King. Among the several women appointed to the

King's Privy Council was Princess Kaiulani's godmother, Princess Ruth Keelikolani, whom Kaiulani fondly referred to as her *Mama Nui*. Princess Ruth served on the Privy Council of King Kamehameha V. She was an imposing figure to all who knew her. One of the last of the Kamehameha dynasty, she was over six feet tall and weighed an imposing 400 pounds. Possessed of an imperious personality she could be intimidating to people of a lesser social status. There is a story that during the eruption of the Mauna Loa volcano in 1881, Ruth and a small party journeyed to the scene of the eruption, which was then endangering the town of Hilo, on Hawaii Island. Ruth prayed and chanted, challenging the volcano goddess, Pele. She kept a solitary vigil before the lava front during the night and the next morning when her attendants came for her the lava flow had stopped.[13] The story, probably apocryphal, nevertheless reflects the strength of character of this remarkable Hawaiian royal woman.

Female *alii* were also appointed as Governors (often styled Governesses) of the individual island territories of the Kingdom of Hawaii. There were four such territories, Kauai (including Nihau), Oahu, Maui (including Molokai, Lanai, and Kahoolawe) and Hawaii Island. The appointment of women as Governors was most striking in relation to Hawaii Island, where five of the last seven governors to hold office during the monarchy were women, including Kaiulani's godmother, Princess Ruth, and Kaiulani's mother, Princess Likelike, who was Governor of Hawaii in 1879-80.

Perhaps the most striking example of the political equality of high-born Hawaiian royal women with their male counterparts concerned the eligibility for the Hawaiian throne itself. In the reign of King Kamehameha III a Chief's Children's School, later called the Royal

School, was established to educate a select group of young Hawaiians whom the King and high *alii* had determined were potentially suitable for ascension to the throne. On June 29, 1844, the King, with the advice of leading Chiefs of the realm, appointed a group of students with first rights to the throne and that list, supplemented by one or two more designations from 1847, formed the pool of candidates for the Hawaiian throne throughout the nineteenth century. The complete list of candidates was equally divided between males and females: [14]

Male Candidates	Female Candidates
Moses Kekuaiwa	Jane Loeau
Alexander Liholiho*	Abigail Maheha
James Kaliokalani	Mary Paaaina
David Kalakaua*	Lydia Kamakaeha*
Lot Kamehameha*	Bernice Pauahi
William C. Lunalilo*	Elizabeth Kekaaniau
Peter Y. Kaeo	Emma Rooke
William Kinau Pitt	Victoria Kamamalu

*Denotes a person who ascended the throne as King or Queen.

From that list would be drawn five Sovereigns of Hawaii,[15] two heiresses apparent,[16] a *Kuhina Nui*[17] and a Queen Consort.[18] Emma Rooke was particularly interesting because she was not only the Queen Consort of Hawaii during the reign of her husband, King Kamehameha IV, she also stood for election to the throne when it became vacant in 1874, a full 142 years before the consort of a former US President would stand for election to the presidency, the highest office in the United States of America.

As *Kuhina Nui*, Kinau was heavily influenced by the missionaries, and by Christian principles, while the King was more libertarian in outlook. In particular, Kinau took a hard line against attempts by Roman Catholic missionaries from France to establish a Catholic mission and to proselytize in Hawaii. In part, the issue concerning the Catholic missionaries was political. Two prominent *alii*, Boki and Liliho, who were opposed to the government, sided with the Roman Catholic missionaries, which motivated the government to suppress the Catholic mission to avoid a threat to their political control of the country.[19] However, the attempted suppression of the Catholic mission led to an episode of gunboat diplomacy, as France quickly despatched a warship to Honolulu to force equal treatment for French catholic missions in Hawaii with the American protestant missions. The *Kuhina Nui* was forced to submit to the French demands, and to grant religious toleration to Roman Catholics, under the threat of French force, a decision that was subsequently ratified by King Kamehameha III.

The three major powers in the Pacific at the time, Great Britain, France, and the United States, maintained a wary concern that one or the other of them would attempt to seize Hawaii. In 1827 the despatch to the Pacific by the United States of the 92-gun ship of the line USS *North Carolina* caused the Royal Navy's Rear Admiral

Sir Graham Eden Hammond, commander in chief on the navy's South American station, to record: "These Yankees are sly dogs and I suspect they have some intention of seizing upon the Sandwich Islands."[20] But the USS *North Carolina* confined its operations to South American waters, and never approached Hawaii.

Conflict with western powers raised concerns about the constitutional structure of the government, primarily owing to the fact that Hawaii continued to have an unwritten constitution. An early initiative to modernize the Hawaiian political institutions led to the development of a written constitution. A missionary, Reverend William Richards, was appointed as an advisor to the King and he worked with a number of educated Hawaiians to draft a declaration establishing the rule of law, and the rights of Hawaiians in 1839, including property rights, and religious toleration in the country. That was followed by a formal written constitution in 1840, that established representative government in the islands. As a result, the Kingdom of Hawaii became a constitutional monarchy, with power divided between the Sovereign, the *Kuhina Nui*, the chiefs, who now constituted the House of Nobles, and an Assembly that was elected, in a rather informal manner, by enfranchised Hawaiians. A Privy Council to advise the Sovereign was also created in 1845. Executive administration was carried out by a Cabinet consisting of the *Kuhina Nui*, as Premier, who also took the post of Minister of the Interior. Other cabinet officers consisted of a Minister of Foreign Affairs, an Attorney-General, a Minister of Finance and (briefly) a Minister of Public Instruction.

A Supreme Court staffed by trained lawyers, mostly in the Anglo-American common law tradition, was established in 1841, and John Ricord, who was appointed Attorney-General in 1844, established courts of chancery, probate, and admiralty, and helped to adapt British constitutional principles to Hawaiian circumstances. William Lee, who became Chief Justice in 1847, created a code of criminal law by following precedents from the American states of Massachusetts and Louisiana.[21]

Increasing penetration of the Pacific region by western powers concerned the Hawaiian Government and efforts were undertaken at mid-century to secure international recognition for the independence of the Kingdom of Hawaii. Around this time, Sir George Simpson, the powerful and autocratic Governor of the Hudson's Bay Company, arrived from Canada on a tour of the Hawaiian Islands. The 'Little Emperor', as he was called in Canada, was the absolute master of a vast empire of Canadian wilderness that incorporated the colonies of Rupert's Land and the Northwestern Territory, where Simpson's word was virtually law, and where he brooked no disobedience to his authority.[22] The Hudson's Bay Company had been present in the Hawaiian Islands since 1830, mostly trading in lumber and provisions from the Pacific coast of North America. Simpson became interested in the diplomatic recognition project being promoted by the Hawaiian Government. He feared that a loss of independence by Hawaii would lead to its annexation by France or the United States, neither of which would be beneficial to the Company's business interests in the islands.[23] Simpson advised the Hawaiian Government to send commissioners to three of the great powers, Great Britain, France, and the United States, seeking the establishment of formal diplomatic relations with the Kingdom. The Hawaiian Government took his advice and despatched three commissioners, two to Washington, who were afterwards to cross the Atlantic to London, and Simpson himself, who went to directly to London by crossing Siberia, after first stopping at Alaska.[24]

Meanwhile, a festering dispute over a land claim between the government and the British consul in Honolulu, Richard Charlton, finally erupted and led Charlton to leave for London to seek redress for his claim, and for those of other British subjects in Hawaii, before formal diplomatic recognition was established between the two kingdoms. Charlton left the British consulate in the charge of Alexander Simpson, an estranged relative of Sir George Simpson.

As a result of previous reports about trouble facing British subjects in Hawaii the commander of the British Pacific squadron at Valparaiso, Chile, despatched a frigate under the command of Captain Lord Paulet to Honolulu. Arriving in Hawaii, and being unfamiliar with its local politics Paulet took advice from Acting Consul Simpson, who only succeeded in inflaming the situation. Negotiations between the British and the Hawaiians began and under the malign influence of Alexander Simpson Paulet eventually decided to take possession of the Hawaiian Islands for Great Britain. Faced with a British determination to annex his kingdom, and the overwhelming power of the Royal Navy, King Kamehameha III and his advisors reluctantly agreed to cede Hawaii to Great Britain. A formal cession ceremony took place on February 25, 1843, whereby the King conceded sovereignty to Great Britain but assured his people that he would continue to make every effort to restore the independence of Hawaii. From February to July 1843, the royal government of Hawaii governed the nation under the supervision of a British commission but late in July Admiral Richard Thomas, the British Pacific squadron commander, arrived in Honolulu from Valparaiso after receiving word of Paulet's actions at Honolulu.

Admiral Thomas immediately took steps to restore Hawaiian independence, after first obtaining assurances from the King that the rights of British subjects would continue to be respected, and that they would be treated equally with other foreigners. On July 31, 1843, the British flag was hauled down over Honolulu and the Hawaiian flag was restored to its rightful place. At a thanksgiving service that followed King Kamehameha III uttered the words that subsequently became the national (and now the state) motto of Hawaii "*Ua mau ke ea o ka aina I ka pono*" ("The life of the land is perpetuated by righteousness").

Meanwhile, the Hawaiian commissioners sent abroad were continuing their efforts to seek recognition for the independence of Hawaii in the capitals of the great powers, and were oblivious to what had happened in Honolulu. In Europe they obtained success – primarily because none of the great powers wanted to embroil themselves in potential conflicts with other powers by conquering Hawaii. On his way to London Sir George Simpson stopped at Brussels and in company with the other Hawaiian commissioners who had now arrived in Europe he went to see King Leopold who was the influential widower of the late Princess Charlotte, at one time the Heiress Apparent to the British throne. Leopold was also influential with the British Government, owing to the fact that he was also the uncle of Prince Albert, Queen Victoria's consort. King Leopold agreed to recognize the independence of Hawaii, on behalf of Belgium.[25] Next, Simpson and the other commissioners stopped in Paris where Foreign Minster Guizot also agreed to extend diplomatic recognition to the Kingdom of Hawaii on behalf of France. Finally, in London Simpson made his pitch on behalf of Hawaii for British recognition to the Foreign Minister, Lord Aberdeen. On April 1st Lord Aberdeen advised that, "Her Majesty's

Government are willing and have determined to recognize the independence of the Sandwich Islands under their present sovereign."[26] His mission accomplished, Sir George Simpson sailed for Canada on April 3rd.[27]

Meanwhile, Richards, and Haalilio, the two commissioners sent to Washington from Honolulu, had also obtained some success from the United States. In January,1843, the United States, while not formally recognizing Hawaii, stated through Secretary of State Daniel Webster that: "The United States have regarded the existing authorities in the Sandwich Islands as a Government suited to the condition of the people, and resting on their own choice; and the President is of opinion that the interests of all commercial nations require that that Government should not be interfered with by foreign powers . . ."[28]

President Tyler thereupon enunciated the Tyler Doctrine by which the United States pledged to support the independence of Hawaii, and to forestall any European power from obtaining possession, or a colonial advantage, with respect to the island kingdom. In his subsequent Message to Congress the President stated:

"December 30, 1842

To the Senate and House of Representatives of the United States:

I communicate herewith to Congress copies of a correspondence which has recently taken place between certain agents of the Government of the Hawaiian or Sandwich Islands and the Secretary of State.

The condition of those islands has excited a good deal of interest, which is increasing by every successive proof that their inhabitants are making progress in civilization and becoming more and more competent to maintain regular and orderly civil government. They lie in the Pacific

20

Ocean, much nearer to this continent than the other, and have become an important place for the refitment and provisioning of American and European vessels.

Owing to their locality and to the course of the winds which prevail in this quarter of the world, the Sandwich Islands are the stopping place for almost all vessels passing from continent to continent across the Pacific Ocean. They are especially resorted to by the great number of vessels of the United States which are, engaged in the whale fishery in those seas. The number of vessels of all sorts and the amount of property owned by citizens of the United States which are found in those islands in the course of the year are stated probably with sufficient accuracy in the letter of the agents.

Just emerging from a state of barbarism, the Government of the islands is as yet feeble, but its dispositions appear to be just and pacific, and it seems anxious to improve the condition of its people by the introduction of knowledge, of religious and moral institutions, means of education, and the arts of civilized life.

It can not but be in conformity with the interest and wishes of the Government and the people of the United States that this community, thus existing in the midst of a vast expanse of ocean, should be respected and all its rights strictly and conscientiously regarded; and this must also be the true interest of all other commercial states. Far remote from the dominions of European powers, its growth and prosperity as an independent state may yet be in a high degree useful to all whose trade is extended to those regions; while its near approach to this continent and the intercourse which American vessels have with it, such vessels constituting five-sixths of all which annually visit it, could not but create dissatisfaction on the part of the United States at any attempt by another power, should such attempt be threatened or feared, to take possession of the islands, colonize them, and subvert the native Government. Considering, therefore, that the United States possesses so large a share of the intercourse with those islands, it is deemed not unfit to make

21

the declaration that their Government seeks, nevertheless, no peculiar advantages, no exclusive control over the Hawaiian Government, but is content with its independent existence and anxiously wishes for its security and prosperity. Its forbearance in this respect under the circumstances of the very large intercourse of their citizens with the islands would justify this Government, should events hereafter arise to require it, in making a decided remonstrance against the adoption of an opposite policy by any other power. Under the circumstances I recommend to Congress to provide for a moderate allowance to be made out of the Treasury to the consul residing there, that in a Government so new and a country so remote American citizens may have respectable authority to which to apply for redress in case of injury to their persons and property, and to whom the Government of the country may also make known any acts committed by American citizens of which it may think it has a right to complain." [29]

After negotiations resolved the outstanding issues faced by British subjects in Hawaii (mostly in favour of the position taken by the Hawaiian Government, although Charlton's land claim was conceded) a joint declaration was issued by the Kingdoms of Great Britain and France on November 28, 1843, which recognized the independence of the Hawaiian Islands:

"Her Majesty the Queen of the United Kingdom of Great Britain and Ireland and His Majesty the King of the French, taking into consideration the existence in the Sandwich Islands of a government capable of providing for the regularity of its relations with foreign nations, have thought it right to engage reciprocally to consider the Sandwich Islands as an independent state, and never take possession, either directly or under the title of a protectorate, or under any other form, of any part of the territory of which they are composed . . .".[30]

Hawaii was thus formally admitted to the community of nations by those declarations but the treaties subsequently entered into by

22

the western powers with Hawaii were unequal treaties, advancing western interests at Hawaii's expense. The first fair and honourable treaty that was negotiated by Hawaii was a treaty of recognition between Hawaii and Denmark, that was negotiated with Danish Captain Bille of the Danish corvette *Galathea* on October 19, 1846.[31]

After 1843, the Hawaiian government grew in sophistication, and many foreigners became naturalized Hawaiians and, obtained positions in the Kingdom's public administration. The role of the King became more dignified, and was magnified by westernized royal pomp and circumstance, and he began to interact with foreign representatives and native Hawaiians more formally, as at levées. The capital city of the Hawaiian Kingdom moved from Lahaina on Maui to Honolulu on Oahu in 1844.

Another great change came in 1848 when the Great *Mahele* revolutionized landholding in Hawaii. A feudal landholding system under which grants from the King or the *alii* to commoners remained revocable titles was unacceptable to western immigrants, who were beginning to make a greater claim to the Hawaiian economy, and they pressed for change. Foreign residents in Hawaii who desired to own land wished to obtain a fee simple title under common law principles. Under the Great *Mahele* a major land division occurred. A Land Commission converted oral titles to land into written titles. Then a major division was made of lands that belonged to the King from those that belonged to *alii*, who were required to file formal claims with the Land Commission to obtain their individual land titles. Next, the King divided the lands that were allocated to him into the so-called Crown lands that belonged to him personally, and a larger portion which became government lands held separately by the government from the Crown. In 1850, commoners in Hawaii were granted fee simple titles to the lands that they occupied, and used, provided that they submitted their claims to the Land Commission. Finally, foreign residents were permitted to obtain fee simple titles in 1850, a change that was initially much opposed by ordinary Hawaiians, and by the legislature.[32]

The western settlers hoped to promote economic development through the infusion of foreign capital in Hawaii by promoting the Great *Mahele* but they also envisaged social change by encouraging the development of an indigenous middle class, as had occurred in western nations. Of course, they also had their own interests in mind, as they wished to obtain real estate for themselves, but by and large the key promoters within the Hawaiian Government of the Great *Mahele* hoped to improve the economic conditions of the Kingdom for all of its members. The *alii* and other members of the Hawaiian elite also favoured the Great *Mahele* because they could monetize an important asset – land, which they could not previously monetize. The impetus for change from the Hawaiian perspective can be traced to the acquisition of temporary sovereignty over the islands by Lord Paulet for Great Britain, and the general aggrandizement of European powers that was now beginning to take place in the South Pacific Ocean. Many indigenous Hawaiians doubted that the independence of the Kingdom could be maintained, and so they sought to convert fixed assets, such as land, into more liquid assets, such as money, lest they be deprived of anything of value by the force of western colonialism.[33]

As the country developed the need to modernise the constitution of 1840 became more pressing and, in 1852, a new constitution was proclaimed. Under the 1852 constitution the most important provisions were:

- The legislature would consist of two houses, sitting separately,

- Both the King and the *Kuhina Nui* had to sign legislation enacted by the legislature in order for it to become law,

- The members of the House of Nobles, numbering 30 were to be appointed by the King for life,

- The members of the lower house would be elected by universal male suffrage,

- The Privy Council was established as a body separate from the House of Nobles,

- The Supreme Court would consist of the Chief Justice of Hawaii, and two Associate Justices,

- There would be four circuit courts, and a petty judge for each district in the country.[34]

The new constitution also prohibited slavery within the Kingdom, and provided for the manumission of any slave who entered the territory of the Kingdom. It also created a mechanism for judicial references to the Supreme Court, whereby the government could obtain an advisory opinion from the senior level of the judiciary. Although of little use during the Kamehameha dynasty, it was frequently resorted to during the subsequent reigns of King Kalakaua, and Queen Liliuokalani.[35]

As the American policy of Manifest Destiny reached a crescendo in the 1840's and 1850's, and talk of American filibusters arriving from California to overthrow the government of the Kingdom abounded in Honolulu, a weary King Kamehameha III began to contemplate the possibility of an American annexation. Renewed tensions with France were also occurring, and the Kingdom was subjected to bullying by the French navy in the Pacific. The weary King authorized tentative annexation negotiations with the United States but his policy was strongly opposed by the Heir Apparent, Prince Alexander Liholiho, a Hawaiian nationalist with an anti-American outlook owing to his first-hand experience of American racial prejudice during an official visit that he and his brother had once made to the United States.[36]

The Crimean War between Britain and France with Russia broke out at this time and, during 1854, a combined British and French squadron visited Honolulu on their way to attack Russia. It was the largest naval squadron to visit Hawaii, consisting of the 50-gun *HMS President*, the 40-gun *HMS Pique*, the 24-gun *HMS Amphitrite*, the 6-gun *HMS Virago*, the 60-gun *FS Forte*, the 30-gun *FS Artemise*, the 30-gun *FS Eurydice* and the 22-gun *FS Oligado*. The visit of the combined Anglo-French squadron served to enhance the influence of Great Britain and France, and both the British and French admirals spoke to the King to encourage him to maintain the independent sovereignty of his Kingdom.[37] With cares and worries weighing down upon him death came to King Kamehameha III in December, 1854, after a brief illness, and with his death all formal discussions about American annexation were terminated by his successor Prince Alexander Liholiho, who now became King Kamehameha IV.

Of King Kamehameha III, the longest reigning Hawaiian monarch at 29 years on the throne, Professor Alexander stated "He loved his country and his people. He was true and steadfast in friendship. Duplicity and intrigue were foreign to his nature. He always chose men of integrity for responsible offices, and never betrayed secrets of state even in his most unguarded moments."[38]

The reign of King Kamehameha IV proved a quieter time diplomatically for Hawaii. Relations with Britain and France remained stable, and the United States began to be consumed by the dread of its pending civil war, which began in December 1860, with the secession of South Carolina. Hawaii quickly declared its neutrality in the war between the American states.

King Kamehameha IV and his consort, Queen Emma, were both pro-British and sought to increase ties with Great Britain. They brought the Anglican church to Hawaii, which angered the Congregationalists in the entrenched New England missionary church. But the King had learned first-hand about American racial prejudices towards people of darker skin during the visit he had made to the United States as a young man, and the poor impression he formed of Americans remained with him throughout his reign.[39] The Hawaiian economy continued to progress and sugar cane production began to replace the declining whaling industry as a mainstay of the economy.

A serious domestic incident occurred during Kamehameha IV's reign when the King became jealous of his private secretary, Henry Nielsen, whom he accused of having an illicit affair with Queen Emma. After a bout of heavy drinking the King approached Nielsen at the house in which he was staying and shot him in the chest with the intent of killing him. Nielsen was very seriously wounded but he survived with medical assistance. The King immediately became filled with remorse for his precipitate and ill-thought action. However, Nielsen never fully recovered from his wound and died of its consequences two years later. The Queen denied the affair, and the King came to realize that he had been the victim of malicious gossip and he contemplated abdicating the throne, and submitting himself to a trial, but the Privy Council dissuaded him.[40]

As a Sovereign, the King could not be prosecuted under the common law principle that the King can do no wrong, which was firmly established in the jurisprudence of England, and was equally applicable under the laws of the Kingdom of Hawaii. Thus, the King could never be charged, or prosecuted under the criminal law. The King did express his remorse to Nielsen, which must have been a cold comfort to his former secretary. The King made some public amends by assisting his consort in her desire to establish a hospital in Honolulu for the Hawaiian people. When public fund-raising proved to be insufficient the King went door to door with Queen Emma seeking subscriptions for a building fund from members of the public. Queen's Hospital became an important legacy of their reign, and especially of Queen Emma.

The royal couple had one child, Prince Albert, the Prince of Hawaii, who was designated as the King's direct heir. He was greatly loved by his parents but sadly the young prince became ill and died at the age of four. His loss devastated his parents but the King felt the loss most keenly, and coupled with his remorse, and grief, over the injury he caused to Henry Nielsen, he succumbed to depression. His longstanding asthma worsened, and he passed away at the age of 29 in November, 1863.

King Kamehamha IV had not designated a new heir before he died, so the *Kuhina Nui*, Princess Victoria Kamamalu, sister of the late King and the next highest official in the government met with the Privy Council to canvass their advice to the Crown. With the advice and consent of the Privy Council, Princess Victoria Kamamalu convened the Legislature, and then proclaimed her brother, Prince Lot, as the next King of Hawaii, under the regnal name of King Kamehameha V.[41]

Although he had been passed over for the throne upon the death of King Kamehameha III, despite being older than his brother Prince Liholiho, Prince Lot proved to be an effective, if unduly strong-willed governor of the Kingdom, and he successfully maintained its independence.[42] Very Hawaiian in his outlook, and tastes, the new King showed his wilfulness early in the reign by refusing to take the constitutional oath of office,[43] and expressing his intention to create a new constitution to replace the 1852 constitution granted by King Kamehameha III. The new King even took the view that he was not bound by the 1852 constitution, and that the grant of a constitution by King Kamehameha III was a precedent allowing him to promulgate a new constitution.

A royal proclamation was issued in May, 1864, calling together a constitutional convention in Honolulu to establish a new constitution. The convention met in Honolulu in July. However, when difficulties within the convention stymied efforts at reaching agreement among the delegates King Kamehameha V acted unilaterally, and dismissed the convention on August 13, 1864, declared the Constitution of 1852 abrogated, and reserved to himself the right to impose a new constitution by royal fiat.[44] The autocratic tendencies of King Kamehameha V were on full display when he promulgated a new constitution later in August, and only then did the King swear an oath to uphold the constitution, a constitution of his own making.

The new constitution abolished the post of *Kuhina Nui*, and restricted the powers of the Privy Council, while enhancing the powers of the executive, and of the Sovereign. For the electors, the new constitution imposed both a property requirement, and a literacy requirement, and it directed that the two houses of the Legislature should sit and vote together.

Before 1819, Hawaii possessed an absolute monarchy, and after 1819, an executive monarchy that shared power between the Sovereign and the *Kuhina Nui* and was, although no longer absolute, still an autocratic monarchy. But by 1840, Hawaii had become a constitutional monarchy with constitutional advisors established to assist the King in his Privy Council, and subsequently Cabinet Ministers to exercise the executive functions of government. The 1852 Constitution further liberalized the constitutional monarchy of 1840. However, with his autocratic outlook King Kamehameha V did not respect the constitutional principles that had evolved over time in the unique circumstances of Hawaii. He desired to restore the full prerogatives of the monarchy that had been freely given up by King Kamehameha III when the latter modernized the political structure of the state.

A key change was King Kamehameha V's decision to abolish the office of the *Kuhina Nui*, which had been present in the constitutional structure since the accession of King Kamehameha II in 1819. The abolition of the post of *Kuhina Nui* was regrettable, because it removed a potential internal check on the powers of the Sovereign from within the indigenous Hawaiian community. Additionally, the

Kuhina Nui was the head of the Cabinet, and presided over the Privy Council, and thus provided a level of supervision over the executive organs of the Hawaiian government that did not directly engage the Sovereign in political matters, providing a dignified and useful separation between the throne and the politics of government. In Great Britain, the separation between the Crown and political administration was described by the constitutional theorist Walter Bagehot as a difference between the dignified and the efficient components of the British Constitution. It was a distinction that was intended to protect the monarch from being drawn into politics, where one or two serious missteps could undermine the majesty of the Crown.

Once the position of *Kuhina Nui* was abolished executive decisions, whether popular or unpopular, were politically owned by the Sovereign. Although King Kamehameha V would successfully govern the Kingdom under his 1864 Constitution, the seeds planted by the King in the new constitution, and in the manner in which he imposed it, would become a dangerous precedent under his successors.

King Kamehameha V came to the throne as a bachelor and while he did have feelings for his widowed sister-in-law, Queen Emma, the King did not marry during his reign.[45] In 1864 he named his sister, Princess Victoria Kamamalu, as the Heiress Apparent but she died two years later. On his deathbed in 1872, the King named his half-sister, Princess Bernice Pauahi Bishop, as his successor but the Princess refused the appointment. The King would consider no other candidates, and he passed away without naming an heir.

Under the 1864 Constitution, a vacancy in the throne required the

Legislature to convene and elect a new Sovereign. Accordingly, the Hawaiian Cabinet of the late King called the Legislature into session to elect a new monarch from among four candidates, William Lunalilo, David Kalakaua, Ruth Keelikolani, and Bernice Pauahi Bishop. The best claim to the throne was held by Bernice Pauahi Bishop, as she was a great grand-daughter of King Kamehameha the Great but she had refused the throne when it was proffered to her by King Kamehameha V, and no nineteenth century legislature filled with men would think of forcing an unwilling female candidate to ascend the throne. Lunalilo had the next best genealogical claim to the throne based on descent, as he was the grandchild of the half-brother of King Kamehameha the Great. Ruth Keelikolani was the late King's half-sister but elements of her genealogy rendered her unsuitable in the view of many indigenous Hawaiians. David Kalakaua had no direct connection to the Kamehamehas but he was descended from *alii* who had been close supporters of Kamehameha the Great in the Hawaiian unification wars.

Prince Lunalilo asked that a public vote of electors be held before the matter was taken up by the Hawaiian Legislature and in that popular election Lunalilo was the clear favourite of the electorate. Taking its cue from public opinion, the Hawaiian Legislature unanimously elected Lunalilo as Sovereign, with only one abstention. The election of this popular *alii* received near universal popular acclaim, and King Lunalilo ascended the throne with the good wishes of all the people of Hawaii.

King Lunalilo perceived the dangers in the more autocratic reforms that King Kamehameha V had made to the constitutional structure of the islands in the 1864 Constitution, and he wished to roll back a number of the changes made by Kamehameha V. He asked the legislature to consider changes to the constitution but the King was in poor health, and his reign lasted just over one year before he passed away, once again without designating an heir, and without obtaining the changes to the constitution that he sought. He left his personal estate to establish a charitable home for poor, aged, or invalided Hawaiians.

Once again, the legislature was required to hold an election for a new monarch. Again both David Kalakaua and Bernice Pauahi Bishop were considered suitable candidates but this time Dowager Queen Emma, the widow of King Kamehameha IV, decided to seek the throne for herself. With Princess Bernice Pauahi Bishop once again forswearing any ambitions for the throne, the contest came down to two candidates, Queen Emma, and David Kalakaua. There was a general consensus that Queen Emma had a superior genealogical claim to the throne, and she was the popular choice of the Hawaiian people.[46]

David Kalakaua had the support of the *haole* business community however, and considerable experience in government. King Lunalilo had insisted on a special election before the legislative election that was required by the 1864 Constitution in order to confirm his acceptability to the Hawaiian public, an election that Lunalilo easily won. However, the 1874 election did not involve a special popular election and it was therefore strictly a legislative election. As such, the Hawaiian Legislature did not have electoral proof of the acceptability of one or the other of the two leading candidates to the general public. A bitter campaign ensued between David Kalakaua and Queen Emma over a period of nine days to sway the votes of the legislators.

Among the foreign community there was a sense that the election of Queen Emma would result in a pro-British tilt in Hawaii's foreign relations while the election of Kalakaua would mean a pro-American foreign policy for Hawaii. However, the American commissioner, Henry Peirce considered Kalakaua to be pro-British, and he thought Kalakaua was a flighty and vacillating character. The British consul, Theo Davies, also considered Kalakaua to be pro-British, as well as unprincipled, and of little intelligence, although he recognized that Kalakaua was an educated man.[47] Many of those in the settler community were in favour of Kalakaua's election. In the general population there was support for Queen Emma, the widow of King Kamehameha IV, and a feeling that David Kalakaua was something of an upstart, despite his *alii* background.[48] In the legislative election however, the legislators overwhelmingly favoured David Kalakaua, who was elected on a lopsided 39 to 6 ballot.

Immediately after the results became known a violent riot erupted in Honolulu. The rioters, all of whom were supporters of Queen Emma, did not accept the results of the legislative election and attacked the legislators, injuring several, one of whom one later died. The Legislature was trashed by the mob and the police made no effort to stop the rioters, perhaps in sympathy with their cause. The small Hawaiian military force had been disbanded the previous year by King Lunalilo, following a mutiny over pay, and thus there was no Hawaiian civil, or military, force that was willing and capable of repulsing the rioters. The Hawaiian Government turned to the western powers and sought military assistance from American and British warships in Honolulu harbour. A force of 150 American marines and sailors, and 70 British Royal Marines and sailors came ashore and suppressed the riot, thus restoring order. The western forces were required to arrest many Hawaiians engaged in rioting, and for more than a week the western forces protected the government buildings, lest a new riot erupt.

The day following the riots David Kalakaua took the constitutional oath as Sovereign of Hawaii under the 1864 Constitution in a subdued ceremony, and was recognized as the legitimate ruler of the country by the diplomatic representatives of the United States, Great Britain, and France. That same day Queen Emma, at the request of the western diplomats, sent word to King Kalakaua that she recognized him as the new Sovereign of Hawaii. The new King then paid a courtesy call on Queen Emma in an attempt to bridge the personal divide between them but although public cordiality was restored Queen Emma remained estranged from King Kalakaua, and his court, for the remainder of her life despite fruitless efforts by the King to recognize and accord her a respectful place in Hawaiian society.

The estrangement between Queen Emma and King Kalakaua was not wholly political. Kalakaua's consort, Queen Kapiolani, had been the nursemaid to Prince Albert, the young child of King Kamehameha IV and Queen Emma who had died at the age of four. It seems that Queen Emma may have blamed Kapiolani to some extent for the death of her child, although in truth the young Prince appears to have succumbed to appendicitis, an affliction with which mid-nineteenth century Hawaiian medicine could not cope.[49] Despite the efforts of medical professionals, there was nothing more that could have been done to save the young Prince, and Kapiolani seems to have been faultless with respect to his death.

The estrangement between Queen Emma and the King and Queen divided loyalties among the remaining *alii* and weakened the monarchy at a time when the growing economic strength of the western settlers, and the increasing geopolitical importance of the Hawaiian Islands, required the undivided loyalty to the Crown of the indigenous nobility and commoners. It was only after the death of Queen Emma, in 1885, that King Kalakaua could begin to receive the undivided loyalty of the indigenous Hawaiians and by that time the western settler community had grown immensely powerful in Hawaii.

With the death of King Kamehameha V, and the subsequent defeat of Queen Emma in the election to the throne that followed King Lunalilo's death, the Kamehameha Royal Family, which was the founding dynasty of the Kingdom of Hawaii, played no further role in the governing of the kingdom. Some of the Kamehameha courtiers took the opportunity to leave government service, as the end of the dynasty released them from their royal obligations.[50] A new dynasty now took their place, the Kalakaua, or Keawe-a-Heulu dynasty, and this new Royal Family would play a critical role in the future political development, and the ultimate fall, of the Kingdom of Hawaii.

NOTES

[1] Christopher Lloyd, *Pacific Horizons: The Exploration of the Pacific Before Captain Cook*, George Allen & Unwin Ltd., London, 1946, 24. A map found in the Spanish Archives in Madrid suggests that a Spaniard named Gaetano may have reached Hawaii at an early date, perhaps prior to 1600, but no conclusive evidence to corroborate the event has been found.

[2] Richard A Wisniewski, *The Rise and Fall of the Hawaiian Kingdom, A Pictorial History*, Pacific Basin Enterprises, Honolulu, 1979, 20

[3] Reportedly, as late as 1818 human sacrifices were still authorized under Hawaiian law (W D Alexander, *A Brief History of the Hawaiian People*, Published by Authority of the Board of Education of the Hawaiian Kingdom, American Book Company, New York, 1891, 164)

[4] King Kamehameha II consecrated two new *heiaus*, or temples, after succeeding to the Hawaiian throne, at Kawaihae and Honokohau in north Kona on Hawaii Island but both consecrations were marred by disorder and drunkenness. These were apparently the last *heiaus* created before the fall of the *kapu* system (Alexander, 167).

[5] Allan Seiden, *The Hawaiian Monarchy*, Mutual Publishing, Honolulu, 2014, 20

[6] Riánna Williams, *Queen Lili'uokalani, the Dominis Family, and Washington Place, their home*, Ka Mea Kakau Press, Honolulu, 2015, 16

[7] Elizabeth Kieszkowski (ed.), *Na Hale Ho'ike'ike o Na Mikanele*, Mission Houses Museum, Honolulu, 2001, 22, 39

[8] Alexander, 185

[9] Alexander, 188

[10] Glen Barclay, *A History of the Pacific, from the Stone Age to the present day*, Sidgwick & Jackson, London, 1978, 78

[11] Seiden, 45

[12] Williams, 1

[13] Seiden, 50 The account has similarities to an earlier confrontation of Pele by High Chiefess Kapiolani, namesake of King Kalakaua's consort, whose Christian prayers at the site of

Halemaumau, a crater within the Kilauea volcano caldera, had helped to establish Christianity in the islands.

[14] The names marked with an asterisk all subsequently became a reigning King or Queen of Hawaii.

[15] Alexander Liholiho (Kamehameha IV), Lot Kamehameha (Kamehameha V), William C Lunalilo (Lunalilo), David Kalakaua (Kalakaua) and Lydia Kamakaeha (Liliuokalani).

[16] Lydia Kamakaeha and Victoria Kamamalu. Three women in total were heiresses apparent to the Hawaiian throne, Princess Kaiulani being the third.

[17] Victoria Kamamalu

[18] Emma Rooke (Queen Emma)

[19] Alexander, 207

[20] Quoted in Barry Gough, *The Royal Navy and the Northwest Coast of North America 1810 – 1914*, University of British Columbia Press, Vancouver, 1971, 37

[21] Merze Tate, *The United States and the Hawaiian Kingdom: A Political History*, Yale University Press, New Haven (CT), 1965, 13-14

[22] For a description of Simpson's character see Peter C Newman, *Caesars of the Wilderness, Company of Adventurers Volume II*, Viking, Toronto, 1987, 219-24

[23] Newman, 257

[24] Alexander, 237; Newman, 259

[25] Newman, 259

[26] Quoted in Alexander, 240

[27] The Hudson Bay Company remained active in Hawaii until 1867, when increasing competition from American firms led to the winding up of the HBC's Hawaiian presence.

[28] *Senate Congressional Record*, December 13, 1893, Washington, 198

[29] President John Tyler, *Special Message*, The American Presidency Project https://www.presidency.ucsb.edu/documents/special-message-4235 [accessed May 16, 2020]

[30] Quoted in Alexander, 253

[31] Alexander, 262

[32] Stuart Banner, *Possessing the Pacific, Land, Settlers, and Indigenous People from Australia to Alaska*, Harvard University Press, Cambridge (MA), 2007, 140-3

[33] Banner, 150-1. Land titles granted to Hawaiians as a result of the *Great Mahele* continued to be recognized by the Republic of Hawaii after the overthrow of the Kingdom, and by the United States after annexation in 1898. The sole exception was the land held by the King, the so-called Crown lands, which were originally intended to be held as a private estate by the Hawaiian Sovereign but which subsequently became quasi-public as a result of litigation between King Kamehameha V, and his sister-in-law, Queen Dowager Emma, in 1864. After annexation, the claims of Queen Liliuokalani to the Crown lands were dismissed by the American courts using the 1864 judgment from the Supreme Court of Hawaii as a precedent, and the Crown lands passed to the United States, rather than to ex-Queen Liliuokalani.

[34] Alexander, 272

[35] Tate, 15

[36] Tate, 19

[37] Gough, 113

[38] Alexander, 279

[39] Seiden, 29

[40] Joseph Theroux, *Kamehameha IV and the Shooting of Henry*

Neilson, Honolulu Magazine, Honolulu Magazine.com, Published: 2010.06.01 [accessed March 4, 2020]

[41] King Kamehameha V removed Princess Victoria Kamamalu from the position of *Kuhina Nui* shortly after ascending to the throne and appointed their father Mataio Kekuanaoa as *Kuhina Nui* in her place. Kekuanaoa supported his son's decision to abolish the office of *Kuhina Nui* in the new constitution that the King subsequently imposed on the country. Princess Victoria, staunchly pro-American in her political views, was designated as the Heiress Apparent.

[42] The hereditary inheritance of political power in Polynesian societies did not necessarily follow the rule of male primogeniture. Family councils often determined inheritance by an assessment of the individual (I C Campbell, *A History of the Pacific Islands*, University of California Press, Berkeley, 1996, 15)

[43] The King maintained that article 94 of the Constitution of 1852 conferred a personal discretion on the heir to the throne to take the oath, or not to take it.

[44] Wisniewski, page 57.

[45] Wisniewski, 60

[46] Curtis Piehu Iaukea and Lorna Kahilipuaokalani Iaukea Watson, Niklaus R Schweizer (ed.), *By Royal Command, The Official Life and Personal Reminiscences of Colonel Curtis Pi'ehu Iaukea at the Court of Hawaii's Rulers*, Angel Inc., Honolulu, 1988, 22

[47] Tate, 34

[48] King Kamehameha V apparently considered Kalakaua to be a fool (Wisniewski, 61).

[49] The first abdominal surgery for appendicitis only occurred in New York in 1848, and surgery was not widely promoted as the preferred treatment for appendicitis before the 1880's

[50] Iaukea, 21

2

The Hope Of A Nation

At four o'clock in the afternoon of Saturday, October 16, 1875, the bells of Honolulu pealed to announce the birth of a baby girl to Princess Miriam Likelike Kekauluohi Keahelapalapa Kapili, the younger sister of King Kalakaua, and her husband, Archibald Scott Cleghorn. The birth occurred at the Cleghorn home on Queen Emma Street in downtown Honolulu. The birth was auspicious because it marked the first time since the birth of Prince Albert, the ill-fated child of Queen Emma and King Kamehameha IV, that a child had been born into the family of the reigning sovereign of the Hawaiian Islands. On Christmas Day, 1875, at nearby St. Andrew's Cathedral, the infant girl was christened Victoria Kawekiu Kaiulani Lunalilo Kalaninuiahilapalapa Cleghorn, according to the rites of the Anglican Church, by Bishop Alfred Willis. Her sponsors were King Kalakaua himself, together with his consort Queen Kapiolani, and Princess Ruth Keelikolani Keanolani Kanahoahoa, the half-sister of both King Kamehameha IV, and King Kamehameha V. A diplomatic reception and a champagne toast were held afterwards at the old Iolani Palace to mark the occasion. The Royal Hawaiian

Band played bandmaster Henry Berger's newest composition, *The Kaiulani March.*

Happiness at the birth of Kaiulani infused not only the Royal Family but all of the people of Oahu, and beyond Oahu to the neighbour islands, and it was a sincere and deeply felt happiness for an important reason. The Hawaiian Islands were in the midst of a demographic calamity that was slowly extinguishing the Polynesian settlement of the islands. Hawaii was, and is, the place that is farthest away from any other point on the surface of the Earth. As a result, the humans that settled there from other parts of the Pacific region had no exposure to the diseases that ran rampant in the more settled parts of both the Old and New Worlds. As a consequence, when sustained contact with the outside world began in the early decades of the nineteenth century, the diseases that outsiders brought to the Hawaiian Islands had devastating consequences for the people who lived there.

At the time of the first European contact during the exploration voyages of Captain James Cook, Hawaii may have had a population of 683,000 according to one estimate,[1] although estimates of pre-contact population in the islands do vary. During his initial voyage of discovery to the Hawaiian Islands Captain Cook was well aware of the degradation that would be caused to the native population if rampant venereal disease was introduced to the islands and he forbade contact between his crews and the local women. Of course, his sailors had not seen women for some time, and the Polynesian women they encountered were both curious and unconstrained by any European notions of sexual morality. Inevitably, there was contact. When Cook subsequently returned to the islands several months later there was clear evidence that venereal diseases were spreading through the population. Venereal disease could kill outright but when it did not kill it often rendered its victims infertile, thus reducing the ability of a vulnerable native population to reproduce itself. That is exactly the result that occurred in Hawaii, where the fertility of the indigenous population was significantly impacted by western contact. Toward the end of the century many indigenous Hawaiians suffered from venereal diseases and, in 1882, the Government physician reported treating 2748 syphilis cases, and 51 other venereal diseases.[2]

Other terrible disease epidemics were to follow, including cholera in 1804, influenza in the 1820's, mumps in 1839, measles and whooping cough in both 1848, and 1849, smallpox in 1853, and leprosy[3], which was introduced from the Orient, in the 1860's.[4] In 1836, the newspaper of the Hawaiian missionaries noted that since the inception of the Hawaiian mission in 1820, a minimum of 100,000 indigenous Hawaiians in every age group had lost their lives to disease.[5]

Other factors may have also contributed to the decline in population. One was the whaling trade which became very active in Hawaii between the 1820's and the 1860's, and which resulted in many young Hawaiian men being recruited for long voyages, as the Hawaiians made excellent sailors. That, too, reduced the population growth by removing young men from the society at a time when they would be expected to engage in family formation.[6] Perhaps less-well documented is an overall sense of malaise, or general depression, produced by Hawaiian contact with a technologically superior culture, which may have affected their confidence in their ability to survive and prosper on their own terms, in their own country. By 1900, there would only be 30,000 indigenous Hawaiians in Hawaii, and a further 7,800 part-Hawaiians.[7]

The absence of children was particularly noticed in the Royal Families of Hawaii. The founding dynasty, the Kamehamehas produced only three direct heirs; King Kamehameha II and King Kamehameha III, the sons of King Kamehameha the Great, and finally Prince Albert, the son of King Kamehameha IV and Queen Emma. As a result, by 1872, the founding dynasty had failed, and King Lunalilo was elected to replace the last Kamehameha, but was himself childless, and when he died scarcely more than a year later another election brought David Kalakaua to the throne. King Kalakaua and Queen Kapiolani were childless, although the Queen adopted her nephews after they were orphaned. Princess (later Queen) Liliuokalani and her husband, the Hon. J O Dominis, were also childless. Thus, during the Kalakaua years, the only Princess of the Blood who produced a child was Princess Likelike, who gave birth to Princess Kaiulani.

Kaiulani's father, Archibald S. Cleghorn, was born on November 15, 1835, in Edinburgh, Scotland, to Thomas Cleghorn, a horticulturalist, and his wife Janet Nisbet. When he was still a child, his father took the family to New Zealand where he was employed by the government. It was while the family was living in New Zealand that Archibald Cleghorn's mother died. When Archibald was sixteen, he accompanied his father to the Hawaiian Islands where his father became a dry goods merchant. Never in good health, Thomas died within a year of his arrival but Archibald stayed on in Hawaii, taking over his father's store and prospering. He entered into a domestic relationship with a Hawaiian woman, Elizabeth Lepeka Kahalaunani, who bore him three daughters, Helen, Rose,

44

and Annie Cleghorn. However, their relationship subsequently failed, and Cleghorn later married into a prominent *alii* family when he won the hand of the younger sister of David Kalakaua, Miriam Likelike.

Miriam Likelike was born on January 13, 1851, the daughter of Analea Keohokalole and Caesar Kapaakea, the *alii* parents of David Kalakaua and his siblings, who would later form the final reigning dynasty in Hawaii in the last decades of the nineteenth century. Raised initially on Hawaii Island by *hanai* parents, Miriam returned to Honolulu for her schooling at the hands of Catholic nuns, and subsequently at Kawaiahao Seminary.

Archibald Cleghorn and Miriam Likelike were married on September 22, 1870, at Washington Place, the residence of her sister Lydia Liliu Loloku Walania Kamakaeha (later to be styled Liliuokalani) and her husband, John O Dominis. As a sign of her highborn status as an *alii*, King Kamehameha V attended her wedding ceremony as a witness.[8] At the time of their wedding the groom was 35 years old, and the bride was 19. The significant differences in their ages, cultural background, and Hawaiian social status inevitably complicated their marriage. Although the marriage was stormy, it endured until the death of Likelike.

As an *alii*, Likelike travelled in the highest circles of Hawaiian society. The various descriptions of her that have come down to us over the years describe a mercurial individual, one who was both vivacious and charming, and very popular in society, but who could also be haughty and arrogant, and possessed of a volcanic temper.[9] Gertrude Gardinier, who became Princess Kaiulani's governess knew Princess Likelike well and described her to her own family as an imperious and impulsive woman who was somewhat haughty but nice and thoughtful to people that she liked.[10] In common with other members of her family Likelike was a talented musician. Publicly, and with charm and poise, she fulfilled the expectations of her role as a member of the Royal Family, even serving as Governor of Hawaii Island for a period in the late 1870's.[11] At her installation ceremony as Governor of Hawaii Island she paraded in a procession of *kukui* nut torches and feather *kahilis* to a flower-bedecked stage amidst chanting within a large crowd. In a blue satin dress trimmed with ostrich feathers she addressed the assembled crowd after her procedural installation and noted that the island of Hawaii was the cradle of Hawaiian nobility and royalty. Afterwards, she watched a pageant of past Hawaiian glories unfold upon the stage .[12]

Kaiulani's father, Archibald Scott Cleghorn, had advanced himself in Hawaii as a businessman in the years since he took over his father's dry goods store. He was described as genial and dignified[13] and like many men of his social standing in that era he focused on his business interests, and remained aloof from household management and responsibilities. As his business interests prospered Cleghorn's firm established outlets on several of the islands of Hawaii. He later served in government under both King Kalakaua and Queen Liliuokalani in multiple capacities, including Privy Councillor, Member of the Boards of Health, Prison Inspectors, and Immigration, Collector of Customs and eventually rising to the position of Governor of Oahu Island under Queen Liliuokalani. Cleghorn also became the first President of The Queen's Hospital, and the first Honolulu Parks Commissioner.[14]

Kaiulani was the only child born to Archibald Cleghorn and Princess Likelike. King Kalakaua announced that Kaiulani would take her place in the order of succession to the throne behind the Heiress Apparent, Princess Liliuokalani, and Kaiulani's own mother, Princess Likelike. As a special child, the highest-born *alii* of her generation, Kaiulani was doted upon and had a retinue of nurses and others to watch over her, and to see to it that no harm came to her. A governess, Miss Marion Barnes, a native of Australia, was engaged to keep charge of her. Under Miss Barnes tutelage Kaiulani learned to read and write in English, and learned the basics of social deportment. From her mother, and her nurses, Kaiulani learned to speak Hawaiian, a skill that never left her.[15]

When she was still very young Kaiulani's parents decided to move out of the city to Waikiki, where they built an estate on land purchased by them, and supplemented by additional lands given by Princess Ruth as a christening gift for her godchild, Kaiulani.[16] At Waikiki, Cleghorn built a home for his family and Likelike christened it Ainahau, meaning a cool place because of the cooling breezes that swept down to the ocean from the mountains of Oahu. Many of the Hawaiian *alii* maintained country homes in Waikiki (which means 'spouting water') and the entrance to the estate of Archibald Cleghorn and Princess Likelike abutted the entrance to King Kalakaua's Waikiki residence.

Here at Ainahau, Cleghorn indulged his interest and his passion in horticulture, a legacy from his father, and planted many special trees and flowering plants on this ten-acre estate. He planted 300 coconut palms to honour Kaiulani's birth, together with eight different types of mango trees, date palms, Washingtonia palms, cinnamon, teak, camphor, Monterey cypress, sago palms, lotus, two types of Hawaiian kamani trees, a Chinese soap tree and a red flowering tiger-claw tree from India, rubber trees, lantana bushes, jasmine, and 14 kinds of hibiscus. He also filled three lily ponds from an artesian well and placed Japanese style bridges over them. Towering over it all was a banyan tree, the original Hawaiian banyan tree, that in time would become a favourite place of Kaiulani's, and where she would sit and read, or listen to the stories of Robert Louis Stevenson when he sojourned in Hawaii.

As a final touch, Cleghorn added a giant tortoise, and a muster of peafowls from India as natural wardens of the verdant paradise he was creating. Kaiulani would fall in love with the peacocks, and peahen, learning to feed them by hand. Her affection for the peafowl was such that she is sometimes known as the Princess of the Peacocks in Hawaiian memory. She also had a St. Bernard dog, and a beloved pony named Fairy.

Kaiulani's father built a large, spacious, single story home on the property with a sizeable lanai. It was a comfortable home, though not majestic in any royal sense. Portraits of Hawaiian royalty lined the walls of the Ainahau villa. A traditional grass house was also constructed on the property in the old Hawaiian style, with plaited grass walls, and a thatch roof.[17] Here, the young Kaiulani would spend her happy childhood days. She formed friendships with other, carefully vetted girls, such as Kate de Vida and May Atkinson, and the Parker girls. She paddled an outrigger canoe on the Apuakehau, a stream that flowed through Ainahau to the ocean. And it was there where she first swam out into the Pacific from the beautiful beach at Waikiki and in the ocean that she learned to become a proficient swimmer. As her skills in the water grew she took up surfing and became a good wave rider, maintaining the tradition of *hee nalu,* or wave sliding, as it was called in the Hawaiian language. In the late nineteenth century it was uncommon for females to take up surfing, although in ancient times both male and female Hawaiians of all classes had participated. Surfing was discouraged by the missionaries in the early nineteenth century but it never died out as a sporting activity. The Hawaiian cultural renaissance that occurred during the reign of King Kalakaua helped to restore the tradition, and Kaiulani became part of that as an early role model for Hawaiian female surfers in the late nineteenth and early twentieth centuries.[18] Ainahau also provided the young Kaiulani with a tennis court and space for a croquet field – a sport that became all the rage in the late nineteenth century genteel Hawaiian society.

Kaiulani was trained from an early age to be an excellent horsewoman. A family retainer, Sam Alapai, who had once trained Princess Likelike to ride when she was young, now instructed her daughter, Kaiulani, in horsemanship. In reminiscing about her childhood, Kaiulani recalled that Alapai was a strict taskmaster who forced her to learn to ride without a pommel, and when she had mastered that he removed the stirrups, and later he even took away the saddle and scolded Kaiulani if she failed to sit a horse well. Nevertheless, under his demanding tutelage Kaiulani became an excellent rider at an early age. Kaiulani's parents gave her a white pony which she named Fairy, and whom she came to dearly love. On Fairy's back she began to explore Waikiki. On the weekends she would ride out to Diamond Head with her governess as far as the lookout station, and then travel back along the seashore searching for seashells.

Apart from Ainahau, Kaiulani also spent time on Hawaii Island, where her mother had spent her early years and where she served as Governor while Kaiulani was a young girl. Princess Likelike owned a cottage at Kaawaloa on Kealekekua Bay, where Britain's Captain

James Cook had lost his life in a dispute with Hawaiians many years before. Kaawaloa was an attractive place for the young girl to explore and there she swam in a natural basin filled with cool water, as the presence of sharks offshore rendered the ocean too risky for the young Princess.

At an early age Kaiulani began to realize that she was different from other children. Social conventions applied to her much differently than to other children. Reflecting on her childhood later she said:

"I don't think I quite understood it at all, but I knew I was – well, somebody different, you know, because I was *tabu* . . . not to be touched – sacred – you know. No one was supposed to touch me except persons of my own rank and of course the servants who dressed me, and my foster mother . . . I found out very early that I could be as naughty as I liked with my nurses and I enjoyed that very much, because I was naturally naughty, I suppose. I had one nurse that I hated and I used to love to beat her . . . But even that got tiresome after awhile. I was the only one you know and very delicate and every one feted me at home and at the Palace, but still I was very lonely. I missed something that all my friends who were allowed to come to play with me seemed to have. They could not use my chair, or sit on my bed or touch me even when we played tag in the garden. I could never be alone with them. I had always six or seven women watching and watching me. I was not allowed to climb trees as they were, or to race about down to the beach, or to do any of the things that children have to do alone among themselves without any nurses or elders fussing about. . . . I had a friend, a very jolly, careless little girl, and one day when we had been playing together we went up to my bedroom and she threw herself down on my bed. I remember how my nurse rushed at her across the room, 'How dare you,' she said, and she took hold of her roughly and pulled her to the floor. 'Sit there!' she said 'that is the place for you.' . . . The little girl went home and I thought about it a long time. I never had seen my nurse angry and it made a great impression on me. 'Why

50

is the floor the place for her?' I asked, and my nurse said . . . 'Because you are a Princess and the others are not."[19]

Kaiulani was also introduced to the duties that came with the status of a Princess of Hawaii. She was instructed in the obligations of an *alii* to practice *haawi ke aloha* – the respectful recognition of other Hawaiians, even when she was seated in a carriage. Rather than looking elsewhere she must look at passing Hawaiians and acknowledge them with a short bow. On Sundays there would often be a carriage drive and she would have the opportunity to show that she understood this responsibility to recognize other Hawaiians, regardless of their social status.

As a princess, Kaiulani was expected to participate in public events held within the Kingdom. Thus, she attended events such as official picnics, receptions, graduation ceremonies, and luaus at Iolani Palace. She attended the funeral of Queen Emma in the company of King Kalakaua, (and she found it disturbing), and Kaiulani also had a prominent place in the Coronation Ceremony for the King and Queen in 1883, which she attended attired in a pale blue dress with lace trim, and wearing blue ribbons in her hair.

Although Kaiulani seems to have had a happy childhood, she did experience loss, and sometimes profound losses, that deeply affected her. The first time she experienced a direct loss was the passing of her godmother, Princess Ruth Keelikolani, which occurred in the spring of 1883, shortly after Princess Kaiulani had returned to Honolulu after a visit with her parents to Hawaii Island, where her mother, the former Governor of the island, had unveiled a statue of King Kamehameha the Great at Kohala, near the birthplace of the great king.[20] Kaiulani mourned her godmother, who had been a larger than life presence in her early years. Then, in the summer of 1883, her governess, Marion Barnes, remembered for her "graceful and charming manner" died suddenly after a bout of pneumonia.[21] Thus, in a very short space of time two of the women who had loomed large in young Kaiulani's life were gone.

To replace Miss Barnes a series of new governesses were tried but none were satisfactory until Mrs. George Wallace, the wife of the rector at St. Andrew's Cathedral, recommended Miss Gertrude Gardinier of New York as a replacement for Miss Barnes. Arrangements were duly made and Miss Gardinier sailed for Honolulu, where she commenced her duties as Kaiulani's new governess in May, 1884.[22] Between Kaiulani and her young and pretty governess there was an immediate bond, a mutual liking that helped to dispel the loss of Miss Barnes. Writing to her own family back in the United States, Gardinier described her new charge as fragile but high-spirited and affectionate, with large and expressive eyes, a vivacious and generous girl but wilful, and impulsive, although possessed of a refined and quick-witted mind.[23]

On weekdays Miss Gardinier would lead Kaiulani in her lessons and in music instruction in the mornings. In the afternoon, there would be time for a swim, or surfing in the ocean, or a carriage ride. On occasion, Miss Gardinier would take Kaiulani to the theatre if a visiting production was in Honolulu, and together they would watch a play from the Royal Box. On Sundays there would be Bible and catechism classes, often held under the great Banyan tree on the Ainahau estate that was a favourite of Kaiulani. After Sunday services at St. Andrew's Cathedral, there might be a carriage ride in her mother's fine carriage, with its tortoise shell panels, and gilt-garlanded horses with white reins, which was driven by a household liveryman dressed in black with white gloves. Princess Likelike took great pride in the appearance of her carriage, which she embellished with her own personal coat of arms. If the appearance of her carriage suffered, her explosive temper would come forth, and on one occasion she used a riding whip to lash a household groomsman who failed to polish the carriage to Princess Likelike's satisfaction.[24]

Miss Gardinier was able to influence Kaiulani's choice of dress. She persuaded Princess Likelike that the formal frocks that Kaiulani routinely dressed in were unsuited for everyday life in a tropical climate, and as a result lighter dresses became Kaiulani's normal everyday fashion. As Kaiulani approached her tenth birthday, Miss Gardinier thought that a change of scene from Waikiki would do her some good and Princess Likelike was happy to oblige by taking Kaiulani and Miss Gardinier with her to Hawaii Island, where Kaiulani, free of any lessons, could enjoy the pleasures of the Village of Kaawaloa on Kealekekua Bay, where Great Britain's Captain Cook had met his demise many years before.[25]

At Kaawaloa, Kaiulani celebrated her tenth birthday with a grand luau attended by both native Hawaiians and the foreign-born settler community. Likelike had a new lanai built on her cottage for the luau. Afterwards, upon returning to Honolulu the shore battery at Honolulu harbour fired a salute as Kaiulani's ship arrived, and there was another party to celebrate Kaiulani's tenth birthday that same day at Ainahau. The King and Queen attended the party and it was there that King Kalakaua presented Princess Kaiulani with her very own personal royal standard, the shield from the Hawaiian royal coat of arms surmounted by a crown that was placed in a vertical white rectangle on a background of red silk.[26] The Premier of Hawaii, Walter Gibson, also appeared, and he gave the young princess ten gold coins as a birthday present.[27]

As time passed Kaiulani's self-professed naughtiness reared itself and she challenged her governess on more than one occasion but Miss Gardinier would have none of that behaviour. When a serious lack of obedience manifested itself, Gardinier insisted on her right to discipline Kaiulani, notwithstanding the fact that she was a princess. Her insistence brought on a conflict between Miss Gardinier and Princess Likelike, a dispute that almost caused Gardinier to resign her position in the household. However, after a cooling-off period between the two women, Princess Likelike asked Miss Gardinier to stay on and Gardinier, after reflecting, agreed to remain. Princess Kaiulani was compelled to apologize to Miss Gardinier for misbehaving, and she pleaded with Miss Gardinier to remain as her governess. In this way the young girl came to learn the behavioural limits expected of a girl-child in an upper-class home in the late nineteenth century, notwithstanding her exalted social position in the larger Hawaiian society.

Another year passed, and Kaiulani's eleventh birthday was again celebrated at Ainahau. The King attended the party for his niece and there were ample dishes from both Hawaiian cuisines as well as foreign fare. The King rose from the table to toast his future heir, expressing the hope that she would bring credit to Hawaii. In response Samuel Wilder, a Member of the House of Nobles, the upper house of the Hawaiian Legislature, and a firm monarchist, responded to the King's toast to Kaiulani by wishing that the young Princess may be the 'Hope of the Nation,' and that she would some day reign with wisdom, and always keep the love of the Hawaiian people.[28]

Another pleasant year in Kaiulani's childhood was passing when very disquieting news came in October. Miss Gardinier announced her engagement to Albert W Heydtmann, with the wedding to take place the next year. Another loss! And a very personal one for the young Princess, who was deeply attached to her governess. Much worse news soon followed.

Around Christmastime of 1886, Kaiulani's mother, Princess Likelike, became ill and took to her bed. Ominously, Princess Likelike began to refuse all food. Her physicians could find nothing that was physically wrong with her and yet her health continued to decline. Superstitious Hawaiians began to mutter that a *kahuna*, a Hawaiian sorcerer, was praying against Likelike. That feeling was reinforced when Hawaiians on Hawaii Island reported the presence of a school of red *aweoweo* fish, historically viewed as a sign of impending death of a great *alii*. Kaiulani's mother began to lose interest in the ordinary circumstances of life. Then, on January 16, 1887, Mauna Loa, the great volcano on Hawaii Island erupted and that was seen by many Hawaiians as an important portent. Princess Likelike began to fear that the Hawaiian volcano goddess, Pele, wished to take her life, much to the consternation of the King, and those close to her. Premier Gibson recorded in his diary: "The Princess Likelike said to be in danger – refuses food – affected by her native superstition that her death is required by the spirit of Pele of the Volcano. The King is angry with his sister on account of her obstinacy in refusing food."[29]

As smoke filled the atmosphere, and lightning traced across the sky from the volcano, Princess Likelike sank further. On the morning of February 2, 1887, Princess Kaiulani was summoned to her mother's bedroom for a private farewell. At four o'clock on February 2, 1887, Princess Likelike, the second in line in the succession to the Hawaiian throne, passed away at the age of 37.[30] Her mother's sudden and mysterious death was crushing to the young Kaiulani, and it was fortunate that she had both a friend and a governess in Miss Gardinier to help her cope with her devastating loss. Reflecting much later on the death of her mother, Kaiulani explained how deeply she was affected by this loss, and the strain on a young daughter of the elaborate funeral arrangements that were made for her mother:

"I idolized my mother she was charming: very brilliant, very happy and sunny; we worshipped each other. And I have missed her every day from the first dreadful day she died. It was a dreadful day in every way. I was taken to the Palace. I remember when she lay for three weeks in state. I can see her dead face now laid against the cloak feathers. Everything is black against that white, white room. The four royal *Kahilis* were held by the *kahili* bearers, one at each corner of her bier and six at each side. Six others dressed all in velvet waved the *Kahilis* over her body. You know we have a superstition about the dead. No insect must touch our dead. I remember shrieking out once I saw her and then never finding voice, it seemed to me, to shriek again or a tear to cry. I used to be awake at night and listen to the wailing. It never ceased, you know, by day or night for those three weeks. I thought I should go mad of it. A child suffers on so many ways that it cannot tell. No one understood, I think, what I suffered in that time. I missed her so. . . ."
[31]

Hawaiian protocol required that the body of Princess Likelike lie in state for several weeks and that all those *alii* of the same rank ought to be present throughout the lying in state. Consequently, Princess Kaiulani was compelled to reside at Iolani Palace until the funeral, exacerbating the effects of her personal loss. However, Miss Gardinier came to the palace every day and took Kaiulani out for walks in the gardens of the palace. Finally, on February 27, 1887, the funeral of Princess Likelike took place. After a service conducted by the Anglican Bishop, and the other denominational clergy of

Honolulu, a long two-hour procession was conducted out to the Royal Mausoleum at Mauna Ala in the Nuuanu Valley, as minute guns fired from the battery at the Punchbowl. There, Princess Likelike was laid to rest in a coffin made of wood from the *koa* and *kau* trees, and embossed with the Princess's personal coat of arms and motto: *I hii I ke Kapu* (The sacred one will be held in the protecting arms).[32]

Princess Kaiulani returned to Ainahau from Iolani Palace and resumed her life but she was no longer free of adult cares. At Ainahau, she strove to take her mothers place and for a brief time she retained the support of her governess, Miss Gardinier, until the day of Gardinier's wedding in the spring of 1887. She missed her governess but Miss Gardinier would at least stay in Honolulu and Princess Kaiulani could still visit her. Other losses soon followed. Former Premier Gibson died and Kaiulani was required to attend his lying-in-state to pay her final respects. Closer to home and harder to bear was the death of one of Queen Kapiolani's *hanai* children, Prince Edward Abnel Keliiahonui, who died of typhoid fever in September of 1887, at the age of only eighteen years.

So many losses, and yet there was one notable addition to Kaiulani's circle of acquaintances. Robert Louis Stevenson, perhaps the most well-known author of the times, arrived in Hawaii on his private yacht, the *Casco,* on January 24, 1889, with the members of his immediate family, including his wife, mother, and stepson, and reunited with his stepdaughter, Isobel Strong, who was married to Joseph Strong, the Court Painter to the Royal Hawaiian Court. Archibald Cleghorn soon invited Stevenson and his family to supper at Ainahau and an adoring friendship developed between Stevenson and Cleghorn's lively young daughter.[33] Thereafter, Stevenson, who resided with his family nearby in Waikiki, often visited Kaiulani in the afternoons when her studies, now overseen first by Mademoiselle Acala, a Frenchwoman, and then Fraulein Reisenberg, a German, were completed. Kaiulani and Stevenson would sit under the great Banyan tree at Ainahau and Stevenson, whose Samoan nickname was *Tusitala* ('teller of tales') would regale his young friend with many stories as she sat enthralled under the Banyan tree.[34]

Princess Kaiulani continued with her royal duties during this time and one special event occurred in the spring of 1888. On the evening of March 23, 1888, Kaiulani, accompanied by Crown Princess Liliuokalani, and escorted by the Minister of the Interior, Lorrin Thurston, proceeded to the new electrical station built out in a valley, away from the city of Honolulu. While standing on a chair, and following the instructions of the Station Superintendent, Kaiulani threw the switches that brought electricity to Honolulu, and illuminated the city. Honolulu was certainly as progressive, and as modern, as any western capital city.

Her thirteenth birthday was another prominent affair. *Kukui* torches burned, and strolling musicians wandered through the exotic plants and trees of Ainahau, with its grove of 300 coconut palms, and still ponds accented by the floating pink lotus amidst statuary, as the wafting fragrance of jasmine, the Princess' favourite flower, flowed over the grounds. Above Ainahau, Princess Kaiulani's personal royal standard flew as diplomats, and foreign naval officers in full dress uniforms called to pay their respects. The Princess, dressed in a soft blue satin dress received them and Hawaiian Government officials, and many well-wishers from both the indigenous Hawaiian and the settler Hawaiian communities.[35]

The year 1888 passed into 1889, and Kaiulani was now thirteen years old. Her early childhood was behind her. She would now have to begin transforming herself into a young lady of the Victorian period, and to become a woman fit someday to assume the throne of the Kingdom. Consideration was now given by her father, and the King, to the education that would best prepare her for the days ahead when she would reign over Hawaii. It was decided that the Princess should go to Great Britain to receive a polished education. Arrangements began to be made for her departure from Hawaii.

Not everyone thought it would be a good idea for Kaiulani to move to Britain, including Kaiulani herself. Robert Louis Stevenson had warned Archibald Cleghorn that the climate of Great Britain was unsuitable for maintaining the health of a delicate girl like Kaiulani.[36] Nevertheless, it was decided that Princess Kaiulani should go abroad. The *hanai* children of Queen Kapiolani, Princes David Kawananakoa, and Jonah Kuhio Kalanianaole, had both gone abroad to the United States, and to Great Britain, to complete their education and the *hanai* child of Princess Poomaikelani, Edward Abnel Keliiahonui, prior to his tragic young death, had also studied in California. Thus, in the latter years of the Kalakaua dynasty, it was viewed as virtually *de rigeur* for the younger members of the Royal Family to obtain a foreign education to complement their earlier studies within Hawaii.

Soon afterwards an announcement of Kaiulani's forthcoming journey appeared in the *Honolulu Advertiser* newspaper; "Princess Kaiulani will leave for England in May in charge of Mrs. R. Walker, and will be accompanied by Miss Annie Cleghorn. The young Princess will obtain a governess in England, and on returning will visit the principal cities of the United States."

Although Kaiulani would travel in the company of Mrs. Walker, the wife of the British Vice-Consul, while in Great Britain arrangements were also made by Kaiulani's father for Theophilus Harris Davies, a prominent British businessman who had extensive interests in Hawaii, to act as Princess Kaiulani's official guardian while she was abroad as a minor.[37]

Sad to see this young island maid, who delighted in his stories, depart for his own homeland, Robert Louis Stevenson wrote a poem about her departure:

"Forth from her land to mine she goes,

The Island maid, the Island rose;

Light of heart and bright of face:

The daughter of a double race.

Her islands here, in Southern sun,

Shall mourn their Kaiulani gone,

And I, in her dear banyan shade,

Look vainly for my little maid.

But our Scots islands far away

Shall glitter with unwonted day,

And cast for once their tempests by

To smile in Kaiulani's eye."[38]

As a royal princess, Kaiulani could not make a quiet departure from Honolulu. A rigorous adherence to protocol and etiquette was required. Therefore, the beautiful tortoiseshell carriage that had belonged to her mother once again came out and in it Kaiulani took her formal farewells of the Hawaiian Government, and of Honolulu society. Riding in her carriage through the streets of Honolulu, Princess Kaiulani made formal farewell calls on the chief government departments, the foreign diplomatic missions, the members of King Kalakaua's cabinet, the Justices of the Supreme Court of Hawaii, and the major educational institutions, including Oahu College, St. Andrew's Priory, and the Kawaiahao Seminary. She called upon the Heiress Apparent, Princess Liliuokalani at her home at Washington Place where she found her aunt still in mourning over the recent death of her mother-in-law, Mrs. Dominis. Her last official calls, according to precedent, were to Iolani Palace to see the King and Queen. As second in line to the throne of Hawaii, Princess Kaiulani could not leave the realm without the King's permission, which he granted to her by a document of formal permission:

"I Kalakaua King of the Hawaiian Islands do hereby give my consent and approval for My Niece Her Royal Highness Princess Victoria Kaiulani, to leave the Hawaiian Kingdom and proceed to England, on or about the month of May 1889 in charge of, and under the care and control of Mrs Thomas Rain Walker, and be accompanied by Miss Annie Cleghorn.

The Princess to travel entirely incognito. Her return to the Hawaiian Kingdom to be during the year of Our Lord One thousand eight hundred and ninety

Signed Kalakaua Rex

Iolani Palace

Honolulu, March 20th 1889."[39]

Kaiulani also had to make social calls to bid farewell to her dear friends and perhaps none was more important to her than her former governess, Gertrude Gardinier, now married and the mother of an infant child, whom Kaiulani held in her lap while bidding an emotional good-bye to her former governess, who was now Mrs. Heydtmann. Saddest of all was her private leave-taking of her special pet, her pony Fairy, whom she dearly loved. And then she was off. A diverse crowd filled the dock at Honolulu harbour as she boarded the steamer *SS Umatilla* that would take her on the first leg of her journey to San Francisco, accompanied by Mrs. Walker and Annie Cleghorn who would travel with her all the way to Great Britain, and her father, who would travel with them as far as San Francisco. The *Umatilla* got up steam and at dockside the Royal Hawaiian Band struck up the national anthem, *Hawaii Ponoi,* as the ship proceeded out of Honolulu harbour, and away from Hawaii.

Kaiulani watched Oahu Island slowly slip away into the distance. She would not see her homeland for another eight years. When the time came for her return she would find a Hawaii that had changed in ways beyond her reckoning.

NOTES

[1] David A. Swanson, University of Washington, *The Number of*

Native Hawaiians and Part-Hawaiians in Hawaii, 1778 to 1900: Demographic Estimates by Age, With Discussion, Paper Presented at a Conference of the Canadian Population Society, Calgary, Alberta, June 2016

[2] Tate, 47

[3] The Hawaiian Government established a leper colony on an isolated coast on the island of Molokai, where a Belgian priest, Father Damien, later ministered to the community until he contracted the disease and died from it.

[4] Doug Herman, *Shutting Down Hawai'i: A Historical Perspective on Epidemics in the Islands,* March 25, 2020, Smithsonianmag.com, Washington [accessed March, 2020]

[5] Herman, ibid

[6] Campbell, 64

[7] Swanson, ibid

[8] Nancy Webb & Jean Francis Webb, *Kaiulani, Crown Princess of Hawai'i,* Mutual Publishing, Honolulu, 1998, 21

[9] Webb & Webb, 23

[10] Webb & Webb, 29

[11] Dorthea Woodrun, *Governor Cleghorn, Princess Kaiulani and Ainahau; Recollections of a Gracious Era in Hawaii's History,* Island Development Corp., Honolulu, 1964, 13

[12] Kathleen Dickenson Mellen, *An Island Kingdom Passes, Hawaii Becomes American,* Hasting House, New York, 1958, 81-82

[13] Webb & Webb, 29

[14] Woodrun, 1

[15] Kristen Zambucka, *Princess Kaiulani, The Last Hope of Hawaii's Monarchy,* Mana Publishing Co., Honolulu, 1976, 119

[16] Stan Cohen, *Princess Victoria Kaiulani, and the Princess Kaiulani*

Hotel in Waikiki, Pictorial Histories Publishing Co., Missoula (MO), 1997, 15

[17] Woodrum, 11

[18] Kaiulani's 7-and-one-half foot *alaia koa* surfboard is preserved at the Bishop Museum in Honolulu.

[19] Alice Rix, *The Princess Who Wanted to be Queen*, San Francisco Call, August 7, 1898, San Francisco (CA), 17.

[20] That statue has an interesting history. It was commissioned by the government to stand outside the Aliiolani Hale in downtown Honolulu but the statue was lost at sea near the Falkland Islands in the south Atlantic Ocean while it was being transported to Hawaii. The government immediately commissioned a replacement, and the replacement was later successfully installed in Honolulu. In the meantime however, salvagers had retrieved the first statue from the ocean depths and it was sold to the Hawaiian Government, which decided to place it on Hawaii Island, where Kamehameha was born and raised.

[21] *Honolulu Advertiser*, March 8, 1884, 2

[22] Webb & Webb, 26

[23] Webb & Webb, 29

[24] Maxine Mrantz, *Hawaii's Tragic Princess, Kaiulani, The Girl who Never Got to Rule*, Aloha Publishing, Honolulu, 1980, 12

[25] While serving as the Governor of Hawaii Island Princess Likelike had directed that a monument be constructed on Kealekekua Bay to mark the fall of the great Captain Cook at the hands of Hawaiian warriors. Later, that monument and the title to the patch of land upon which it was constructed were deeded to the British Government. Landing parties from British Commonwealth naval ships periodically visited the monument over the years to maintain it

(William Graves, *Hawaii*, National Geographic Society, Washington, 1970, 122)

[26] Douglas V Askman, *Royal Standards of the Kingdom of Hawai'i, 1837-1893*, The Hawaiian Journal of History, vol. 47 (2013), 61 at 72-73

[27] Walter Murray Gibson (Jacob Adler and Gwynn Barrett ed.), *The Diaries of Walter Murray Gibson 1886, 1887*, University Press of Hawaii, Honolulu, 1973, 78

[28] Webb & Webb, 41

[29] Gibson (Adler and Barrett), 120

[30] Mrantz, 14; Webb & Webb, 47

[31] Rix, 17, 29

[32] Webb and Webb, 51

[33] Mellen, 222

[34] Mrantz, 15. For the history of Kaiulani's banyan tree, see Ralph Thomas Kam, The Legacy of Ainahau, *The Geneology of Ka'iulani's Banyan*, The Hawaiian Journal of History, vol 45 (2011)

[35] Mellen, 219

[36] Mrantz, 15

[37] The firm of Theo H Davies & Co. Limited was one of the 'Big Five' sugar firms in Hawaii and would come to have an oversized role in the Hawaiian economy.

[38] Quoted in Mindi Reid, Princess *Ka'iulani, Rose of Two Worlds*, Electric Scotland, https://electricscotland.com/history/women/wh36.htm [accessed April 2, 2020]

[39] Untitled Document, Cleghorn File, HSA

3

The Glittering Court of Polynesia

Nineteenth century Honolulu presented an unusual spectacle to the casual visitor from a western country due to the presence of the Royal Court of Hawaii. From very modest beginnings, the Royal Court of the island kingdom grew in scope and sophistication to reach its apogee under King Kalakaua and his consort, Queen Kapiolani, in the 1880's. Although the original foundations of the court and its ceremonies were based on Polynesian customs, the exposure of Hawaii to western customs, and the necessity of integrating Hawaii into the international community of nations, compelled the monarchs of Hawaii to increasingly incorporate western emblems of royalty into the framework of the Hawaiian monarchy.

Traditionally the Hawaiian *alii* were the recipients of a larger share of the resources of the kingdom. The finer things in Hawaiian life such as the finest household objects, the voices of chanters, and the graceful, enchanting movements of the hula dancers, were provided for their pleasure. They wore the best clothing, including beautiful capes borne by the high *alii* that were made from the feathers of colourful Hawaiian mountain birds. The famous feather capes reached their finest, and most striking form, in the yellow and red feather capes worn by the island kings. Their magnificent regalia was much commented upon by the early western visitors to Hawaii for their beauty, and for the devotion, and craftsmanship, required by the artisans who created them. The prized yellow feathers of such cloaks were taken by specially trained bird catchers only from particular birds:

> "These birds were honey-suckers, living on the nectar of flowers of the *okia*, the banana and the large *lobelias*. The yellow feathers were taken from two species of birds, viz. the *O'o* (*Acrulocercus nobilis*), which has one little tuft of yellow feathers under each wing, and the still rarer *Mamo* (*Drepanis pacifica*), which has also larger golden-yellow feathers on its back . . . The scarlet feathers were obtained from the *Iiwi* (*Vestiaria coccinea*), a song bird with gorgeous scarlet coat and black wings; and from the *Akakane* (*Fringilla coccinea*)."[1]

The *O'o* bird, and the *Mamo* were captured and released after surrendering their feathers but the unfortunate *Iiwi* was predominantly covered in brilliant red feathers and was therefore slaughtered for them.[2] The great yellow cloak worn by King Kamehameha the Great has been calculated to have required feathers from 80,000 birds.[3]

Feathers were also used to construct *kahilis*, a unique Hawaiian royal standard that was borne before the *alii* as they made their social progressions through Hawaiian society. The *kahilis* consisted of colourful feather clusters constructed in a cylindrical design and placed atop a long pole, as much as 20 or 30 feet in height. The *kahilis* were present at feasts whenever the *alii* dined and in rooms where the *alii* were present. They were also carried before them as they walked. From the time of King Kamehameha the Great until the fall of the monarchy, and even afterward, they remained a visible public symbol of Hawaiian royalty. Social distinctions between commoners and chiefs were clear and strictly enforced during the Kamehameha dynasty. No one could touch something that belonged to the Sovereign, or serve them in a close manner if they were not of chiefly rank themselves, and there was a clear difference between common servants, and the servants of more exalted rank.[4]

Another visible royal symbol was the *mahiole*, or Hawaiian helmet crown that was borne by the senior *alii* at public events, and during wars. Made from the roots of the *Ieie* vine woven together, the helmets were completed with red and yellow feathers in a tufted line along the middle of the woven cap, or pressed together to form an elevated crest, which provided a visible symbol of the presence of a high *alii*.[5] Also important was the sash borne by the high chiefs and kings, which was covered in feathers.[6]

Each of the royal dynasties during the nineteenth century also adopted some natural phenomena as a sigil, or symbol, of their extraordinary status. For the Kamehameha dynasty it was the torrential rain that pummelled the Hawaiian Islands. For Lunalilo it was a red mist and for the Kalakaua line it was the sun, reflected in the burning *kukui* nut torches in daylight, but also sometimes portrayed with golden flowers.[7]

An example of the early pageantry of the Hawaiian monarchy was contained in a description of the annual celebration of King Kamehameha II's accession to the throne in 1823:

"The head queen, Kamamalu, was seated in a whaleboat, fastened to a platform of spars, and borne on the shoulders of seventy men. The

68

boat and platform were covered with fine broadcloth, relieved by richly coloured native cloth. The bearers marched in a solid phalanx, the outer ranks of which wore scarlet and yellow feather cloaks and helmets. The queen wore a scarlet silk *pa'a* and a coronet of feathers, and was screened from the sun by a huge umbrella of scarlet damask, supported by a chief wearing a scarlet *malo* and a feather helmet. On one quarter of the boat stood Naihe, and on the other Kalanimoku, similarly clad, and each holding a scarlet *kahili*, or plumed staff of state thirty feet in height."[8]

Apart from the feather capes and *kahilis* however, the Hawaiian royalty increasingly adapted themselves to western ways as nineteenth century contacts with western nations increased. Male clothing styles changed from the wearing of loincloths into the wearing of western military style uniforms by the princes and kings of Hawaii, and western dresses and gowns representing missionary modesty became *de rigeur* for princesses and queens, instead of the traditional topless *pa'a*. The *mahiole*, the traditional Hawaiian feathered helmets worn by King Kamehameha the Great as an expression of royalty and sovereignty was replaced in subsequent reigns by western-style crowns as a new symbol of sovereignty.[9]

The process of western acculturation that became apparent in the visible symbols of the Royal Court in Hawaii began to accelerate by mid-century, during the reign of King Kamehameha IV. Hawaiian royalty began to model themselves closely on British royalty. One of the ways that the Hawaiian royalty borrowed from the monarchical template of Great Britain was in the establishment of royal orders for merit and service to the Crown of Hawaii.

Orders of chivalry began in the middle ages as institutional bodies of knights who owed allegiance to a lord, and to their fellow members of the order. They embodied the values of exclusive admission, loyalty to their prince, and inclusion in an elite community. In subsequent centuries European monarchs established modern royal orders of knighthood that were modelled on the medieval concept of an order of chivalry. The characteristics of British orders of chivalry included formal admissions to an order, the use of prefix titles and post-nominal letters, the payment of fees by members of the order, the appointment of officers to administer an order, and regular meetings of the membership to instill both a sense of community and to reinforce loyalty to the Crown. There was also a strong religious element operative in British orders of chivalry, a reflection of both the medieval values of such institutions, as well as the establishment of a state religion in Great Britain.

The Hawaiian monarchy wished to establish a system of royal orders in Hawaii to recognize both loyalty and service to the Hawaiian Crown, and individual merit in promoting the interests of the Kingdom of Hawaii.[10] The first step was undertaken by King Kamehameha V in 1865, when he established the first royal order in the Hawaiian Islands, the Order of Kamehameha I, named for his illustrious grandfather, who was responsible for the creation of the modern, unified, Kingdom of Hawaii. All of the Hawaiian royal orders were modelled on the royal orders of the United Kingdom, both institutionally as well as in their basic design elements. All of the physical decorations were manufactured by jewellers employed by the firm of A Kretly in Paris.[11]

In 1865, shortly after his unilateral promulgation of the 1864 Constitution, King Kamehameha V established the Royal Order of Kamehameha I with three classes, the Knight Grand Cross, the Knight Commander, and the Knight Companion. This Order was conferred for service to the Royal House of Hawaii, or to the people of Hawaii. The King was the Grand Master of the Order and other officers, including a Chancellor of the Order, a Secretary, and a Treasurer, were appointed from amongst the members of the Order. The insignia of the Order consisted of a white enamelled gold cross with a shield in the center upon which was placed several stylized letters K.

For the Knight Grand Cross, the highest class of the Order, the cross was placed upon an eight-point star. The Knight Commander, and the slightly smaller Knight Companion, were accentuated by rays of gold between the arms of the cross. Both examples were worn suspended from the neck by a ribbon of red and white. The Knight Companion cross was sometimes manufactured of silver rather than of gold. The grant of the Order carried no prefix title with it (such as Sir) but the recipients were permitted to use post-nominal letters attached to their surnames; KGCK (for the Knight Grand Cross), KCK (for the Knight Commander) and CK (for the Knight Companion class). Members of the Order resident in the Hawaiian Islands were annually summoned to attend a meeting of the Council of the Order. This Order was conferred 57 times by King Kamehameha V and 82 times by King Kalakaua but it was not conferred during the short reigns of King Lunalilo, or Queen Liliuokalani. To the end of the monarchy, this Order remained the preeminent royal order of the Hawaiian Kingdom.[12]

Among the prominent Hawaiians who received this Order were Mataio Kekuanaoa, the father of Kings Kamehameha IV and V; Charles Kanaina, father of King Lunalilo, and Caesar Kapaakea, father of King Kalakaua and Queen Liliuokalani. Prince Lunalilo, David Kalakaua, Governor Kanoa of Kauai, and Governor Nahaolelua of Maui were also honoured with this Order. Several awards were made to Emperors and Kings, and to other grand royalty in Europe and Asia, as well as to the President of France. The settler community in Hawaii was well represented with Orders given to men prominent in business and society, such as Charles R Bishop, the banker and husband of Princess Bernice Pauhi Bishop, Hawaiian historian Abraham Fornander, and bandmaster Henry Berger.[13]

When King Kalakaua came to the throne in 1874, he embarked upon the creation of a series of additional royal orders. Firstly, he created the Royal Order of Kalakaua I to mark his own assumption of the Hawaiian throne. Similar to the Royal Order of Kamehameha I this new award was intended to reward distinguished and meritorious service rendered to the throne, or to Hawaii. There were four classes, Knight Grand Cross, Knight Grand Officer, Knight Commander and Knight Companion. The Knight Grand Cross consisted of a blue and white enamelled cross of gold fixed upon an eight-pointed breast star. Surmounted on the cross was a shield with a centred *kahili* and surrounding the shield was a banner reading "Kalakaua February 12, 1874". The award also came with a pendant cross attached to a bowed blue ribbon sash.

The Knight Grand Officer was initially of a different design but was subsequently changed to match the Knight Grand Cross, albeit slightly smaller. The Knight Commander award and the Knight Companion award both consisted of a blue and white enamelled gold cross (silver for the Knight Companion) placed upon a gold wreath with crossed Hawaiian royal staffs (*puloulou*). The shield on the crosses contained the same design as the two senior classes but the cross in each case was surmounted by a Crown. On the reverse side of the cross the inscription '*Keola*' ('eternal life') was inscribed, together with the year 1874, the year of Kalakaua's accession to the throne of Hawaii. The Knight Commander award was worn around the neck suspended from a collar ribbon, while the Knight Companion was fixed to a breast ribbon that was worn over the chest.

In addition, the Royal Order of Kalakaua I had a special feature associated with the rank of a Knight Grand Cross. The Sovereign of Hawaii, as Grand Master, could award a Chain consisting of linked stylized KIK ciphers separated by *kahilis* in red and gold with a front-piece of gold leaves wreathing the royal cipher KIK, as a special mark of distinction. This award seems to have been patterned on the Royal Victorian Chain of Great Britain, which is closely associated with Britain's Royal Victorian Order. As with the Royal Victorian Chain, the Kalakaua Chain was an award that was intended to be bestowed on foreign princes, rather than on Hawaiian subjects, though there was no formal restriction on awarding the Kalakaua Chain to a Hawaiian subject. The only recipient (other than King Kalakaua himself) was Britain's Prince of Wales, Prince Albert Edward, later King Edward VII.[14] The Kalakaua Chain that King Kalakaua wore was presented to him as a gift from the Hawaiian military, and contained 466 diamonds, as well as opals and rubies.[15]

Most of the awards of this Order went to foreign royalty or to diplomats both Hawaiian and foreign. Among indigenous Hawaiians, awards were made to Prince Leleiohoku and Charles Kanaina, Princess Poomaikelani, Prince David Kawananakoa, and Prince Kuhio Kalanianaole, Governor Kapena of Maui, and Governor Kipi of Hawaii, John and Samuel Parker, and Curtis Iaukea. High government officials also received the award, such as the Chief Justice, as did some members of the settler community. Perhaps the most prominent local recipient was Father Damien of the lepers' settlement on Molokai, who was made a Knight Commander of the Order in 1881.

In 1880, Kalakaua created the Royal Order of Kapiolani, a novel approach to royal orders in that it commemorated a great female *alii*, Kapiolani the Great, who was the first, and most senior Hawaiian *alii* to be converted to Christianity by the protestant missionaries that came to Hawaii shortly after the rejection of the *kapu* system. This award was particularly intended to honour those Hawaiians who had distinguished themselves in the fields of science, art, and humanity. It was divided into six classes, including a special class of Lady Companions, although Hawaiian female royalty, and foreign female royalty, were also appointed to the most senior class of the Order. The classes of this Order were the Grand Cross, High Grand Officer, Grand Officer , Commander, Officer and Companion.

The Grand Cross of the Order consisted of a red-enamelled gold cross interspersed with crowns between the arms of the cross, the whole surmounted by a portrait medallion of the commemorated *alii*, Kapiolani the Great, above the upper arm of the cross. Superimposed on the centre of the cross was a shield enamelled in red, with a white enamelled banner surrounding it. Upon the shield there was centred two stylized letters K and on the surrounding banner was the inscription '*Kulia I Ka Nuu*' ('Strive for the Summit'). The Grand Cross came with a yellow sash bordered by a red, white, and blue fringe, and a pendant cross suspended from the bow of the sash. The High Grand Officer award was distinguished from the Grand Cross only by the wearing of the small pendant cross suspended from the neck, while the Grand Officer class omitted the sash and pendant cross. The Commander class was identical, and was surmounted by a crown and suspended from the neck by a red and yellow striped collar ribbon. In addition, the word 'Kulia,' the first word in the motto of the Order, was inscribed on the reverse side of the cross. The Officer class was the same as the Commander class but smaller and suspended from the chest by a breast ribbon of red and yellow stripes. The final class, the Companion award, was divided into divisions. The first, a general division presumably intended for males, received the identical cross as the other classes but in silver instead of gold. It was suspended from the chest by a breast ribbon of red and yellow stripes. The second division, a ladies division, provided for a silver cross of the same design as the other crosses of the Order but it was worn suspended from a red and yellow striped bow.[16]

A medal was also associated with this Order containing the same cross but without crown supporters, or a surmounting crown, and was to be worn on the chest suspended from a red and yellow striped breast ribbon. As with some British orders that also contained a medal (i.e., the Royal Victorian Medal of the Royal Victorian Order) the Kapiolani Medal was intended as a junior award and did not confer any of the privileges of the Order itself on the recipients. The Medal was awarded in both a first and second grade.[17]

The Grand Cross of this Order was conferred on Queen Kapiolani, and on Princesses Liliuokalani, Poomaikelani, and Kekaulike, and on Princes David Kawananakoa, Edward Keliianhonui, and Kuhio Kalanianaole. Most of the awards went to foreign naval officers, and government officials. Among government officials, Henry Berger, the Royal Hawaiian Bandmaster, was honoured with this Order. Other local awards went to the members of the settler community who were engaged in commerce in Hawaii. Given that this Order honoured a Hawaiian *alii* woman, the largest number of awards made to females among the Hawaiian Royal Orders was of the Royal Order of Kapiolani. Among the female recipients was Mother Superior Marianne of the Roman Catholic convent, a woman much adored by Premier Walter Gibson.[18]

To mark the occasion of his forthcoming coronation as King in February, 1883, King Kalakaua created the Royal Order of the Crown of Hawaii in September, 1882, to recognize meritorious and distinguished service to the Crown and to Hawaii. There were five classes in this Order, as well as a medal. The Grand Cross of the Order, consisted of a white enamelled gold cross with a centre shield possessing a superimposed gold crown with a blue enamelled ring around the shield and bearing an inscribed banner stating 'Hawaii Ke Kalaunu' ('Crown of Hawaii'). The Grand Cross was placed upon a diamond-shaped silver breast star and worn with a white sash bordered in blue stripes, with a pendant cross suspended from the bow of the sash. The Grand Officer award was a smaller version of the Grand Cross *sans* pendant cross and was sometimes awarded without the sash. The Commander award consisted of the cross without the breast star and was worn from the neck on a collar ribbon of white, with blue stripes. The Officer award was similar but was worn on the chest from a white breast ribbon with blue borders. The cross was surmounted by a crown. The Companion level was the same as the Officer award but the cross was manufactured in silver.[19]

A Crown of Hawaii Medal in two grades was also associated with this Order, and was intended as a junior award for long service. A gold medal was prescribed for 20 years of military service to the Crown, and a silver medal was prescribed for 20 years of civil service.

Appointments to this Order included Queen Kapiolani, and

Princesses Liliuokalani, Likelike, Poomaikelani and Kekaulike. Among government personnel, Premier Gibson and Cabinet Members received it. Colonel Iaukea, was also honoured with this Order for his diplomatic efforts. Queen Liliuokalani employed this Royal Order to honour indigenous members of the Royal Hawaiian Band.[20] The usual foreign awards were also made and, in this instance, there were quite a number of awards made to officials of the Persian Government, as well as to Japanese and western naval officers. A number of appointments were also made from among the settler business community in Hawaii.

The final royal order created by King Kalakaua was the Royal Order of the Star of Oceania, which he created in 1886, and which he seems to have intended to be primarily a reward for diplomatic achievement in the carrying out of the Primacy of the Pacific Policy of the King and his Premier, Walter Murray Gibson. It was given to those persons who displayed meritorious service in promoting Hawaii in the islands of the Indo-Pacific region, and on the neighbouring continents. There were six classes in this Order, all similar in name to the Royal Order of the Crown of Hawaii but differing in design. The Grand Cross was actually a five-pointed green and white enamelled star, with a green and white enamelled shield representing the ocean, and a beacon, and stars above. The star itself was placed upon a five-point silver breast star. A red-enamelled ring surrounding the shield bore the inscription 'Ka Hoku O Osiania' ('The Star of Oceania'). It was worn with a sash of green, bordered in white, and with a pendant cross suspended from the bow of the sash. The Grand Officer class was the same as the Grand Cross class *sans* the sash and the pendant star. The Commander award was essentially the same, with the star surmounted with a crown and worn from the neck suspended from a collar ribbon of light green with white borders. The Officer class was similar to the Commander class but smaller in size and worn on the chest suspended from a breast ribbon of pale green with white borders. The Companion level was divided into two divisions. Recipients in the (male) general division received a star without the surmounting crown that was borne upon a looped ribbon of pale green and white and worn on the chest suspended from a breast ribbon. The ladies' division was similar but worn suspended from a bow of the same colours.

Associated with the Order was a medal in two grades, one of gold and the other of silver. The medals did not carry the privileges of the Order. A set of formal court dress was prescribed for the recipients of this Order, and according to the Hawaiian Government Gazette it was to consist of; ". . . a black dress coat, with the cuffs and . . . collar trimmed with green and gold cord; white satin vest [and] knee breeches; garters ornamented with gems; black silk stockings; patent leather slippers; a court rapier . . . and [a] court chapeau without plume."[21]

The Star of Oceania was the rarest of all Hawaiian Royal Orders and only 25 awards were made during the reign of King Kalakaua. The Order was not conferred at all by Queen Liliuokalani. The Grand Cross was never conferred on a recipient, and even King Kalakaua never wore it. Although Premier Gibson was the architect of Kalakaua's Primacy of the Pacific Policy, he never received this Order. Staunch monarchists Sydney Hoffnung, the Hawaiian Charge d'affaires in Great Britain, and Paul Neumann, a prominent attorney in Honolulu, both received the Grand Officer award. Only two appointments were made to the Lady Companion Division, one of them to Isobel Strong, the stepdaughter of Robert Louis

Stevenson, whose husband was the Court Painter at the Royal Court of Hawaii.[22]

As in the case of British Royal Orders, awards were generally open to men rather than to men and women together. However, King Kalakaua did not wish to exclude women from appointment to the Hawaiian Royal Orders and therefore in two of the orders, the Royal Order of Kapiolani, and the Royal Order of Oceania, the King created a separate Lady Companion division so that Hawaiian women could be honoured for their contributions to Hawaii, and to the Crown. A total of 21 female appointments to the Royal Order of Kapiolani were made by the King between 1883 and 1885, and two women were appointed by King Kalakaua to the Royal Order of Oceania between 1887 and 1890. Although there was no Lady Companion division in the constitution of the Royal Order of Kalakaua I, Queen Liliuokalani purported to make one such appointment in 1892.[23]

Although women were not appointed to the Royal Order of Kamehameha I, the preeminent Hawaiian honour, King Kamehameha V and King Kalakaua both granted permission to high-ranking female royalty to wear the highest insignia of the order. Those so honoured included Queen Emma, Queen Kapiolani, and Princess Victoria Kamamalu, Princess Ruth Keelikolani, Princess Bernice Pauahi Bishop, Princess Liliuokalani, and Princess Likelike.[24] Likewise, King Kalakaua granted permission to Queen Kapiolani and Princess Bernice Pauahi Bishop, Princess Liliuokalani, Princess Likelike, and Princess Kekaulike to wear the insignia of the highest division of the Royal Order of Kalakaua I.[25] Curiously, Princess Virginia Poomaikelani was formally appointed a Knight Grand Cross of that Order in 1890.[26]

As might be expected, the Royal Order of Kapiolani, established in honour of a notable female *alii* did have several royal female appointments, including two foreign royal women, Queen Maria Cristina, the Regent of Spain, and Princess Higashi Fushiminaya of Japan.[27] The Grand Cross of the Royal Order of the Crown of Hawaii was also conferred on Hawaiian female royalty, in the persons of Queen Kapiolani and Princesses Liliuokalani, Likelike, Poomaikelani and Kekaulike.

Finally, there was also a private royal order established by the Kalakaua dynasty, the Kalakaua Royal Household Order. Formal royal orders are usually worn with a uniform, and since women did not ordinarily dress in uniform, it has often been seen to be necessary in monarchies to provide for some indicia of royal status for women when they are wearing a gown. The solution has been an ornamental badge to be worn by women to denote their royal status. Such household orders are still used in the British monarchy, where a new Order is created for each succeeding reign. Since household orders are only conferred on female members of a royal family, and they are awarded only at the discretion of a monarch, examples of such orders are rare. Hawaii adopted the practice of a royal household order during the reign of King Kalakaua and a small gold and white enamelled badge was created with a stylized K in the centre and surrounded by a banner containing the inscription '*Kulia Kanuu* ('*Kulia Ka Nuu*' – the summit, was a personal motto of Queen Kapiolani). It is unknown how many badges of this Order were issued to the female members of the Royal Family but it is known that both Queen Kapiolani, and Princess Virginia Poomaikelani, possessed this Order.[28]

Many of the Hawaiian Royal Orders were conferred on foreigners, especially foreign royalty, official visitors to the islands, and visiting foreign naval officers. Awards of honours to foreigners were a common practice among nineteenth century monarchies, and Hawaii was no different in this respect. From the list of awards however, it is apparent that Hawaii made a particular effort to use a foreign conferral as a means to establish favourable diplomatic relations with Asian states that were successfully striving to maintain their independence against the onslaught of nineteenth century western imperialism. Thus, many awards were made to foreign royalty and other important persons in Japan, Siam, and Persia.

One notable person who is absent from the lists of appointments made to the royal orders of Hawaii is Princess Kaiulani. It seems she did not even possess the Royal Household Order, although it would have been natural for her to receive it. It is unclear why the Princess was omitted from the list of appointments made to the Royal Orders although her youth, and the fact that she was abroad from the age of thirteen, may have been a factor. Nevertheless, it is notable that King Kalakaua appointed the Princes David Kawananakoa, Kuhio Kalanianaole, and Edward Keliianhonui to the Royal Order of Kapiolani in 1883, while they were still teenagers.[29]

King Kamehameha V, who established the first of Royal Orders of Hawaii was also responsible for the establishment of another important institution of the Hawaiian Royal Court that continues to function even in the present day, the Royal Hawaiian Band, a brass, wind and (eventually) string ensemble, that plays both western-style marches, as well as more traditional Hawaiian music.

Acceding to popular wishes, King Kamehameha V sought the services of an accomplished bandmaster from Germany through diplomatic channels to reconstitute a public band in Honolulu (an earlier public band had disbanded). Kaiser Wilhelm I asked a German Army bandmaster, Henry Berger, to undertake the Hawaiian assignment.[30] Berger came with excellent references, having served in the Prussian Army as the bandmaster of the Kaiser's 2nd Life Guards. After accepting his selection for the new post Berger arrived in Honolulu in June, 1872. Scarcely one week later Berger was required to lead the small band that had awaited his arrival in Hawaii in the first-ever Kamehameha Day celebration. The occasion was a success, and Berger never looked back. Over the next 43 years he would lead the Royal Hawaiian Band under the Sovereigns of Hawaii, the Provisional Government, the Republic of Hawaii, the Territory of Hawaii and, after 1905, the City of Honolulu. Not only would he bring sprightly European marches to Hawaii but he would grow to love Hawaiian music, and he would preserve a great deal of it for musical posterity. Berger notably added female singers to accompany the band, one of the first formal bands to do so. He is most famous for arranging the music for *Hawaii Ponoi*, the national anthem of Hawaii for which King Kalakaua supplied the lyrics in 1874. Always on good terms with Hawaii's Sovereigns, Berger experienced his most poignant performance as bandmaster in 1898, when he led the band in playing *Hawaii Ponoi* for its final time as Hawaii's national anthem during the annexation ceremonies held at Iolani Palace in Honolulu.

The greatest, and the most enduring symbol of the Hawaiian Royal Court became its centerpiece, Iolani Palace, in downtown Honolulu. When Honolulu was restored to the status of the capital city of the Kingdom in 1845, King Kamehameha III obtained a fine house recently built by the Governor of Oahu, Mataio Kekuanaoa, and originally intended by him as a residence for his daughter, Victoria

Kamamalu, which the King thereafter established as his official royal residence. It remained the official royal residence of the Hawaiian Sovereigns during several subsequent reigns, and was named Iolani (the royal or heavenly hawk) by King Kamehameha V.[31]

After the accession of King Kalakaua in 1874, the new King found the old palace compound to be in poor condition and he asked Archibald Cleghorn, the consort of his sister Princess Likelike, to begin a process of renovation and demolition on the palace compound, which resulted in the removal of the old palace. In 1878, the legislature appropriated funds for a new palace, and work began on a design prepared by Honolulu architect Thomas J Baker, with revisions by San Francisco architect Charles J Wall. Iolani Palace is sometimes architecturally described as American Florentine in style but its design elements can be seen in many other late Victorian colonial buildings across the tropics.

The new Iolani Palace was quite striking, with high ceilings pierced with many windows, some of them etched with Hawaiian motifs. Long lanai on both the main and the second floor of the palace admitted natural light, and cooling breezes. Six towers dominated the overall building design, with the four corner towers preventing the lanai from completely wrapping around the building. A large tower centred in the front of the building (and matched by a similar tower at the rear) added a sense of grandeur to the front and rear stairs of the palace. There was an attic and a basement level in the palace, and an excavation around the base of the palace allowed for light and soft breezes to reach the basement level, where court and household officials maintained their offices and establishments.

The King was determined to create a palace for Hawaiian Sovereigns that would be on a par with the palaces he had seen in Europe during his world tour, and that would symbolize the royal authority of his independent Kingdom. Therefore, little expense was spared in the design and construction of the new palace. A master carpenter in Honolulu, George Lucas, supervised much of the woodwork that went into the new Iolani Palace and the building incorporated many beautiful native Hawaiian woods such as *koa, kamani,* and *kou.*[32] American walnut and white cedar obtained from Oregon were also used in the interior of the palace.[33] The exterior of the palace was completed in concrete to ensure that the structure would be long-lasting. Iolani Palace was equipped with the most modern plumbing available in the 1880's, with several full bathrooms and functioning water closets that provided Italian marble washbasins, and copper baths. Running water was supplied from an artesian well located on the grounds of the palace. Although it was initially designed for gas lighting at night, the King ordered the gas lines ripped out after his 1881 round-the-world tour introduced Kalakaua to the marvels of a new invention, electricity. At a substantial additional cost King Kalakaua directed that the new palace be equipped with electric lighting. Thus, Iolani Palace had electric lighting by 1887, only four years after electricity had begun to be installed in Buckingham Palace, the official royal residence of the sovereigns of Great Britain.

In entering Iolani Palace visitors rose above the ground on the stone stairway and reached the grand entry hall where they faced the impressive grand staircase leading up to the second level. To their left was a reception room decorated with blue upholstered sitting furniture and drapes, and thus attracting the name, the Blue Room. From the Blue Room visitors could proceed into the State Dining Room, which was lined with portraits of European monarchs that were gifted to Hawaii by those monarchs themselves. A special portrait, much treasured, was that of British Rear Admiral Thomas of the Royal Navy who stepped in to quash the ill-advised seizure of the Kingdom by Lord Paulet during the reign of King Kamehameha III. Here in the State Dining Room both King Kalakaua and Queen Liliuokalani presided over state dinners with local and foreign dignitaries.

Upstairs there were bedrooms for the King, the Queen, and their guests. A library *cum* office was the place where the Sovereigns conducted the business of state, and where the meetings of the Privy Council were held. In another sign of forward thinking by King Kalakaua, a telephone system was installed in this location and through it the King could telephone both within the palace and outside within the city through the Hawaiian Bell Telephone Company.

The Gold Room was a place of private entertainment for the Royal Family. Here they retreated and enjoyed music, and all of the members of the Kalakaua Royal Family were accomplished musicians. The members of the Royal Family composed notable Hawaiian music, and the King himself, while serving as a colonel on the staff of King Lunalilo, collaborated with the Royal Hawaiian bandmaster Henry Berger to create Hawaii's beautiful national anthem, *Hawaii Ponoi*.[34] Equally talented, Princess Liliuokalani created Hawaii's most popular ode, *Aloha Oe* and, as the deposed Queen she created the *Queen's Hymn*, which continues to be played in the twenty-first century at religious services in Hawaii.

Finally, there was a magnificent Throne Room, decorated in crimson. Two carved and crimson upholstered thrones stood upon a dais at the head of the Throne Room, with side chairs ranged along the windows and a circular sofa in the centre of the room. In the Throne Room the Hawaiian Sovereigns held formal audiences for diplomats and important visitors, received petitions from their subjects, and issued royal proclamations. The Throne Room was also the scene of many splendid balls and formal receptions, all much enjoyed by King Kalakaua.

Iolani Palace was a very advanced centre of government for its day and it was on a par with the facilities afforded to heads of state in the capitals of the major western powers. However, giving Hawaii a functioning royal palace on a par with European countries came at a substantial cost. Furthermore, King Kalakaua's penchant for making changes to incorporate the latest technology, as in his decision to replace gas lighting with electrical lighting in the palace, contributed to massive cost overruns. Those cost overruns created very real tensions between the commercial interests that were represented in the Hawaiian Legislature, and the King, souring the loyalty of many of the Hawaiians of foreign ancestry and especially those who traced their origins to the United States of America. For many in the *haole* community the substantial financial outlays required for the completion of the palace called into question the King's financial judgement.

The Iolani Palace compound did not consist of Iolani Palace alone. There were other buildings in the compound, including the barracks for the Royal Guard, which had been constructed in 1871, and a bungalow known as the Hale Akala adjacent to the palace where the royal couple could live more informally. The bungalow was often used as a retreat by Queen Kapiolani. Father afield, the King maintained a boathouse down at the harbour front, which he used as a personal retreat and where he frequently entertained informally. In addition to the Iolani Palace compound, King Kalakaua and Queen Kapiolani purchased a summer residence on Hawaii Island, Hulihee Palace, from the estate of Princess Bernice Pauhi Bishop, as the heir of Princess Ruth Keelikolani, in 1885. Hulihee Palace was originally leased from Princess Ruth by King Kamehameha IV, and it had also been used after that King's death by his widow Queen Emma, and then subsequently by King Lunalilo.[35]

The King and Queen moved into the completed Iolani Palace in December, 1882, and plans were already underway at that point for a formal coronation of the King and Queen. Hitherto, Hawaiian monarchs had not been formally crowned in a public ceremony because coronations were a European tradition. Nevertheless, with his reign now seemingly secure Kalakaua wanted to arrange a public ceremony to confirm his, and his family's, possession of the Hawaiian throne. A coronation ceremony would also serve to underscore that the Hawaiian monarchy was the monarchy of a modern state, and the Hawaiian Court was as sophisticated as any of the European monarchies half a world away. Such symbolism was important because it confirmed Hawaii's place in the community of nations in the nineteenth century. The Hawaiian Premier, Walter Murray Gibson, defended the expenditures necessary for the coronation ceremony in the Hawaiian Legislature as a patriotic necessity that would assert the national spirit of the Hawaiian people, and entrench their claim to national independence.[36]

Although the ceremony of a coronation was culturally alien to the ancient traditions of Hawaii, Gibson tried to relate it to the traditional ceremonies for the installation of a Hawaiian high chief stating that in ancient ceremonies a new Sovereign was anointed and decorated with *maile* in a ceremony called *poni,* which Gibson maintained was the Hawaiian equivalent of a coronation in a European monarchy.[37] The coronation ceremony conceived by Kalakaua and Gibson was, however, ill-received by the settler community. John Mott-Smith, a member of the House of Nobles deplored the ceremony as one that was alien to Hawaiian history and sentiment.[38]

The coronation pageantry in Honolulu stretched over many days and involved a number of events and celebrations, including the coronation ceremony itself, a state dinner at Iolani Palace, public fireworks, the dedication of a statue of King Kamehameha the Great, a *Hookupu* or gifting ceremony, in which Hawaiians presented a gift to a chief, in this instance, the King, a Grand Ball at Iolani Palace, a Regatta at the harbour, horse races at Kapiolani Park, a diving contest, hula performances, and a Grand Luau.[39]

In preparation for the ceremony the King, by Letters Patent,[40] formally granted royal titles to those near and dear to him who had not previously been so honoured, and granted rights of precedence to the members of his family. The titles and precedence established by the King for the members of the Royal Family were (in their order of precedence):

Her Majesty Queen Kapiolani

Her Majesty Queen Dowager Emma

Her Royal Highness Princess Liliuokalani

His Excellency John Owen Dominis (husband of Liliuokalani)[41]

Her Royal Highness Princess Likelike

88

The Honourable Archibald S Cleghorn

Her Royal Highness Princess Victoria Kaiulani

Her Royal Highness Princess Virginia Kapooloku Poomaikelani

Her Royal Highness Princess Victoria Kinoiki Kekaulike

His Royal Highness Prince David Kawananakoa

His Royal Highness Prince Edward Abnel Keliiahonui

His Royal Highness Prince Jonah Kuhio Kalanianaole[42]

February 12, 1883 dawned bright and sunny for the only formal coronation ceremony to be held under Hawaiian skies (and the only royal coronation ceremony ever to be held on a territory that would eventually become part of the United States of America). A Coronation Pavilion had been constructed on the grounds of Iolani Palace, and a raised platform was constructed from the first floor of the palace lanai to connect to the pavilion. Surrounding the Coronation Pavilion on three sides was a giant wooden-covered amphitheatre to accommodate the invited guests in comfort. The eight columns of the Coronation Pavilion represented the eight inhabited islands of the Hawaiian Islands chain. On each side of the octagon was inscribed the name of the Sovereigns of Hawaii surrounded by a laurel wreath. The armorial bearings of Hawaii, and of the major western powers were displayed on the outside of the pavilion, emphasizing that the Kingdom of Hawaii was an accepted member of the community of nations.

School children and members of civil societies began marching onto the palace grounds by 9:00 A.M. over reeds cast upon the muddy streets, still damp from the rains of the preceding three days.[43] At 10:15 in the morning the palace gates were opened and invited guests began taking their places at the direction of the Grand Master of the Coronation Ceremony, Hon. J A Cummins, and his staff of ushers. Three thousand people took their assigned places within the amphitheatre and another 1000 people, primarily schoolchildren, were accommodated on the raised platform. In addition, to those guests, a further three thousand people from amongst the general public were permitted to enter the grounds to watch the ceremonies from afar.[44]

Diplomatic representatives attending the ceremony included a special representative from Japan sent for the occasion, Sugi Magoshichiro, Envoy Extraordinary and Minister Plenipotentiary of Japan. The western countries merely left it to their existing diplomatic and consular representatives accredited to Hawaii to attend the ceremony on behalf of their respective countries. In attendance were the Minister of the United States, the Commissioner and Consul General of Great Britain, the Commissioners of France and Portugal, the Consuls of Italy, Germany, Sweden and Norway, the Netherlands, Belgium, United States, Mexico, Denmark, Austria-Hungary and Russia.

The domestic attendees included the members of the Privy Council of Hawaii, Premier Gibson and the Hawaiian Cabinet, the members of the Supreme Court of Hawaii, and the judges of the District Courts, the Governors of the individual islands, government officials, members of the Legislature, the clergy, and many members of the general public, most of whom were indigenous Hawaiians. As the preparations for the formal Coronation Procession continued inside the palace, an elderly Hawaiian woman began chanting a *mele* extolling the King's genealogical lineage to demonstrate his highborn *alii* status, and thus his eligibility for the throne, as well as his personal accomplishments.

At 11:00 A.M. the sky clouded over but no rain fell. At 11:30 A.M. the King's Chamberlain appeared with the royal heralds who announced the approach of their Majesties and as the Royal Hawaiian Band began to play the national anthem, *Hawaii Ponoi*, the Coronation Procession emerged from Iolani Palace, and proceeded to the Coronation Pavilion in the following order:

The Marshal of the Royal Household, Hon. J M Kapena

The Marshal of the Kingdom of Hawaii, Hon. W C Parke

The Chaplain of the Royal Household, Rev. A MacIntosh

The President of the Legislative Assembly, Hon. Godfrey Rhodes

The Chancellor of the Kingdom of Hawaii, Hon. A Francis Judd[45]

HRH Princess Victoria Kaiulani, bearing flowers

HRH Princess Miriam Likelike and her consort Hon. A S Cleghorn

HRH Princess Lydia Liliuokalani and her consort Governor the Hon. J O Dominis

Bearer of the King's Jewels and Decorations

Bearer of the Sceptre

Bearer of the Sword of State[46]

Bearer of the Crowns[47]

Bearer of the Robes

Bearer of the *Palaoa*

Bearer of the *Puloulou*

Bearer of the Torch of Iwikauikaua

Bearer of the *Kahili* of Pili

The King's Chamberlain

Their Majesties the King and Queen

Bearers of Her Majesty's Train

The Ladies in Waiting to Her Majesty[48]

Ladies in Waiting to HRH Princess Liliuokalani[49]

Ladies in Waiting to HRH Princess Likelike[50]

The King was dressed in the uniform of the Royal Guard, in a white jacket and blue pants, and wore the Royal Order of Kamehameha I, and several of his foreign Orders. The Queen was dressed in a gold embroidered white satin gown with a crimson and black velvet train, her hair immaculately coiffed with a diadem. The choir began to sing *Almighty Father, hear! The Isles do wait on Thee* as the royal party took their places on the Coronation Pavilion after which the Marshal of the Royal Household began a recitation of the King's formal names and decorations and then declaimed that David Kalakaua was "the rightful occupant of the Hawaiian Throne and Sovereign Chief of the Hawaiian Islands and their Dependencies, as heretofore claimed by his predecessors, chosen by the Nobles and Representatives of the Kingdom" and called upon those present to "render unto His Majesty all fealty and loyal obedience under the laws of the Realm."[51]

Following the pronouncement of the Marshal, Princess Poomaikelani advanced toward the throne, and taking the Hawaiian regalia presented to King Kalakaua a *Puloulou*, a *Palaoa* on a cushion, the Torch of Iwikauikaua, and the *Kahili* of Pili, as ancient symbols of Hawaiian supremacy which the King accepted, and which were then placed to the side of his throne. The *Puloulou* was made from the tusk of a Narwhal, and tipped in gold and it bore a gold orb. Suspended from the orb was gold plate upon which was the Royal Coat of Arms of Hawaii, the colours being enamelled, and beneath the Royal Arms a gold ribbon upon which was inscribed the Hawaiian heraldic motto "The life of the land is preserved in righteousness." The ancient symbolic importance of the *Puloulou* was as an emblem of the bearer's *kapu* status and thus of Kalakaua's right to the Hawaiian throne.[52] In the contemporary western context the *Puloulou* was said to represent the royal protection afforded to everyone by Hawaiian law.[53] The *Puloulou* was the first piece of royal regalia presented to King Kalakaua because it established his status.[54]

The *Lei Niho Palaoa* was a whale tooth pendant (always ideally taken from a sperm whale) that was strung on a necklace of braided human hair and was a visible symbol of the very highest ranking Hawaiian *alii*. The tooth was carved in a manner representing a hook, which also represented the tongue, and was therefore symbolic of the oratorical importance of the King's pronouncements.[55] The *Palaoa* was considered to be a vessel of the King's *mana*.[56]

The Torch of Iwikauikaua was representative of Iwikauikaua, a great chief of Hawaii's past who began a tradition of burning *kukui* torches during the daylight hours whenever royalty was present during official ceremonies. It was symbolic of the high *alii* status of Kalakaua, and of his descent from Iwikauikaua. While any Hawaiian could burn torches made of *Kukui* nuts (*Aleurites moluccana*) at night, only those Hawaiians who were descended from Iwikauikaua could claim the right to burn *Kukui* torches during the daylight hours, a right that Kalakaua possessed by descent.[57]

The *Kahili* of Pili, made of white feathers, was an ancient symbol of Hawaiian royalty and was once possessed by Chief Pili of Hawaii Island.[58] The *kahilis* were most often made of the wood of the *Kauila* tree (*Alphitonia ponderosa*) and only the chiefs in the Hawaiian Islands were entitled to use them. Chief Pili of Hawaii Island was said to have lived in the 12th or 13th century and Kalakaua also claimed descent from him.[59]

The Chancellor then approached the King and asked if His Majesty was prepared to reaffirm the oath he had taken nine years before at his accession ceremony and upon his assenting to that request the King arose and stood before the Chancellor. King Kalakaua raised his right hand and repeated:

"I, David Kalakaua, King of the Hawaiian Islands, having on the 12th day of February, A.D. 1874, in conformity with the provisions of the Constitution of the Kingdom, been duly elected by the Legislative Assembly of the Hawaiian Islands in the Legislature of the Kingdom assembled to the Throne of Hawaii, and having on the following day taken the oath prescribed by Article 24 of the Constitution, do hereby of my own grace and motion solemnly reaffirm the same, and I do hereby solemnly swear in the presence of Almighty God to maintain the Constitution of the Kingdom whole and inviolate, and to govern in conformity therewith."[60]

The King then signed the oath and returned to his place on the throne.

The Chancellor then presented to the King the Sword of State, as the emblem of Kingly justice and mercy, and received it back from the King. The Chancellor thereupon entrusted the sword to its bearer, Colonel Iaukea, and instructed him to unsheathe it for the duration of the ceremony. The Hawaiian Sword of State was closely modelled on the English Sword of State and was manufactured of fine Damascus steel with the Royal Arms of Hawaii inlaid in gold on the blade. The sword hilt and guard were also of gold, and were finely engraved. A sheath of purple velvet held the sword.

Princess Kekaulike, the Governor of Hawaii Island, and a younger sister of Queen Kapiolani, then approached bearing the Royal Mantle and presented it to the Chancellor who draped it over the King's shoulders stating: "Receive this ancient Royal Mantle of your predecessors as the ensign of knowledge and wisdom." The Royal Mantle consisted of a feather cloak made from the yellow feathers of the O'o bird and was approximately 4 feet in length and semicircular in design with a total area of approximately 25 square feet.[61] The feathers were fixed on a bark underlay and created a shimmering and magnificent symbol of Hawaiian royal status and authority.[62] Scarlet Iiwis (Vestiaria coccinea) feathers lined the neck line of the cloak, which was embellished further by a purple velvet neck border.[63] Although there were other lesser feather capes, only the Sovereign was permitted to wear this one.[64]

After receiving the Royal Ring from its bearer, the Chancellor placed it on the King's fourth finger stating: "Receive this ring, the ensign of Kingly dignity." The King's ring was weighty – almost one ounce, and made of fine Etruscan gold and holding an engraved Carnelian bearing the Royal Arms of Hawaii with a one carat diamond on each side of the supporters on the Royal Arms.

Next the Chancellor, upon receiving the Royal Sceptre from its bearer, presented it to the King as the "ensign of Kingly power and justice." The sceptre was more than two feet in length, and constructed of gold with a base designed as an Ionic column possessing entwining laurel leaves embedded in the polished shaft with three ram heads forming the capital. The grip was covered in velvet, and crowning the top of the sceptre was an orb bearing a dove with outstretched wings, symbolic of peace, in this instance the King's Peace, that was enforced within the realm by the authority of the Sovereign.

At this point, the choir began to sing the hymn *Almighty Father! We do bring, gold and gems for the King*, as Prince Kawananakoa and Prince Kuhio approached bearing the Royal Crowns and the King rose from the throne. The Princes presented the Royal Crowns to the President of the Legislative Assembly, Godfrey Rhodes, who took the King's Crown and held it up before the assembled public, and then placing it in the Chancellor's hands stated: "I present this Crown to the rightful King of these Islands, approved by Acts of the Legislative Assembly in the Legislature of the Kingdom assembled of the years 1880 and 1882." The Chancellor thereupon took the Crown from the President and passed it to the King with the words: "Receive this Crown of pure gold to adorn the high station wherein thou hast been placed." Then the King took the Royal Crown and placed it on his own head before the dignitaries and the people of Hawaii who had assembled for the purpose of bearing witness to that event. Next, the King took the slightly smaller Crown provided for Queen Kapiolani and before her the King stated: "I place this Crown upon your head to share the honours of my throne." Now at this point in the Coronation Ceremony there was a quasi-comical interlude because it was discovered that the Queen's Crown could not be seated upon her head because of the elaborate coiffure that she had arranged for this, the most auspicious occasion of her life. Immediately, her ladies-in-waiting attended her, and they sought to rearrange the coiffure to permit the Crown to sit easily upon her head but it was all to no avail. The King, now frustrated, took the Crown and jammed it down on his consort's head with sufficient force to seat it but causing the poor Queen to wince in pain.

The Crowns were made in England and each Crown consisted of a band of gold studded with diamonds, opals, and polished *kukui* nuts. A Maltese cross adorned the front and back of each Crown and from the band rose eight bars of gold over a crimson velvet cap, the eight bars symbolizing the eight inhabited islands of the Hawaiian chain. The bands were interspersed with gold taro leaves. A globe of dark red enamel studded with pearls sat atop the meeting point of the eight gold bars and was surmounted by a Maltese cross of gold set with diamonds. The Queen's Crown was slightly smaller in dimensions than the King's Crown. Each Crown had embedded within it 521 diamonds, 54 pearls, 20 opals, 8 emeralds, 6 polished *kukui* nuts and a carbuncle (probably a red garnet).[65] As the ceremony proceeded, clouds briefly obscured the sun and a single star appeared in the sky, a favourable omen that was later remarked upon by the participants and observers of the coronation.[66]

Reverend MacIntosh then intoned a prayer:

"Almighty Father, who crownest thy faithful servants with mercy and loving kindness, look down upon these, thy servants, Kalakaua and Kapiolani, who now in lowly devotion bow their heads to Thy Divine Majesty; and as Thou dost this day set crowns of pure gold upon their heads, so enrich their royal hearts with Thy Heavenly Grace, and crown them with all princely virtues which may adorn the high stations wherein Thou hast placed them, and Thine the honour and glory for ever and ever. Amen."[67]

The King and Queen, now crowned, resumed their thrones and at a signal, cannon in the batteries at the waterfront, and at the Punchbowl crater, boomed in celebration and were answered by the guns of the British, French, and American warships anchored in Honolulu harbour. The choir sang *Cry out O Isles with Joy* as the Coronation Procession reformed, and retired into Iolani Palace. The King then received the Privy Council, government officials, members of the diplomatic corps, and the foreign naval officers attending the ceremony but the Queen retired upon returning to the Palace, and therefore the women who attended the ceremony were not formally received. So ended the first, and only, Hawaiian coronation ceremony.

Although the Coronation Ceremony was modelled on European practices, and particularly on the British coronation ceremony, it departed from the coronation procedure followed in the United Kingdom in one significant aspect. Unlike a British coronation, there was an absence of the anointing of the Sovereign, thus omitting what is the most overtly religious and mystical element of a British coronation ceremony. Its absence from the ceremony was significant, as under the ancient Hawaiian religion an anointment of a new King (*poni*) was a feature of a new King's ascension to a Hawaiian throne. Perhaps the King thought that the European medieval religious imagery of a sovereign selected by God to reign would not be suitable for a King who was elected to the office rather than born to it. However, it is more likely that the King felt politically challenged by the settler community, which had strong connections to the missionary church in Hawaii centred on Kawaiahao Church. That may explain the use of a Coronation Pavilion on the palace grounds for the ceremony rather than the use of a religious institution, which is the British practice.[68] In any event, King Kalakaua himself was not a particularly devout man. Thus, despite the prayers offered at the ceremony the Hawaiian Coronation was much more a secular, rather than a religious ceremony.

Two important elements of Hawaiian society held themselves aloof from the Coronation Ceremony. The divide between the former Royal House of Kamehameha and the new Royal House of Keawe-a-Heulu remained a fault line in Hawaiian society. None of the surviving high *alii* of the former royal family, Dowager Queen Emma, Princess Ruth Keelikolani, or Princess Bernice Pauahi Bishop, attended the Coronation Ceremony, although all of them received invitations to attend. Their absence was particularly unfortunate because it exposed the royal fault lines in Hawaiian society to a settler community that was hardening its attitude toward the Hawaiian monarchy. The bitterness that followed David Kalakaua's election to the throne over Dowager Queen Emma in 1874, also continued to contribute to a belief among some segments of indigenous Hawaiian society that Kalakaua was an upstart.

Although King Kalakaua did try to mend relations with the remaining members of the Kamehameha dynasty, his efforts remained unappreciated by any of the grand ladies who carried on the traditions of their dynastic house. In fact, the rivalry continued between the two royal houses to the bitter end. When King Kalakaua built Iolani Palace as a showcase for the Kalakaua line Princess Ruth built Keola Hale, a palatial mansion of her own in downtown Honolulu to rival the King's grand mansion.[69] In her memoirs, Queen Liliuokalani maintained that the Kalakaua family had to present itself at a public ceremonial, such as the coronation, in order to publicly establish the new stirps of the reigning family upon the failure of the Kamehameha line.[70]

The second group that dismissed the King's coronation was the settler business community, which saw the coronation as an extravagant and unnecessary expense. As more and more of the economic life of the Kingdom passed into their hands, they grew less and less tolerant of the political control that native Hawaiians continued to exercise over the government of Hawaii. The settlers, concerned for their wealth, feared that indigenous control of the government would lead to increased taxation, directly threatening their wealth. Many were descendants of Americans who hoped for the future annexation of Hawaii by the United States. Ceremonies such as the coronation, which were designed to foster national pride, and a celebration of Hawaiian patriotism, were rejected by this community. Few of the American-descended business, or professional, leaders in Hawaiian society attended the Coronation Ceremony[71] and the national press that opposed the King's government actively sought to disparage the event, even criticizing the manner in which the King placed his crown upon his head.[72]

Nevertheless, the Coronation Ceremony was a great success for the Keawe-a-Heulu dynasty, and it was followed up by a ceremony to dedicate a specially-commissioned statue of King Kamehameha the

Great in front of the Aliiolani Hale, then the seat of the Hawaiian Legislature, and where the statue remains to this day. The King and Premier Gibson had ordered the statue to commemorate the centennial of Captain Cook's European discovery of Hawaii and in their nationalist mode of thinking they wished to emphasize that it was Kamehameha, the founder of the Kingdom, who was among those that had met Captain Cook on Hawaii Island.[73] The unveiling of the statue had been delayed both by the time the sculptor took to complete the project, and by the fact that the statue was lost at sea near the Falkland Islands, requiring that a replacement be cast and sent out to Hawaii. So the unveiling ceremony coincided with Kalakaua's coronation celebrations. The King made a speech, the statue was unveiled, and "Great enthusiasm was manifested by the people," according to American Minister Rollin M. Daggett in his report to the President of the United States on the coronation festivities.[74]

In the days following the coronation a state dinner and a state ball were held at Iolani Palace, and there were public fireworks, a regatta, and commemorative horse races, hula dances, and a grand Hawaiian luau attended by 5000 people.[75] The coronation state dinner was unfortunately marred by an incident involving the King's sisters. Princess Liliuokalani was upset that Dowager Queen Emma was to be given precedence at the dinner over her, the Heiress Apparent to the throne, and, as result, Liliuokalani refused to attend the state dinner, as did her sister Princess Likelike, the mother of Princess Kaiulani. However, their husbands, J O Dominis, and A S Cleghorn, did attend the dinner.[76]

Heraldry played a role in the Hawaiian monarchy similar to the European royal houses. The Royal Arms of Hawaii were publicly displayed, as were the personal standards of various monarchs, and the members of the Royal Family. In 1842, Reverend William Richards and *alii* Timoteo Haalilio were in Europe as representatives of King Kamehameha III's government and while they were there they commissioned the College of Heralds in London, England, to prepare formal armorial bearings for the Kingdom of Hawaii. The result, slightly modified, was adopted by Hawaii in 1845, as the Royal Coat of Arms and they were used, with minor modifications, until the downfall of the monarchy in 1893.

The subsequent seals of the Republic, Territory, and State of Hawaii, were all derived from the Royal Arms of Hawaii. In heraldic terms the shield of the Kingdom was quartered with the first and fourth quarters displaying stripes from the National Flag of Hawaii and the second and third quarters containing in each a *puloulou* or, in heraldic terminology, *a ball argent on a staff sable*. In the centre of the shield was a smaller shield of a green background with a triangular device lying across two spears, or, in heraldic terms, *in escutcheon oct, triangular banner argent, leaning on a cross saltire*, which represented an ancient banner used by Hawaiian chiefs when they were at sea, before European contact. Above the shield was a crest in the form of a crown and on each side of the shield was a supporter in the form of a man, one bearing a *kahili* and the other a spear. Both were clothed with feather cloaks, and were representations of Hawaiian *alii*. Beneath the shield ran a banner and upon it was inscribed the motto of Hawaii, *Ua mau ke ea o ka aina I ka pono* which means: *The life of the land is perpetuated by righteousness.*

In addition, monarchs of both the Kamehameha and Keawe-a-Heulu dynasties employed personal flags to represent the monarchy, and the particular members of the Royal Family. Such flags, or personal standards, were flown both on land and at sea when particular members of the Royal Family were present. The first historical evidence of the use of a Royal Flag occurs in the reign of King Kamehameha III. Although the precise description of that flag is unknown there is a general knowledge of it from a sketch made by one Alexander Adams, probably in the late 1840's. The flag apparently had eight alternating stripes taken from the national flag with the Shield of the Royal Arms centred on a white square that was superimposed on the stripes of the flag. The Royal Flag was intended to be hoisted on ships bearing a member of the Royal Family, and to be flown on land whenever a member of the Royal Family was present for a public event. Thus, the Royal Flag was an institutional flag rather than one personally associated with a member of the Royal Family. The historical evidence suggests that this Royal Flag continued to be used during the reigns of Kings Kamehameha III, IV, V, and King Lunalilo.

During the Keawe-a-Heulu dynasty, the Royal Flag also continued to be used but with modifications. The Keawe-a-Heulu versions of the Royal Flag omit the two supporters on either side of the shield on the coat of arms, as well the banner containing the national motto.

In addition, King Kalakaua adopted a personal standard consisting of a white flag with the shield of the Royal Arms centred in the middle of the flag. This personal standard was also used by Queen Liliuokalani as her personal standard. Both monarchs also continued to use the Royal Flag, as well as their own personal standard.

King Kalakaua also granted personal standards to two other members of the Royal Family. A personal standard was authorized for Princess Likelike, consisting of alternating red and white stripes with a white square in the middle upon which was contained a version of the shield from the coat of arms surmounted by a crown but with a modification to the shield. Rather than the ancient device of a *puela*, or triangular device borne by the ancient chiefs at sea the Princess's shield displayed a *puloulou* in the centre. Finally, a personal standard was granted to Princess Likelike's daughter, Princess Kaiulani, and consisted of a solid red background with the shield and crown as displayed on her mother's standard upon a white square, centred on the flag.[77]

The last great public ceremonial of the Kalakaua years occurred in the autumn of 1886 when King Kalakaua celebrated his fiftieth birthday with a Golden Jubilee celebration. For two weeks commencing on November 16, 1886, a series of public events were held including fireworks, bonfires, royal receptions, parades, regattas, athletic competitions, hula dancing, balls, and athletic competitions to mark the King's birthday. A historical parade from the corner of King and Nuuanu streets to Iolani Palace included historical floats, costumed warriors, hula dancers, fishers demonstrating their netting techniques, and musical bands.[78] The birthday festivities ended with a formal state dinner. All of the events combined cost $15,000, a source of consternation to those in the commercial elite, who continued to oppose what they considered to be royal mismanagement.[79]

NOTES

[1] Alexander, 86

[2] Despite the practices of the ancient Hawaiians, the *I'iwi* still

survives but the *O'o* and the *Mamo* are extinct. Habitat loss and species collection contributed to their loss.

[3] Seiden, 7

[4] Iaukea, 8

[5] Barclay, 12

[6] Seiden, 8

[7] Mellen, 21, 25

[8] Quoted in Alexander, 181

[9] Seiden, 9–10

[10] The main source for the description that follows of Hawaiian Royal Orders is Gordon Medcalf, *Hawaiian Royal Orders*, Oceania Coin Co., Honolulu, 1963. Medcalf's work is the primary source for information concerning Hawaiian orders of chivalry.

[11] Williams, 140

[12] Medcalf, 7–8

[13] Medcalf, 9–12

[14] Medcalf, 15

[15] Gibson (Adler and Barrett), 95

[16] For a list of the recipients of this Order see Medcalf, 25–26

[17] Medcalf, 26

[18] A list of the recipients of this Order may be found in Medcalf, 27–30

[19] A list of the recipients of this Order may be found in Medcalf, 33–34

[20] A list of the recipients of this Order may be found in Medcalf, 35–40.

[21] Quoted in Gibson (Adler and Barrett), 95

[22] A list of the recipients of this Order may be found in Medcalf, 45–46.

[23] Medcalf, 23

[24] Medcalf, 8

[25] Medcalf, 15

[26] Medcalf, 17

[27] Medcalf, 27

[28] Gordon Medcalf and Ronald Russell, *Hawaiian Money, Standard Catalogue, 2nd ed.*, Honolulu/Washington, 1991, 158.

[29] Medcalf, 27. Queen Liliuokalani appointed Prince Kawananakoa and Prince Kalanianaole to the Royal Order of Kalakaua I in 1892, when they were respectively aged 24 and 21.

[30] Scott C. S. Stone, *The Royal Hawaiian Band, Its Legacy*, Island Heritage Publishing, Waipahu (HI), 2004, 11

[31] Rhoda E A Hackler, *Iolani Palace*, Friends of Iolani Palace, Honolulu, 2016, 3.

[32] Hackler, 8

[33] Wisniewski, 75

[34] Stone, 19

[35] J Patricia Morgan Swenson, *Treasures of the Hawaiian Kingdom*, Daughters of Hawai'i, Honolulu, 2007, 12-14

[36] Stacey L Kamehiro, *The Arts of Kinship: Hawaiian Art and National Culture of the Kalakaua Era*, University of Hawaii Press, Honolulu, 2009, 29

[37] Kamehiro, 30

[38] Kamehiro, 29

[39] Kamehiro, 31

[40] Letters Patent are a formal document issued in the name of the Sovereign under the Great Seal of the Kingdom and in the common law they are an ancient legal form for the exercise of a Sovereign's royal prerogatives. Most commonly they are issued where the Sovereign wishes to grant a discretionary privilege to a subject.

[41] Precedence granted to the non-royal spouses of the Princesses would only last during the joint lives of the married couples. The precedence established for those of royal birth was permanent.

[42] *By Authority*, The Pacific Commercial Advertiser, February 17, 1883, Honolulu, 5

[43] Workmen installed a corrugated tin roof over the amphitheatre between 4 AM and 6 AM on the day of the coronation when it became obvious that the roof was not water resistant, and that guests would be drenched if it rained during the ceremony.

[44] Author unknown, *Coronation of Their Majesties the King and Queen of Hawaiian Islands, at Honolulu February 12, 1883* [hereinafter "Coronation"], Advertiser Steam Printing House, Honolulu, 1883, 2

[45] Judd was Chief Justice of the Supreme Court of Hawaii. The Chancellorship was an associated position that acknowledged his role as the head of the Hawaiian judiciary.

[46] Colonel Iaukea of the King's staff was given this honour.

[47] Colonel Boyd of the King's staff was given this honour according to *Coronation* at p. 4.

[48] Mrs. C H Judd, Mrs. C P Iaukea, Mrs. Colburn, Mrs. L Pohaialii, Mrs. A N Tripp, and Mrs. M King

[49] Mrs. C B Wilson, and Miss S Sheldon

[50] Miss Clara, and Miss L Coney

[51] *Coronation*, 4

[52] Kamehiro, 36-37

[53] *Coronation*, 7

[54] Kamehiro, 39

[55] *Necklace (lei niho palaoa)* early 19th century, accession of the Metropolitan Museum of Art, New York, https://www.metmuseum.org/art/collection/search/313842 [accessed March 19, 2020]

[56] Kamehiro, 39

[57] Kamehiro, 42

[58] *Coronation*, 7

[59] Kamehiro, 41

[60] *Coronation*, 5

[61] Kamehiro gives dimensions of 56 inches in length and 148 inches in width for the mantle.

[62] Kamehiro, at 46, states that 450,000 feathers were used in making the cloak.

[63] Kamehiro, 45

[64] *Coronation*, 7

[65] *Coronation*, 7. After the Hawaiian coup thieves entered the palace (quite likely the Provisional Government's own guards) and stole the jewels in the King's Crown, leaving it wrecked. It has since been restored with fake jewels for display at Iolani Palace. The Queen's Crown was in the private possession of Dowager Queen Kapiolani at the time of the coup and it remains intact.

[66] Liliuokalani, *Hawaii's Story by Hawaii's Queen*, Mutual Publishing, Honolulu, 1990, 103

[67] *Coronation*, 5

[68] The coronation of a British monarch is held in Westminster Abbey in London.

[69] Princess Ruth lived in her new mansion only very briefly following its grand opening in the spring of 1883. She became ill and decided to return to Hawaii Island where she died on May 24, 1883.

[70] Liliuokalani, 104

[71] One who apparently did attend was Sandford Dole whose wife said it was "a glorious day" and there was "much pageantry." (Sarah Vowel, *Unfamiliar Fishes*, Riverhead Books, New York, 2011, 187/ 234)

[72] *Crowned! Kalakaua's Coronation Accomplished! A Large But Unenthusiastic Assemblage*, Hawaiian Gazette, Honolulu, February 14, 1883, 2. The King crowned himself because it was considered *kapu* for a commoner to pass his or her hands over the head of a great chief (Kamehiro, 53).

[73] Kamehameha was also present at the death of Cook, and was injured when Captain Clerke of HMS Discovery, having assumed command of Cook's expedition, fired a four-pounder cannon into a mass of Hawaiians on the shore (Gavan Daws, *Shoal of Time, A History of the Hawaiian Islands*, University of Hawaii Press, Honolulu, 1968, 22).

[74] Rollin M Daggett, Daggett to Frelinghuysen, *Papers Relating to the Foreign Relations of the United States*, Transmitted to Congress, With the Annual Message of the President, December 4, 1883, No. 329, Washington, 1883.

[75] Seiden, 11

[76] Iaukea, 50

[77] A complete discussion of Hawaiian royal standards is contained in Askman, *Royal Standards of the Kingdom of Hawai'I, 1837-1893*, The Hawaiian Journal of History, vol. 47 (2013), 61

[78] Gibson (Adler and Barrett), 87

[79] Wisniewski, 80; Webb and Webb, 43

4

The Reign of Kalakaua Rex

In many ways, the reign of Princess Kaiulani's uncle, King Kalakaua, marked a change in the character of the Hawaiian monarchy from the royal reigns that had preceded it. An intelligent man, David Laamea Kamanakapuu Mahinulani Naloiaehuokalani Lumialani Kalakaua was educated locally at the Chief's School, which was established for those *alii* who were considered to be the potential future sovereigns of Hawaii. Kalakaua also read law under the guidance of Honolulu lawyer Charles C Harris but he interrupted his legal education to take on a number of positions in the Hawaiian public administration, eventually becoming the Hawaiian Postmaster-General, and subsequently the King's Chamberlain under King Kamehameha V. Upon completing his legal education he was called to the Hawaiian Bar as an attorney. He was appointed a colonel in the Hawaiian military under King Lunalilo, and he afterwards retained a great fondness for military uniforms and accoutrements. Though intelligent, politically astute, and committed to the progress of his country, Kalakaua also displayed several less desirable character traits, including a lack of self-discipline, a spendthrift nature, and a certain naivete in his personal judgements about the character of the people that he appointed to important offices. As a well-known *bon vivant*, King Kalakaua enjoyed gambling, alcohol, music, sports, the company of beautiful women, and a life of luxury.[1] As King, those personal characteristics soon brought him into conflict with the austere and dour temperament of the missionary-descended Caucasian settlers from the United States.

By the time that David Kalakaua ascended to the throne of Hawaii in 1874, the country had largely become a modern, westernized state. However, westernization would prove to be a weak barrier against the arrival of American imperialism. Early in the nineteenth century the missionaries despatched from the United States had assisted the Hawaiians by creating a model constitutional monarchy, as a bulwark against foreign claims that Hawaii was an uncivilized state. The early work of the missionaries enabled Hawaii to resist the depredations of adventurers from both Europe and North America.[2] However, the strategic position of Hawaii in the North Pacific Ocean made it a desirable acquisition by western countries, and Hawaii was always at some risk of a foreign invasion by Russia, France, Britain, or America, during the first half of the nineteenth century. Unequal treaties pressed on Hawaii by the major powers also threatened its independence, and a Hawaiian diplomatic mission undertaken during the reign of King Kamehameha III seeking the redaction of those treaties failed. However, the controversy over Lord Paulet's seizure of the country for Great Britain in the 1840's, subsequently led to the Anglo-French convention that recognized Hawaii's independence. When the United States also agreed to recognize Hawaiian statehood in the Tyler Doctrine, international *de jure* recognition of Hawaii's independence was assured.[3]

Although Hawaii became an internationally recognized country, and a member of the worldwide community of nations by the time King Kalakaua came to the Hawaiian throne, the new King faced many challenges, both domestically and internationally, in maintaining Hawaiian independence. In domestic policy, his chief challenge was to maintain the indigenous Hawaiian monarchy as a bulwark against the political effects of the declining indigenous population, the demographic impact of increasing immigration from western and Asian countries, and the increasing control over Hawaii's economy that American and European settlers were establishing. Yet, maintaining overall prosperity in the islands was also an important challenge, and it was essential to ensuring the continued loyalty of the western settlers. Prosperity required the Hawaiian Government to ensure a welcoming environment for the inflow of foreign capital, and to provide for an adequate labour supply for agriculture, which became the main economic driver following the decline of the whaling industry.

Economic access to the US domestic market for Hawaiian agricultural products, primarily sugar cane, was essential to Hawaiian prosperity and that put trade relations with the United States at the top of King Kalakaua's foreign policy agenda. Rapid increases in the consumption of sugar in the United States, amounting to a five-fold increase in American sugar consumption, drove the expansion of both the US domestic sugar producers as well as foreign sugar producers. The importation of raw sugar became the largest single import into the United States in the late nineteenth century.[4] Increasingly, a small number of sugar barons came to dominate the Hawaiian economy as the century wore on.[5] Their outsize influence impacted both domestic and foreign policy in Hawaii, and an imbalance began to grow between those who held economic power in Hawaii, principally in the white settler community, and the repository of political power in the country, the indigenous Hawaiians. That power imbalance contributed to an erosion in harmonious relations between different ethnic groups in Hawaii.[6]

The sugar cane industry was labour intensive, and the continual demographic decline in the indigenous Hawaiian population, together with an aversion by indigenous Hawaiians to the hard labour entailed in the harvesting of cane, created significant constraints on the development of the sugar cane industry in Hawaii. The solution adopted was to import foreign labour, and beginning in the reign of King Kamehameha V foreign labour was brought into Hawaii. Initially Chinese immigrants were accepted under labour contracts that lasted several years. When those contracts expired most of the Chinese workers went home to China with their earnings but some of them opted to settle in Hawaii, where they married indigenous Hawaiian women.

The insatiable drive by the sugar industry to obtain labour to work in the cane fields eventually brought significant numbers of Japanese, Portuguese, and Pacific Islanders into Hawaii throughout the latter part of the nineteenth century. During that period there was also continued immigration from Europe and North America. In a short period of time the complexion of the Hawaiian population changed forever. The census data from this period underscores the magnitude of the demographic changes that transpired in the Hawaiian Kingdom. The table below illustrates this.

1876 Hawaiian Population Demographics

Hawaiian	46,500
Part-Hawaiian	3,000
Caucasian	3,500 (450 Portuguese)
Chinese	2,500
TOTAL	55,500

1900 Hawaiian Population Demographics

Hawaiian	30,000
Part-Hawaiian	10,000
Caucasian	27,000 (18,000 Portuguese)
Chinese	26,000
Japanese	61,000
TOTAL	154,000

The precipitate decline in the population of indigenous Hawaiians was heartbreaking, especially as so many Hawaiian parents suffered the loss of their children to diseases that were hitherto unknown to Hawaiians and brought into the kingdom by travellers and immigrants from Europe, Asia, and the Americas. When King Kamehameha III came to the throne, he presided over a kingdom of about 150,000 indigenous inhabitants but by the close of King Kalakaua's reign there were only about 35,000 indigenous Hawaiians, a loss of 115,000, and that loss deprived the monarchy of its strongest base of political support, and endangered the independence of the islands during an era of western imperialistic encroachments in the Pacific Ocean.[7] Hawaiian Sovereigns characterized the fall in the indigenous population as the most serious issue facing the country.[8] King Kalakaua encouraged the Board of Health to work toward a reduction in the rate of infant mortality, and he suggested tax incentives for people who had a large number of children.[9] In his first royal tour of the Kingdom, Kalakaua emphasized again and again to his people that the decline in the population was a very serious challenge for the Hawaiian Kingdom.[10] The King called his policy to reverse indigenous demographic decline *Hooulu Lahui*, meaning "increase the nation."[11]

Another challenge that King Kalakaua and his government faced was the integration of disparate ethnic and racial groups into Hawaii in a way that avoided social and cultural tensions. Part of the domestic political challenge faced by the Kalakaua dynasty was a growing divide between ethnic groups within the Hawaiian population. Although Americans and British residents controlled the majority of foreign investments in Hawaii, the country was experiencing a large influx of Chinese, Japanese, and Portuguese immigrants. In campaigning for the throne Kalakaua had deliberately associated himself with a policy of 'Hawaii for the Hawaiians,' thus emphasizing a preferential policy toward the indigenous population that was potentially detrimental to the growing settler community. Once on the throne King Kalakaua quickly adjusted his policy to maintain the loyalty of the economically powerful Caucasian settler community, although he continued to promote the indigenous culture of his Kingdom. As a result, the policy of the Kamehameha Dynasty, which was to effect a fusion of the indigenous and settler populations, was no longer emphasized.[12]

Among the foreign-born, or foreign-descended class, a sugar plantation economy had been firmly established, and the planters and the mercantile and professional classes perceived their common interests. Linkages between these groups were fortified by intermarriage between the settler families. Although some Caucasian males in the settler community, such as Archibald Cleghorn, Princess Kaiulani's father, did marry into prominent indigenous Hawaiian families, the opposite did not occur. Caucasian settler women generally did not marry into prominent indigenous families. Instead, they married into other settler families, reinforcing a Caucasian settler ethnicity that saw itself as separate (and superior to) the indigenous Hawaiian community.

Immigration had another pronounced effect. Early visitors to the islands noted the great ability and effectiveness of the Hawaiians as farmers.[13] The food supply of the major towns was adequately supplied by the domestic market farming sector of the economy. However, the importation of contract labour into the islands resulted in new competition for the indigenous Hawaiians within the agricultural sector. Most of the foreign contract labourers came from peasant stock in their home countries and when their contracts expired some elected to remain in Hawaii, where they became small farmers, and competed with the indigenous Hawaiians. As a result, the indigenous Hawaiians lost their dominance in the market farming sector of the economy.[14]

Many of the immigrants from east Asia prospered as settlers in Hawaii, and like some of the Caucasian men they also took Hawaiian wives and contributed to the mixture of races in the Kingdom. Among the most prominent in the Chinese-Hawaiian community was Afong Chan, who married a Hawaiian woman and sired four sons and 12 daughters, the latter renowned for their beauty. Afong Chan obtained substantial wealth and eventually became the first settler of Chinese ethnicity to be appointed to the King's Privy Council.[15] The loyalty expressed by the Chinese-Hawaiian community to King Kalakaua was noted by the western settler community.[16]

As foreign immigration changed the demography and culture of the Kingdom, King Kalakaua became particularly concerned about the loss of indigenous Hawaiian traditions and he sought to ensure that the cultural treasures of the Hawaiian people would not be lost in the race to develop a modern country. He rescued classical hulas, a form of dance that promoted the expression of the soul in the movement of the body from the underground obscurity to which the disapproval of missionaries had earlier banished it. The missionaries regarded the hula as dangerously lascivious. However, hulas remained a major cultural flashpoint between the indigenous population and the strait-laced settler community through the remainder of the nineteenth century. The King also wished to rescue the ancient stories of Hawaii from oblivion and to that end he authored a book of Hawaiian myth and legends.[17]

All of the members of the Royal Family during the era of the

Kalakaua dynasty were capable and talented musicians who contributed substantially to the development of Hawaiian music. The King himself collaborated with Henry Berger, the Royal Hawaiian Bandmaster, to create *Hawaii Ponoi*, the National Anthem of the Kingdom of Hawaii. Kalakaua's successor, Queen Liliuokalani, is also justly famous for her composition *Aloha Oe*, the most widely recognized, and cherished, of Hawaiian songs.

King Kalakaua's promotion of Hawaiian independence and Hawaiian indigenous culture increasingly brought him into conflict with the settler community in Hawaii. The obvious decline in the indigenous population, and the economic necessity of accessing the US sugar market, encouraged the settler community, and particularly those from an American-descended, or American-born, origin to push for closer economic integration with the United States through a trade reciprocity treaty. A growing minority of those with American roots also hoped for a political union with the United States. Those in the settler community who hailed from the United States, or whose ancestors did, also retained a strong American cultural aversion to monarchy, as the creation narrative of the United States portrayed monarchy, in the person of King George III of Great Britain, as tyrannical. As time went on American and European immigrants, and their descendants in Hawaii, found more and more faults with the political structure of the country. Those attitudes were increasingly coupled with a rising sense of white racial superiority as rapid industrialization in western countries made Asian, African, and Oceanic countries seem backward by comparison, and therefore ripe for colonizing by the western powers.

In the Pacific Ocean, the acquisition of control over many of the remaining independent Pacific islands fuelled the political aspirations

118

of elements of the Hawaiian settler community who sought political control over Hawaii. In 1840, the Maori of New Zealand had ceded the sovereignty of their islands to the British Crown, and subsequently the New Zealand Government supported a Polynesian Chartered Company as a vehicle to extend British control over Polynesia. Their ultimate goal was the creation of an autonomous dominion, with New Zealand at the centre, similar to the political project that had created Canada in 1867.[18] Further to the east, in 1842, pressure by France on Queen Pomare IV of Tahiti produced an ultimatum requiring that she accept a French protectorate over the Kingdom of Tahiti. The timing of the French ultimatum was somewhat unfortunate for the Queen, as she was late in a pregnancy and expecting to give birth shortly.[19] With only moral support available from Great Britain, the Queen of Tahiti was unable to resist the French pressure and she was forced to concede the protectorate.[20] [21] In 1881, three years after the Queen's death France annexed Tahiti outright, after Queen Pomare's alcoholic son and heir, King Pomare V, ceded the entire sovereignty of the kingdom to France.[22]

In 1867, the United States acquired territory much closer to the Kingdom of Hawaii by laying formal claim to the Midway Islands, which are located at the northernmost extension of the Hawaiian Island chain. The annexation of the Midway Islands followed an earlier American claim under the US Guano Act.[23] Secretary of State William H Seward wanted the Midway Islands as a potential naval station in the mid-Pacific but after their acquisition it was discovered that they would not provide a useful harbour for US naval vessels. Nevertheless, the US maintained its sovereignty claim over the islands.

In 1887, French pressure compelled Queen Amelia of Uvea, in the Wallis and Futuna group, to concede a French protectorate over Uvea.[24] A Catholic priest was designated as the French Resident to handle matters concerning foreign relations and issues involving Europeans on the island. The following year France extended its protectorate over the smaller neighbouring kingdoms of Alofi and Futuna, thus bringing the entire Wallis and Futuna group into the French Empire.[25] In 1888, Great Britain established a protectorate over Rarotonga, and then subsequently extended that protectorate over all of the Cook Islands in the South Pacific before transferring the protectorate to the jurisdiction of the colony of New Zealand.[26] Britain had previously annexed the islands of Fiji in 1874, after American pressure on Fijian King Cakobau for compensation for damages incurred by the American consul compelled the King to cede his sovereignty to Queen Victoria. The British established protectorates over the Gilbert and Ellice Islands in 1892 and over the Solomon Islands a year later.[27] Only Hawaii, in the North Pacific, and the Kingdom of Tonga, in the South Pacific, remained under the political sovereignty of their original inhabitants.[28] The annexation of the South Pacific islands fortified a growing sentiment of white supremacy that was not lost on the settler community in Hawaii, who began to view indigenous rule in Hawaii with increasing disdain.

In 1867, the United States acquired Alaska, including the Aleutian Islands in the North Pacific, from the Russian Empire. That acquisition was stage-managed by US Secretary of State William H Seward and although the acquisition of Alaska was decried in the American Press as Seward's Folly, it actually gave the United States a commanding strategic position across the northernmost reaches of the North Pacific Ocean.

In 1871, a new political entity emerged on the Pacific coast of North America when the colony of British Columbia joined Canada. Although Canada was a self-governing country, it remained linked to Britain which continued to administer Canada's defence and foreign affairs. In the coming struggle over Hawaii's future the Hawaiian Government would occasionally look to Canada as an alternative economic partner for the Kingdom whenever it seemed that the Reciprocity Treaty between Hawaii and the United States was in jeopardy.

In the eastern North Pacific Japan had continued to emerge from self-isolation following the forcible opening of the country by Commodore Matthew Perry of the United States Navy in 1853. In 1868, the shogunate, the hereditary military government which exercised the delegated powers of the Emperor of Japan, fell from power and the ultimate political authority was restored to the Emperor, and to officials who were answerable to him. Thereafter, Japan embarked upon a significant modernization program to ensure that it would have the economic and military strength to match the Western powers, in order to ensure its independence. But like the western powers Japan was not averse to taking advantage of weaker island nations. In 1879, Japan compelled the incorporation of the neighbouring Ryukyu Kingdom into the Empire of Japan.

The international pressures faced by King Kalakaua were equally matched by the domestic imperative of providing for the prosperity of his country. Foremost among the challenges facing the King and his government after his accession was the negotiation of a reciprocity treaty with the United States to allow the duty-free importation of Hawaiian sugar into the United States. In that endeavour the government of Hawaii was successful, and a reciprocity treaty was negotiated with the United States in June, 1875. While the reciprocity agreement with the United States provided economic stability to the Kingdom of Hawaii it also brought the position of the island kingdom to the forefront of American foreign policy interest, and it foreshadowed a growing desire on the part of some Americans to acquire the Kingdom. When the American Minister to Hawaii, Henry A Pierce, returned to Washington to testify on the proposed reciprocity treaty before the Senate Committee on Foreign Relations he reflected the desires of those Americans who actively sought to colonize the islands, telling the Committee that:

> "The acquisition of the Hawaiian Islands by the United States, sooner or later, must become a national necessity, to guard the approaches against hostile attempts on the Pacific States . . . the future necessities and exigencies of the United States will cause the Hawaiian Islands to become part and parcel of our great republic, either through the course intimated, or, if need be, through cost of much blood and treasure necessary for their conquest; and considering the critical position of political and commercial affairs in that quarter, I desire to strongly urge upon you to consummate a treaty with the Hawaiian Islands, and thereby bind them to this country with all the force of gravitation and self-interest."[29]

If the positive argument for Hawaiian annexation based upon a strategic necessity in connection with the future domination of the Pacific was insufficient to sway uncertain senators, Pierce went on to paint a picture of the potential for British aggrandizement toward Hawaii, always a useful shibboleth in nineteenth century American politics, by suggesting that Hawaii would be forced into intimate commercial relations with Canada, New Zealand, Fiji, or Australia if the United States failed to approve the proposed Reciprocity Treaty.[30]

To ensure that the United States would ratify the reciprocity treaty King Kalakaua undertook a state visit to the United States, leaving his brother Prince Leleiohoku to govern Hawaii as Regent. The King arrived aboard a US warship in San Francisco in late November, 1874, and proceeded across the United States by train, giving the King a personal view of the vast size of the United States.[31] King Kalakaua was well received by Americans across the country, and in Washington he was met at the railway station by Secretary of State Hamilton Fish and two US Marine battalions serving as an escort. The King was received in a Joint Meeting by the US Congress, although illness prevented him from reading the speech that he had prepared for the occasion. President Grant held a state dinner for the King at the White House, the first American state dinner for a visiting head of state.

Throughout his journey Kalakaua's position as a foreign potentate put to rest for the moment the racial prejudices of American society, and the King's darker complexion did not bring out racial stereotyping. In fact, King Kalakaua became so popular with Americans that rumours began to circulate that he was actually the son of a Caucasian American sea captain, and that his mother was a Hawaiian Princess.[32] Much later, when the settler community in Hawaii had turned against the King, and the missionary party in Hawaii could no longer reliably manipulate him, new rumours would be put out suggesting that Kalakaua was actually the son of an African-American barber who had sojourned in Hawaii, in an attempt to besmirch his public reputation in racially-prejudiced America.[33] In this, his first official visit, however, the King's

123

personal diplomacy undoubtedly smoothed the path for the eventual ratification of the reciprocity treaty by the United States, and the King returned to Honolulu in February, 1875, satisfied with the results of his trip, and lauded by all elements and classes of Hawaiian society for his efforts.

However, there was one significant result of the King's trip to Washington and the resulting Reciprocity Treaty with the United States that did not bode well for the future independence of Hawaii. The fourth article of the treaty contained a new restriction on the powers of the Hawaiian Sovereign that limited Hawaii's sovereignty:

> "It is agreed on the part of His Hawaiian Majesty, that, so long as this treaty shall remain in force, he will not lease or otherwise dispose of or create any lien upon any port, harbor, or other territory in his dominion, or grant any special privilege or rights of use therein, to any other power, state, or government, nor make any treaty by which any other nation shall obtain the same privileges relative to the admission of any articles free of duty, hereby secured to the United States."[34]

For the first time, the United States had made a claim to the islands of Hawaii by restricting the right of the Hawaiian Government to grant any formal concession, or transfer of land, to another foreign power. The American claim was crafted in the negative in order to prevent other nations from making a claim to Hawaiian territory but nevertheless it reflected the increasing American interest in the strategically placed islands. That concession to the United States actually caused a temporary rift in Hawaii's relations with other nations, especially Great Britain, and while it was soon smoothed over the British attitude to it remained disapproving, a feeling was concurred in by other European powers.[35]

It was on his American trip that King Kalakaua came into contact with a fantastic adventurer who would have a significant impact on the political stability of the Kingdom. Celso Caesar Moreno was born in the Italian Kingdom of Piedmont and Sardinia, and became a soldier in the Crimean War before attending university to become a civil engineer. Abandoning that career, Moreno went to sea as the captain of his own steamship, eventually settling in the Dutch East Indies where he married the daughter of a local Sultan. However, Moreno came into conflict with the Dutch colonial administration and he was forced to flee, abandoning his wife. He showed up in Washington in 1868, where he claimed that he was the elected ruler of an unclaimed Malayan island that he proposed to sell to the United States for $500,000. When that scheme failed he became involved in various projects to create a trans-Pacific cable, and he was able to meet with key congressional decision-makers, and with President Grant. Although he obtained legislative authorization from Congress to lay a trans-Pacific cable, he was unable to obtain financial backers, and his scheme failed. It was around this time that King Kalakaua travelled to America and Moreno took advantage of the opportunity to acquaint himself with Kalakaua, and to make a favourable impression on the impressionable King. Kalakaua was quite taken by the smooth-talking Moreno, and Moreno quickly made arrangements to travel to Hawaii to take advantage of his next big opportunity.

In Hawaii, Moreno tried but failed to obtain a subvention to support his cable scheme. However, his ingratiating personality fit perfectly with that of the convivial King Kalakaua, and Moreno became a court favourite. Moreno obtained Hawaiian nationality on August 14, 1880, and on that very day King Kalakaua appointed him to be the Foreign Minister, and effectively the Premier of Hawaii, after dismissing the competent and loyal Samuel Wilder, whose Cabinet had only recently obtained a vote of confidence from the Legislature. In appointing Moreno to such an important post King Kalakaua displayed an obvious sense of naivety toward someone who was transparently a bounder, and a main-chancer. Samuel Wilder was treated shabbily by the King, who sent one of his courtiers, Curtis Iaukea, to deliver a letter of dismissal to Wilder, rather than dismissing Wilder in person. For his part, Premier Wilder expressed no personal animosity toward the King over the treatment he received from him, and he remained loyal to his adopted country.[36]

Moreno's appointment energized the opposition in Hawaii to King Kalakaua's administration of the government and mass meetings were held in Honolulu to protest the Moreno appointment. Royalist courtier Curtis Iaukea later wrote that the dismissal of the Wilder Cabinet destroyed the faith of the mercantile community in the competence of the King, and put Kalakaua on a collision course with the American missionary descendants in Hawaiian society.[37] After Moreno held office for a mere four days, the King was compelled by the public clamour to dismiss him.

A program to send deserving Hawaiian youth abroad to further their education had recently been established and, as a consolation, Moreno was appointed as the guardian of several youths that were being sent to Italy, including Robert W Wilcox, a future Hawaiian insurrectionist. Moreno subsequently misrepresented his charges in Italy as members of the Hawaiian Royal Family in order to enhance his own status, resulting in his removal as their guardian. However, Moreno kept in contact with Robert Wilcox, and he might have recovered his standing in Hawaii if any of Wilcox's rebellions had actually succeeded in overturning the Hawaiian Government.

At the same time that public criticisms emerged of the King's appointment of Moreno there were continuing objections from the settler community about royal expenditures. Construction of the new Iolani Palace was underway in 1880-81, and costs of the building were high, attracting much public attention. The construction costs of Iolani Palace reached $343,545.00 by 1884.[38] That was a huge cost, and in the minds of many citizens it was an unnecessarily lavish expenditure for a small kingdom. But King Kalakaua wanted a palace that could keep company with the modern royal households of Europe, and that would speak to the modernity of the Kingdom of Hawaii. Most of the other expenses associated with the monarchy, such as the coronation ceremony, and the King's jubilee, also came in for stern criticism from the settler community, which did not favour expenditures designed either to enhance the profile of the King, or the Kingdom of Hawaii itself. There was also criticism over the expenses of maintaining a large number of missions and legations in foreign capitals.[39]

Faced with growing tensions at home, and concerned about enhancing the standing of Hawaii in international affairs, King Kalakaua decided in 1881 to embark upon a world tour. The new cabinet of William Greene thought it made good political sense for the King to leave the realm for a time to allow the Cabinet to restore political harmony in the Kingdom, following the uproar over Moreno.[40] Leaving the Kingdom in the hands of his sister, Crown Princess Liliuokalani,[41] the King travelled to California, where he arrived in January, 1881, before doubling back across the Pacific and proceeding to visit China (March-April), Hong Kong and Siam (April), Singapore, Malaysia, and Burma (May), India (May – June), Egypt (June), Italy (June-July) England and Belgium (July), Germany (July-August), Austria-Hungary, France, Spain and Portugal

127

(August) and Scotland (September) before returning home by crossing the United States (September–October). The King arrived home in Honolulu on November 6, 1881.

It was in Japan where the young Princess Kaiulani entered into the King's calculations concerning the future of his island Kingdom. During a private meeting with the Emperor Mutsuhito, King Kalakaua suggested that one way to enhance the relationship between the Empire of Japan and the Kingdom of Hawaii, possibly resulting in an alliance, would be through a royal marriage between the Royal Families of Japan and Hawaii. King Kalakaua had been much impressed with a young member of the Japanese Imperial Family, Prince Yamashina Yorihito, and Kalakaua proposed that a marriage be arranged between that Prince, and Princess Kaiulani, when the Hawaiian Princess came of age. Emperor Mutsuhito was noncommittal, suggesting that he would take the matter under advisement.

In Hawaii, Princess Kaiulani was quite naturally alarmed by the suggestion of a foreign dynastic marriage, and her mind was not put at ease when an important Japanese official, Lord Michinori Nagasaki, the Master of Ceremonies for the Imperial Court, subsequently made an official visit to Hawaii. However, Lord Nagasaki was engaged in more prosaic diplomatic discussions with Hawaiian officials, and so there were no further discussions about a possible marital union between the two royal families. But Kaiulani was not forgotten by the Japanese Government. Lord Nagasaki presented to Princess Kaiulani several beautiful Japanese kimonos, as well as silk rolls.[42]

In many ways, King Kalakaua's round-the-world trip became a

personal triumph for him. He was the first reigning monarch to circumnavigate the Earth, and everywhere he went he was received with the respect due to the Sovereign of an independent country. In addition to the reception that he received in Japan from the Emperor and high state officials he was met in China by the leading statesman of the late Manchu Empire, General Li Hung-Chang, and the mannered and well-educated Hawaiian King received favourable reviews in the Chinese media.[43] An elaborate reception for the King was held by the British Governor of Hong Kong, Lord Hennessey, and his wife, when the King visited the key British colony in the Far East. His visit to Siam, modern Thailand, enthralled King Kalakaua, who found many similarities in the temperaments of the Siamese and the Hawaiians, especially in their joint love of flowers and music. The King was much impressed by the riches of that country, displayed as adornments on the temples and palaces of the Siamese Kingdom.[44] The round the world voyage of the King allowed him to interact with monarchs and statesmen, and King Kalakaua's genial personality stood him well in his meetings with foreign leaders. His status as a Sovereign prevailed over any question of western racial superiority in the protocol of European courts, or the American government.

There was an increase in interest by other countries in Hawaii as a result of the King's visits to foreign lands. The trip also gave the King an opportunity to smooth over relations with Great Britain, which was still smarting over the terms of the Reciprocity Agreement with the United States that prevented Hawaii from alienating its territory, or entering into a similar trade agreement with any other country.[45]

Perhaps because a world tour by a reigning monarch was so

unprecedented the trip also gave rise to many unfortunate and negative rumours about the King's real purpose in undertaking such an extensive journey. Spurious rumours were started that the King planned to sell his Kingdom to a European power. King Kalakaua denied the rumours (which would have been unconstitutional if there had been any truth to them). Nevertheless, those rumours caused some consternation in US Government circles, where the new Secretary of State, James G Blaine, weighed in on the subject in an instruction to the American Minister to Hawaii: "If they [Hawaii] drift from their independent station it must be toward assimilation and identification with the American system, to which they belong by the operation of natural laws, and must belong by the operation of political necessity."[46]

Blaine also made plain his views about the Kingdom of Hawaii to the British Minister to the United States, Sir Edward Thornton, stating to him that "sooner or later" Hawaii would have to fall "under the protection of the United States" leaving Thornton with the impression that the United States would do anything to prevent another country from obtaining a sovereign position in the Hawaiian Islands, including, if necessary, seizing them for the United States.[47]

Travelling with the King on his world-girding journey, Curtis Iaukea, now a Hawaiian diplomat, as well as a royal courtier, found that European opinion also encouraged close relations between Hawaii and the United States. In Paris, the French Foreign Minister encouraged Iaukea to think of the United States as the best friend of Hawaii and that while France would always remain friendly to Hawaii, its interests in the Hawaiian Islands were now limited, and Hawaii could only anticipate diplomatic support from France.[48]

Thornton's report to London on his interview with Secretary Blaine also ended up in the files of the British Consul in Honolulu, James H Wodehouse, who through his long sojourn in Hawaii became familiar with several of the leading personalities in the country, including Dowager Queen Emma, to whom he showed Thornton's despatch to London. The Dowager Queen was aghast and reported to Wodehouse that the despatch caused her "great grief and anxiety" and that Hawaiians loved their country and were "determined not to let Hawaii become a part of the United States of America."[49] Members of the Royal Family also saw that despatch and its release to senior Hawaiian personages led to a diplomatic incident between London and Washington, which resulted in Consul Wodehouse receiving a knuckle-wrapping from his superiors in London. In particular, London did not like the fact that Wodehouse had summoned a British warship from Canada to Honolulu as a warning to the Americans. Meanwhile, Secretary of State Blaine wrote to the American Minister in Honolulu making it clear that the United States sought no derogation of Hawaiian independence despite its great interest in the fate of the country.[50]

King Kalakaua returned from this, the major foreign trip of this reign, more politically aggressive, and imbued with a renewed sense of his paramount position in Hawaii. He had a determination to mold the Hawaiian monarchy as much as he could into the monarchical forms he had seen in Europe.[51] Consequently, there was a significant increase in public expenditures on the monarchy, particularly for the completion and furnishing of the new Iolani Palace, the coronation ceremony, and its related expenditures, the creation and ordering of insignia of the new Royal Orders, and the creation and ordering of a set of coinage for the Hawaiian realm.

King Kalakaua also arranged for his private purchase of Hulihee Palace on Hawaii Island in 1885.

Even the King's trusted Premier, Walter Gibson, was concerned about King Kalakaua's tendency toward spendthrift ways, complaining in his diary about the cost of the funeral of Princess Kaiulani's mother, Princess Likelike, which cost $23,000. Gibson felt that the King had no real conception of the true value of money, and that he needed to do substantially more for the public welfare of his people.[75]

Money to support the Royal establishment, and to undertake the policy initiatives that Kalakaua sought, increasingly became a pressing concern within the Hawaiian Government. Unlike the Kamehameha dynasty, the Kalakaua Royal Family did not have significant private financial resources at their disposal, and were to a great extent dependent upon the appropriation of funds by the Hawaiian Legislature, and on public borrowing.

During and after the *Great Mahele* in the 1840's the Kamehameha Royal Family had acquired significant land wealth, and through subsequent deaths and inheritances the wealth of the Kamehameha family had become concentrated in Princess Bernice Pauhi Bishop who, at her death, controlled more than 375,000 acres, equivalent to a ninth of all land in the Kingdom.[52] Had Princess Bernice taken the throne when she was nominated as the heir by King Kamehameha V on his deathbed she (and her designated heirs) would not have been financially dependent on the Hawaiian Legislature for expenditures connected with the dignified maintenance of the Royal Family.

Much of the fortune that Princess Bernice possessed she inherited from her cousin, Princess Ruth Keelikolani, a half-sister of King

Kamehameha V. Princess Ruth had informally adopted a son through the Hawaiian *hanai* practice, William Pitt Leleiohoku II, the younger brother of David Kalakaua. Later, Princess Ruth legally adopted Leleiohoku, and made him her heir-at-law in her will. When David Kalakaua ascended to the throne of Hawaii, he designated Prince Leleiohoku as the Crown Prince of Hawaii. If Prince Leleiohoku had survived Princess Ruth, and King Kalakaua, her considerable fortune would have been inherited by a member of the Kalakaua dynasty in the direct line, which would have meant that the dynasty would not have had to rely solely on financial appropriations by the Hawaiian Legislature. As it was, Prince Leleiohoku died before Princess Ruth, and her fortune went instead to Princess Bernice, compelling King Kalakaua to rely on the appropriation of funds by the Legislature to support the Royal establishment, such as the construction of the new Iolani Palace and his coronation ceremony. Those appropriations caused severe resentment within the settler community in Hawaii, who became upset with the King over the level of public expenditures.[53] Whether public events such as the coronation ceremony truly inspired a stronger loyalty of the indigenous community to King Kalakaua remains an open question.[54]

The need for revenues to meet the policy and other objectives of the government, and to sustain the royal establishment, led to significant government borrowing and a large part of the Hawaiian public debt came to be held by one of the chief sugar barons in the islands, Claus Spreckels, a Californian who exercised an excessively influential position in the affairs of the Hawaiian Government during the 1880's. Spreckels eventually held two million dollars of Hawaiian Government debt by the middle 1880's.[55]

When King Kalakaua arranged for an issue of Hawaiian coinage, in part to enhance the independence of the Kingdom, Claus Spreckels arranged to act as Hawaiian agent in procuring the coinage from the US mint in San Francisco. In legal terms Spreckels arranged to lend one million US dollars to the Hawaiian Government at a considerable discount. To add to his achievement, he also succeeded in pocketing the seigniorage associated with the issue, obtaining an additional $100,000 dollars in profit. A strong reaction against Spreckels and his hold on the country began to spread amongst the settler community.

King Kalakaua was also notorious for his love of a good party, and for his many entertainments, especially those held at his private retreat in his boathouse,[56] which caused much angst among the more prudish settlers whose forebears had come to the islands as missionaries to establish a firm Christian morality in Hawaii. There was little social mixing between the indigenous Hawaiians and those settlers who were monarchists, with the commercial settler community that was descended from the missionary families.[57] The King himself was not a regular churchgoer.[58] However, even the King's loyal Hawaiian Premier, Walter Murray Gibson was concerned about royal carousing and Gibson mentions in his diary occasions when the King was too indisposed from the previous nights entertainments to attend a scheduled appearance, leading the King to suffer public disrepute over his nocturnal activities.[59]

In reporting to Washington on the political stability of Hawaii in the mid-1880's, the America Minister to Hawaii, Rollin Daggett, identified four recurring political threats to King Kalakaua. Firstly there was the threat posed by those who continued to support the Kamehameha Dynasty, which was represented in the person of Dowager Queen Emma. Although that group continued to be a threat to Kalakaua, Daggett believed that in the wake of the recent immigration into the islands its importance could be discounted because of the dilution of the indigenous population. Secondly, Daggett saw a threat in the rising number of young and zealous Americans who wished the United States to annex Hawaii. Thirdly, there was a large group of American and European planters and men of property in Hawaii who sought competent government but otherwise did not seek radical change if their demands could be met through monarchical government. Lastly, Daggett pointed to a group that he described as the "missionaries," a group of settlers who reflected the American missionary influence in Hawaii and who (a) had been dismissed from previous government positions, or (b) wanted to obtain new government positions that were now held by others.[60]

Another outsider who rose to considerable prominence in King Kalakaua's reign but who also attracted the hatred of segments of the settler community was Walter Murray Gibson, who served as a Minister, and as Premier, in several of the cabinets appointed by the King during the 1880's. Gibson, like Moreno before him, was something of an adventurer who followed a twisting path that ultimately reached Honolulu.

Gibson was born in Great Britain but while still young his family emigrated to Canada, settling near Montreal, in Lower Canada (now Quebec). Somewhat later, the family emigrated again, this time to New York, and shortly afterwards Gibson was on his own, settling in South Carolina where he married and began to raise a family. The early death of his wife prompted him to seek a more adventurous life and he purchased a ship in which he sailed to the Dutch East Indies, running into misadventure and mutiny along the way. He then fell in with a local Sultan in the East Indies but ran afoul of the Dutch authorities, who tried him for treason and sentenced him to twelve years imprisonment at Batavia. Escaping from the Dutch authorities he ended up in Europe where he passed himself off as a person associated with the US embassy in France, and subsequently went to Great Britain, where he claimed he was of noble parentage but had been switched at birth with the child of a lesser family on board a ship at sea.

After arriving back in the United States Gibson persuaded the Mormon Church to commission him as an elder to establish a Mormon colony in the Pacific. He sailed for Hawaii and on the island of Lanai he took control of the Mormon Church. He succeeded in building up a ranch on Lanai but Gibson ran afoul of the Mormon leadership in Utah, and he was effectively excommunicated. Despite that setback, Gibson kept for himself the legal title to the lands he had acquired on Lanai as part of the Mormon mission. Later, Gibson moved to Maui where he won an election to the Legislature, and where he became a strong supporter of King Kalakau. In the Legislature Gibson promoted the advancement of the indigenous Hawaiian population. In doing so he ran afoul of the western settler community that increasingly regarded Gibson as a white renegade, disloyal to his race. He was attacked in the settler-owned press but he remained a heroic figure to the indigenous Hawaiians throughout his political career. The settler community became so exercised over Gibson's promotion of the development of the indigenous Hawaiians that there was some official concern around the time of King Kalakaua and Queen Kapiolani's coronation ceremony about a plot to assassinate Gibson.[61]

Gibson became closely associated with Claus Spreckels although

Gibson recognized that Spreckels was both shrewd and ruthless.[62] In 1886, the King and Gibson fell out with Claus Spreckels. In October of that year, Spreckels came to Honolulu from California when he learned that the Hawaiian Government was attempting to place a significant loan in London. Spreckels insisted that the statute authorizing the London loan must specify that any bonds floated in London would be subordinated to the debt owed by Hawaii to Spreckels. An amendment to that effect failed to pass in the Legislative Assembly, prompting harsh words from Spreckels, and the subsequent resignation of the Hawaiian Cabinet, in order to allow Spreckels' men to withdraw from their ministerial positions. Ultimately, a complete break occurred in the relations between the King and Gibson with Spreckels.[63] The London loan went ahead at great cost to the Hawaiian exchequer, and the monies obtained from the loan were used to discharge the debts owed by the Hawaiian Government to Spreckels, thus breaking his hold on the government forever. But the damage was done. The public perceived that the government was, or at least had been, beholden to a rich outsider and that caused significant damage to the reputations of both the King and Gibson. The political result was to strengthen public support within the settler community for the missionary-dominated Reform Party.[64]

Gibson entered King Kalakaua's cabinet in 1882, and through the remainder of the decade until the eve of the 1887 revolution he held all of the senior posts in the government, including Premier. He was both intelligent and articulate, fluent in both English and Hawaiian, and he positioned himself as a Hawaiian nationalist. It was Premier Gibson who articulated the Primacy of the Pacific Policy by which the Kingdom of Hawaii sought to play a leading role in the Pacific, and to limit the western powers from seizing further colonial territory in the Pacific. Gibson was the author, in 1883, of a memorandum circulated by Hawaii to foreign governments asking them to recognize the right of Polynesian states to self-government, which was essentially a protest against western colonialism in the Pacific, and was predictably ignored by the major powers.[65] The Primacy of the Pacific Policy encouraged King Kalakaua to attempt to position himself as the leader of a new Pacific confederation, with disastrous consequences. Under the policy, the Kingdom of Hawaii attempted to insert itself into great power rivalry over the Samoan Islands, where civil order was imperilled by a German-backed rebellion against the King of Samoa. The Hawaiian government expended $100,000 to purchase a vessel, the HHMS *Kamiloa*,[66] which the government converted into a warship manned by reform school students under the command of experienced mariners, and despatched it to Samoa to assist a Hawaiian special commissioner who was appointed to negotiate a Hawaiian-Samoan confederation with the Royal Samoan Government.

Gibson was determined to press forward with his Polynesian-centric foreign policy, writing in his diary after the purchase of the HHMS *Kamiloa* that Hawaii could be "a commanding Polynesian state,"[67] and decrying "European bullies" who reserved unto themselves the right to "grab, and partition" as they liked throughout the islands of Polynesia.[68]

Three great powers, Germany, the United States, and Great Britain were circling the Samoan Islands with the object of colonizing them, although none of them were in a position to take the islands outright. The presence of Hawaii as an international actor in this drama was a novel event in Pacific diplomacy. At first it seemed that Great Britain might support a Hawaiian intervention in Samoa. Lord

Rosebery, the Foreign Minister in Prime Minister Gladstone's short-lived 1886 Ministry, stated to the British Minister in Washington that Great Britain would not be opposed to Samoa retaining its independence, and being aided in developing a settled government by the Kingdom of Hawaii.[69] Later, however, when the Conservatives returned to power in London under Lord Salisbury, Wodehouse, the British Consul in Hawaii, was instructed by London to discourage any attempt by Hawaii to involve itself in Samoan affairs.[70] Gibson tried to align his Hawaiian policy in Samoa with the United States, even suggesting that the US consul in Samoa be cross-appointed as the Hawaiian consul but the US consul ruined his reputation in Washington by accepting a proposal made by King Malietoa to place Samoa under a US protectorate, and the American consul was recalled by Washington, leaving Gibson without any convenient access point into the Washington decision-making machinery necessary for the resolution of the Samoan question.[71]

Although a confederation treaty between Samoa and Hawaii was entered into in February, 1886, the German Empire sent its warships to Samoa, and the Samoan King was deposed. Germany warned Great Britain, and the United States, that Hawaiian intervention could provoke a war between Hawaii and Germany. Thus the Hawaiian intervention in Samoa failed in the face of superior German military force, and the acquiescence of Great Britain and the United States to the German policy of colonizing Samoa. Furthermore, indiscipline aboard the HHMS *Kamiloa*, became a public embarrassment in Hawaii, and was one of the complaints raised against the Hawaiian Government that led to the 1887 Hawaiian revolution, and the fall of Premier Gibson. In the wake of the Samoan fiasco the Hawaiian Government ceased any attempts to promote Hawaii as the centre of a wider Pacific polity. Premier

Gibson summed up his appreciation of what had happened in Samoa by writing in his diary that unfair advantage of the weak and ignorant had been taken by the strong and intelligent nations of the west.[72] Hawaii ratified the convention that its diplomats had signed with King Malietoa's Samoan government but that ratification was subject to the obligations that Samoa had accepted in treaties with Germany, the United States, and Great Britain. In the result, the Samoan treaty with Hawaii had no practical effect.[73]

During this period a financial scandal also appeared to tarnish the reputation of the King. A payment in the sum of $71,000 had been made to the King by one Aki, at the behest of Junius Kaae, the Registrar of Land Conveyances, for the grant of an opium licence but subsequently the licence was given to someone else who promised to pay the King more money than Aki had paid for the grant of the licence. The payment to the King of a sum of money for a public licence raised serious concerns that bribery had reached into the highest levels of the state.[74] Concerns about the payment made by Aki were only increased when King Kalakaua did not return the money to Aki, stating that it had been a gift. The opium licence affair severely damaged the personal reputation of the King in the settler community, and in the more radical quarters there were calls for the King to be deposed.

In 1887 matters began to come to a head and there was an increase in calls for substantive reform in Hawaii. The opinion of almost the entire settler community coalesced around the subject of political reform and found its voice in the Hawaiian League, a group of European and American businessmen who wanted political change in Hawaii by any means necessary. Foremost amongst the Hawaiian League were three Hawaiians of American descent, Lorrin Thurston,

Sandford Dole, and William R Castle. Thurston and Dole were descendants of the missionaries who originally came to Hawaii to proselytize to the Hawaiians. Both Dole and Thurston attended Punahou High School, an elite institution for the settler community on Oahu. Both spoke Hawaiian in addition to English, and both obtained their higher education in the United States, Dole at Williams College, an Ivy League school in Massachusetts, and Thurston at the Columbia University Law School in New York, which he put himself through with funds he earned while working at the Wailuku Sugar Company in Hawaii. Both men returned to Hawaii after their studies (Dole after clerking in a Boston law office for a year) where Dole practised as a Notary Public, and Thurston practised law in Honolulu with his friend, William Smith. Gravitating to Hawaiian politics, both men found themselves in opposition to the King, and to the King's party in the Hawaiian Legislature. Although a definite political chasm would exist between the Kalakaua monarchs and Thurston, Sanford Dole occupied a more ambivalent position. While Dole never held cabinet office under the Kingdom, he did serve on the Supreme Court of Hawaii, and in the Privy Council of Queen Liliuokalani.

King Kalakaua was always fond of the military and he encouraged its development in Hawaii. Although the proposed Hawaiian navy proved to be a failure in the *Kamiloa* affair, Kalakaua had high hopes for the Hawaiian army, and to enhance and strengthen the army beyond the permanent King's Guard, the government encouraged the formation of volunteer companies under the sanction of the government. Possibly, the King sensed that growing internal discontent required that the government have sufficient forces available for its own security.[76] Six volunteer companies were organized under the laws of the Kingdom as a militia force that the government could call upon in an emergency to supplement the only permanent military force, the King's Guard.[77]

King Kalakaua appointed his brother-in-law, John O Dominis, as Lieutenant General and Commander in Chief of the Hawaiian forces. However, Dominis had no military experience, or military competencies for that matter. The volunteer units were not organized as blended companies, a significant mistake, and therefore one of the companies, the Honolulu Rifles, came to be manned largely by men from the Caucasian settler community.[78] They became a very efficiently trained unit under Lieutenant Colonel Volney Ashford, a Canadian who practised law in Honolulu with his brother, Clarence Ashford. Volney Ashford had left Canada to join the Union Army during the American Civil War where he gained military training and experience. After the Civil War, he returned to Canada and joined the Canadian militia, where he rose to the rank of Captain. He was particularly effective as a military trainer and the Honolulu Rifles became the most efficient component of the fledgling Hawaiian Army. However, since the Honolulu Rifles consisted mainly of volunteers from the Caucasian settler community on Oahu, it shared the political views and aspirations of that community, rendering it highly susceptible of being infiltrated by men opposed to the royal government of the islands. Thus within the Hawaiian Forces, which were ostensibly subject to the orders of the King, the Premier, and Lieutenant General Dominis, the Honolulu Rifles actually became answerable only to the officers of the secretive Hawaiian League that was established by the western settler community. On the eve of an insurrection, the best trained and the most capable component of the Hawaiian Army was in the hands of insurrectionists.

By the middle of 1887, rumours abounded of public unrest in the settler community against the King's government, and there was near universal support among the settler community for some type of political action to ensure that competent government would prevail in the Kingdom. Premier Gibson was tired, and ill, as the storm approached. He still retained the affection and loyalty of the indigenous Hawaiians however, and when efforts were made by the settler community to co-opt the Mormon community to join in attacking Gibson for his past transgressions as a Mormon elder the Mormons refused to do so.[79]

Within the Hawaiian League there was a great debate over whether the Hawaiian monarchy should be reformed, or deposed, but ultimately conservative views prevailed and it was decided that the monarchy should be reformed, if that was possible. As matters reached a fever pitch, the Hawaiian Government called out the Honolulu Rifles to maintain public order, oblivious to the fact that the Honolulu Rifles were actually disloyal to the King and his government. Thus, the Hawaiian Government played directly into the hands of the Hawaiian League.[80]

Realizing now that he was in great political danger the King demanded and received the resignations of Premier Gibson and the other members of the Cabinet, and the King stated that he would form a new Cabinet under more acceptable Ministers. However, jettisoning Gibson and his pliable team of Ministers came too late and a public meeting on June 30th demanded that the King respond to all the grievances of the people, and the meeting called for a new constitution. Gibson was arrested, and both he and some members of his family were abused by a mob as chaos reigned briefly in Honolulu.[81] The British Commissioner, Wodehouse, was forced to threaten the Honolulu mob with British retaliation if they harmed Gibson, who remained a British subject.[82] Foreign diplomats urged King Kalakaua to accede to the demands of the people, as expressed in the June 30th mass meeting, and the King conceded to them that he was politically isolated. The King appointed a new Reform Party Cabinet under a moderate, W L Green, which proceeded to restore a semblance of order within the capital, and then quickly drafted a new constitution which was submitted to King Kalakaua on the afternoon of July 6th.

The new constitution, which would come to be called the Bayonet Constitution of 1887 because it was forced upon the King, left King Kalakaua shorn of most of his powers. Far from exercising real authority as the chief executive of the government of the Kingdom of Hawaii, Kalakaua was now to be confined to the role of a symbolic figurehead, with most of his powers of government transferred to the Cabinet Ministers. The King was now to exercise political power only by and with the advice and consent of the Hawaiian Cabinet, and he would no longer be able to act of his own volition, with two exceptions. The King's two unencumbered powers were the power to appoint as Cabinet Ministers whoever he liked, subject to those appointees obtaining a vote of confidence from the Hawaiian Legislature, and the power to veto bills passed by the Legislature. The King lost the power to dismiss his Ministers so long as they held the confidence of the Legislature. Thus, the power to oust a government would now rest with the Legislature instead of the King. As to the veto power, while the King would be able to veto legislation his veto could be overturned by a two-thirds vote of the Legislature. Nevertheless, the King was still left with substantial power, despite being reduced to the role of a figurehead, rather than a chief executive.[83]

Many other changes were made to the Hawaiian government by the 1887 Bayonet Constitution, such as extending the franchise for elections to the Legislative Assembly to any male resident of Hawaii, in addition to Hawaiian subjects, which greatly expanded the electoral franchise of the Caucasian settler community.

Membership in the House of Nobles was no longer by appointment of the King but now members would be elected by an electoral franchise of substantial property owners, which again favoured the Caucasian settler community over the indigenous Hawaiians. The King objected to these provisions of the new constitution and he remonstrated with the Reform Cabinet for two hours on July 6th but faced with a united front amongst the settler community, the lack of diplomatic support from either Great Britain, or the United States, and with the Honolulu Rifles poised outside ready to depose him if he failed to approve the new constitution the King conceded. Wisely, the King signed the new Constitution, which came into effect the next day.

The actions that led to the 1887 Constitution were revolutionary actions, and there was a *pro forma* protest by the Judges of the Supreme Court. However, the broad acquiescence of the Hawaiian Legislature and Hawaiian society to the new constitutional arrangements, and the subsequent ability of the Hawaiian Government to govern the Kingdom under the terms of the new constitution, gave it validity despite its revolutionary origins.[84] Now, for the first time, the political power of the Kingdom was aligned with the economic power of the growing settler community. The 1887 Bayonet Constitution was by no means fairly wrought, or broadly acceptable, as the fundamental law of the Kingdom. The native Hawaiians as well as immigrants from China and Japan lost political rights under the new constitution, while immigrants from North America and Europe, especially in the growing Portuguese community, gained political rights. The political imbalances created by the 1887 Bayonet Constitution would bedevil the political landscape of Hawaii until the fall of the monarchy six years later.

The 1887 Bayonet Constitution ushered in a period of marked political instability in Hawaii because it was the first time that the legitimate political authority of the Hawaiian Sovereign had been successfully challenged. Chief Justice Judd thought that the constitutional coup by the Hawaiian League, as well as the much earlier royal constitutional coup by King Kamehameha V in 1864, had weakened the respect of all Hawaiians for their constitution.[85] King Kalakaua was now politically isolated but he began a rear guard fight against the Reform Cabinet by deferring, or refusing to sign state documents that he disagreed with, even when the Supreme Court pointed out that he was under a duty to sign them. Kalakaua had some gifts of political brinkmanship, and he was able to play an obstructionist game with the Reform Cabinet to gain some advantages, and to win back some of his former power, but the King always gave way when he perceived that personal ruin would ensue if he failed to give way. His relations with the individual members of the Reform Cabinet remained strained, so much so that Lorrin Thurston, the Minister of the Interior, later stated in his memoirs that he always carried a revolver with him when he met alone with the King because he recalled that King Kamehameha IV had once shot his secretary with legal impunity.[86]

From San Francisco the King's ex-Premier, Walter Gibson, was surprised at how adept the King was in using his remaining powers to foil the excesses of the Reform Cabinet.[87] But the King was in a weakened financial position because he no longer had a pliable Cabinet to arrange loans to finance government deficits. In fact, the Reform Cabinet moved promptly to put the public finances of the Hawaiian Kingdom on a firm footing. The Reform Cabinet also dealt with King Kalakaua's personal financial position. It was discovered that the King had very heavy personal debts, and he was forced to accept a trusteeship over his personal property in order to liquidate his debts. The money claimed by Aki for the opium licence was litigated, and the court found that the King was personally liable to Aki's estate for the payment of the $71,000 that Kalakaua had received. The King's trustees discharged the debt.

Queen Kapiolani and Crown Princess Liliuokalani had been abroad in Great Britain during the 1887 revolution while attending Queen Victoria's Golden Jubilee but they hurried home when rumours of political instability in Honolulu reached them. Princess Liliuokalani, in particular, despaired over the 1887 Bayonet Constitution, and she held a strong view that her brother had been too weak when he gave in to the demands of the Hawaiian League, and the insurrectionists. A new division would now appear in the Royal Family over the extent to which the King had conceded the powers of the monarchy to the Cabinet, and to the Legislature.

While all these developments of great import were occurring, young Princess Kaiulani was largely oblivious to them, as she enjoyed the halcyon days of childhood and youth. However, political shadows now crept into her life, and she would have been all too aware that all was not well within the sun-blessed isles of her uncle's kingdom. Yet the bulk of the Hawaiian population, including the settler community, remained respectful of the Royal Family, and the young

147

Princess had no cause to be concerned about the feelings of the people toward her, as she remained popular amongst all elements of Hawaiian society.

NOTES

[1] Mellen, 154-55

[2] Campbell, 78-79

[3] Campbell, 141-42

[4] A G Hopkins, *American Empire*, Princeton University Press, Princeton, 2018, 388

[5] Campbell, 87

[6] Hopkins, 425

[7] Seiden, 68

[8] Seiden, 30

[9] Seiden, 62

[10] Wisniewski, 67

[11] Gibson (Adler and Barrett), 125

[12] Ralph S Kuykendall, *The Hawaiian Kingdom, Volume III, 1874 – 1893, The Kalakaua Dynasty*, University of Hawaii Press, Honolulu, 1967, 186-87

[13] Donald D Johnson with Gary Dean Best, *The United States in the Pacific, Private Interests and Public Policies, 1784-1899*, Praeger, Westport (CT), 1995, 107

[14] Johnson and Best, 109

[15] Mellen, 80

[16] Mellen, 117

[17] His Hawaiian Majesty Kalakaua, *The Legends and Myths of Hawai'i*, Honolulu, 1888

[18] W David McIntyre, *Winding Up The British Empire In The Pacific Islands*, Oxford University Press, Oxford, 2014, 11

[19] Barclay, 87

[20] Campbell, 137

[21] Queen Pomare IV also wrote to her Hawaiian counterpart, King Kamehameha III, who wrote back to her expressing his anguish at her situation but he admitted that he had no power to help her.

[22] Campbell, 143

[23] Johnson and Best, 131

[24] Matt K Matsuda, *Empire of Love, Histories of France and the Pacific*, Oxford University Press, Oxford, 2005, 87

[25] Matsuda, 88

[26] Campbell, 147

[27] McIntyre, 14

[28] Great Britain entered into a treaty with Tonga in 1901 that made it a protected state. Tonga retrained internal self-government under its monarchical government.

[29] Henry A Pierce, *An Argument before the Committee on Foreign Relations of the Senate of the United States, with regard to a treaty of reciprocity between the United States and the Hawaiian Islands*, Proceedings of the Senate Committee on Foreign Relations, Washington, January, 1875, 868, 871.

[30] Kuykendall, 27

[31] Previously, in 1860, before Kalakaua had become King, he visited California and the Pacific coast colony of British Columbia before that colony became a province of Canada.

[32] Mellen, 43

[33] Mellen, 162. Such an individual did reside for a time in Hawaii but the dates of his sojourn did not correspond with the birth of Kalakau, whose actual indigenous Hawaiian birth parents have been correctly recorded in history. King Kalakaua was not the last Hawaiian born head of state to face allegations concerning his birth. Hawaiian born US President Barack Obama faced allegations that his birth was outside Hawaii (and the United States) and that he was therefore not eligible to become the US President.

[34] Library of Congress, *Commercial Reciprocity Treaty between the United States of America and the Kingdom of Hawaii*, loc.gov/law/help/us-treaties/bevans/b-hawaii-ust000008-0874.pdf [accessed September, 2020]

[35] Iaukea, 29

[36] Iaukea, 54

[37] Iaukea, 39

[38] Hackler, 5

[39] Wisniewski, 81

[40] Iaukea, 41

[41] Prince William Pitt Leleiohoku, the King's younger brother, and his Heir Apparent, died of rheumatic fever in 1877, following which Kalakaua appointed the eldest of his two sisters, Lydia Kamakaeha to be Heiress Apparent under the name and style of Liliuokalani.

[42] Webb and Webb, 22

[43] Mellen, 100. The King was not however, able to meet with the Dowager Empress, the true ruler of China, who was not holding audiences during the King's visit.

[44] Mellen, 101

[45] Iaukea, 43

[46] James G Blaine to Comly (No. 113), in *Foreign Relations of*

the United States, 1894, Appendix II, Affairs in Hawaii, Office of the Historian, Department of State, https://history.state.gov/historicaldocuments/frus1894app2/d394 [accessed September, 2020]

[47] Kuykendall, 239

[48] Iaukea, 98

[49] Kuykendall, 242

[50] Blaine to Comly (No. 113) *Foreign Relations of the United States*

[51] Iaukea, 47

[52] This concentration of lands was caused by the ongoing failure of the senior *alii* in the Kamehameha line to propagate themselves. A good example pertains to lands awarded to Moses Kekuaiwa in the Great *Mahele* in 1848, which were subsequently passed to his sister, Princess Victoria Kamamalu, when Moses Kekuaiwa died without children at the age of 19. Victoria Kamamalu passed those lands, together with other property she owned to her brother Prince Lot Kapuaiwa, later King Kamehameha V, when Princess Victoria Kamamalu died at the age of 27, without children. King Kamehameha V in turn passed those lands, together with other lands he possessed, to his half-sister Princess Ruth Keelikolani, when he died without issue, and Princess Ruth Keelikolani in turn passed those lands and many other properties she owned to her cousin Princess Bernice Pauahi Bishop when Princess Ruth died without surviving children. When Princess Bernice Pauahi Bishop died without children, her lands were left to an educational trust, which is today the Kamehameha Schools. (*Restoring Bishop Museum's Hawaiian Hall, Ho'i Hou Ka Wena I Kaiwi'ula*, Bishop Museum Press, Honolulu, 2009, 1)

[53] King Kalakaua and his successor, Queen Liliuokalani did have land wealth associated with their office, in the Crown lands. Those lands were originally intended by King Kamehameha III to constitute

the private domain of the Hawaiian Sovereign but after the death of King Kamehameha IV Dowager Queen Emma commenced litigation against King Kamehameha V to assert her dower rights, and thus to obtain a right to one-half of the Crown estate. The Supreme Court of Hawaii allowed the dower claim but dismissed her title claims. That prompted the Legislature to impress the Crown lands with restrictions to prevent the alienation of the Crown estate except by way of 30 year leases. That law, and the Supreme Court jurisprudence, had the legal effect of transforming the Sovereign's private domain into a quasi-public land domain. When the monarchy fell, and Queen Liliuokalani tried to retain the Crown lands as her personal domain, the US Supreme Court denied her petition because the Crown lands were no longer private as a result of the earlier Hawaiian jurisprudence and legislation. (See Banner, 160–61).

[54] Iaukea, 50

[55] Seiden, 66

[56] Wisniewski, 78

[57] Mellen, 132

[58] Gibson (Adler and Barrett), 122

[59] Gibson (Adler and Barrett), 109

[60] Kuykendall, 268

[61] Mellen, 134

[62] Mellen, 147

[63] Gibson (Adler and Barrett), 77–78

[64] Tate, 71

[65] Gibson (Adler and Barrett),, xvi

[66] HHMS stood for His Hawaiian Majesty's Ship

[67] Gibson (Adler and Barrett), 116

[68] Gibson (Adler and Barrett), 123

[69] Gibson (Adler and Barrett), 37

[70] Gibson (Adler and Barrett), 119

[71] Gibson (Adler and Barrett), 70

[72] Gibson (Adler and Barrett), 132

[73] Gibson (Adler and Barrett), 134

[74] Kuykendall, 354

[75] Gibson (Adler and Barrett), 124

[76] Gibson (Adler and Barrett), 25

[77] Gibson (Adler and Barrett), 34

[78] Apparently there had been an earlier militia company by the same name that had been a blended company of indigenous Hawaiian men and men from the settler community but that version of the Honolulu Rifles had been disbanded.

[79] Mellen, 171

[80] The Commander-in-Chief, Lieutenant General Dominis, it should be noted, was abroad and returning from London where he had accompanied Queen Kapiolani and Crown Princess Liliuokalani to Queen Victoria's Golden Jubilee.

[81] Gibson was formally arrested and charged but the charges were subsequently dropped when no evidence of criminal conduct against him could be found. His real crime was that as a white man he took the side of the indigenous people in their efforts to strengthen and sustain the Kingdom. Gibson died in exile in San Francisco a few months after the 1887 revolution, and his body was returned to Honolulu for a state funeral. The young Princess Kaiulani was among those in the Royal Family who paid their formal, final, respects to the late Premier of the Kingdom.

[82] Mellen, 199

[83] The powers of the King under the 1887 Bayonet Constitution actually exceeded the powers that Queen Victoria, for example, was

capable of exercising under the British Constitution at this time. Queen Victoria could select her own Ministers but as in Hawaii they had to obtain the confidence of Parliament in order to govern. However, the more cohesive structure of British political parties reduced the scope of her personal discretion in selecting her Ministers. While the Queen also had a theoretical power of veto, a veto had not been cast by a British monarch in more than 150 years and, according to constitutional convention, that power could no longer be exercised by the Queen of her own volition by the 1880's.

[84] Kuykendall, 372. That was the view later expressed by Chief Justice Judd.

[85] Tate, 93

[86] Lorrin A Thurston, Andrew Farrell (ed.), *Memoirs of the Hawaiian Revolution*, Advertiser Publishing Company, Honolulu, 1936, 214

[87] Gibson (Adler and Barrett), 177

5

The Boarding School Student

The *SS Umatilla* sailed eastward towards the California coast bearing the young Princess Kaiulani and her half-sister Annie Cleghorn on the first leg of their journey to England. Whether from seasickness, or homesickness, or both, Kaiulani spent a lot of her time on the voyage to San Francisco resting and recuperating in her cabin. Finally, the ship raised the coast of California, and the City of San Francisco gave Kaiulani her first view of a major world city. After a whirlwind tour of San Francisco, it was time for the sisters to begin their journey by train to New York, and for Kaiulani and Annie to part from their father, whom they would not see again for a long time.

Leaving San Francisco in the care of Kaiulani's temporary guardian, Mrs Thomas Rain Walker, the wife of the British Vice-Consul to Hawaii, the small party paused at Chicago before arriving at New York City, their final US destination. As her train bore her eastwards, farther and farther away from Hawaii, Kaiulani came to appreciate the immense scale of the United States, a true giant of a country in comparison to her own tiny realm of Hawaii.

After a brief stay in New York, Kaiulani and Annie boarded an ocean liner for the Atlantic crossing, which was not as rough as the voyage across the Pacific to San Francisco from Honolulu. Kaiulani was able to walk the decks and relax on the voyage to Great Britain. After arriving in Liverpool they went on to Manchester and then, finally, on June 18th, the Princess and her sister arrived in London, then the imperial capital of the greatest empire in the world. Here, they spent several days looking about and Kaiulani and Annie were able to see many of the major sights in the British capital. They also glimpsed Queen Victoria, the preeminent monarch of the age, as she drove past in her royal carriage, and it was a thrill to see the woman who was the dominant monarch in Europe.

Princess Kaiulani was raised as a highborn *alii* in a society that lent itself to female participation in public affairs. In her mother, and even more so in her godmother, Kaiulani could look upon female role models who exercised influence and power in the government of her country. However, with the exception of Queen Victoria, who was enthroned at the apex of public life in Great Britain, women did not play a major role in the public life, or the constitutional government, of Great Britain. In fact, now that Kaiulani was away from Hawaiian society she found herself in a different world where the roles of women were much more constrained, especially in government. Victorian society was patriarchal, and gender roles were clearly assigned and socially enforced. Men and women lived essentially separate lives, with the men focused on business, politics, and the military, while women concentrated on their households and their family, charity works, and the nascent bodies of civil society.

Sometimes, the lives of men and women in the same household only interconnected socially at their evening meal.

Kaiulani now had to assimilate the restraints and strictures of this western Victorian society, a feat that she would sometimes have difficulty in accomplishing! But even in Hawaii, the role of women was changing, and as time progressed, and western ideas about the proper role of women in Hawaiian society overtook the traditional respect and power that female *alii* obtained, there were increasing restrictions on the participation of women in public life in Hawaii. By the 1890's, women had disappeared from the Hawaiian legislature and, with rare exceptions, they ceased to hold public offices.[1]

Kaiulani spent her first summer in Great Britain touring around England but as August turned to September it was time for the Hawaiian Princess and her sister to go to their boarding school to continue their education. Mrs. Walker's responsibilities for Kaiulani and Annie ended when they enrolled in their boarding school, and for the remainder of her time in Great Britain as a schoolgirl Princess Kaiulani was watched over by Theophilus H Davies. Born in England to a Welsh minister and his English wife in 1834, Davies entered business in 1857 as an employee of Janion, Green and Company, a British firm with interests in Hawaii, where Davies went and stayed until 1862. Davies had a good head for business and by the late sixties he was a partner in the firm and had sole control after 1881. Over time Davies gained an important position in the sugar industry and he expanded into dry goods, groceries, and hardware. Eventually, Theo H Davies & Company became one of the largest and most dominant firms in Hawaii. As a prominent

British businessman Davies often made business trips to Hawaii, and he and Archibald Cleghorn became familiar with each other. Davies was a natural candidate for the position of the legal guardian of the future Hawaiian monarch while she sojourned in Great Britain because of his prominent economic position in Hawaiian business circles, his knowledge of Hawaiian politics, and his acquaintance with the prominent personalities in Hawaii.

Education played a key role in the socialization of young upper class females in British society. Kaiulani now entered this world as a student of Great Harrowden Hall School for Girls. The estate upon which Great Harrowden Hall was located was in Wellingborough, Northamptonshire, England, and was the ancestral estate of the Barons Vaux, although by the time Kaiulani came to study at the hall the estate had been out of the hands of the Vaux family for almost two centuries.[2] The hall itself, in which Princess Kaiulani lived and studied, was a fine three-story stone structure built in 1719, by Thomas Wentworth, the son of a British aristocrat. Much of England's history was to be found memorialized on this estate. There were mounted heraldic shields of the gentry that had lived in the house, and the drawing room concealed an entrance to a hidden chamber. A magnificent oak staircase led to the upper floor. According to the lore of the estate, a meeting of the Gunpowder Plot conspirators who sought to blowup King James I in Parliament was held at the estate. Later, King Charles I held a council in the mansion on the estate, and the King played lawn bowling there before the English Civil War removed both his crown and his head.[3] In 1876, a school for girls was established in the formal country house, and it was here that Princess Kaiulani and her sister Annie came to study in 1889, under the care of the proprietress of the school, the seventy-two year old Caroline Sharp.

For the first time in her life Kaiulani found herself in a formal classroom setting with other girls, and in an environment where her social rank as an *alii* gave her no special privileges. Kaiulani and Annie studied several languages, French, German, some Latin, and English Literature, as well as Mathematics and History. Physical activities were not ignored, and the students took tennis lessons, and learned to play cricket. The large estate contained beautiful gardens and the girls could walk through and enjoy them when they were not engaged in their studies. Kaiulani gathered seeds from some of the plants that she found there to send home to Ainahau for her father to plant. Princess Kaiulani was a good student and performed well in her academic studies. In one letter home, Kaiulani reported that she had done particularly well in her studies of the French language. By all accounts Kaiulani and Annie enjoyed their studies at Great Harrowden Hall, and the opportunity it gave Kaiulani to live and study with other girls of a similar age greatly contributed to Kaiulani's development as a young lady in a Victorian society.

Her legal guardian in Great Britain, Theophilus Davies, was pleased that the Princess was thriving in the environment at Great Harrowden Hall. He reported to Archibald Cleghorn that Kaiulani was obtaining both increased knowledge and a good character development at the school.[4] However, Kaiulani's studies brought out one deficiency, which had not previously been noted – poor eyesight. It quickly became apparent that Kaiulani was quite nearsighted, and that she needed to wear glasses in order to see properly at a distance.[5]

Her first Christmas away from Hawaii found Princess Kaiulani and Annie in London, where they had a visit from Prince David Kawananakoa, now twenty-one, who was also finishing his education in England. Prince David and his brother, Prince Jonah Kuhio Kalanianaole, were attending the Royal Agricultural College in Gloucestershire. His visit brought back many memories of happy times in Hawaii. Prince David admitted to Kaiulani that he was homesick for Hawaii, and that he looked forward to returning home.[6]

During school breaks Davies invited Kaiulani to stay with his family at their estate in Southport. There, Kaiulani became friends with Theo Davies' daughter Alice, who much later in life recalled Kaiulani as a boisterous schoolgirl who liked to tease, and who once chased Alice with a hair brush. Alice also recounted that Kaiulani liked to chase Alice's brothers up and down the household stairs. However, the young Kaiulani did not always take to being teased herself, once expressing "haughty indignation" when a visiting boy teased her.[7]

Although King Kalakaua had initially given his niece permission to study outside of the Kingdom for only one year, it was thought that Kaiulani would benefit by continuing her education in England for a further period of time. Therefore, when the spring arrived in 1890, there was no thought of Kaiulani returning to Hawaii as was originally envisaged. However, the expense of maintaining both Kaiulani and Annie in England was too much for Archibald Cleghorn to bear (although Kaiulani also received an allowance from the Hawaiian Government to cover the basic costs of her stay in England). Cleghorn ordered Annie to return home to Hawaii in the fall of 1890. It was a sad occasion when Kaiulani bid farewell to her sister but Kaiulani bore the loss well, and her schoolmistress, Mrs. Sharp, complemented Kaiulani in a letter to Archibald Cleghorn, noting that Kaiulani had restrained her tears in parting from Annie, which was just the type of commendable behaviour that Victorian England expected from a royal personage.[8]

The autumn of 1890 also brought an unusual letter to Kaiulani from her uncle, the King. His Majesty wrote to Kaiulani and, after first inquiring about her progress at school, he turned both serious and mysterious advising Kaiulani to be wary of "certain enemies" whom the King did not wish to name in his letter. The warning came as a shock to Princess Kaiulani. The King did not provide any further details that could allow Kaiulani to decipher the meaning of the mysterious letter and she wondered whom he could have meant? Certainly not her legal guardian, Theo Davies, who had been more than kind to her, and who was a supporter of the Hawaiian monarchy. The King must have been referring to people at home in Hawaii where one day Kaiulani was expected to reign as the Queen. Perceiving that the King's warning was something that she should take seriously she immediately wrote back to him to say: "I am quite at a loss to know to whom you refer as 'not to be relied upon' – I wish you would speak more plainly, as I cannot be upon my guard unless I know to whom you allude . . ."[9] She wished to assure the King that Mr. Davies was treating her well and she wrote to tell the King that she had lunch with Davies, and he had kindly invited her to visit his family. But no response to her letter came from the King.

While she waited for a response from the King, Kaiulani continued with her studies, alone now that Annie had returned home, and she prepared to take her Christmas holidays with Davies' family. She was becoming more independent-minded and more daring. When she arrived at Southport for the holidays she was to be met by the Davies' family governess, who waited in vain for her charge to appear after the train arrived. Finally, Kaiulani dashed up in the company of two young gentlemen who were attending her, much to the chagrin of the governess! Other changes were in the offing as Christmastime approached. Mrs Sharp, now seventy-four years old, had announced that she would close her school at the end of 1891. That meant only one more full year of boarding school for Kaiulani at Great Harrowden Hall.

Returning to her school after the holidays, Kaiulani soon received some very bad news from home. Her uncle, King Kalakaua, was dead at the age of 54. The King had journeyed to California in an attempt to recover his failing health but his condition had worsened, and he died in San Francisco on January 20, 1891. The next day Theo Davies came to Great Harrowden Hall and told Kaiulani the sad news about her uncle. Davies took Kaiulani out of the school temporarily, and brought her back to his home at Hesketh Park, in Southport, so that she could mourn privately.

Princess Kaiulani actually learned of her uncle's death before her people in Hawaii had learned of it because of the modern miracle of the transatlantic cable, which quickly carried the news from the United States to Europe. Using the same mechanism, Kaiulani was able (with Theo Davies assistance) to send a cable to a florist shop in San Francisco and deliver instructions for a funeral wreath of orchids from Kaiulani to accompany her uncle on his final journey home to Hawaii aboard the American warship, USS *Charleston*. She had the wreath beribboned with the words: '*Aloha me ka paumake*,' which meant 'My love is with the one who is done with dying.'[10] On the evening of January 21st she sat down and wrote to her aunt, now Queen Liliuokalani, expressing her sadness at the loss of her uncle, and asking Queen Liliuokalani to give her love to her aunt, now the Dowager Queen, Kapiolani.

NOTES

[1] Apart from Queen Liliuokalani, the most prominent woman in the Hawaiian Government in the 1890's may have been Emma Metcalf Nakuina, who served as Water Commissioner during and after Queen Liliuokalani's reign, adjudicating claims on riparian rights and other allocations of water. She became a noted authority on Hawaiian water customs and laws.

[2] Surprisingly, the Vaux family repurchased the estate in 1895, after the school closed.

[3] L T Meade, *Girl's Schools of Today II, St. Leonard's and Great Harrowden Hall,* The Strand Magazine, London, 1895, 457 at 461

[4] Kuykendall, 478

[5] Mrantz, 19

[6] Webb & Webb, 78

[7] Marilyn Stassen-McLaughlin, *Unlucky Star: Princess Kaiulani,* The Hawaiian Journal of History, vol.33 (1999), 21, at 24-25

[8] Stassen-McLaughlin, 24

[9] Kaiulani to Kalakaua, November 13, 1890, BMA

[10] Webb & Webb, 81

6

The King Beset

In the aftermath of the Bayonet Constitution, and the entrenchment of a Reform Cabinet, Kaiulani's uncle, King Kalakaua, was a considerably diminished figure. The transition from chief executive of the Hawaiian government to a constrained constitutional figurehead was abrupt, and unsettling, and led to further political instability within the Kingdom. Within the administration, King Kalakaua fought a rearguard defence of his remaining royal prerogatives to maximize the remaining powers of the crown under the 1887 constitution. Although the 1887 Bayonet Constitution had focussed on restraining the powers of the Hawaiian Sovereign, it still left considerable powers in the hands of the King. The King retained the power to appoint the Ministers of the Hawaiian Cabinet, and his discretion in doing so was not limited by any objective standards. Thus the King could appoint as Ministers men that were at least neutral, if not friendly to the Crown. However, the Legislature could dismiss the Cabinet for a want of confidence, which meant that the King had to ensure that any Cabinet he selected could win a vote of confidence in the Legislature.

King Kalakaua's power to appoint a cabinet compared favourably to the powers of the British monarch, Queen Victoria, who at this point in time also had the power to appoint her own ministers but by the established conventions of the British constitution she was required to call upon the leader of the political party that controlled the greatest number of seats in the House of Commons to form a cabinet. Should a British cabinet lose a vote of confidence in the House of Commons the Queen could call upon an opposition party to form a new cabinet but only if the opposition leader could satisfy the Queen that he had a reasonable prospect of winning a vote of confidence in the House of Commons. Otherwise, the Prime Minister of the cabinet that had lost the confidence of the House of Commons would be entitled to a royal dissolution of the House of Commons, and a new election, to determine which political party would be able to command a majority in the House of Commons.

In contrast, King Kalakaua could appoint whomever he wished to the Hawaiian Cabinet, and he was not precluded from selecting men who did not hold a seat in the Legislative Assembly, or who were not affiliated with a political party or group.[1] While his Cabinet selections had to meet with the subsequent approval of the Legislature, he was otherwise unrestricted in his choices, and thus the King of Hawaii under the 1887 Bayonet Constitution possessed a wider discretion than Queen Victoria possessed under the British Constitution, with respect to the appointment of a government. The key feature of the new Hawaiian Constitution from the settlers perspective was that the House of Nobles would now be elected rather than appointed, and a substantial property qualification was required for the electors of a Noble. That meant that the settlers could control the upper house of the Hawaiian Legislature, and thus enjoyed a reasonable prospect of blocking any unfavourable measures, such as new debt obligations, or an increase in taxation.

The other important power that King Kalakaua retained was the power to veto bills passed by the Hawaiian Legislature. In the early months after the new constitution was proclaimed a conflict developed between King Kalakaua and the Reform Cabinet over whether the King, in exercising his veto power, was required to act on the advice of his ministers. That conflict was placed before the Judges of the Supreme Court of Hawaii for resolution by a reference, and a majority of the court ruled that the King was not obliged to take advice from his ministers before exercising his veto power. Although King Kalakaua thus retained a personal discretion to veto legislation, his veto could be overturned by a two-thirds majority vote of the Hawaiian Legislature. The power to veto legislation was an important power that the King could exercise to delay, or even upend, legislation and was a power that the monarchs of Great Britain could no longer exercise. No British legislation had been vetoed by a King or Queen since Queen Anne vetoed a bill passed by the British Parliament in the early years of the eighteenth century. By the reign of Queen Victoria it was considered that by the conventions of the British Constitution the Queen had to assent to legislation passed by the British Parliament, and the power to veto, if was at all still exercisable, could only be performed on the advice of her ministers.

Thus, despite the revolution that brought about the 1887 Bayonet Constitution, the Hawaiian monarch could still exercise substantial powers, and King Kalakaua took full advantage of the powers left to him. One tactic he used was to defer proposals from his Cabinet in order to obtain changes to proposals, and thus maximize the role of the Sovereign under the new constitutional arrangements. As one might imagine, his obstructionism created severe strains in his relations with his Cabinet Ministers. Matters came to a head when the Cabinet collectively sent a missive to the King stating that the King was required by the constitution to sign any public documents that his ministers advised him to sign, and that they had sent to him for his approval. The Cabinet insisted that:

"The government in all its departments must be conducted by the cabinet. Your Majesty shall, in future, sign all documents and do all acts which, under the laws of the constitution, require the signature or act of the sovereign, when advised so to do by the cabinet, the cabinet being solely and absolutely responsible for any signature of any document or act so done or performed by their advice."[2]

The King refused to agree with what was in reality a correct formulation of the principle of responsible government in a constitutional monarchy. The Cabinet referred the question to the Supreme Court of Hawaii, which ruled that in this matter the Cabinet was correct, and the King had to approve the public measures that the Hawaiian Cabinet advised him to approve.

Of course, a great deal of the tension between the King and the Reform Cabinet revolved around the fact that the Cabinet consisted of people that Kalakaua considered to be his enemies, and they returned the sentiment. Over time, the strains in the relationship between the Cabinet and the monarch, and the need for efforts to persuade the King to provide his approval for decisions that he was now constitutionally obligated to approve, led some among the members of the Reform Party to contemplate removing the King from the Hawaiian throne, and substituting his sister, Crown

Princess Liliuokalani, in his place. The subject was discussed within the Hawaiian Cabinet.[3] In her memoir Liliuokalani, while the Crown Princess, relates that she was approached by two members of the Reform Party, including W R Castle, a prominent Hawaiian businessman, to determine whether she would agree to take the throne if her brother was deposed. Liliuokalani states that she refused Castle point-blank, out of loyalty to the King, and nothing further was heard of the matter.[4]

However, Liliuokalani was more accommodating to indigenous Hawaiians who also contemplated the removal of the King. Secret societies were formed by persons who considered King Kalakaua to have been weak in dealing with the 1887 insurrection, and who sought to replace him with the Crown Princess. In response to entreaties from them Liliuokalani told them to approach the King with respect, and explain to him that the conditions of the country might be changed if he were to abdicate the throne, possibly to return later when political conditions were more stable.[5] The Reform Cabinet heard of these attempts and they promised the King their support to maintain his position on the throne if he would cooperate with them.

The most serious sign of political instability in Hawaii was the Wilcox Rebellion, in which a young *hapa-haole* named Robert W Wilcox attempted to overthrow the Reform Cabinet by force of arms. Wilcox was one of the young Hawaiians who had been sent abroad to be educated in western institutions early in King Kalakaua's reign in the charge of the Italian adventurer, Cesar Moreno, whom King Kalakaua had once tried to make Premier of Hawaii. After the Reform Party took office all of the Hawaiians being trained abroad were recalled home, and Wilcox returned home with notions of himself as a kind of Hawaiian revolutionary. Born to an American father and a Hawaiian mother, Wilcox was tall and thin, with dark eyes and although he was mentally sharp he was emotional, dramatic, temperamental, and rebellious.[6] In short, he was an unstable personality.

Wilcox, along with his fellow foreign student returnee, Robert Boyd, were disgruntled to discover that the responsible government positions they had expected to receive were no longer on offer to them, causing them to contemplate an insurrection.[7] In 1889, Wilcox brought together a secret group of insurrectionists who were financed, at least in part, by the Chinese-Hawaiian community, and who had the avowed purpose of overthrowing the 1887 Bayonet Constitution, and the Reform Cabinet. In this endeavour Wilcox received some support from Princess Liliuokalani, at least to the extent of having her provide him with the use of one of her residences in which to hold his conspiratorial meetings. King Kalakaua learned about his sister lending her house for what the King termed "treasonable projects" and he informed the Cabinet. It appears that Wilcox had in mind not only the overthrow of the Reform Party Cabinet, as well as the 1887 Bayonet Constitution, but also the replacement of the King by his sister Liliuokalani on the throne of Hawaii.[8]

An insurrection was mounted by Wilcox and his confederates on July 29, 1889, which involved the seizure of Iolani Palace. King Kalakaua had foreknowledge of the pending insurrection because a participant in the meetings held by Wilcox, one J K Kaunamana, a legislator, secretly reported on them to the King. Late on the night before the insurrection the King was in the office of his Chamberlain, Colonel Iaukea, when Kaunamana came to them and reported that Wilcox had announced his intention on the morrow not only to depose the Reform Cabinet but to depose Kalakaua himself, and to place Princess Liliuokalani on the throne. Upon receipt of that information the King and Colonel Iaukea departed Iolani Palace at once, and the King left instructions for the King's Guard not to support Robert Wilcox in the pending uprising.[9] The King retreated to his boathouse at the harbour to await the outcome of the rebellion. Meanwhile, the Cabinet called out the volunteer militia, and US troops were landed from the guard ship in the harbour, with the permission of the Hawaiian Government, ostensibly to help maintain public order.

The Wilcox Rebellion was put down with the loss of seven rebel lives, and Wilcox himself was arrested and charged but he was later acquitted by a jury consisting of indigenous Hawaiians.[10] An inquiry exposed the links between Princess Liliuokalani and Wilcox but since there was no evidence of overt acts of treason by the Princess she did not suffer any personal consequences. Nevertheless, the King called her a *kipi*, meaning a rebel, and according to the British Consul the King contemplated removing her as the Heiress Apparent to the throne of Hawaii, and replacing her with his wife's nephew, and *hanai*-adopted son, Prince David Kawananakoa.[11]

In the spring of 1890 there were new rumours of a forthcoming coup circulating in Honolulu. It was centred on Wilcox again, and on Volney Ashford, formerly the Colonel of the Honolulu Volunteers who had suffered a falling out with the Reform Party (though he was still supported by his brother Clarence, the Attorney General of Hawaii in the Reform Cabinet). Security in Honolulu was heightened for a time but there was no insurrection. During this period political instability had a marked effect on the morale of the Hawaiian civil service, whose members began to despair over the lack of political harmony, and wondered what would happen next. A school of pink *aweoweo* fish also appeared in the harbour at Honolulu, a traditional supernatural sign of an *alii's* forthcoming death, sparking new concerns about the King's health.[12]

In mid-June 1890, internal dissension brought down the Reform Cabinet[13] and King Kalakaua appointed a Cabinet more to his liking, although it still operated in accordance with the 1887 Bayonet Constitution. With the Reform Party out of office there were renewed calls to rollback the 1887 constitutional changes, and King Kalakaua started on the path toward changing the constitution by referring petitions for constitutional change, and petitions calling for a constitutional convention, to the Legislature without consulting his ministers. The sending of the petitions to the King had been orchestrated by prominent indigenous politicians, notably Joseph Nawahi.[14] The American and British diplomatic representatives immediately counselled the King against direct actions without the support of his Cabinet, much to Kalakaua's displeasure. The King went so far as to suggest to the British government that Wodehouse, the British Consul, should be recalled but Lord Salisbury, the British Foreign Minister, refused on the grounds that Wodehouse had acted properly in advising the King.[15] In the end, King Kalakaua did follow the advice of the British and American diplomats, and the King's message to the Legislature was reported out from a committee with a recommendation that no action be taken on account of his proposals being contrary to the 1887 Constitution.

After the 1887 coup that brought the Bayonet Constitution into force the near universal consensus amongst the white settler community began to break down. There was an increasing divergence of political opinion concerning the future of Hawaii, and the future of the monarchy, both subjects that were inextricably entwined. On the one hand, there were those, such as Lorrin Thurston and William R Castle, who favoured the abolition of the monarchy, and the establishment of a republic, as a way station on the path to the annexation of the country by the United States. On the other hand, there was a more conservative group who wished to establish responsible government under a constitutional monarchy to ensure efficient and honest government. It was the latter group that had been paramount in the 1887 revolution and the constitution that King Kalakaua endorsed was largely the result of their handiwork. That divergence among the settlers was certainly reflected in the business community in Hawaii, and there was by no means a consensus amongst Hawaiian businessmen concerning a policy of annexation by the United States.

Those favouring American annexation tended to be Americans, or American-descended Hawaiians, such as Thurston and Castle but there were also some of that view who were not connected to the United States by birth or heritage. Those who were more conservative and who favoured the continuation of the monarchy tended to be primarily British, Canadian, or Europeans, to whom a monarchical form of government was more familiar. The fact that there was a growing difference of opinion in the settler community meant that the King could find a base of support among some of those who had supported the 1887 Bayonet Constitution. It also meant that those who wanted annexation to the United States would have to take greater risks in order to bring about the resolution of Hawaiian affairs that they desired.

The effects of political turmoil in Honolulu were of concern to all those who loved their island country but the near-continual presence of British and American warships in the harbour, with their implied threat of intervention, prevented matters from getting too far out of hand.

Meanwhile, a much greater threat to the stability and independence of the Kingdom was taking shape outside of the Hawaiian Kingdom. The renewal of the reciprocity agreement with the United States engaged a large portion of the attention of both the Gibson Cabinet and the Reform Cabinet that replaced it. The dominant sugar industry needed the reciprocity agreement to be renewed before its ten-year expiration date was reached and the negotiations to renew it proved to be both difficult and controversial. While the Cleveland Administration in the United States was amenable to a renewal of the reciprocity agreement, the US Senate wished for the United States to obtain rights to establish a naval base at Pearl Harbour. The United States had become aware of the value of Pearl Harbour as a potential naval base in 1873, after Secretary of War William Belknap sent Major (later General) John Schofield as a spy, masquerading as a tourist, to scout out the potential strategic value of the Hawaiian Islands to the United States. Major Schofield recommended that the US should establish a naval harbour at Pearl Harbour. The Senate now proposed that as the price of a renewed reciprocity treaty with Hawaii and the following amendment was proposed and adopted by the US Senate:

"His Majesty the King of the Hawaiian Islands grants to the Government of the United States the exclusive right to enter the harbour of Pearl River in the island of Oahu, and to establish and maintain there a coaling and repair station for the use of vessels of the United States, and to that end the United States may improve the entrance to said harbour and do all other things needful to the purpose aforesaid."[16]

King Kalakaua was opposed to the grant of a concession over Pearl Harbour to the United States, as Walter Gibson, who noted in his diary on February 8, 1887; "The King is disposed to temporize on the Pearl Harbour cession question. Says we must never consent to the cession – but to appear to entertain the matter for a while. Don't like temporizing about this matter, I will oppose the cession under all circumstances."[17]

The British Government was also opposed to Hawaii parting with rights to establish a US naval station at Pearl Harbour. Rear Admiral Sir Michael Culme-Seymour told King Kalakaua that Britain "could not approve of any other nation having a coaling station or other establishment in the Sandwich Islands."[18] In reality Britain would have also liked to have a coaling station in Hawaii because a reappraisal of ship traffic in the North Pacific Ocean disclosed that Hawaii would be an ideal point to coal ships traversing the ocean between Panama (assuming a transoceanic canal was built) and Japan, as well as between Vancouver, Canada, and Sydney, Australia.

However, the 1887 Bayonet Constitution, and the imposition of the Reform Cabinet, changed the perspectives of the Hawaiian Government. The Reform Cabinet was, of course, closely allied with the Hawaiian sugar industry and for that industry the renewal of the reciprocity agreement with the United States was essential, no matter what price had to be paid by Hawaii.

In London, the British Foreign Office perceived the US demand for rights to Pearl Harbour as the first step in acquiring the country, and Sir Julian Pauncefote, the Undersecretary of State at the Foreign Office wrote a despatch to the British Consul in Honolulu, James H Wodehouse, advising him that Great Britain and France were committed to Hawaiian independence but if the United States acquired a concession at Pearl Harbour it would mean the inevitable loss of independence for Hawaii, and the extinguishment of Hawaiian nationality. Consequently, Wodehouse was instructed to impress upon the Hawaiian authorities the great danger of conceding a concession at Pearl Harbour to the United States.[19]

To obtain negotiating leverage with the United States, the Gibson Cabinet went so far as to explore negotiations for a reciprocity treaty with Canada, an initiative that was supported by the King.[20] The Canadian Government was certainly aware of the strategic location of the Hawaiian Islands, sitting astride the sea routes between Canada and the southern British dominions of New Zealand and Australia. And the completion of the transcontinental Canadian Pacific Railway late in 1885 had opened up new markets in the eastern Canadian provinces for goods landed at the port of Vancouver.

In March, 1886, the Canadian Government sent Walker Powell, a prominent businessman, and the Adjutant General of the Canadian Militia, to Hawaii to explore potential Canadian-Hawaiian links. However, Powell had meetings with British Consul Wodehouse, who disabused him of any potential growth in Hawaii-Canada trade by pointing out that there was little possibility of an increase in trade while the reciprocity agreement between Hawaii and the United States remained in force.[21] Powell himself concluded from his own inquiries that Canada could not replace the American market for Hawaiian sugar, and that Hawaiian exports to eastern Canada would face stiff competition from sugar imports from the British West Indies.[22] Powell decided to return home to Canada and report to the Canadian Government without opening any direct trade discussions with the Hawaiian Government.

When the Reform Cabinet came into office, it also considered opening trade negotiations with Canada, but mostly as a form of negotiating leverage to use against the United States.[23] Hawaiian Attorney General Clarence Ashford, who had been born in Canada, was sent to Canada by the Hawaiian Government to discuss trade. Ashford was feted by Prime Minister Sir John A Macdonald, and by the head of the Canadian Pacific Railway, Lord Mount-Stephen. Their blandishments had some effect on Ashford because upon his return to Honolulu Ashford displayed a changed attitude, and he now stood opposed to the efforts of the Hawaiian Minister in Washington, Henry A P Carter, to negotiate a broader free-trade agreement with the United States.[24] Undoubtedly, Prime Minister Macdonald of Canada was open to the possibility of a reciprocity treaty between Canada and Hawaii but the economics of such a treaty simply did not work for Hawaii.[25] Only the American market could absorb the totality of Hawaiian sugar production, and nothing came of any Hawaiian trade initiatives involving Canada.

Faced with a situation of unequal bargaining power the Reform Cabinet decided that Hawaii had no choice but to accept the American demand for Pearl Harbour, and they advised the King to sign a reciprocity renewal that accepted the concession concerning Pearl Harbour. The King signed the treaty renewal on October 20, 1887, and President Cleveland ratified the treaty on behalf of the United States on November 7, 1887.[26] For the first time, a foreign power had obtained territorial rights within the Hawaiian Kingdom, and as Sir Julian Pauncefote had tried to warn the Hawaiians, imperial powers, like the sharks found in Hawaiian waters, did not necessarily stop after taking the first bite.

All that Great Britain could now do was to remind the Hawaiian

Government that under Hawaii's existing treaties with Great Britain warships of the Royal Navy could "enter into all harbours, rivers and places within those islands to which ships of war of other nations are or may be permitted to come to anchor there and to remain and refit."[27] But of course Pearl Harbour would now be controlled by the United States, rather than by Hawaii, and it was to the United States that Great Britain would have to address any request to use facilities at Pearl Harbour. The grant of special rights to the United States at Pearl Harbour began a process of reappraisal within the British Foreign Office of the future of the Hawaiian Islands. Although Great Britain continued to favour the independence of Hawaii, the growing power of the United States, and its determination to achieve and retain paramountcy in Hawaii, could not be ignored.

The world that was emerging as it entered the last decade of the nineteenth century was very different from the world that the monarchs of the Kamehameha Dynasty had known. The full fruits of the industrial revolution were increasingly apparent and Hawaii was no longer as remote as it had once been. Western imperialism had come at last in a large way to the Pacific Ocean and during King Kalakaua's reign almost all of the remaining independent indigenous states in the Pacific were taken over by the more advanced nations as protectorates, or colonies. Hawaii had hitherto escaped foreign control because of its strategic position in the North Pacific Ocean, which had forced Britain, France, and the United States to forswear from taking it to avoid a conflict, as each of them coveted it, or at least wished to deny it to any other power. However, by the start of the 1890's the relative strength and position of the three powers were rapidly changing. France now focussed its efforts on the South Pacific, and had only a peripheral interest in the Hawaiian Islands.

Hawaii remained of importance to Great Britain but the United States was growing in economic strength by leaps and bounds and it was increasingly clear to British policymakers that Great Britain could no longer allow itself to be drawn into a conflict with the United States over Hawaii, or any other issue.[28] Japan had emerged from obscurity to rapidly industrialize and it was beginning to take its place amongst the great powers. However, Japan still laboured under unequal treaties with western powers.[29] The Chinese Empire was in a condition of terminal decline, and the European powers began to circle around it, establishing commercial spheres of interest.

Rapid changes were also taking place in the United States. Manifest Destiny, the dominant American ideology of the nineteenth century, gave justification to the westward movement of the United States. The Revolutionary War had been fought in large part over access to the land beyond the Appalachians, and land hunger continually drove the American population farther west. Awareness of the breadth of the continent was brought to public attention by the explorations of Lewis and Clark, and the imagination of the American public was fired with the thought of possessing the entire continent. Although Manifest Destiny was never articulated as official government policy, it animated American political objectives in the nineteenth century with respect to the acquisition of new territories.

By the 1890's, Manifest Destiny had largely run its course across the United States between the Canadian border and the Rio Grande River. Populated Mexico was unwanted as part of the union, and although Canada was still coveted by some policymakers, the continuing suzerainty of Great Britain over Canada forestalled any American acquisition of that country. The US Army had been extensively deployed in the west and the last major aboriginal conflict occurred in 1890, at Wounded Knee, South Dakota. That same year the US Census Bureau declared that the American frontier was closed, and the country was now settled. The loss of the frontier caused many to wonder how the character of the American people would evolve in the absence of the tension between a settled America and a wilderness frontier. In the late 1880's President Cleveland's Secretary of State, Thomas F Bayard, noted that Americans had become aware of their country's growing national power and began to exhibit an appetite for bursting the borders of the republic to acquire new lands.[30]

One pointer to the future of the United States appeared in the guise of a hitherto unknown US naval officer, Captain Alfred Thayer Mahan, a lecturer at the US Naval Academy. In 1889, Mahan published an immensely influential book entitled *The Influence of Sea Power Upon History, 1660-1783*, which drew attention to the importance of naval power in securing national security and overseas expansion. His premise was that a great power required a great navy and nowhere was that truer than in relation to the United States. According to Mahan:

"Is it meant, it may be asked, to attribute to sea power alone the greatness or wealth of any State? Certainly not. The due use and control of the sea is but one link in the chain of exchange by which wealth accumulates; but it is the central link, which lays under contribution other nations for the benefit of the one holding it, and which, history seems to assert, most surely of all gathers to itself riches."[31]

Policymakers in both Washington and European capitals were strongly influenced by the publication of Mahan's book, and it drew particular attention to America's continuing lack of substantial sea power. In December, 1890, Captain Mahan wrote an article for the Atlantic Monthly entitled *The United States Looking Outward* in which he emphasized the importance of the Hawaiian Islands to the military security of the USA, and noted that political unrest in Hawaii had implications for American security.[32] In Washington, President Cleveland's Secretary of State, Thomas F Bayard, quietly opined that the United States only had ". . . to wait quietly and patiently and let the islands fill up with American planters and industries until they should be wholly identified with the United States. It was simply a matter of waiting until the apple should fall."[33]

In 1889 a new administration took office in Washington. The first Democrat elected since the US Civil War, Grover Cleveland, had been defeated for reelection as President in the 1888 election by Republican Benjamin Harrison. A native of Ohio, Harrison, the grandson of former President William Henry Harrison, was a lawyer of some renown in Indianapolis where he had settled after attending Miami University in Ohio. Harrison served with distinction in the US Civil War and he had reached the rank of Brigadier General by the end of it. He was elected to the Senate after the war and then was nominated for the Presidency by the Republican Party in the 1888 election. Although he lost the popular vote to Cleveland, Harrison prevailed in the US Electoral College, and he was sworn in as the 23rd President of the United States on March 4, 1889. Harrison believed that Providence had made possible his victory but one of the Republican Party stalwarts remarked that the new President did not realize that a number of men came close to entering the penitentiary in order to put him in the White House![34] Harrison began the march of the United States toward imperial expansion beyond its borders and its reach for worldwide power and influence.

Conforming to the ideas of Captain Alfred Thayer Mahan, the Harrison Administration, guided by Secretary of the Navy Benjamin F Tracy, promoted the rebuilding of the US Navy as a blue-water fleet. The US Navy had almost fallen into a third class state in the years after the US Civil War, and the American merchant marine had largely disappeared from the seas. To a large extent the loss of the US merchant fleet was a result of the wartime depredations of Confederate naval raiders such as the CSS *Alabama*, and the CSS *Shenandoah*, the latter having made port at Honolulu during the hostilities. Now the Harrison Administration obtained congressional approval for the building of new, modern, warships, and the result was the laying down of the *Indiana*-class coastal battleships, and the battleships/protected cruisers USS *Maine* and USS *Texas*. By the end of the nineties, the United States would possess a modernized navy capable of projecting force well beyond the coasts of the United States.

The Harrison Administration also began to project a new, aggressive foreign policy for the United States. In the Caribbean, and in the Pacific, the United States began to exert its weight in foreign affairs. Harrison's Secretary of State was James G Blaine, a party stalwart from Maine who had previously served as Secretary of State in both the Garfield and the Arthur Administrations. Blaine favoured the acquisition of the Hawaiian Islands by the United States. Now, with the expansion-minded Benjamin Harrison in office Blaine moved American foreign policy in the Pacific towards a more aggressive stance, contending with both Germany and Great Britain over the future of the Samoan Islands, and preparing the way for the United States to acquire Hawaii.

As the new American Minister to the Kingdom of Hawaii, Blaine nominated his friend and former journalistic colleague, John L Stevens, who was also from Maine. Blaine and Stevens had worked together as editors of a newspaper in Maine for 14 years before Blaine entered the House of Representatives in 1863. Both Blaine and Stevens had assiduously promoted the fortunes of the Republican Party in Maine and Stevens had served as a senator in the Maine Legislature. Stevens' party connections helped him to obtain a position in the United States diplomatic service after the Civil War, and he served as the American Minister to Paraguay, Uruguay, and Sweden, before his appointment as American Minister to Hawaii on June 20, 1889. Subsequently, Blaine raised Stevens from Minister to Hawaii to the rank of Envoy Extraordinary and Minister Plenipotentiary to Hawaii on July 30, 1890.[35] Princess Kaiulani's legal guardian in England, Theo Davies, described Stevens to Kaiulani as a potential enemy.[36]

Both Blaine and Stevens held compatible views about the desirability of the United States acquiring the Kingdom of Hawaii, and with Steven's appointment to Honolulu the Harrison Administration began to foster the conditions that would make that acquisition possible. The event that acted as the catalyst to the annexation involved a tariff change. At this period of time the Federal Government in the United States obtained most of its revenue from tariffs, and the most lucrative tariff was the tariff on sugar. Hawaii had natural advantages in the production of sugar, which accounts for the fact that it so dominated the Hawaiian economy in the latter part of the nineteenth century. The reciprocity agreement that King Kalakaua had obtained early in his reign, and which was renegotiated and extended under the Reform Cabinet, in 1887, gave Hawaiian sugar preferential market access to the United States. But the surplus revenues that the tariffs produced in the United States led to political embarrassment because it pushed up domestic prices. However, reducing the tariff would have a negative impact on domestic sugar producers in the American south. Some way was required to square the circle of the high tariffs required to protect domestic producers with the excessive revenue generation which hurt American consumers.

The solution to this quandary was proposed by Representative William McKinley of Ohio, a protectionist politician who was sometimes referred to as the Tariff Napoleon for his aggressive promotion of tariff barriers. McKinley and other Republicans thought that the best way to reduce the tariff revenue surplus that the Federal government was experiencing was to raise tariffs to reduce imports, and thereby spark domestic production. Their Democratic opponents took the opposite view that the best way to reduce the tariff revenue surplus was to reduce the tariffs. During the Harrison Administration the Republicans controlled Congress so their theory was one that was enacted in the Tariff Act of 1890, otherwise known as the McKinley Tariff.

The effect of the existing tariffs on raw sugar combined with the Hawaiian reciprocity treaty was to give Hawaiian sugar a significant advantage in the US market, and it accounts for the explosive growth of the sugar industry in Hawaii in the latter part of the nineteenth century. Now, in the McKinley Tariff, the United States decided to eliminate the tariff on imports of raw sugar but to protect American domestic sugar producers by providing them with a subsidy of two cents per pound on raw sugar. The effect of this change was to eliminate the economic advantage of Hawaiian sugar in the US domestic market and plunge the Hawaiian economy into a severe recession. Did McKinley or the United States government foresee that result? There is no evidence that either did but those officials who followed Hawaiian conditions closely, such as Secretary of State Blaine, must have been aware that any damage to the Hawaiian economy could produce political instability at a time when the Kingdom was still attempting to consolidate the political changes brought about by the 1887 Bayonet Constitution.

For the people of Hawaii the McKinley Tariff posed a direct challenge to the economic health of the Kingdom and it called for a response. A number of those in the business community, and particularly those who had emigrated from the United States, or who were descended from Americans who had earlier settled in the islands, began to seriously contemplate how to bring about the annexation of the Kingdom by the United States. It was thought by the annexationists that the only hope of preserving wealth based on the production of sugar in the islands lay in placing Hawaii inside the US domestic tariff barrier. If the Kingdom became part of the United States it would never again be subject to the imposition of US tariffs on sugar and, as an American possession, the islands would have some claim to participate in any subsidy provided by Congress to American raw sugar producers.

For the government of Hawaii the challenge posed by the McKinley Tariff was profound, and it called for some creative thinking about how to adjust to the loss of revenue. From the perspective of domestic policy there was, of course, a renewed focus on identifying new sources of tax revenue. From a foreign policy perspective,

Hawaii needed to find a way back into the US market for its sugar products. Foreign Minister Jonathan Austin hoped to leverage Hawaiian-Canadian relations to open up the US market. He wrote to the Hawaiian Minister to the United States, Henry A P Carter, stating that Hawaii could develop closer relations with Canada and if it did so the resulting diversion of passenger and freight traffic to Canadian ports and railways would diminish the favour in which the Hawaiians currently held the United States.[37] Austin hoped that the United States would be alarmed by the thought of closer relations between Hawaii and Canada, and offer relief from the negative effects of the McKinley Tariff. Although Canada could not absorb the entire Hawaiian sugar production it could be a market for at least some of the Hawaiian sugar production, and therefore closer relations seemed to have merit. Early in 1890, Attorney General Clarence Ashford, originally from Canada, was despatched to North America to visit the United States and Canada and Ashford subsequently reported to his fellow members of the Reform Cabinet that Canadian Prime Minister Macdonald had a great interest in Hawaii. In his later memoirs Lorrin Thurston traced Clarence Ashford's change in attitude and tone towards the other members of the Reform Cabinet, which ultimately led to a breach in Cabinet solidarity, from the time that Ashford made his visit to his homeland.[38]

Although it seems surprising, from a great historical distance that American officials feared that Hawaii might link its future to Canada, the record does show that this was of concern to American officials in Honolulu at the time. The American Minister Plenipotentiary to Hawaii, John L Stevens, reported to Secretary of State Blaine that: "So long as the islands retain their own independent government there remains the possibility that England or the Canadian Dominion might secure one of the Hawaiian harbours for a coaling station. Annexation excludes all dangers of this kind."[39]

However, nothing of substance came out of the flirtations between Canada and Hawaii. The simple matter was that the small Canadian market for Hawaiian products could never be an effective substitute for the US market. In 1891, Canadian Prime Minister Sir John A Macdonald, died in office, and his death ushered in an era of political instability in Canada that would see the country governed by five different Prime Ministers between 1891 and 1896. Under such circumstances, the forging of an expanded trade relationship by Hawaii with Canada was not feasible.

In Hawaii, King Kalakaua's health declined through the remainder of 1890, and it was publicly stated that he would visit California to recover his health.[40] He left for San Francisco on November 25, 1890, and although he intended to vacation in California, the Hawaiian Minister to the United States, Henry A P Carter, arranged to come out to California from Washington to brief his Sovereign on the McKinley Tariff problem. King Kalakaua was well-received in California, and the Southern Pacific Railway placed a private rail car at his disposal for his journeys around the state.[41] The King's health began to deteriorate significantly during a visit he made to southern California and he returned to San Francisco to prepare for his return to Honolulu. His condition worsened precipitously however, and on January 20, 1891, he died in his hotel in San Francisco, at the age of 54. Attending the King at his bedside, in addition to his personal servants, were his military aides Colonel George Macfarlane, and Colonel Hoapili Baker, and prominent Hawaiian financiers Charles R Bishop, and Claus Spreckels. Admiral George Brown provided an official US Government presence.

President Harrison ordered that the King be given a state funeral with full military honours in San Francisco, and the USS *Charleston* was directed to return the body of the late monarch to Honolulu, where Hawaii's King completed his final journey. The body of the King arrived to a shocked and mournful nation on January 29, 1891.

Although he was perhaps too flawed as a man to be considered a great King, Kalakaua nevertheless strove mightily against formidable odds to preserve his country's independence within the community of nations, and to advance its standing as a modern state. His state visits to the United States, and to the capitals of Asia, and Europe, on his 1881 world tour succeeded in placing Hawaii firmly within the firmament of recognized independent states. King Kalakaua set a course toward a diverse multi-ethnic country, albeit without necessarily knowing where that would ultimately lead. He recognized that demographic trends portended disaster for his country if steps were not taken to bolster its population and so he opened Hawaii to immigration. The cosmopolitan society of modern Hawaii can be traced to decisions he made during his reign.

The true legacy of King Kalakaua lies in his efforts to foster the preservation of the history and cultural traditions of the indigenous Hawaiian people. Had he not sought to capture and collect the chants and *meles* of ancient Hawaiians, and especially the *Kumulipo*, the Polynesian Chant of Creation, and had he not brought back the hula, and inspired a renaissance in Hawaiian music much of the old Hawaiian culture would probably have been lost to time. Even the extravagances of the coronation had the benefit of giving scope to native Hawaiian artisans to create works of art and embellishment, and thus helped to preserve the traditional crafts of the country.

The survival of an indigenous Hawaiian culture in the twenty-first century owes much to the memory of this extraordinary man.

NOTES

[1]Hawaiian Cabinet Ministers were *ex officio* members of the Legislative Assembly and could vote on all legislative proposals, except votes of confidence in the Hawaiian Cabinet.

[2] Quoted in Liliuokalani, *Hawaii's Story by Hawaii's Queen*, Lothrop, Lee & Shephard Co., Boston, 1898, 191

[3] Kuykendall, 415

[4] Liliuokalani, 188

[5] Kuykendall, 415

[6] Mellen, 226

[7] Tate, 98

[8] Kuykendall, 426

[9] Iaukea, 130

[10] Mellen, 233. Indigenous Hawaiians could only be tried by a jury consisting of indigenous Hawaiians, according to Hawaiian law.

[11] Kuykendall, 416 *fn*

[12] Iaukea, 132

[13] Much of that dissension was caused by a breach between Attorney General Clarence Ashford and the other members of the Cabinet over the appointment of the Attorney-General's brother, Volney Ashford, as commander of the Honolulu Rifles. Volney Ashford seems to have been a main-chancer, and his demands for patronage unsettled the Reform Cabinet whose members were concerned that the loyalty the Rifles displayed towards him could

make him a potential threat to the Reform Ministry. His brother Clarence disagreed and supported Volney.

[14] Tate, 103

[15] Kuykendall, 463

[16] Senate of the United States, *Report of the Committee on Foreign Relations, the United States and the Hawaiian Islands*, Washington, February 24, 1888, 3

[17] Gibson (Adler & Barrett), 123

[18] Gough,, 232

[19] Kuykendall, 398

[20] Gibson (Adler & Barrett), 123

[21] Merze Tate, *Canada's Interest in the Trade and the Sovereignty of Hawaii*, Canadian Historical Review, vol. XLIV, No. 1, March, 1963

[22] Tate, *Canada's Interest*, 26

[23] Tate, *Canada's Interest*, 27

[24] Tate, *Canada's Interest*, 29

[25] Tate, *Canada's Interest*, 30

[26] Kuykendall, 396-97

[27] Gough, 232

[28] Gough, 237

[29] Including one with the Kingdom of Hawaii.

[30] Tate, 106

[31] Captain A T Mahan, USN, *The Influence of Sea Power Upon History 1660 – 1783*, London, Sampson Low, Marston, Searle & Rivington, 1890, 225

[32] Johnson and Best, *The United States in the Pacific*, 106

[33] Quoted in Joseph P Smith, Director, *Hawaii*, Bureau of the American Republics, Document 178, Part 14, Senate, 55th Congress, 2nd Sess. Washington, 1897, 34

[34] Frank Freidel, *The Presidents of the United States of America*,

White House Historical Association/National Geographic Society, Washington, 1964, 52

[35] A Minister is a diplomat accredited to the head of the receiving state. The Envoy Extraordinary and Minister Plenipotentiary (also informally referred to as Minister) is a diplomat accredited to the receiving state but the difference is that Envoy Extraordinary is enabled with plenipotentiary powers to enter into agreements with a host government, and those agreements will be accepted and carried into fruition by the government of the country which despatched the Envoy Extraordinary. The elevation in the status of the American diplomatic chief of mission in Honolulu in 1890, may have reflected Blaine's desire and anticipation that Stevens would move quickly to secure the annexation of Hawaii if such an opportunity arose.

[36] Sharon Linnéa, *Princess Kaiulani, Hope of a Nation, Heart of a People*, Eerdmans Books for Young Readers, Grand Rapids (MI), 1999, 101

[37] Kuykendall, 437

[38] Thurston, 209

[39] Senate Committee on Foreign Relations, *Annexation of Hawaii*, 55th Congress, 2nd Sess., Senate Report 681, Washington, March 16, 1898, 272

[40] The Canadian Prime Minister, Sir John A Macdonald, was concerned that the King's visit to the United States might be a prelude to the annexation of Hawaii by the United States and he asked Sir Charles Tupper, the Canadian High Commissioner in Great Britain to have the Foreign Office instruct the British Consul in Honolulu, Wodehouse, to oppose any Hawaiian moves towards US annexation. (Tate, *Canada's Interest*, 31)

[41] Mellen, 246

7

The Education of a Victorian Princess

In the summer of 1891, Princess Kaiulani was reunited at last with her father who had come to England to make new arrangements with Theo Davies concerning Kaiulani's future education. The Princess spent the summer of 1891 touring about Great Britain with her father. They started in London, visiting Parliament, Windsor Castle, and the Royal Gardens, and then she and her father went north to Archibald Cleghorn's ancestral homeland of Scotland. Afterwards, they wound their way back to England through Wales.

During the summer Archibald Cleghorn and Theo Davies made arrangements for the continuation of Kaiulani's education. With the forthcoming closure of Mrs. Sharp's Great Harrowden Hall School for Girls it was decided that Kaiulani would profit from private instruction, through tutors, and arrangements were made for Kaiulani to live with a woman in the village of Hove, a suburb of the town of Brighton, in Sussex County. Her new governess would be Phebe Rooke, a relative of the late Dowager Queen Emma.[1]

The summer also brought some further sad news from home. The Prince Consort, Kaiulani's uncle, John O Dominis, the husband of Queen Liliuokalani, died at the age of 59, after being ill for several weeks. It was another harsh blow for her aunt, the Queen. Her uncle had been an important and steadfast advisor to her aunt, and he was one of the few people whose status allowed him to be candid with the Queen, an important role in the charged political atmosphere of Honolulu in the early 1890's. Liliuokalani wrote to Kaiulani with the sad news telling her that "you and Papa [i.e., Archibald Cleghorn] are all that is left to me." The Queen's feelings of isolation were growing, and she admitted to her heiress that "I shall look forward to the time when you finish your studies with all due satisfaction to your teachers, and then come home and live a life of usefulness to your people."[2]

Her father returned to Hawaii, and Kaiulani went back to Great Harrowden Hall to finish her year before joining the Davies family for the Christmas celebration at the end of 1891. It had been a momentous year for Princess Kaiulani, with the death of two of her uncles, the King, and the Prince Consort. She was now the heiress to the throne of Hawaii and that knowledge helped her to grow and mature. She began to look beyond her education to the assumption of the long-planned role that awaited her when she returned home. Plans were now afoot for her to complete her education privately, through tutors, in 1892-93, before a formal coming out in society in early 1893, and then, potentially, an audience with Queen Victoria. She would return home in time for her eighteenth birthday in October, 1893, when she would assume her responsibilities as Crown Princess of Hawaii.

Kaiulani described her new governess, Mrs. Rooke, to the Queen as a "thorough lady." To help her settle in at Brighton Alice Davies accompanied her there. Kaiulani now began a full range of private studies to finish off her formal education. During her first term of private studies in the winter and spring of 1892, Kaiulani received instruction in German and French, English literature, grammar and composition, music and singing, and in history.[3] In her correspondence with the Queen she also reported that she had received, as a gift from Mr C R Bishop, the widower of Princess Bernice, a copy of a recent publication from Hawaii by Professor W D Alexander entitled *A Brief History of the Hawaiian People*.[4] Kaiulani found the book very useful because it filled in gaps in her own knowledge about Hawaii, and of the Royal Family of which she was a prominent member. ("In fact I knew nothing about our family until I read Prof. Alexander's Book."[5])

The Queen took an interest in the education that Kaiulani was receiving and she wrote back to the Princess recommending the study of history in particular, because it was of great importance in the exercise of statecraft. She approved of Kaiulani's study of Professor Alexander's book, and she noted its careful description of her Keawe-a-Heulu dynasty's genealogy, which was so essential for the legitimacy of the royal line. The Queen explained that:

"I am very glad that you have a copy of Prof Alexander's book – You will find in the latter part of the Genealogical tree of the Kamehameha line, and it contains one of ours also – but there are many interesting facts not mentioned in his book in regard to our family. Our great great Grandfather Keaweaheulu was one of Kamehameha's 1st Counsellors . . . From that time until the death of the last Kamehamehas there have always existed a friendship and for that reason I think that it is only our due to sit on the throne of the Kamehamehas – but we must be worthy of it."[6]

The Queen also endorsed her study of languages, and she noted that both French and German were used extensively in diplomacy. However, she pointed out to Kaiulani that the Hawaiian Foreign Office had within it personnel who were skilled at foreign languages, and they would always be available to help Kaiulani with foreign languages when she became Queen. She did think that Kaiulani should attempt to acquire a talent for writing, which would serve her well in the future, and she closed by telling her to work hard and to complete her studies by the spring of 1893, before returning home to Hawaii.

In early spring, 1892, Kaiulani was given a break from her studies and Mrs. Rooke took her on a short two-week vacation to Jersey, one of the Channel Island dependencies that lie close to France in the English Channel. There she found the climate to be ideal, and she enjoyed herself exploring the quaint island, a last remnant of William the Conqueror's Duchy of Normandy, from which he had plotted his conquest of England in the year 1066. She attended the local church, where the service was conducted in French, and she found to her satisfaction that she was able to understand the service quite well.

Kaiulani liked Jersey, and about the only thing that she wished she had with her was her horse, Fairy, as the local mounts she considered to be in quite poor condition.[7] Then it was back to Brighton until June when Theo Davies took Kaiulani and Alice Davies to spend a couple of weeks in London. After London, Kaiulani returned to Mrs. Rooke in Brighton to finish off her study term, and then she went to spend her summer holidays with the Davies family at their various estates. While in Brighton Kaiulani took up the pastime of stamp collecting, and she found that philately helped her in learning about geography.

With the summer of 1892 behind her, Kaiulani returned to Brighton for her next term of studies. In the new term she received lectures three time per week from a Mr. Loman, who taught her history, English literature, and physics, while Fraulein Kling, her language teacher, tutored her in reading, speaking, and translating in both German and French, the two European languages in which Kaiulani sought to develop a conversational fluency.

Madame Lancia was Kaiulani's arts teacher, and she instructed Kaiulani twice a week in singing, music, and painting. Kaiulani also received instruction in subjects that were essential for a nineteenth century future monarch – dancing, horseback riding, and deportment, which was the art of carrying oneself in an admirable way.

Kaiulani's days also required two hours of lesson preparation, or homework, each day.[8] The Princess wrote to the Queen to say that she felt that she learned much better now through private tuition than in her previous formal classroom setting with other girls at Great Harrowden Hall. Kaiulani did, however, continue to keep in touch with Mrs. Sharp, her former headmistress at Great Harrowden Hall.

She was maturing now, as she approached seventeen years of age, and she had a new appreciation for the role that she would be destined to assume someday in her homeland. She liked Brighton, and she was amused that all the shopkeepers addressed her as Miss Rooke, assuming that she was the daughter of Mrs. Phebe Rooke, with whom Kaiulani lodged. Kaiulani did well in her studies and her fluency in German, her favourite foreign language, was particularly improved. She became more and more aware of how she was being perceived by society at large and she concentrated on improving her deportment. "Do you not think that to learn to walk and move gracefully is very important? I do hope that by the time I come home, you will think I have improved" she told the Queen in a letter.[9] She wanted to be seen to have a graceful walk and she took note when her friends and acquaintances told her that she walked much more beautifully when she was outside, on the street, then when she entered a drawing room, so she practised making quiet and graceful interior entrances.[10] She also took up charitable work, and while she could not devote as much time to it as she wished, because of her studies, she was happy to participate in fund-raising for worthy causes. Slowly she began to enter formal society, telling the Queen that she planned to call upon the Duke of Connaught, the son of Queen Victoria, when he visited Brighton, and that she had accepted an invitation from Lady Wiseman to visit her and her husband, Rear Admiral Sir William Wiseman, over the Christmas holidays in 1892. Kaiulani thought that the Wisemans were refined people, who displayed very good manners, and she realized that she could learn much from observing refined people.[11]

The picture that emerges from Kaiulani's life in Brighton is that of an earnest young woman on the cusp of adulthood who has fully realized the importance of her future constitutional role in Hawaii, and who was displaying a great determination to prepare herself for it. As she gained a greater maturity she left behind some of the more carefree, or child-like, aspects of her personality, and that can be seen in a heartfelt letter she received from one of her former school friends from Great Harrowden Hall, Maude Wright, who, like Kaiulani, also hailed from Honolulu. Wright wrote plaintively to Kaiulani and complained that the Princess now seemed distant toward her, and she feared that Kaiulani had lost her affection for her. Maude said that even if Kaiulani no longer found value in their friendship Maude would always remember Kaiulani as "jolly" and "open-hearted."[12]

Kaiulani's course of studies had been laid out by her guardian in consultation with her father, and they were the kind of studies that a young, Victorian, upper class woman in Britain was expected to follow, and excel in. Mainly, the course of studies she followed was designed to educate upper class women to function in society in support of their husbands, who would be expected to concern themselves with the more masculine nineteenth century pursuits of politics and commerce. Probably, the studies that Kaiulani undertook were similar to the studies that Theo Davies would have arranged for his own daughter Alice. But Kaiulani's studies were also appropriate for a woman who would subsequently be a constitutional monarch, a Queen who was symbolic of the sovereignty of her country, instead of its actual ruler.

Nor was Kaiulani's study plan greatly different from the kind of tutoring that was often provided by European royalty to their own daughters. A good example of the education of a princess who was a contemporary of Princess Kaiulani was that given to Princess Alix of Hesse-Darmstadt, a favourite granddaughter of Queen Victoria, who was born in 1872, only three years before Princess Kaiulani. Like Princess Kaiulani, Princess Alix had also lost her mother to illness when Alix was very young, and Queen Victoria thereafter took a strong interest in the upbringing and education of the granddaughter the British Royal Family nicknamed 'Sunny'. An intelligent student, Princess Alix took tutoring in history, geography, English literature, German literature, and music (piano). Prodded by Queen Victoria's steady stream of advice from England, Princess Alix's character and opinions were molded to fit those expected of a young royal lady of the Victorian age.[13] Although the subjects that Princess Alix was taught were similar to those that were set for her Hawaiian contemporary, it was not yet thought to be desirable to instruct young princesses in the arts of politics and government. Later, Alix would marry the heir to the Russian throne and become the Empress Alexandra of Russia.[14]

Thus, Princess Kaiulani's education followed the main features of an education that European royalty, and the British upper class, provided to their own daughters. That she lacked any specific instruction in Hawaiian constitutional law, and Hawaiian governance, was a major and surprising omission but one that was expected to be remedied after she returned home and began to act as an understudy to Queen Liliuokalani. Nor did Princess Kaiulani obtain any formal education in international relations, also a notable omission for the future monarch of a small country that had to balance its relations with foreign powers in order to maintain its standing among the independent nations of the world.

Although Kaiulani was exposed to foreign languages, she was only taught European languages. However, with the strong current of immigration into Hawaii from Asia, a basic introduction to the Japanese and Chinese languages would not have been out of place. Indeed, with respect to the European languages relevant to Hawaii an obvious gap was her lack of exposure to Portuguese, given the level of immigration from Madeira, and the Azores, into Hawaii. Those gaps would not necessarily have proved damaging if Kaiulani had succeeded to the throne of Hawaii, but a knowledge of them might have also helped a future monarch of a country that was undergoing significant demographic changes.

By and large however, Kaiulani's education in Great Britain made her into a modern Victorian lady who would be able to enter into high society and perform any of the ceremonial functions that would have been expected of her as the Princess of Hawaii. She might have also looked forward to a long apprenticeship before she was called upon to ascend to the Hawaiian throne, and that would have given her plenty of time to assimilate the contours of Hawaiian politics, and to grasp the essentials of Hawaiian constitutional government. Although her education was valuable, and she appreciated it, she was also increasingly homesick, and she yearned to return to Hawaii.

For the time being, putting aside the problems that she could not do anything about, Kaiulani looked forward to spending the 1892 Christmas Season and the New Year holiday, with her guardian, Theo Davies, and his family, and also with her friends Lord and Lady Wiseman, before returning to Brighton to complete her studies. In the spring of 1893 she would make her formal social debut in England, following which there were plans for Kaiulani to tour the continent and to obtain an audience with Queen Victoria before she began her return journey to Hawaii, where she was expected to arrive in time for her eighteenth birthday in October.

But before all of that there was more sad news from home. Her sister Annie, after returning from England to Hawaii had married Hay Wodehouse, the son of the senior British diplomat in Hawaii, and Annie had subsequently given birth to a son, giving much joy to the Cleghorn family. Now, in December of 1892, Kaiulani's friend in Honolulu, May Atkinson, wrote to tell her that Annie's baby had died. May wrote that Annie's eyes were "wells of sadness" and she felt a great sorrow that her sister Kaiulani would never see her baby.[15]

199

Even more dreadful news would soon reach Kaiulani in England.

NOTES

[1] Stassen-McLaughlin, 26

[2] Liliuokalani to Kaiulani, September 18, 1891, HSA

[3] Kaiulani to Liliuokalani, February 3, 1892 and March 20, 1892, BMA

[4] Kaiulani to Liliuokalani, March 20, 1892, BMA

[5] Kaiulani to Liliuokalani, May 18, 1892, BMA

[6] Liliuokalani to Kaiulani, April 25, 1893, HSA

[7] Kaiulani to Liliuokalani, May 18, 1892, BMA

[8] Kaiulani to Liliuokalani, September 25, 1892, BMA

[9] Kaiulani to Liliuokalani, September 25, 1892, BMA

[10] Kaiulani to Liliuokalani, October 9, 1892, BMA

[11] Stassen-McLaughlin, 29

[12] Stassen-McLaughlin, 31

[13] Robert Massie, *Nicholas and Alexandra*, Dell Publishing, New York, 1967, 30-31

[14] Both royal women would suffer a loss of status afterwards – in Kaiulani's case when the Hawaiian monarchy fell and she became a former princess and in the case of Princess Alix, who rose to become Empress Alexandra of Russia, her execution in the aftermath of the Russian Revolution, which was the tragic fate of the Russian Imperial family.

[15] Stassen-McLaughlin, 31

8

The Annexation Plot

The year 1892 was crucial in the history of the Kingdom of Hawaii. Political instability in the Kingdom had not been quelled by the passing of the throne from King Kalakaua to his sister, Queen Liliuokalani. If anything, Liliuokalani was more determined than Kalakaua to wrest political authority back to the monarch from the Cabinet, where it had rested in the years following the imposition of the 1887 Bayonet Constitution. The Queen used her remaining executive powers to the fullest by attempting to put into office Cabinets that would be pliable to monarchical control. However, her attempts were often foiled by the Legislature, which experienced its longest session in the history of the Kingdom during 1892-93. From May, 1892, to January, 1893, seven non-confidence motions were made against the governing Cabinets appointed by the Queen, and four of those non-confidence motions succeeded in ousting the sitting Cabinet.[1]

The monarchy was under threat from two sources during Queen Liliuokalani's reign. A political party, the Liberal Party, had been established by indigenous politicians led by John Bush and Robert Wilcox and became disaffected from the monarchy because its leaders had either found themselves blocked from public appointments (Wilcox), or cashiered from high public office (Bush).[2] Bush and Wilcox pressed for the abolition of the monarchy and its replacement by a republic, as well as US annexation, thinking that with annexation indigenous Hawaiians would be able to control a US territorial legislature, and reap the rewards of political patronage. Bush promoted these ideas in a newspaper that he edited.

Wilcox, having failed to mount a successful insurrection to put Princess Liliuokalani on the throne in place of her brother now found himself aggrieved at being shut out from important government positions after Liliuokalani became Queen. The Queen now seemed to have no further use for him. Reacting to this failure to obtain high office Wilcox displayed a newfound scorn for the Queen in vituperative statements that he made to the Liberal Party faithful. He complained that she had disregarded him, and that Hawaii was ruled by "dolls." He suggested that women were "brainless," and that he and his associates could never be satisfied with Liliuokalani on the throne because she was plainly against Wilcox and his companions.[3]

Personal attacks were also made against the selection of Charlie Wilson as the Marshal of the Kingdom, and some of the Liberal Party complaints about him were racial in tone because Wilson was half Tahitian. The Liberals complained that the Queen had lowered the dignity of the Hawaiian throne by making a Tahitian a court favourite.[4] Among the settler community there were also allegations that Wilson was corrupt, and that he was in league with elements of the opium trade in the Kingdom.[5]

The attacks on the throne, and the promotion of annexation to the United States by the Liberal Party in the Legislature, were particularly damaging because for the first time a block of indigenous Hawaiian politicians denigrated the monarchy and called into question the country's independence. The situation was not helped by threats of an insurrection made by the Liberal Party leaders if they could not get what they wanted through the democratic processes of the Legislature. American officials present in Honolulu took note of these developments. Acting Rear Admiral George Brown, returning to his country from Honolulu said there was an indigenous faction within the Legislature that contemplated the overthrow of the monarchy but the presence at Honolulu of the USS *San Francisco* prevented them from treading the road of rebellion.[6]

Political instability in the Kingdom meant a golden opportunity for political firebrands in the settler community like Lorrin Thurston. Thurston, who had adopted the Hawaiian name Kakina was the grandchild of New England missionaries, and was born and raised in the Kingdom of Hawaii, and fluent in the Hawaiian language. He had attended Punahou School, the secondary school popular with the settler community, and then worked as a clerk at the Wailuku Sugar Company where he earned enough money to finance an American education. Thurston attended Columbia Law School, where he was a contemporary of Theodore Roosevelt,[7] and then returned to Honolulu where he practised law with William O Smith. He became a leader of the Hawaiian League, and was a member of the Reform Cabinet that took office after the successful imposition on King Kalakaua of the Bayonet Constitution. Thurston served successfully as Minister of the Interior for three years. He believed in white rule over the islands as a matter of patriotism, and he consistently opposed the monarchy throughout his political career.[8]

After leaving the Cabinet Thurston returned to private law practice, although he was elected to the House of Nobles where he continued to sit as a member of the Reform party. His political views had evolved, and he no longer sought to reform the government of his country but rather he now sought the annexation of his country by the United States. With that object in mind Thurston convened a meeting of like-minded men in his law office in early 1892, and formed a secret society known as the Annexation Club. The objects of the club were to obtain the annexation of the Hawaiian Islands by the United States, and the perpetuation of the rule of the islands by the Caucasian settler community.

Thurston had a willing accomplice for his plans in Hawaii in the person of John L Stevens, the accredited Minister of the United States to the Kingdom of Hawaii, and America's senior diplomatic representative to the Hawaiian Royal Court, and the Hawaiian Government. Stevens was an experienced American diplomat who was now, at the age of 71, approaching the end of his public service career. He had previously represented the United States abroad as American Minister in Paraguay, Uruguay, and the United Kingdom of Sweden and Norway. Before becoming a US diplomat Stevens, a native of the state of Maine, had been a journalist, and the co-editor with his fellow Mainer, James G Blaine, of the *Kennebec Journal*. After their journalism careers both Stevens and Blaine went into politics, Blaine into Federal politics, and Stevens into state politics. When his political career fizzled Stevens used his connections to move into the US diplomatic service.

Blaine was a rising star in Republican political circles in Washington, and he would find himself successively as a Congressman, the Speaker of the House of Representatives, a US Senator from Maine, the US Secretary of State under President Garfield and President Arthur, and the Republican candidate for President in the 1884 presidential election, which he lost to Grover Cleveland. When Benjamin Harrison, the Republican standard bearer in the 1888 presidential election, succeeded in ousting Cleveland Blaine returned to Washington as Harrison's Secretary of State. Blaine was an avowed believer in American Manifest Destiny, and he applied that ideology to the distant Hawaiian Islands. In his friend John L Stevens, Blaine had an ally in the cause of Hawaiian annexation within the federal bureaucracy, and Blaine personally selected Stevens for the sensitive appointment to Honolulu knowing that Stevens shared his views about the annexation of Hawaii.

From the outset Stevens was unyielding in his contempt for the Hawaiian monarchy, which only increased when Queen Liliuokalani came to the throne. He was rude and arrogant toward the Queen and her royal officials, creating a tense environment for the conduct of diplomatic relations. He spoke in a very slow and patronizing way to the Queen, as if she was an obtuse person, and he clearly tried her patience. It seems evident that Stevens, like so many of the men of his time, was unable to accept the idea of a woman in a high political office and he exhibited a degree of misogyny that interfered with his ability to represent the United States in a neutral and professional manner to a female head of state.

As a man of strong religious morals, Stevens was also more comfortable identifying with the descendants of the New England missionaries to Hawaii, rather than with the indigenous population.

Stevens openly favoured those in Hawaiian society who promoted the American annexation of Hawaii, and he tended to avoid contact with those who harboured different views.[9] Although he was a poor example of a diplomatic representative from an ostensibly friendly power, Stevens was wildly successful as a foreign subversive agent encouraging domestic coup plotters. Thurston and his confederates lost no time in bringing Stevens up to speed with their ideas for the annexation of Hawaii, although Thurston later denied that there was any overt conspiracy involving Stevens in the annexation of Hawaii.[10]

New intelligence from Thurston, along with the anti-monarchical and pro-annexations proposals of the Liberal Party, prompted Stevens to write twice to Washington for formal instructions in the event of a *coup d'état* occurring in Honolulu, although presumably his long and close association with his friend Secretary Blaine had left him with little doubt as to how he should proceed. Nevertheless, he wrote formally to the Secretary of State on March 8, 1892, to say that a secret society had been formed in Honolulu that was opposed to Queen Liliuokalani and the entire Royal House. It was organizing against the Queen and would be opposed to the future accession to the throne of Princess Kaiulani. Stevens asked; What are my instructions? Stevens followed up that letter with another on March 25, 1892, in which he asked Secretary Blaine point blank for instructions about the possibility of the annexation by the US of the Kingdom, stating "are you for annexation?" To both of those missives Stevens received no answer from Blaine.

Blaine was too intelligent to put in writing instructions to undermine a foreign state with which the United States had enjoyed friendly relations for many decades. In any event Blaine doubtless knew that Stevens comprehended where Blaine stood on the question of annexation, and Blaine knew that with or without instructions Stevens, who shared many of the same views as Blaine, would lend whatever support the annexationists needed from the United States. Meanwhile in April, 1892, Secretary Blaine met with the John Mott-Smith, the Hawaiian Minister to the United States and told Mott-Smith that he expected a revolution to occur in Hawaii.[11] In the same month, during a meeting with the British Minister, Sir Julian Pauncefote, Secretary Blaine said to Pauncefote that the United States might undertake measures to make secure US influence in Hawaii in view of the trouble that could be caused by the existence of dual governments in the islands.[12] Blaine did not clarify to Pauncefote what he meant by a dual government. The year before, Secretary Blaine had briefed President Benjamin Harrison on the prospects of acquiring the Hawaiian Islands, telling President Harrison that only three foreign territories were valuable enough to warrant the US taking them; Hawaii, Cuba, and Puerto Rico, and that of the three, Hawaii was ripe, and a need for a decision to take them could arise at any time.[13]

Secretary Blaine thought that Hawaiian annexation would come, and would come fairly soon, despite the efforts of the Hawaiian Government to maintain the independence of their country. His view was also shared by an American military commander on a rotational station at Oahu, Captain Gilbert C Wiltse of the USS *Boston,* who noted that the Hawaiian sugar planters were all either foreign, or of foreign descent, and were in favour of US annexation although they did not think annexation was imminent.[14]

While the Harrison Administration was moving toward an acquisition stance, official policy continued to lull the Hawaiian

Government into thinking that the United States supported its continued independence. The Hawaiian Minister in Washington reported to Honolulu on a conversation he had with Secretary Blaine in which Blaine assured him that the United States would support the authority of the Queen to preserve internal order, and that it would not interfere with internal Hawaiian affairs unless the Queen requested America's assistance. If America did provide assistance to the Hawaiian Government, at its request, the US would promptly withdraw as soon as any crisis had passed.[15]

As an example of the kind of help that the Americans could provide, the acting Rear Admiral of the US Pacific Squadron, George Brown, arranged for a drill in which 300 US sailors were landed in Honolulu from a US warship. The sailors marched in a parade past Iolani Palace. This demonstration by the US military concerned Wodehouse, the British diplomat in Hawaii, who reported it to the Foreign Office and expressed the view that the American Admiral did not have the Queen's best interests at heart.

Of greater concern perhaps was the fact that in late 1890, the British Government made a decision that it would no longer station a British warship more or less semi-permanently at Honolulu, and that in the future it would only arrange for periodic visits by warships of the Pacific Squadron based at Esquimalt in British Columbia, Canada.[16] One such visit, requested by Wodehouse, was made in the spring of 1892, when HMS *Champion* came from Canada to help settle the political conditions in the country after the latest Wilcox-Ashford Liberal Party insurrection plot was stopped by a series of arrests.[17]

The Hawaiian Government had to contend with more trouble from

Robert Wilcox, and from Volney Ashford, now a Liberal Party stalwart, who were attempting to foment another rebellion. The Marshal of the Kingdom used undercover police officers to infiltrate the insurrectionist organization and to discern their plans, after which they were arrested on charges of treason. However, the charges of treason were dropped against the majority of those who were arrested because the Attorney-General's Department decided that there was insufficient evidence to secure a conviction. Volney Ashford was released and he immediately fled the Kingdom. Eventually, the Attorney General concluded that his department would be unlikely to secure a conviction of Wilcox from a Hawaiian jury, given his oratorical gifts, and the esteem in which he was held by a large segment of the indigenous Hawaiian population.[18] The court was advised that the Attorney-General's department would not proceed against Wilcox, and he and his confederates were released.

The Annexation Club decided to send Thurston to Washington in May, 1892, to make contact with senior American decision-makers in order to determine their willingness to support them and to accept the annexation of Hawaii. Thurston had been appointed by the Hawaiian Government as a special commissioner, along with Edwin M Walsh, an agent of the sugar industry, to prepare for Hawaii's participation in the 1893 Chicago Colombian Exhibition. The Colombian Exhibition provided a convenient cover for Thurston to travel to Washington and to meet with US officials, and it also allowed Thurston to charge the majority of his trip expenses to the Hawaiian Government. (The Annexation Club did pay for the expenses of Thurston's side trip to Washington.)

Thurston and Walsh stopped in San Francisco where Thurston met with a number of prominent people including the Hawaiian Consul in San Francisco, and Claus Spreckels, before moving onto Salt Lake City, Utah. There, Walsh took it upon himself to make a statement to the press about the prospects for annexation, saying to the press that the pressure put on the country by the McKinley Tariff was forcing all in Hawaii to contemplate annexation, either with the United States, or with Canada, or Great Britain.[19] The threat of a potential annexation of Hawaii by Canada and/or Great Britain was a continual theme of the Americans, and those Hawaiian-Americans who favoured the annexation of Hawaii by the United States in the run-up to the 1893 *coup d'état*. It was used by the annexationists as a political tool to create a sense of urgency for American action, lest Hawaii slip from America's grasp.

On his way to Washington Thurston stopped in New York, where he met with the Hawaiian Consul, Elisha Allen, and with William N Armstrong, an attorney who had once lived in the islands, and who had been the Attorney General in one of King Kalakaua's cabinets. Armstrong had always opposed both the Hawaiian monarchy and the independence of the islands, and he was quite willing to advise Thurston on the latter's annexation efforts. Thurston then moved onto Washington, the main purpose of his North American trip. Obedient to protocol, he met with the Hawaiian Minister to the United States, Dr. Mott-Smith, and in his company Thurston met with the senior party leaders from both of America's two main political parties. Thurston's meetings included Senator Cushman Davis, the senior Republican on the Senate Foreign Relations Committee, and Democratic Representative James Blount, the Chairman of the House Committee on Foreign Affairs. The subject of the annexation of the Hawaiian islands was discussed at both meetings. Senator Davis, being a Republican, was supportive. Representative Blount, however, put Thurston off, saying that from a political perspective the issue of annexing the Hawaiian Islands was a national question, instead of a partisan one, and he suggested that Thurston go and see Secretary of State Blaine. Blount later described Thurston as "uppish."[20]

Afterwards Thurston went alone to see Secretary of State Blaine, and in his memoirs states:

"I called at the State Department and presented a letter of introduction from John L Stevens, United States minister to Hawaii. I made a full explanation to Mr. Blaine; we had no intention of precipitating action in Honolulu, but conditions had gone so far that we felt the maintenance of peace to be impossible; we believed that Liliuokalani was likely at any time to attempt the promulgation of a new constitution. If she tended toward absolutism, we proposed to seek annexation to the United States, provided it would entertain the proposal. A nucleus had been formed in Honolulu to bring the plan to a focus, should occasion arise; that nucleus had sent me to Washington to ascertain the attitude of the authorities there."[21]

Blaine asked Thurston with whom among the Washington power-brokers had he spoke to. Thurston told him that he had seen both Senator Davis and Representative Blount. Secretary Blaine then responded to Thurston, saying: "I am somewhat unwell, but I wish you would call on B. F. Tracy, secretary of the navy, and tell him what you have told me, and say to him that I think you should see the President. Do not see Mr. Blount again. I will attend to him. Come to me after you have seen President Harrison."[22]

Thurston did as he was bid to do and he went to see the Secretary of the Navy, Benjamin F Tracy. After hearing Thurston out Tracy escorted him to the White House to discuss his plans with President Harrison. Tracy went into a private meeting with the President in the President's office while Thurston remained outside. When Tracy emerged he beckoned Thurston out of the presidential mansion and said to him:

> "I have explained fully to the President what you have said to me, and have this to say to you: the President does not think he should see you, but he authorizes me to say to you that, if conditions in Hawaii compel you people to act as you have indicated, and you come to Washington with an annexation proposition, you will find an exceedingly sympathetic administration here."[23]

As Thurston remarked in his memoirs, "That was all I wanted to know."

Whether President Harrison had any scruples about seeing Thurston or, as is more likely, he wished to retain some measure of plausible deniability in case of the failure of an American-backed physical assault on the government of a friendly country, it was now clear that the United States government had committed itself to support the overthrow of a government with which it had enjoyed decades of close and friendly relations, and with the ultimate purpose of annexing that country. Furthermore, despite some earlier protestations to the contrary in Thurston's memoirs, the statement by Secretary Tracy that "if conditions in Hawaii compel you people to act as you have indicated . . . " clearly indicates that some form of insurrection in Honolulu was discussed between Thurston and Tracy. It also seems clear that the substance of that conversation, and the intentions of the Annexation Club, were conveyed to the President of the United States who endorsed the outcome by promising a favourable reception from his administration to any subsequent annexation proposal that it might receive from Thurston and his confederates.

Lorrin Thurston crossed his Rubicon on that fateful May day in Washington. Thurston, and Hawaiian members of the Annexation Club who sent him to Washington were committing treason by engaging in a conspiracy with the government of a foreign country to extinguish Hawaii's national sovereignty. Sadly, President Benjamin Harrison and his Cabinet officers chose to abandon decades of honourable diplomatic relations with Hawaii and to seek to destroy the Hawaiian Kingdom's sovereignty by holding out the promise of annexation to Thurston and his confederates in Honolulu. From that day onward the Kingdom of Hawaii faced external and internal threats to its independence.

Thurston did not see Secretary Blaine again. Before leaving the United States and returning home to Hawaii however, Thurston met again with New York attorney William N Armstrong, who suggested that an appropriate back channel should be set up for communications between the US government and the Hawaiian conspirators. In that way, it would be unnecessary to involve Stevens, the American Minister in Hawaii, who could thus rely on plausible deniability if the annexation plot failed. Armstrong suggested that a friend of his, Archibald Hopkins, Esq. the Clerk of the Court of Claims in New York City would be an appropriate conduit for back-channel communications between Thurston and the US government. Thurston agreed and Hopkins was engaged at a salary of $75.00 per month, "with the expectation of further compensation proportionate to results if any were reached."[24]

On his way back to Hawaii, Thurston penned a policy paper to Secretary Blaine in which he analyzed the political situation in Hawaii for the Secretary's benefit. Thurston said there were six competitive political groups in the islands:

1.   Non-resident foreign investors

2.   Hawaiian-born and resident foreign investors

3.   Liberal Party agitators

4.   The general indigenous Hawaiian population

5.   The Queen and royalists

6.   A pro-British faction.

In Thurston's view, the first three groups would support US annexation while the last two would not. The general indigenous population, in Thurston's opinion, was undecided. Why would annexation by the United States be a good idea at the present time? Thurston enumerated a number of points:

1.   The McKinley Tariff had caused a recession

2.   The largely indigenous Liberal Party supported it

3.   The indigenous population formed the greater part of the electorate but the whites had the money and they needed political control to protect their money. The natives were unhappy with ceding political control to the whites and refused to accept the political *status quo*. Irresponsible foreigners fomented political trouble and left the country in a state of expectant revolution.

Thurston's conclusion was that the monied class needed political protection, and political stability, and only annexation by the United States could provide them with that.[25] Thurston suggested to Secretary Blaine that the Queen might be pensioned off in order to further the annexation effort but there might be a need for a coup, and the formation of a provisional government if she refused, or if the indigenous population failed to support the annexation project.[26]

By the time Thurston wrote his memorandum to the Secretary of State there had been new political developments in Hawaii. Some members of the Liberal Party had been extremely uncomfortable with their party's position on the monarchy, and on US annexation, and those members led by Joseph Nawali, and William White, mounted a successful effort to wrest control of their party away from Bush and Wilcox, who were banished from its leadership. Nawali and White held more moderate positions and focused on promoting constitutional changes that would enhance the political position of the indigenous population. They supported the institution of the monarchy. Part of their political strategy called for organizing a process to generate petitions to the Queen to plead with her for a new constitution for Hawaii.[27]

Lorrin Thurston returned home to report on the outcome of his trip to his confederates in the Annexation Club. The consensus amongst the annexationists was that they needed a pretext in order to take action against the government. Fortunately for the annexationists, Queen Liliuokalani was also working on a project that would give them their pretext for action – a new constitution for Hawaii. Working with the new Hawaiian Liberal Party leaders Joseph Nawahi, and William White, and also with input from Samuel Nowlein, the Captain of her Royal Guard, a draft constitution was prepared by the Queen and was ready by August 2nd. Foiled in her attempts to persuade the Legislature to convene a constitutional convention where her new draft constitution could be debated, and hopefully adopted, the Queen decided that she would unilaterally

215

impose a new constitution by royal fiat at the next prorogation of the Hawaiian Legislature.

The Queen was primarily motivated by her desire to sustain and enhance the prerogatives of the Crown through the recovery of those powers that her brother, King Kalakaua, had surrendered in the 1887 Bayonet Constitution. Unilateral proclamation of a new constitution by royal authority would contravene the existing, 1887 Bayonet Constitution but the Queen was well aware of the political precedent of 1864, when King Kamehameha V had promulgated his own constitution in defiance of the existing constitution. And of course, the 1887 Bayonet Constitution itself had been imposed on the country without any reference to the Hawaiian Legislature, or adoption by a constitutional convention.

One outcome of Thurston's trip was the curious attitude of the Hawaiian Minister to the United States, Dr. John Mott-Smith. He had attended several of the initial meetings that Thurston had with US legislative representatives and he heard what Thurston was hoping to achieve, although it seems that Thurston's more radical ideas, such as a coup, and the establishment of a provisional government, were not mentioned by Thurston in the presence of Hawaii's diplomatic representative. When US newspaper articles began to mention Mott-Smith's name in connection with the promotion of US annexation of Hawaii there were demands in the Hawaiian press for his recall. Foreign Minister Parker at first demanded explanations from Mott-Smith, and then he ordered Mott-Smith to publicly refute any statements attributable to him that alluded to, or promoted, the annexation of Hawaii by the United States. Mott-Smith was instructed to ensure that the American Government understood that the Queen, the Hawaiian Government, and the people of Hawaii, were determined to maintain the independence of their country.[28]

Annexation remained a live issue in Washington however, due to the continual reports about it by American officials in Hawaii. In the autumn, Stevens published an anonymous article in the *Kennebec Journal* in Maine, the same newspaper that he had once co-edited with James Blaine, on the subject of an American annexation of Hawaii. In it Stevens said: "The time is near when we must decide who shall hold these islands as part of their national territory. It is not possible for them much longer to remain alone." Although the writer was described as anonymous, few knowledgeable people were fooled.

Political discord continued in Honolulu during the second half of 1892, with the Queen and the Legislature vying for control of the Cabinet. The Cabinets selected by the Queen were not supported by the Legislature, which led to unstable governments. Mainly that was a result of an unholy alliance between the Reform and Liberal Parties in the Legislature, where the Liberals, under the leadership of Wilcox and Bush until October, were temporarily opposed to the monarchy, and aligned with the political views of the settler community (and with the sentiments of the secret Annexation Club). The Legislature presented a resolution to the throne calling upon the Queen to recognize, as a constitutional principle, that the monarch should call upon the leader of the majority in the Legislature to assemble a Cabinet to govern the country.[29] That resolution was the operative principle of British constitutional government as practised in Great Britain, and in Pacific rim countries such as Canada, Australia, and New Zealand. However, the 1887 Bayonet Constitution was clear in stipulating the Sovereign had a personal discretion to appoint a Cabinet, and the Queen would not surrender that power easily.

The Queen escaped from a difficult political position by sending a Message to the Legislature ostensibly accepting the principle and, after consulting the British Minister, Wodehouse, appointing a Reform Party Cabinet under George Wilcox that did not contain any annexationists. The Wilcox Cabinet was able to secure the confidence of the Legislature and a significant result of the Wilcox appointment was that it broke the alliance between the Reform Party and the Liberals. The Liberals were chagrined because they failed to secure any of the Cabinet posts in the Wilcox Ministry, which made them look like fools for allying with the Reform Party in the Legislature. The appointment of the Wilcox Cabinet was successful in restoring a measure of political stability to Hawaiian politics.

In Washington, Secretary Blaine's health continued to decline and he was forced to retire from office. He was replaced as Secretary of State by John W Foster. President Harrison ran for reelection in the fall against Grover Cleveland, whom he had defeated in the 1888 presidential election. This time however, the effects of the McKinley Tariff had begun to bite amongst consumers and it contributed to Harrison's defeat by Cleveland in the general election. Cleveland thus became the only US President to serve two non-consecutive terms in the White House. Cleveland's election satisfied the sugar interests in Hawaii because the Democrats opposed the McKinley Tariff, as they were not as beholden to the US domestic sugar cartel as the Republicans were, and therefore the sugar industry in Hawaii had no immediate need to support political change in the Hawaiian islands.[30]

Lorrin Thurston continued his back channel communications with the Harrison Administration through Archibald Hopkins in New York. On November 15, 1892, Hopkins wrote to Thurston, likely in response to the paper that Thurston had earlier sent to Blaine, and said: "I am authorized to inform you that the United States Government will pay Queen Liliuokalani, and those connected with her,[31] the sum of two hundred and fifty thousand dollars for the assignment to the United States of the Sovereignty of Hawaii."[32]

The Annexation Club considered this proposal but determined that it would not be worthwhile to present it to the Queen for two reasons. Firstly, it was not thought to be a large enough sum to entice the Queen to accept it and, secondly, for the indigenous population, from which the Hawaiian monarchy was derived, there was a profound love of country that was resistant to the blandishments of annexation. Thurston wrote to Hopkins:

> "The opposition to annexation by the natives is not based so much upon personal support of royalty as it is on a strong sentimental feeling in favour of independence intertwined with a strong race prejudice against foreigners, and the fear that with the loss of independence the control of their Government would be more likely to pass out of their hands, and that less offices would be filled by Hawaiians . . ."[33]

And concerning the proposed compensation to the Queen, Thurston stated:

> ". . . she is in a more independent frame of mind than she was six months ago, and unless forced to take that or nothing, there is no probability that, under existing circumstances, she would take so small a sum . . . this disposition to resist to the last ditch the demands for popular control of the government . . . is a trait which stands in the way, of negotiations for purchasing her rights as long as she feels no fear

of losing the position by force, except for a much larger sum than the one named."[34]

After conferring with Washington, Hopkins wrote back to Thurston on December 29th to advise him that: "Should unexpected changes make it seem best for you to act immediately, everything possible to second your plans will be done at this end of the line in the short time that remains."[35]

Meanwhile, with the defeat of the Republicans, John L Stevens was preparing to be replaced as American Minister to the Kingdom of Hawaii and he prepared a transition memorandum for his successor, whoever that was to be, in which Stevens outlined his thoughts on the coming events in the Hawaiian Islands. America's interests, Stevens thought, will demand change in Hawaii and perhaps decisive measures to secure American supremacy.[36]

As his attitude toward the government to which he was accredited as a US diplomat continued to decline Stevens engaged in a conflict with the Marshal of the Kingdom over the arrest of one of his servants, and he maintained a close association with the Hawaiian annexationists, a treasonous group. Stevens continued to be disparaging toward Hawaiian royal officials with whom he dealt. His general relations with Queen Liliuokalani remained particularly bad, and his reports home to the United States were full of unsubstantiated gossip.[37] Eventually, Secretary of State John W Foster instructed Stevens to write two separate reports, one that would be straightforward and suitable for official purposes, and a second report in which Stevens could submit all of his secretive gossip, unverifiable intelligence, and complaints against royal personages.[38]

As one year passed into another from 1892 to 1893, the Hawaiian powder keg was full and the fuse was ready. All that was required for a political explosion was for someone to light the fuse. That would not be long in coming.

NOTES

[1] Gavan Daws, *Shoal of Time, A History of the Hawaiian Islands*, University of Hawaii Press, Honolulu, 1968 (1974), 268

[2] Bush had been appointed envoy to Samoa during King Kalakaua and Premier Gibson's ill-fated attempt to create a Polynesian confederation. Bush had embarrassed the Hawaiian Government by his behaviour in Samoa, which served as the cause for his dismissal by Premier Gibson.

[3] Kuykendall, 528

[4] Kuykendall, 529

[5] Tate, 113

[6] Kuykendall, 526

[7] Vowel, 188

[8] Stephen Kinzer, *Overthrow, America's Century of Regime Change From Hawaii to Iraq*, Times Books, Henry Holt and Company, New York, 16

[9] William Michael Morgan, *Pacific Gibralter, U.S. – Japanese Rivalry Over the Annexation of Hawai'i, 1885 – 1898*, Naval Institute Press, Annapolis, MD, 2011, 61

[10] Thurston, 91. After American annexation one would, as a matter of course, expect Thurston to say as much to protect the reputation of the United States and its officials.

[11] Morgan, 66

[12] Kuykendall, 527

[13] Morgan, 67

[14] Morgan, 67

[15] Kuykendall, 526

[16] Kuykendall, 471

[17] Kuykendall, 531

[18] Morgan, 62

[19] Kuykendall, 534

[20] Kuykendall, 535; Daws, 266

[21] Thurston, 230

[22] Thurston, 230

[23] Thurston, 230

[24] Thurston, 243

[25] Kuykendall, 536

[26] Kinzer, *Overthrow*, 266-67; Kuykendall, 537

[27] Kuykendall, 548

[28] Kuykendall, 539

[29] Kuykendall, 552

[30] Morgan, 67

[31] This was undoubtedly a reference to Princess Kaiulani who, as the Heiress Apparent, had a future claim to the throne.

[32] Thurston, 234

[33] Thurston, 236

[34] Thurston, 236

[35] Thurston, 243

[36] Morgan, 64

[37] In one report to Washington referencing Princess Kaiulani Stevens referred to Archibald Cleghorn as Kaiulani's putative father, inferring that her biological father was actually an American naval officer (and, like Stevens, from Maine no less). This report was a

slander of Kaiulani's deceased mother, Princess Likelike, and was probably made by Stevens with the intention of diminishing Princess Kaiulani's standing in Washington. (William Adam Russ, Jr., *The Hawaiian Revolution (1893 – 1894)* Susquehanna University Press, Selinsgrove, Pa, 1959, 44)

[38] Morgan, 65

9

The Heiress Apparent

As a Princess of Hawaii, and one who would in due course succeed to the throne of the Kingdom, it was natural that Princess Kaiulani would develop a sense of the politics of her native country, and be anxious to play a role in its governance when the time came for her to return home and assume her public responsibilities. The Cleghorn family was a politically sophisticated family and growing up Kaiulani was exposed to Hawaiian political matters. From her own early correspondence one can see that even at the age of twelve, Kaiulani was developing an understanding of the politics of Hawaii, and of the comings and goings within the country's public government. Writing, in May, 1888, to her aunt, Princess Liliuokalani, who was then travelling with Queen Kapiolani to London for the celebration of Queen Victoria's Golden Jubilee, Kaiulani reported that her father had secured an important government position; "Papa has got the position of Collector general of customs because Kapena is put out."[1] Apparently, scandal had engulfed Kapena, a favourite of King Kalakaua, and the King and Cabinet had decided to appoint the King's brother-in-law, Archibald Cleghorn, to the post in place of

Kapena. Undoubtedly this appointment was welcomed by Kaiulani's household, because it gave the Cleghorn family an additional degree of financial stability.

In October of 1890, the Princess reached a milestone in her personal life, and a milestone that also had political implications. She undertook the ceremony of confirmation before the Bishop of Leicester, according to the rites of the Anglican Church.[2] In an era of strong religious affiliation the act of joining a particular church was also a declaration of identity. Princess Kaiulani's act of confirmation in the state of Church of England reinforced the impression, held by many pro-annexation Americans in Hawaii affiliated with the Congregationalist church, that the young Princess was much too British for their liking.

Many of those opposed to the continued independence of Hawaii thought that her future ascension to the throne carried with it the prospect of a greater British influence in the affairs of Hawaii, and that it would be detrimental to the cause of US annexation.[3] International rivalry between Great Britain and the United States over influence in Hawaiian affairs remained a feature of geopolitics in the Pacific during the last years of the Hawaiian monarchy, and it was the real, or perceived, British influence on the throne that constantly worried the American Minister in Honolulu, John L Stevens, and his boss, Secretary of State James G Blaine in Washington.

After Kaiulani's departure from Honolulu, and her enrollment at Great Harrowden Hall, she was cut off from the daily discourse on Hawaiian political issues but as she matured a greater effort was made by those who were close to her to keep her abreast of the ongoing dramas of Hawaiian politics. Kaiulani, for her part, also reported home on any meetings she had in England with notable Hawaiians, especially those who played important roles in the politics of the Kingdom. Thus, for example, she wrote home about a visit she had received from Dr. John Mott-Smith, a former cabinet minister, and a future Hawaiian diplomatic minister to the United States.[4]

With the death of her uncle, King Kalakaua, her aunt Princess Liliuokalani now became Queen Liliuokalani, the reigning monarch of Hawaii. Her uncle's will stipulated that Princess Kaiulani should be named as the next heir to the throne and, after her, Prince David and the heirs of his body.[5] Early in 1891, following the death of King Kalakaua, and the accession of her aunt as Queen Liliuokalani, Princess Kaiulani learned of the formal change in her status within the Royal Family. She had been formally proclaimed as the new Heiress Apparent to the throne of Hawaii. In Honolulu on March 9, 1891, the House of Nobles of the Hawaiian Kingdom had been convened in the Throne Room of Iolani Palace before Her Hawaiian Majesty, Queen Liliuokalani, and His Royal Highness, Prince Consort John O Dominis. They were accompanied by the father of the Princess, Hon. Archibald S Cleghorn, the Court Chamberlain J W Robertson, the members of the Cabinet, Samuel Parker, Minister of Foreign Affairs, H A Widemann, Minister of Finance, C N Spencer, Minister of the Interior, W Austin Whiting, Attorney-General, and the aides-de-camp to the royal couple Colonel J Boyd, Major J D Holt, Major H K Bertelsmann, and Colonel John Parker, and Mrs. Clark, a lady-in-waiting to the Queen.

Following a prayer delivered by the Reverend J Kauhane the Queen declared to the Nobles assembled that she had brought them together to announce that she was nominating her beloved niece, Her Royal Highness Victoria Kaiulani, as her successor to the throne of Hawaii, and the Queen expressed the hope that the House of Nobles would approve of her appointment:

> "Nobles of my Kingdom: I have called you together to deliberate on a grave matter of State. Article Twenty-Two of the Constitution calls upon me to appoint a successor to the Throne. The same Article calls for the approval of your Honourable Body of my appointment.
>
> I now announce to you Our Beloved Niece, Her Royal Highness Victoria Kawekiu Kaiulani Lunalilo, as my successor the Throne of the Kingdom and I hope that your deliberations will lead you to approve of my appointment."

After the royal party had retired, the Nobles remained in the Throne Room of Iolani Palace to consider the nomination and almost immediately the House of Nobles concurred in the Queen's nomination of Princess Kaiulani as the Heiress Apparent. The Nobles then repaired to the Blue Room of the Palace where the Queen awaited them. The President of the Legislature, the Hon. J S Walker, announced to the Queen and those assembled with her that:

> "We the assembled Nobles of the Kingdom, hereby approve the appointment by Her Majesty Liliuokalani, Queen of the Hawaiian Islands, of Her Royal Highness Princess Victoria Kawekiu Kaiulani Lunalilo as Successor to the Throne of this Kingdom. Done at Iolani Palace this 9th day of March, A. D. 1891."

As expected, the nomination of Princess Kaiulani as the new Crown Princess had been unanimously confirmed by the Hawaiian House of Nobles. Afterwards, the Queen issued a Royal Proclamation:

> "We, LILIUOKALANI, by the Grace of God, Queen of the Hawaiian

Islands, agreeably to Article twenty-second of the Constitution of the Hawaiian Kingdom, do hereby appoint, failing an heir of Our body, Our beloved Subject and Niece Her Royal Highness VICTORIA KAWEKIU KAIULANI LUNALILO KALANINUIAHILAPALAPA to be Our Successor on the Throne after it shall have pleased God to call Us hence.

Done at Iolani Palace in Honolulu, this ninth day of March, in the year of Our Lord one thousand eight hundred and ninety-one.

LILIUOKALANI.

By the Queen:

Samuel Parker,

Minister of Foreign Affairs."[6]

Around noon, three heralds were sent out into the city on horseback to proclaim to the people of Honolulu the appointment of the Princess Kaiulani as Heiress Apparent to the throne of Hawaii. Colonel J H Boyd, the chief of the Royal staff, together with Majors Holt and Bertlemann, all in full dress uniform, rode through the streets preceded by a bugler from the Royal Guards. Colonel Boyd read out the proclamation, in a loud voice, in both Hawaiian and English, at the Aliiolani Hale, the Government Building, and at the Post Office and the Customs House. The Royal Hawaiian Band played *Hawaii Ponoi*, the national anthem, and then *The Kaiulani March*, which Bandmaster Henry Berger had originally composed for the birth of the Princess. Hawaiian artillery fired cannon in salute to their new heiress, and the American warships in Honolulu harbour, USS *Mohican*, and USS *Iroquois*, responded with a 21-gun salute to the Princess.

The *Honolulu Commercial Advertiser*, a newspaper that was not generally supportive of the Hawaiian monarchy nevertheless proclaimed that: "The nomination of Her Royal Highness Princess Victoria Kaiulani as Heir Apparent to the throne, will receive the hearty endorsement of the entire population, native and foreign."[7] Theo Davies wrote to Kaiulani and told her that she was the one figure in the islands whom everyone approved of and that she was already performing a great service to Hawaii just by being her "own well-beloved self."[8]

The announcement of her formal position as Crown Princess brought a flood of emotions to the breast of the young Princess. Looking back on it several years later she told Alix Dix, a San Francisco reporter for *The Morning Call*, that:

"I was mad with joy when the news of the proclamation declaring me heiress to the kingdom reached me abroad. I said to myself like a little girl, 'Now some day I shall be a Queen.' And meantime, after the Queen, I would come first in the kingdom. . . . [I] made all sorts of vows and plans you can think of. I dreamed of all that I would do for my people. I was sure that I could make them the happiest people in the world."[9]

Now, as the Heiress Apparent to the royal throne of Hawaii, Kaiulani's correspondence with her aunt became focussed increasingly, though tentatively, on important matters relating to the condition of the country, and its political circumstances. In a letter to the Queen in March, 1891, Kaiulani reports that she had been in communication with Prince David, and Prince Kuhio, and was led to understand that both of them had been summoned home, leaving unstated the question of whether she should now return to Honolulu to assist the Queen in matters of state.[10] Prince David had asked

229

Kaiulani if she had been recalled to Hawaii, now that she was the new Heiress Apparent. Kaiulani had been forced to admit to David that "I have no instructions to return home at present. I may have letters next week and if I do go home, I will let you know."[11] But no summons to come home came for Kaiulani from the new Queen.

The Queen's reign got off to a tense start when she called for the resignations of the over-holding cabinet ministers from her brother's reign. The ministers objected to being dismissed by the Sovereign, as the Bayonet Constitution of 1887 provided that only the Legislature could dismiss the Cabinet, and then only for want of confidence. However, the constitution had to be read together with older common law principles, and it was a legal principle, inherited from the common law of England, that the death of a monarch terminated the commissions of appointment of public officers unless a statute had been enacted to provide for their continuation in office upon the death of the preceding monarch, or unless they were reappointed by the new sovereign.

The Supreme Court of Hawaii upheld the legality of the Queen's position and a new Cabinet was appointed by the Queen but the episode caused unease between the monarch and the Legislature, particularly among the members of the Reform Party, and their supporters, who now saw that the Queen could not be manipulated by them. Kaiulani's guardian, Theo Davies wrote to the Princess to warn her of even more serious clashes between the Queen and the Americans who were now entering the country in increasing numbers, and who refused to become naturalized subjects of the Queen, or to pledge their loyalty to their adopted country.[12]

Meanwhile, in the summer of 1891, Kaiulani was reunited with her father, Archibald Cleghorn, who had journeyed to Great Britain in the summer of 1891, to discuss with Theo Davies Princess Kaiulani's placement with Mrs. Rooke at Brighton to finish her education. Kaiulani also met up with two old friends from home, the Parker sisters, Eva and Helen, whom she now found to be very mature, and worldly, compared to herself. She wrote to the Queen and said that in comparison to the Parker girls Kaiulani felt that she was a mere child.[13] Despite that, Kaiulani remained good friends with both of them.

Tragedy struck the Royal Family again in the autumn of 1891, when the Queen's husband and Prince Consort, John O Dominis, died after an illness. The death of the Prince Consort opened up a vacancy in the office of the Governor of Oahu, and Princess Kaiulani wanted her father, Archibald Cleghorn, to obtain the position. Kaiulani was too well aware of the fact that her immediate family was not wealthy, although they were well enough. The cost of maintaining Kaiulani in Great Britain, beyond what the Legislature provided as a subsidy, was a financial burden to her father and if there was a way that Kaiulani could help him to defray some of those costs she was determined to do it. So she decided to write to her aunt and to lobby for the appointment of her father to the vacant post of Governor of Oahu. Kaiulani wrote to the Queen in October, not long after the death of her uncle, after rumours began to circulate in the Hawaiian expatriate community in Europe that Prince David was to receive the post. Kaiulani asked the Queen to excuse her presumptuousness in making this request but she would like her father to obtain the office of Governor, and she was quick to note that she had never before asked anything of the Queen for herself. She closed by saying that she hoped that she would be of use to the Queen when she returned to Honolulu.[14]

Queen Liliuokalani was touched, and perhaps amused, by her niece's lobbying on behalf of her father and she quickly wrote back to the young Princess:

"I quite enjoyed your last letter for there was a good deal for me to think of especially about the Governorship of Oahu. My dear child, I am very glad that you did mention it in your letter but I am happy to say that it had already been decided upon by myself in Cabinet and was only waiting for your fathers return. We had no idea of making David governor at all, it was a report made up outside. David and his brother have had no experience in anything whatever and it would be impossible for one to think of giving them any billet of importance at present until they showed their intelligence in some way or other & let their capability in mind or speech or actions be known but they are still young and I have placed them where I think they might have a chance to improve and learn."[15]

As to the role that Kaiulani might play when she returned to Hawaii, her aunt wrote that the Princess should not rush matters, and that she should concentrate on her studies, and on the development of her character:

". . . as you mentioned about wishing or hoping to be able to help me, I find your natural intelligence prompted you to write it, but it will all come to you in time. The main thing my dear niece is to be good. There is a good deal in that word for it obliges you to guide your actions, your thoughts, to help you in your studies, to be dutiful to your teachers and to gain their love and also of your friends. To study all those qualities that would be the making of a Noble woman. It is necessary that you should acquire all these to fit you for the position you have to take."[16]

Kaiulani was delighted to learn that the Queen had agreed that her father should be the new Governor of Oahu. However, when new rumours reached Britain that the Queen also intended to relieve Kaiulani's father of his responsibilities as the Collector of Customs when he assumed the Governorship of Oahu Kaiulani intervened again, writing to the Queen, and pleading that the Cleghorns could not live in their customary manner without the customs house salary because the salary of the island Governor was only half that of the Collector of Customs. She pointed out that her father was subsidizing her educational sojourn in England and that she did not want her father to fall into debt.[17] In the end, Archibald Cleghorn was rewarded with the Governorship of Oahu while retaining his office as Collector of Customs, so Kaiulani's fears for her father, and his finances, never came to pass while the Kingdom lasted.

In another letter to Princess Kaiulani that autumn the Queen touched upon both international and dynastic issues, expressing concern to Kaiulani about the drift of American opinion toward Hawaii, and rumours of the Queen's ill-health. She wrote: "I find in your father's letter that it is his intention to visit the President and Mr Blaine. I am glad of it because he might be able to [establish] many things about our country which they might not know about."[18]

Turning to the dynastic issue of succession the Queen addressed reports that she was in failing health; "As I write I am enjoying the best of health. The local newspapers say that I am sick and in danger of dying any moment and the foreign papers have copied it, but I can write and am happy to say to the contrary." And as for the two princes, the Queen reports that they were both now employed in the public administration – Prince David in the Department of Foreign Affairs and Prince Kuhio in the Department of the Interior.[19]

As the months passed in 1891, it seems that Kaiulani grew

increasingly homesick, and she hinted in a letter in November that she felt she had been away long enough, saying of Prince David that "I suppose you were very glad to get Kawananakoa home. He had been away such a long time," an unstated appeal for her own summons home. In the same letter she mentioned that she had received a visitor at Great Harrowden Hall, Matthew Makalua, one of the young Hawaiians that King Kalakaua had sent abroad to be educated. Makalua asked Kaiulani to send his respects to the Queen and he hoped she would not think that presumptuous of him. (Makalua had married an English woman and after completing medical studies he decided to remain in England as a physician, rather than to return home to Hawaii.) Perhaps as a sign of the influence her English education was having, she signed her letter as Victoria Kaiulani.[20]

Early in 1892 the Queen wrote again to the Princess discussing the efforts underway at Ainahau to replace the house that Kaiulani grew up in with a more prominent house befitting the beauty of the surrounding estate. Archibald Cleghorn looked forward to Kaiulani's return to Hawaii and he wanted the Heiress Apparent to the throne to have a home on a scale befitting of her social and political position in the Kingdom. The Queen, however, had her own views on how Kaiulani should live after her return home to Hawaii, telling the Princess that:

> "Your father is talking of raising your house at Ainahau. I daresay it will be a grand house when raised but I told him you ought to come to the palace and stay, of course Ainahau will be very nice for a country residence. . . . I look forward to the time when we may have you back to us and in that respect time hangs heavily. Write me again."[21]

Clearly, the Queen was envisaging that after her return home

Kaiulani might live with her at Iolani Palace, where the Queen could mold the future monarch to her royal duties. The Princess however, was looking forward to returning to the home she knew, emphasizing in her reply to the Queen's letter that she had always hoped to have a home in Waikiki that reflected the grandeur of the garden at Ainahau; "I am so glad to see that Father is putting up a proper house at Ainahau. It has always been my ambition to have a house at Waikiki worthy of the beautiful garden."[22] Quite naturally, Kaiulani sought to maintain her personal independence upon her return by living in her own family residence.

In April the Queen wrote to Kaiulani about her studies, advising her about the utility of certain of her subjects, and expressing her approval of Kaiulani's study of Professor Alexander's book on Hawaiian history. In that letter she also mentioned the expertise that would be available to the Princess from the public servants employed in the various departments of the Hawaiian state.[23] By writing so, the Queen wished Kaiulani to know that her future public functions would not be solitary burdens, and that she would be well supported by the institutions of the state.

Kaiulani's visits with her English guardian, Theo Davies, and his family, together with Davies' letters to Kaiulani also kept her up to date on Hawaiian affairs. Davies was acquainted with all of the major actors in Hawaiian politics during the period of Kaiulani's life, and his frequent business trips to the country kept him abreast of the current political developments. As Kaiulani's legal guardian in England, Davies was an excellent source of political information for the Princess, and he became her most important political mentor.

As 1892 progressed, Kaiulani continued to mature as a young and self-aware woman. She appreciated art, and she had some skill as an artist. She was surprised, and delighted when, on her seventeenth birthday in October of 1892, her governess, Mrs. Rooke, presented her with a print of a painting by the artist James Sant that Kaiulani loved, entitled *The Soul's Awakening*. The painting was a portrait of a young girl on the cusp of womanhood looking upwards into the light while clutching a book, possibly the Bible. Kaiulani was thrilled with the print, writing to the Queen that it was a beautiful painting, and that she had always wanted it but never had enough funds to purchase. It now hung in an honoured position on her bedroom wall, and the lovely portrayal of the girl was the first thing that Kaiulani saw when she opened her eyes each morning.[24]

Fashion also occupied Kaiulani's thoughts, and she was developing her own sense of fashion style. Apparently dissatisfied with the current trend of female fashions, she wrote to the Queen that: "I am having such very pretty summer dresses made. I do like pretty, dainty things. All the ladies are wearing dresses made like men's clothes. I do dislike them so, they look so very manly."[25]

She enjoyed a springtime visit with Mrs. Rooke to the island of Jersey. Never a good sailor, she was seasick on the way over but she nevertheless enjoyed her vacation in the Channel Islands very much, as she thought that the islands reminded her of the islands of Hawaii.

Back in Hawaii however, trouble was brewing. Her father wrote to her in June about a growing unease over American covetousness concerning Hawaii. Cleghorn reported that the Queen was quite worried about the articles appearing in the American press concerning the possibility of the United States annexing Hawaii. He said that the US press would not let the matter rest, and there were many people in Hawaii who favoured annexation, thinking that they could make more money out of sugar if Hawaii was part of the United States. Although her father hoped that the day of annexation to the United States would never come he worried about disaffected indigenous Hawaiian politicians, such as the Liberal Party leaders Wilcox and Bush, who demonstrated no real love for their country and were doing great harm to it by attempting to promote annexation.[26]

Meanwhile, the Queen wrote to Kaiulani in June to tell her of the plans being made for Kaiulani's return to Hawaii.

"My dear Niece, I always feel happy to hear from you and to know that you are in good health. I find in your last [letter] that you [were] going to Jersey, for a change. I am sure those little trips will do you lots of good.

You say in your letter that you wished that you might be permitted to stay 'till after Christmas then you might travel on the Continent' and it shows that you have not received any letter in which it says that next April of 1893 your father will come for you then you will go to the Continent and be presented to the crowned heads of Europe, then return to England and be presented to the Queen [Victoria], and then you will come to the United States [to] meet the President [and] see what there is to be seen at Boston or other parts of interest in America, visit the Exposition in Chicago then come back in time to be here on your birthday if possible. So now you must not permit yourself to be troubled by homesickness but be cheerful until you can come back to us. I enjoy your letters very much for Papa sometimes reads them to me. He comes over very often and we talk of you and your future.

My health is very good, my dear child and I would like all my friends to know it, for some of our papers make it out that I am sickly and getting old – Of course I am getting old, we all are, but as long as we are well and I feel well and know that I am capable of attending to my duties, it is nothing to me what they say. I am looking forward to the time when I may have you back, which will lessen the feeling of loneliness which at present weighs upon me.

I will write more another time.

Your Affectionate Aunt,

Liliuokalani."[27]

During the latter part of 1892 the Crown was in an almost perpetual conflict with the Legislature over the formation and sustainability of Cabinet Government in the islands. Queen Liliuokalani was increasingly flexing her political muscles to obtain a Cabinet that would do her own bidding, especially with respect to changing, or supplanting, the Bayonet Constitution of 1887, which always remained her personal *bête noire*. Archibald Cleghorn was alarmed by the political machinations that were occurring and at the almost continual reshuffling of the Cabinet, which he perceived as clear evidence of instability in the governance of the country. He kept Kaiulani closely informed of the unfolding series of events, writing to her on September 13, 1892, to advise that:

"yesterday . . . the Queen appointed Sam Parker Minister of Foreign Affairs, Charles T Gulick, Minister of Interior, E C Macfarlane, Finance[,] P Neumann, Atty General . . . Parker and Neumann are from the old Cabinet. The House adjourned yesterday morning till tomorrow at 1[:]00 [o']c[lock] and then they are going to try to remove the new Cabinet as they do not want any of the old one . . . I will tell you the result the next mail. I do not regard the new Cabinet as a strong one, . . ."[28]

The previous year, when the Queen had written to Princess Kaiulani after the death of the husband the Prince Consort, John O Dominis, and acknowledged the great loss she had consequently suffered she had said how much she would thereafter have to rely on Kaiulani's father for advice and assistance in the conduct of state affairs:

> "When your dear Uncle was alive he used to advise me in [a] great many things pertaining to ruling a nation as he had had some experience under the former Kings and under your dear uncle Kalakaua"s reign so when I became Queen he often gave me advice which were valuable to me but now that he is gone, I will have to look to your father who is left to me."[29]

Now, however, after the passage of a year it seemed that Archibald Cleghorn was no longer relied upon for advice as much as he may have been earlier. The Queen was now influenced by new advisers, and she was bent on obtaining a new constitutional settlement to replace the Bayonet Constitution of 1887 that had been forced on her brother. Archibald Cleghorn found himself increasingly marginalized in the Royal Court. Cleghorn had a low opinion of both the Cornwell and Macfarlane Cabinets that briefly held office in 1892, and it seems certain that Queen Liliuokalani rejected his advice when she made those appointments.[30] However, when she faced up to the realities of the Legislature and appointed a Reform Party Cabinet under George N Wilcox, Cleghorn wrote to Kaiulani expressing his approval. Although they were all Reform Party members, George Wilcox and his colleagues were also patriots, who stood staunchly for continued Hawaiian independence. Thus the Wilcox Cabinet was acceptable to both the annexationists and to the monarchists. Archibald Cleghorn commended the Cabinet to Kaiulani, and told his daughter that anyone who wanted to remove the Wilcox Cabinet would not have the best interests of the Hawaii in their hearts.[31]

As the year 1892 began to draw to a close ominous clouds were on the Hawaiian horizon. The political instability that was ushered in by the uprising against King Kalakaua, and that had led to the Bayonet Constitution, was still present, and it was fuelling an increase in annexationist sentiment amongst the immigrants to Hawaii from the United States who were being encouraged in their annexationist sentiments by the American Minister to Hawaii, John L Stevens, an enemy of Hawaiian patriots, according to Theo Davies.[32]

More ominous still was correspondence Princess Kaiulani received from the Queen, in which the Queen advised Princess Kaiulani that she was contemplating the imposition of a new constitution by royal proclamation to replace the Bayonet Constitution of 1887. Although a bill had been introduced in the Legislature calling for a constitutional convention it had been defeated, and the Cabinet Ministers in the Wilcox Ministry had joined those opposed to the venture in turning it down – an act that hardly endeared them to the Queen. There were fears in Hawaii within the settler community that the Queen might act unilaterally on petitions that had been delivered to her by indigenous Hawaiians requesting that she change the constitution by royal fiat, as King Kamehameha V had done in 1864.[33]

Early in 1893, the political atmosphere became more tense with the passage by the Legislature of a Lottery bill. That law was intended to raise funds for the government through a public lottery scheme and it was carried by its proponents in the Legislature over the stern opposition of both the Cabinet and the Reform Party. The Cabinet advised the Queen to veto the bill but she chose instead to give it her Royal Assent and it became law. The opposition to the bill by the Cabinet and the Reform Party was two-fold. Firstly, their religious morals were offended by a measure that encouraged public gambling, which was seen by many in the Christian churches as a moral vice. But more importantly the measure was opposed because the lottery could free the government from obtaining all of its revenues through the legislative budget process in the Hawaiian Legislature. That prospect presented a threat to the Bayonet Constitution of 1887, because it allowed for the possibility of independent Crown action, which was contrary to the intention of the 1887 Constitution that had sought to restrain the powers of the Crown. Archibald Cleghorn perceived the danger in the lottery bill and he wrote to Princess Kaiulani about his concerns, calling the Lottery Bill wretched, and warning that the Queen had received bad advice, and would likely grant Royal Assent to the measure. Cleghorn himself had advised the Queen to have nothing to do with the lottery measure.[34]

What Kaiulani made of all that is unknown, although she certainly now realized the complexities of the politics of her country. Her main focus continued to be on her forthcoming European tour and her return home in 1893. She was to be presented at the European courts and to have an audience with Queen Victoria before returning to Hawaii via the United States. The plans for her grand tour, and for royal audiences were heady things for a seventeen-year-old to contemplate. Archibald Cleghorn wrote to Dr. John Mott-Smith, the Hawaiian Minister in Washington to begin the process of planning Kaiulani's return to Hawaii through the United States. The importance of that country to Hawaii made it all the more imperative for the Princess to make a good impression on American society. On January 13, 1893, Mott-Smith wrote back to Cleghorn advising him that while it was too early to make any definitive plans for the visit of the Heiress Apparent to the American capital; "I am inclined to think that while she is in Washington at least she will be considered a guest of the nation. I will keep the matter in mind and find out unofficially what the prospect is."[35] At the time that letter was written neither the sender nor the recipient could have contemplated that Kaiulani would make her visit to the United States much sooner than anyone expected, and not as a guest but rather as a supplicant, pleading with the American people for the life of her country.

NOTES

[1] Kaiulani to Liliuokalani, May 5, 1888, BMA

[2] Webb & Webb, 79

[3] While many of the pro-American and pro-annexationists in Hawaii were Congregationalists who were descended from the early missionaries to Hawaii not all of them were members of the Congregational church. In particular, Sandford Dole, later the President of Hawaii, attended services at St. Andrews Anglican Cathedral, in Honolulu.

[4] Kaiulani to Kapiolani, October 15, 1890 BMA

[5] Mellen, 251. However, the dispositions made in the King's will were not constitutional decisions because the Hawaiian Sovereign did not have the power to direct the disposition of the crown of Hawaii as if it were private property. Under the Hawaiian constitution, a reigning monarch could only nominate a single heir, and that nomination had to be confirmed by the Hawaiian House of Nobles in order to constitute a valid constitutional appointment. However, the King's will did indicate his own personal preferences and, as the founding head of his royal house, Kalakaua's intentions carried great weight within the Royal Family. Nevertheless, had

242

the Kingdom continued, and had Kaiulani lived to succeed to the Hawaiian throne, she could have nominated as her own heir someone other than Prince David, or the heirs of his body.

[6] *By Authority – Proclamation*, The Hawaiian gazette, Honolulu, March 17, 1891, 3, Chronicling America, Library of Congress

[7] *The Daily*, The Pacific commercial advertiser, Honolulu, March 10, 1891, 2, Chronicling America, Library of Congress

[8] Webb & Webb, 85

[9] Rix, 17

[10] Kaiulani to Liliuokalani, March 1, 1891

[11] Kaiulani to Kawananakoa, March 7, 1891

[12] Webb & Webb. 85

[13] Webb & Webb, 87

[14] Zambucka, 51

[15] Liliuokalani to Kaiulani, November 11, 1891, HSA.

[16] Liliuokalani to Kaiulani, November 11, 1891, HSA

[17] Linnéa, 104

[18] Liliuokalani to Kaiulani, October 21, 1891 HSA. On his return journey to Honolulu Cleghorn did have a meeting with President Harrison but he did not meet with Secretary Blaine because the Secretary of State was absent from Washington.

[19] Liliuokalani to Kaiulani, October 21, 1891 HSA

[20] Kaiulani to Liliuokalani, November 23, 1891

[21] Liliuokalani to Kaiulani, January 14, 1892, HSA

[22] Kaiulani to Liliuokalani, February 5, 1892 BMA

[23] Liliuokalani to Kaiulani, April 25, 1892, HSA

[24] Linnéa, 104

[25] Kaiulani to Liliuokalani, May 18, 1892, BMA

[26] Kuykendall, 541

[27] Liliuokalani to Kaiulani, June 7, 1892, HSA

[28] Archibald Cleghorn to Kaiulani, September 13, 1892, HSA. This new Cabinet held office only until October 17, 1892.

[29] Liliuokalani to Kaiulani, November 11, 1892, HSA

[30] Kuykendall, 562

[31] Kuykendall, 562

[32] Linnéa, 101

[33] There is no evidence of any views expressed by Princess Kaiulani about the possibility of the Crown imposing a revised constitution on the country, nor whether she had discussions about it with Theo Davies, who would no doubt have had grave views on the wisdom of such an action by the Queen. There was great political danger for the Queen in contemplating unilateral action on the constitution but Kaiulani was probably too young and inexperienced, and too far away from events on the ground, to offer any useful counsel to the Queen on this matter.

[34] Kuykendall, 580

[35] Dr. John Mott-Smith to Archibald Cleghorn, January 13, 1893, HSA

10

The Queen's Gambit

Hawaiian philatelists will know that during each new reign of the Hawaiian monarchs beginning with the reign of King Kamehameha III the Hawaiian Post Office issued stamps bearing a portrait of the reigning monarch, and that in subsequent reigns certain stamps from previous reigns were also reissued. Ominously, during the reign of Queen Liliuokalani, only two stamps were issued, one, a new issue displaying the image of the Queen herself, and the other a reissue of a portrait of King Kamehameha V, an earlier King who, like Liliuokalani, was opposed to the constitution under which he ascended the throne, and who imposed a new constitution on the country unilaterally by royal fiat. When it came to the subject of constitutions, Queen Liliuokalani and King Kamehameha V held similar opinions about the proper balance of power in the Kingdom.

Lydia Liliu Loloku Walania Kamakaeha, Queen Liliuokalani, was the oldest person to have ascended the Hawaiian throne when she became Queen of the Hawaiian Islands on January 29, 1891, at the age of 52. She was a complex person, whose life spanned the greater part of the life of the Kingdom of Hawaii. Born on September 2, 1838, she grew up in the shadow of great Hawaiian kings who wielded unquestioned power and authority over the Hawaiian Islands. It was King Kamehameha III who chose Lydia as one of the small number of high *alii* children who were deemed eligible to ascend to the Hawaiian throne. She was sent to the elite Chief's Children's School for her education. As a young woman it was thought that she might marry one of the men who later became King of Hawaii, Prince Lot, or Prince William Lunalilo, but ultimately she married an American, John Owens Dominis. After the election and accession to the throne of her brother David, Lydia was elevated to the dignity of a Princess of Hawaii under the name Liliuokalani and, after the death of her brother Prince Leleiohoku, King Kalakaua appointed her as the Heiress Apparent to the throne of Hawaii. Despite her American connections, arising from her marriage to John Owens Dominis, and her strong Christian faith, she was never politically close to the American settlers in Hawaii.

Liliuokalani had matured in the company of prominent Hawaiian *alii* who knew their place at the apex of the indigenous social structure in Hawaii and she had, as her role models, the most prominent female members of the Kamehameha dynasty, Queen Emma, Princess Ruth Keelikolani, and Liliuokalani's *hanai* sister, Princess Bernice Pauahi Bishop, all of whom occupied the highest social strata, and who could (and did) expect a great deal of deference from indigenous Hawaiians of a lesser social standing. Although the Kingdom of Hawaii was much more open to the participation of women in government than European or American countries, Liliuokalani, unlike her brother Kalakaua, did not have a career in the Hawaiian civil service before she came to the throne.

Liliuokalani, was soft-spoken but firm in her personal views, and she exhibited a certain rigidity of mind perhaps best expressed in her personal motto *Onipa*, meaning steadfast. She was, however, an efficient administrator, and she had proven her effectiveness during the periods in which she had acted as Regent while her brother, the King, was abroad. Despite certain personal limitations, there was a reservoir of good will for the new monarch when she ascended the Hawaiian throne, and even Professor W D Alexander, who was soon to become a stalwart propagandist for the annexationists, said in a book he prepared for use in the Hawaiian schools, "The new reign has opened under most favourable auspices. May it be a long, peaceful, and prosperous one."[1]

Queen Liliuokalani, like King Kamehameha V, did not want to take the accession oath upon learning of her brother's demise. When the members of the Privy Council, the Cabinet Ministers, and the Justices of the Supreme Court, assembled in Iolani Palace for the purpose of administering and witnessing the constitutional oath by the new Sovereign she sought to delay taking it until after Kalakaua's funeral. However, it was a requirement under the 1887 Constitution that every new Sovereign must take the oath upon their accession and so, prodded by her husband, Governor Dominis, Queen Liliuokalani swore the prescribed oath to uphold the Bayonet Constitution of 1887.[2] Yet many Americans in Hawaii refused to take the Queen at her word, and many expected her to make some sort of effort to overturn the 1887 constitution.[3]

Although she later described the administration of the oath as a trap that was sprung upon her the constitutional practice of taking an oath upon the accession of a new Sovereign is well established in constitutional monarchies. For example, a new British Sovereign meets with a body known as the Accession Council in Great Britain within a day or so of the death, or abdication, of their predecessor, and takes the constitutional oaths of office that are prescribed for a British monarch.

One of Queen Liliuokalani's first acts upon ascending to the throne was to sack the over-holding Cabinet from the reign of her brother, King Kalakaua. Although the sacked Cabinet disputed her power to dismiss them, the Supreme Court upheld her power to appoint a new Cabinet upon ascending the throne. During her first year as Queen of Hawaii, Liliuokalani appeared to reign without controversy, guided by the advice of her husband, the Prince Consort and Governor of Oahu, John Owens Dominis. His death, in late 1891, left her bereft of the one member of the Royal Family that she willingly relied upon, and the one person who could approach her as an equal.

On May 28, 1892, the Queen opened the last legislature of the Kingdom of Hawaii with a strong pledge to preserve the autonomy and independence of Hawaii.[4] As the months passed the Queen and the Legislature contested for political control of the Hawaiian executive branch. After dismissing King Kalakaua's last Cabinet the Queen put into office a Cabinet headed by Samuel Parker that lasted eighteen months while the Legislature was prorogued. However, that Cabinet fell on a vote of no confidence when the new Legislature met following the 1892 election. A succession of Cabinets was subsequently appointed by the Queen and then lost office when they were unable to obtain a vote of confidence in the Legislature, as the contest for control between the Queen and the Legislature continued.

There were three groups vying for control in the Legislature in 1892. Firstly, there were the monarchists in the National Reform Party, who sought to maintain the powers of the monarchy and otherwise promoted moderate policies. Secondly there was the Liberal Party, which sought increased political control by the indigenous Hawaiians, and sinecures for its leaders, Robert W Wilcox, and John E Bush, and who opposed the monarchy and promoted US annexation until Wilcox and Bush were finally ousted from their leadership positions. The Reform Party promoted the interests of the Caucasian settler community but was divided between people whose sentiments were pro-American, and those whose sentiments were pro-British, although the American element was increasingly in the ascendant and many of the latter group sought the annexation of Hawaii by the United States.

The Reform Party had control of the upper house, which afforded the settler community the ability to stop all efforts at undue taxation of the (mostly foreign or foreign-descended) propertied class. In the Assembly, the Reform Party entered into an alliance with the mostly indigenous Hawaiian Liberal Party. Lorrin Thurston, a Reform member of the upper House of Nobles favoured such temporary alliances in the belief that efforts should be expended to co-opt as many indigenous Hawaiians as possible into the annexation camp.[5]

Cabinets rose and fell throughout 1892, some of them very quickly, contributing to rising political instability and to rumours of a coup, or a revolution, which some of the American newspapers picked up on. The Reform-Liberal alliance tried to establish a constitutional convention that the Queen must choose the political leader who is best able to command a majority in the legislature to form a government, a principle that was not in accord with the Hawaiian constitution, which gave the Sovereign primacy in the appointment of Cabinet ministers. To force the Queen to accept their proposition, three Cabinets that the Queen put into office were rejected by the Reform–Liberal alliance in the Legislature.[6]

As her reign progressed, the Queen continued to come under strident attacks from the leaders of the Liberal Party, Robert Wilcox and John Bush. Thinking that they would do better if the monarchy was *pau*, or ended, they called for the replacement of the monarchy by a republic, and for the annexation of the islands by the United States. Wilcox and Bush thought that with annexation the indigenous Hawaiians would be able to control the legislature and they (Wilcox and Bush) would finally be able to capture the patronage sinecures that they sought. Since the Liberals enjoyed the support of a substantial portion of the indigenous Hawaiian electorate the disloyalty of Wilcox and Bush stung the Queen deeply. In the case of Wilcox it was worse because Liliuokalani had offered him personal succour when he needed it, even allowing him to use one of her residences for plotting the 1889 insurrection, which caused her own reputation to suffer through her close association with him. Now that she was Queen, Wilcox had hoped for high office and when he did not obtain it he turned in bitterness against the monarchy seeing in a republic, and perhaps US annexation, as the only opportunity for him to achieve the political power that he craved.

His confederate, John Bush, had disgraced himself as Kalakaua's envoy to Samoa during the Primacy of the Pacific initiative, and he resented his subsequent ostracism from government. He nursed his bitterness toward the Kalakaua dynasty through his anti-monarchical editorials in a newspaper that he controlled. Eventually, however, other indigenous members of the Liberal Party began to see that their attacks on the Queen, and on the institution of the Hawaiian monarchy, would not lead to a restoration of indigenous political supremacy within the Kingdom and was creating a dangerous division amongst the indigenous Hawaiian electorate. Wilcox and Bush were ousted from leadership roles in the Liberal Party and two more conservative indigenous leaders, Joseph Nawahi, and William White came to the fore. They moderated the views of the party toward the monarchy but secretly advised the Queen to replace the 1887 Bayonet Constitution through a constitutional convention, or through monarchical authority.

With the political situation deadlocked, the British Minister, Wodehouse, made an effort to guide the Queen out of her political difficulties in the autumn of 1892, and following his advice the Queen appointed a Cabinet under George Wilcox that was largely Reform in its political complexion. The new Cabinet met with the general approval in the Legislature, and in the Hawaiian media. The appointment of the Wilcox Cabinet was shrewd because it broke the tenuous alliance between the Reform Party and the Liberal Party in the Hawaiian Legislature. No Liberal members were among those who were appointed to the Cabinet, and the Liberals could plainly see that they would not obtain any benefits from their political alliance with the Reform Party.

Many political moderates were pleased to see the appointment of the Wilcox Cabinet and Princess Kaiulani's father, Archibald Cleghorn, was quite relieved, as he considered the Wilcox Cabinet to be a very strong Ministry. So did John L Stevens who reported to Washington that the Wilcox Cabinet showed that Americans were in the ascendancy in Hawaii.[7] The Wilcox Cabinet proved to be skilful, and thoughtful observers believed that the country would be safe for the next two years, until elections secured a new Legislature, if the Wilcox Cabinet could only sustain the confidence of the current Legislature until its prorogation at the end of the 1892 session.

Although Stevens crowed about the Wilcox Cabinet being a symbol of American ascendancy in Hawaii he might have been less enthusiastic about it if he knew that it was actually British Minister Wodehouse who, in a private audience with the Queen, had counselled her to appoint Reform members to the new Cabinet. Stevens continued to fret about British and Canadian influence in the islands. He was particularly annoyed by the visit to Honolulu in 1892, of Princess Kaiulani's British guardian, Theo Davies, who met with the Queen during his stay in Honolulu. Stevens was concerned that Davies would strengthen a pro-British and anti-American bias in the Queen, and he was especially exercised over rumours about Davies' connections with the Canadian Pacific Railway, and rumours of efforts by the British and Canadians to secure rights for a transpacific cable between North America and the British possessions in the South Pacific Ocean.[8]

In Washington, the Harrison Administration watched as the Hawaiian chessboard moved in a direction that was much to its liking. In Stevens they had an experienced American diplomat whose close connections with Thurston and his annexationists implied the backing of the top American official in the islands for whatever the settler community attempted politically. Captain Wiltse of the USS *Boston* was likewise an experienced naval officer who could be counted upon to assist the American Minister if it became necessary to take naval action in Honolulu. The silence of Secretary of State Blaine when Stevens sought instructions from him about what to do if an insurrection occurred was necessary only to give the Secretary plausible deniability if it all went awry.

In fact Secretary Blaine had already determined that the royal government in Hawaii was weak and that it presented no real threat to the increasing American penetration, and political assimilation, of Hawaii. What did concern him was Robert Wilcox, and the possibility that he might mount a successful *coup d'état* against the Queen, and thereby increase indigenous control over the Hawaiian Government. American policy seems to have been to offer short-term temporary support the Queen's government against any attempted *coup d'état* by radical indigenous elements, such as Wilcox, while quietly encouraging a *coup d'état* against the monarchy by the pro-American settler community.

Although efforts were made in the Hawaiian Legislature to change the 1887 Constitution, or to convene a Constitutional Convention to draft a new constitution, all efforts failed in the face of political opposition in 1892. Frustrated, the Queen turned to the imposition of a new constitution by way of royal fiat, just as King Kamehameha V had done in 1864. Of course, such an approach was entirely unconstitutional because the 1887 Bayonet Constitution vested the power to change the constitution of the Kingdom solely in the Legislature. The existing Constitution did not give the Queen any legal power to change the existing constitution on her own. And in 1891, Liliuokalani, unlike King Kamehameha V in 1864, had sworn an oath to uphold the Constitution upon her accession to the throne as the Queen of the Hawaiian Islands. The imposition of a new constitution by royal fiat would result in Queen Liliuokalani breaking her solemn constitutional oath of office, one that she had she had freely taken.

The new leader of the Liberal Party, Joseph Nawahi, was completely in accord with the Queen on the necessity for taking royal action to compel the entrenchment of a new constitution. On the hustings in the 1892 election he had stated publicly that Hawaii needed a new constitution and therefore he advised that indigenous Hawaiians should send petitions to the Queen asking for a new constitution because no constitutional reforms could be secured from the Legislature, which he called "a humbug."[9] Together with his colleague, William White, Nawahi and the Liberals arranged for many petitions to be sent to the Queen calling for the restoration of the political dominance of native Hawaiians, and the restoration to the Crown of the powers taken away in 1887. Those petitions could not be seen to come directly from the Liberal Party however, because the settler community would know that they were entirely partisan, so the *Hui Kalaiaina*, an indigenous Hawaiian political association that was dedicated to the promotion of indigenous political dominance became the source of the petitions that were sent to the Queen.[10] At some point in 1892, Nawahi and White, together with Major Samuel Nowlein, the Captain of the Royal Household Guards, became the Queen's private, extra-constitutional advisors for the purpose of drafting of a new constitution for the Kingdom of Hawaii. All three, but especially Nawahi and White, who were members of the Legislature and therefore had a public duty to uphold the existing Constitution, bear a heavy onus before history for encouraging and maintaining the Queen in her desire to impose a new constitution on the country through an unconstitutional action.[11]

Nevertheless, there were reasons why the Queen and the new leaders of the Liberal Party thought they should embark upon the dangerous course of a constitutional *coup de main*. Firstly, the population of indigenous Hawaiians was continuing to drop, and the rapid increases in both the North American/European population, and the Asian population, meant that Hawaiians were no longer the major demographic group in the Kingdom. In the long run it was unlikely that indigenous Hawaiian political power could be maintained. Nawahi and White no doubt thought that it would be best to entrench indigenous political power now, before other groups raised claims to new, or increased, political representation in the Kingdom. Secondly, the Queen feared that the attacks of Wilcox and Bush had undermined indigenous respect for the monarchy and she was anxious to shore up support among the native Hawaiians for the monarchy by forcing through a new constitution that would enhance indigenous powers, thereby undercutting the argument that the Crown was only responsive to settler concerns. Thirdly, with the disbandment of all companies of the Hawaiian military, including the Honolulu Rifles, there was no longer a settler military force that could quickly overthrow of the government if a new constitution was presented as a *fait accompli*. The only military force that was readily available in the Kingdom was the Queen's own Royal Household Guards, which was under the Queen's control, and its commander, Samuel Nowlein, was one of the men advising the Queen to impose a new constitution by fiat. Probably the Queen, and those close to her thought that the forces available to the Crown would be sufficient to intimidate any bold reaction by the settler community, or to suppress any violent dissent.[12]

What the Queen, Nawahi, White, and Nowlein did not realize, of course, was that the United States had quietly changed its position on the question of Hawaiian independence. The Harrison Administration was giving strong covert encouragement to Thurston and the Annexation Club, and the American Minister to the

Hawaiian Kingdom was no longer a neutral diplomat. The Royal Court was blind to the machinations of the Annexation Club because domestic intelligence gathering by Marshal Wilson did not discover this secretive group, although the Queen did perceive an increasing hostility directed towards her, and the Royal Court, from the American Legation.

Blind to the ambitions of both the United States, and a domestic Hawaiian fifth column that wished to see the end of the independence of Hawaii, the Queen embarked upon the dangerous policy of implementing unilateral constitutional change with Nawahi, White, and Nowlein. Her plan, as it developed, was to promulgate the new constitution on her own authority as soon as the Hawaiian Legislature was prorogued at the end of its 1892 session. By August of 1892, a draft of the new constitution was completed, and the Queen awaited only the prorogation of the Legislature before making the attempt to promulgate a new constitution.[13]

What were the contents of the new constitution that Queen Liliuokalani had prepared? In large measure the final version that she sought to implement in early 1893 was a cut and paste effort from the 1864 and 1887 constitutions, with a few changes intended to enhance the power of the Crown. Under Liliuokalani's draft, Cabinet Ministers would serve at the Queen's pleasure, meaning that she could dismiss them whenever she liked. That was contrary to the 1887 Bayonet Constitution, under which the Cabinet could only be removed from office by a vote of non-confidence in the Legislature. The protection afforded to the Cabinet against arbitrary action by the Crown was a key feature of the Bayonet Constitution, and a vital part of the constitutional structure that the 1887 revolutionists considered necessary. The Queen now determined to reject that change, and to revert to the older system of a previous constitution under which the monarch could dismiss her Ministers at will.[14]

The members of the House of Nobles would no longer be elected for a term of office but would once again be appointed by the Sovereign for life. As a result, the settler community would lose its ability to block revenue or taxation measures, thus exposing their investments in Hawaii to financial risk. That change, more than any other change, was certain to produce a push-back by the classes of residents who held substantial capital investments in the Kingdom.

The lower house of the Legislature would continue to be elected but the electoral franchise was to be reformed so that all male subjects born or naturalized in the Kingdom would be eligible to vote. That would have removed the grant of the franchise to foreign residents contained in the 1887 Bayonet Constitution, and would thus have diluted the Caucasian electorate.

The Supreme Court Justices would no longer be appointed to serve for life but would serve for a term of six years. Term-limiting the Supreme Court Justices would almost certainly have meant a loss of judicial independence. Article 78 of the existing Constitution, which provided that the Sovereign must act with the advice and consent of the Cabinet was repealed, meaning that she would be free to act contrary to the wishes of Ministers who were responsible to the Hawaiian Legislature.[15] The draft also addressed the succession to the throne by adding Prince David Kawananakoa, and Prince Jonah Kuhio Kalanianaole, to the order of succession following Princess Kaiulani.[16]

The effect of this draft constitution, if it had been implemented, would have considerably enhanced the powers of the Crown in contrast to the powers of the Cabinet. It was not necessarily an anti-democratic constitution because the Sovereign would not have been able to interfere with the Legislature's jurisdiction, or with its ability to grant or deny the appropriation of funds necessary to carry on the government. However, it was a retrogressive constitution because it diminished the Cabinet powers while providing for the expansion of the royal prerogative powers of the Sovereign.[17] It was a constitution that could never have been enacted through the prescribed constitutional amendment process within the 1887 Constitution because the settler community would have successfully opposed it in the House of Nobles.

Later, Queen Liliuokalani would point to the large number of petitions that she had received calling for constitutional change as a justification for her attempt to replace the 1887 Bayonet Constitution by a constitutional coup.[18] However, even if there was a popular appetite among the indigenous Hawaiian community for constitutional change, the Queen had sworn an oath to the existing Constitution and she was compelled to seek changes to the constitution only through the amendment procedures provided for within the existing constitution, even if the political complexion of the Legislature at any particular time made it unlikely that she could secure the passage of a new constitution.

The Queen allowed no public discussion of the draft constitution that she had prepared. She did not send it the Legislature for debate and consideration. She did not even circulate it to her Privy Council, which might have warned her about the expected reaction of the settler community. Although Attorney General Petersen was given a copy of the document to review he later claimed that he had only given it a cursory look before setting it aside, perhaps thinking that the constitutional amending process combined with the existing political condition of the country rendered it improbable that the draft could ever by adopted.

Colonel Curtis Iaukea later wrote that the Queen's aversion to the 1887 Bayonet Constitution was a controversy that should have been left in the past and he lamented the loss of Governor Dominis, a man of balanced judgment whom the Queen implicitly trusted. Dominis could have dissuaded the Queen from the course that she embarked upon. Perceiving that the Queen was facing a political trap by the petitions for constitutional change that were coming into the palace Colonel Iaukea approached the Queen and asked her if she considered that she was being drawn into a course of action that would create a crisis. But the Queen merely remarked that the people wanted her to change the existing constitutional framework.[19]

As the year 1892 deepened, Governor Cleghorn rapidly declined in influence with the Queen. His letters to his daughter, Princess Kaiulani, reflect his growing unease and concern at the course events were taking. He perceived that the Queen had embarked on a wrong policy and considered that she was taking bad advice. He worried that a crisis would soon break.

In early January, 1893, the Hawaiian Legislature prepared for prorogation, and the Queen's plan for a new constitution was activated. Toward the end of December 1892, Joseph Nawahi demanded that the George Wilcox Cabinet support a measure calling for a Constitutional Convention. The Wilcox Cabinet predictably refused and on January 4, 1893, a motion of non-confidence was moved against the Cabinet but it was unsuccessful.

Frustrated, the Queen's plotters waited a few more days before trying again. Some of the legislators began leaving early to return to their home islands, giving Nawahi and White their best chance. On January 8th, the Queen advised the Marshal of the Kingdom, Charles Wilson, that she planned to promulgate a new constitution on her own authority after prorogation and that he should make security preparations in the event of public disturbances. Around this time she also spoke to Captain Nowlein of the palace guard who had assisted her in preparing a new constitution, warning him to be prepared to put down any violent reaction to it. Both Nowlein and Wilson were commanded to keep the Queen's intentions confidential.

Wilson, to his credit, objected to her intention, and he sought to dissuade the Queen. He thought that she had agreed to defer the matter but the 1887 Bayonet Constitution was her *bete noir* and she had no intention of retaining it. On January 12th, the Legislature succeeded in passing a motion of non-confidence against the Wilcox Cabinet, which immediately resigned. The Queen's intention now was to put into office a Cabinet that would assist her in bringing about a new constitution and on January 13th the Queen appointed a Cabinet led by Samuel Parker as Minister of Foreign Affairs, and including John F Colburn as Minister of the Interior, William H Cornwell, as Minister of Finance, and Arthur P Petersen as the Attorney General. All four were regarded as amiable gentlemen but they were not necessarily the right men to be in charge during a crisis. The new Cabinet was accepted by the population in the Kingdom however, and was it expected that they would hold office throughout the period of time in which the Legislature remained prorogued. On the same day the Queen spoke again with Marshal Wilson about making security arrangements for the next day, when she planned to promulgate a new constitution.

The following day, January 14th, Wilson confirmed to the Queen that all of the necessary security arrangements had been made. At 10 AM the Queen met with her newly appointed Cabinet in Iolani Palace where she informed them that she intended to proclaim a new Constitution from the balcony of Iolani Palace after proroguing the Legislature, and for that purpose she required their countersignatures on the new constitution. The Cabinet immediately voiced objections to her plan, fearing an uprising, and met privately among themselves. Returning, they confirmed to the Queen that they would not countersign any new constitution that was proposed to be promulgated by the Queen without legislative authorization. Colonel Iaukea, who was present in the palace later recalled the strained faces of the Ministers who warned the Queen that any attempt to unilaterally promulgate a new constitution could provoke an uprising by the *haole* community but the Queen was adamant that the people wished her to create a new constitution.[20]

An interesting aspect to this debate between Queen and Cabinet was that Liliuokalani did not actually need the signatures of her Cabinet Ministers if she planned to unconstitutionally abolish and replace the existing constitution. The ministerial countersignatures were only required under the existing constitution where the Ministers had to take responsibility for the legal actions of the Sovereign. Their countersignatures would not be required where the Queen mounted a *coup d'etat* against the constitution. If the Queen had succeeded in abrogating the existing constitution the Cabinet Ministers would have automatically ceased to hold their offices from the moment the 1887 constitution was abrogated. Other than a desire perhaps to show the population that she had some political support for her actions (or to share the responsibility if she failed) the Minister's signatures served no legal purpose but the Ministers did not tell her that because they still hoped to stop the Queen from taking an extraordinary action.

Although the debate between the Queen and her Cabinet might suggest that Queen Liliuokalani had a very imperfect understanding of her constitutional responsibilities and limitations, the secretiveness of her constitutional drafting, her failure to openly consult with her Cabinets, and her Privy Council, her efforts to put in place security arrangements in the event of an uprising, and her sudden demand for Cabinet support, suggests that the Queen knew perfectly well that what she was proposing amounted to a coup against the Hawaiian constitution.

In order for her plan to succeed the Queen required control of the capital city by a superior force. Here, Liliuokalani proved herself to be an inept coup-maker. She left the security arrangements to Marshal Wilson, and Captain Nowlein, but she did not take steps to ensure that those arrangements would be adequate if an insurrection occurred. There was no plan to take control of the major public buildings in the capital, or the electricity station, or the waterworks, and to hold them with a superior armed force, nor was there a plan to control the streets of Honolulu with regular police, or military patrols. No effort was made to round up and confine anyone who might conceivably defy the Queen's plan. Yet the Hawaiian Government was not lacking for armed men to enforce its will in Honolulu. Between the police forces and the Royal Guard the government had at its disposal 500 men, 10 Gatling guns, and 12 breech-loading artillery pieces. What it lacked was a guiding will to enforce its authority. It does not appear that the Queen even brought any of the island Governors into her confidence, although the Governors had a legal responsibility for national defence in case of an invasion, a possibility that soon came to fruition as the crisis unfolded.

The controversy inside Iolani Palace now spilled out into the streets of Honolulu. Faced with their angry and intractable monarch the Cabinet Ministers began fanning out into the city, where they turned for support to men who were prominent in the settler community, and who would lead them to other men who were active in the secretive Annexation Club, most prominently, Lorrin Thurston.

John Colburn met with A S Hartwell, a retired Justice of the Supreme Court who was alarmed at the reports of the Queen's proposed action. Hartwell immediately took Colburn to the law office of W O Smith, where they were joined by Lorrin Thurston and then by Attorney General Petersen. Thurston, Smith and Hartwell all counselled that the Cabinet should stand firm in opposition to the Queen.

Meanwhile, back at the palace, the Queen was rewarding her principal confederates in the drafting of a new constitution for Hawaii by conferring the Royal Order of Kalakaua on Joseph Nawahi, and William White. Both were made Knights Commander in the Order.[21] They were the final recipients of the awards of Royal Orders bestowed by the Kingdom of Hawaii.

It is curious that the Cabinet Ministers chose not appeal to the Legislature for support against the Queen's intention to replace the constitution, as the abrogation of the 1887 constitution would have certainly affected the prerogatives of the Legislature, and of the right of some members to continue to sit in the Legislature. Yet the Ministers assembled in the Legislature for the prorogation ceremony without calling upon the Legislature for support. Perhaps they felt

263

the Legislature, having tossed out the previous Wilcox Cabinet, was in the Queen's pocket. Or perhaps they still trusted that they could dissuade the Queen from the course of action that she had set for herself. The Ministers sat in silence as the ceremony took place.

The colourful ceremony of prorogation included a Royal Procession by the Queen and her courtiers from Iolani Palace to Aliiolani Hale, the seat of the Hawaiian Legislature. Troops in ceremonial dress accompanied the Sovereign, who was preceded by *kahili* bearers and accompanied by the Royal Hawaiian Band. A cannon salute marked the arrival of the Queen who proceeded with her entourage into the legislative chamber. Queen Liliuokalani then read a short speech to close the legislature. Not once did she mention the momentous change to the constitution of the Kingdom that she was planning to announce that afternoon. In her final speech to the Hawaiian Legislature the Queen said:

"Nobles and Representatives:

More than seven months have elapsed since I opened this Assembly. During that time many changes of Cabinets have taken place. The unprecedented length of the session has involved much labour, and I congratulate you on at last having completed your arduous duties.

The Legislation which has now been placed on the Statute Books, will I trust conduce to the advancement of the material interests of the Kingdom, and it gives me pleasure to note that attempts to tamper with the currency and interfere with the established usages of Commerce have been happily averted.

My Ministers will use their best efforts to carry out your intentions as expressed in the numerous acts which have become law.

The appropriations which you have made are on a liberal scale, and it is the hope of Myself and My Constitutional advisors that the revenues of the Government will be adequate for the proper carrying out of your intentions as so expressed.

It will be My earnest endeavour to promote such Treaty relations with our Great and Friendly Neighbour, the United States of America, as may restore to Our agricultural interests that measure of prosperity which we formerly enjoyed.

It is also a source of gratification for Me to notice that liberal encouragement has been extended to some of our infant industries, and it is My hope that the results will prove the wisdom of your action.

Nobles and Representatives, I pray the Almighty may continue to pour out upon you and our Country blessings and prosperity as heretofore.

I now declare this Legislature prorogued."[22]

And with that, the Hawaiian Cabinet was left to its own devices, without the support of the Hawaiian Legislature, in the Cabinet's struggle to maintain the constitution of the country.

While the prorogation ceremony was underway retired Justice Hartwell sent a message to the commanding officer of the USS *Boston*, which only that morning had arrived back in Honolulu harbour after completing an outing to the island of Hawaii, and informed Captain Wiltse of the Queen's intentions, and of the possibility of public discord. Captain Wiltse began making preparations for the landing of US forces at Honolulu. Hartwell then went to the US Legation where he saw Minister Stevens and discussed the Queen's plan for a constitutional coup. Hartwell asked Stevens to seek an audience with the Queen in the company of the British Minister, Wodehouse, to forestall the Queen's plan. Stevens immediately went out to seek out Wodehouse and together they went to call upon the Queen. For some reason that the historical record does not seem to explain they were unable to see the Queen but they did manage to meet with the Hawaiian Cabinet at the Aliiolani Hale. There the senior American and British diplomats advised the Ministers that the Queen must not attempt to create a new Constitution in violation of the existing Constitution. The Ministers were of the same view as the diplomats, and they left for a crisis showdown with the Queen at Iolani Palace.

Back at Iolani Palace a large crowd of mostly indigenous Hawaiians was gathering. They had been prompted to come by knowledge, or speculation, within the *Hui Kalaiaina,* that a new constitution restoring indigenous political primacy in Hawaii was to come to fruition on that day. Inside the palace, a large of number of guests had been specially invited by the Queen, and had assembled in the Throne Room. The invitees included Supreme Court justices, members of the diplomatic corps, and other prominent persons. While the guests cooled their heels in the Throne Room, the Queen met in the Blue Room with her Cabinet Ministers who were united in opposition to any attempt by the Queen to promulgate a new Constitution in violation of the existing Constitution. An angry debate ensued in which the Queen maintained that the Cabinet Ministers had been aware of her plans for some time but now that the moment of decision had come they sought to abandon her.

Foreign Minister Parker stayed with the Queen while the other Ministers went to speak to the diplomatic corps who had been invited for the Queen's promulgation ceremony, and the foreign diplomats were of all of one view that the Queen should not make the attempt. Chief Justice Judd also appealed to the Queen not to take the step of attempting to promulgate a new constitution of her own volition.[23]   Minister Colburn left the palace to meet with a group of prominent members of the settler community, including Lorrin Thurston, A S Hartwell, and E C Macfarlane, all of whom counselled that the Cabinet must stand firm against the demands of the Queen.

The Cabinet reconvened with the Queen in the Blue Room where Attorney General Petersen, having quickly but thoroughly read through the constitutional document that the Queen was proposing, expressed objections to some of its provisions. The Attorney General advised that the Queen's proposal should be deferred to the future. Faced with the adamant opposition of her Cabinet, the Chief Justice, and the diplomatic corps, the Queen relented and agreed not to proceed with the promulgation of a new constitution. Visiting the Throne Room the Queen spoke to her invited guests, telling them that she had proposed to issue a new constitution for the country but on the advice of her Ministers she had agreed to defer the matter to a future day.[24]

The Queen then went on to the balcony of Iolani Palace below which many indigenous Hawaiians had assembled to await the announcement of a new constitution. The Queen spoke to the people in Hawaiian and dismissed them, stating that there would not be an announcement of a new constitution that day, to which William White expressed loud consternation. Then the Queen said words which the annexationists would leap upon to justify their own counter-coup. The Queen, in stating that promulgation would be deferred, used the expression *ma keia man la*, which was ambiguous in English, and could be translated variously as 'a long time from now' or as 'in a few days.' The annexationists took the Queen to mean the latter, which was likely correct, as in her own mind the Queen had not given up her intention to rid the country of the 1887

Bayonet Constitution. The annexationists claimed that the threat of unconstitutional action remained, and so they continued their efforts to organize opposition to the Queen and to her government.

Lorrin Thurston now realized that the moment he had been waiting for had come. He was a man of ability, energy, and resolution, and those were the character traits that would drive the success of the annexation coup. The Queen had now given Thurston the pretext he needed to raise the pro-American settler community in an uprising against her, and to call upon the United States, and its military forces, for support in overthrowing the Hawaiian monarchy. Thurston threw all of his energy and intelligence into the overthrow of his country's government.

On Saturday afternoon an *ad hoc* meeting at W O Smith's law office led to the formation of a Committee of Safety, headed by Thurston and Smith, the thirteen members of which were almost all members of the secretive Annexation Club. There were some changes to the membership shortly afterwards but in its permanent constitution it consisted of six natural-born or naturalized Hawaiian subjects, five American citizens, one British subject, and one German subject. Numerically, the Committee was effectively a balance between Hawaiian subjects and foreigners. However, four of the Hawaiian subjects were descended from American parents and identified themselves as American.[25] The complexion of this committee was therefore overwhelmingly American. There were no indigenous Hawaiians.

The Committee resolved to form a Provisional Government for Hawaii, and a delegation led by Thurston was assigned the task of meeting with US Minister Stevens to determine his position on the developments of the day. Stevens received the delegates and summed up the situation from his perspective. He viewed the Queen as a revolutionary and he would no longer deal with her but he would continue to deal with the Hawaiian Cabinet. The *Boston's* forces were prepared to land and if a Provisional Government was established Stevens would recognize it if it controlled the Aliiolani Hale, the public archives, the government departments, and the city of Honolulu.[26] All of this was subsequently discussed at a meeting Saturday evening involving Thurston, W R Castle, and W O Smith, together with four others that included retired Justice A S Hartwell and a current Supreme Court Justice Sanford B Dole, who would shortly rise to head the movement to overthrow the monarchy.

The next morning, Sunday, January 15th, Thurston met with two of the Cabinet Ministers, Interior Minister Colburn and Attorney-General Petersen, and told them that the Committee of Safety would support them if they declared that the Queen had embarked upon a revolution, declared the throne now vacant, and then sought to rally the people for support.[27] The Ministers demurred for the time being but after consulting with their colleagues they decided that while they wanted to stop the Queen they did not want to mount a revolution against the throne. On Monday they formally rejected Thurston's offer, and decided that what the Committee of Safety was doing was organizing a treasonous plot that the Government should suppress.[28]

On Sunday the Cabinet met with loyal monarchists including F A Schaefer, J O Carter, S M Damon, W M Gifford, S C Allen and E C Macfarlane and it was decided to issue a proclamation to offer reassurance to the population, and to calm political opinion. Issued under the authority of the Cabinet the proclamation attempted to explain the Queen's unfortunate intentions:

"Her Majesty's ministers desire to express their appreciation for the quiet and order which have prevailed in this community since the events of Saturday, and are authorized to say that the position taken by Her Majesty in regard to the promulgation of a new Constitution, was under stress of her native subjects.

Authority is given for the assurance that any changes desired in the fundamental law of the land will be sought only by methods provided in the Constitution itself.

Her Majesty's ministers request all citizens to accept the assurance of Her Majesty in the same spirit in which it is given."[29]

Foreign Minister Parker and Attorney General Petersen went to see US Minister Stevens on Sunday to ask if the US would support the Hawaiian Government if there was a rebellion but Stevens refused to commit the US to support the government. Later on Sunday, Thurston and Smith called on Stevens who told them that he could not, on behalf of the United States, recognize a Provisional Government until that government was actually established.

Both the loyalists and the annexationists now began organizing mass meetings scheduled for the following day to show public support for the government, or to show public support for a revolution. Monday, January 16th was the crucial day. In the morning the Committee of Safety met at Lorrin Thurston's law office to iron out the details for the mass meeting later that day as well as to plan for their *coup d'état* against the Hawaiian Government. While the meeting was underway Marshall Wilson arrived and called Lorrin Thurston out of the meeting to warn him that the Committee's efforts were unlawful, and to assure Thurston that the Queen would be prevented from attempting any further unilateral constitutional changes. According to Thurston he had the following exchange with Marshal Wilson:

> "[Wilson said] 'I know what you fellows are up to, and I want you to quit and go home.' 'We are not going home, Charlie,' I replied. 'Things have advanced too far, and we do not intend to have a repetition of the events of Saturday.' He answered: 'The Queen will not make any further attempt to do away with the present constitution, or to promulgate another one, so there is no danger of repetition.'
>
> 'What assurance have we?' asked I. 'I give you my personal assurance,' he said. 'And of what value is that?' I inquired. 'Suppose that the Queen goes ahead and attempts to do it anyway? What can you do?' 'If it is necessary,' Mr Wilson replied 'I will undertake personally to lock up the Queen to prevent her from doing anything further along those lines.' 'It's no use, Charlie,' I told him."[30]

Far from satisfying the annexationists, Wilson only confirmed them in their intentions because, as Thurston might have told him, a head of state who may have to be locked up by her courtiers to prevent her from taking an extra-constitutional action is not one in whom the general population of a country can have much confidence.

It was now common knowledge in Honolulu that the Queen was riding for a fall at the hands of the Committee of Safety, which prompted another caller to interrupt Thurston. This time it was Governor Cleghorn, who was reading the reality of the situation and tried to protect the rights of his daughter, Princess Kaiulani. He knew that the Queen had broken faith with the constitution, and that residual loyalties would no longer hold where Liliuokalani was concerned. Cleghorn spoke up for his daughter, Princess Kaiulani, and according to Thurston Cleghorn said:

"[Governor Cleghorn:] I do not blame you for what you are proposing to do to Liliuokalani, Mr Thurston, but I wish to submit for the consideration of the committee of safety, whether it is necessary to overturn the monarchy entirely, and to have you take into consideration the claim of Princess Kaiulani. If you remove Liliuokalani from the throne, why not appoint Kaiulani, who is now the heir apparent, to be queen? You can appoint a board of regents to act during her minority, and I assure you that the community will have a very different state of affairs to deal with from that which Kalakaua and Liliuokalani have presented."

"[Thurston replied] 'You know my regard for Kaiulani, Mr. Cleghorn,' I replied. 'I think very highly of her. If conditions were different, I should be glad to help promote your suggestion; but matters have proceeded too far for your plan to be an adequate answer to this situation. We are going to abrogate the Monarchy entirely, and nothing can be done to stop us, so far as I can see."[31]

Thurston said in his memoirs that Cleghorn looked like he might break down and shed tears but he bowed his head in silence and left.[32]

The Hawaiian Ministers convened a meeting of the diplomatic corps to elicit support for the government and the representatives of Britain, France, Japan, and Portugal attended. The representatives of the United States and Germany were noticeably absent. The American Minister was preparing to support the insurrectionists, and the German Consul had taken a position as a member of the insurrectionist Committee of Safety. The diplomats who did attend the meeting with the Cabinet supported the efforts of the government to restore calm in the capital.

The Committee of Safety, taking cognizance of the implied threat in the Marshal's visit to Thurston's office while they were in session, compiled an address to US Minister Stevens, requesting protection:

"To His Excellency JOHN L. STEVENS, American Minister Resident:

SIR: We, the undersigned, citizens and residents of Honolulu, respectfully represent that, in view of recent public events in this Kingdom, culminating in the revolutionary acts of Queen Liliuokalani on Saturday last, the public safety is menaced and lives and property are in peril, and we appeal to you and the United States forces at your command for assistance.

The Queen, with the aid of armed force and accompanied by threats of violence and bloodshed from those with whom she was acting, attempted to proclaim a new constitution; and while prevented for the time from accomplishing her object, declared publicly that she would only defer her action.

This conduct and action was upon an occasion and under circumstances which have created general alarm and terror.

We are unable to protect ourselves without aid, and, therefore, pray for the protection of the United States forces.

Henry E Cooper, F W McChesney, W C Wilder, C Bolte, A Brown, William O Smith, Henry Waterhouse, Theo F Lansing, Ed Suhr, L A Thurston, John Emmeluth, Wm E Castle, J A McCandless,

Citizen's Committee of Safety."[33]

However, the US was already positioning itself to intervene in Hawaiian affairs. Early in the day, anticipating trouble as a result of the competing mass meetings in the city, Captain Wiltse gave orders for the landing of US marines and US sailors later in the day. US Consul General Severance warned Captain Wiltse of potential trouble involving the US consulate and said he would lower the US flag if assistance from the navy was required. At 2:30 PM Minister Stevens boarded the warship and provided Captain Wiltse with a written request on behalf of the US Government for the landing of US forces at Honolulu:

"United States Legation,

Honolulu, January 16, 1893.

Sir: In view of the existing critical circumstances in Honolulu, including an inadequate legal force, I request you to land marines and sailors from the ship under your command for the protection of the United States legation and United States consulate, and to secure the safety of American life and property.

Very truly, yours,

John L. Stevens,

Envoy Extraordinary and Minister Plenipotentiary of the United States.

Capt. G. C. Wiltse,

Commander U. S. S. Boston."[34]

There was actually no cause for the landing of US forces at the time this request was made. The US Minister and the US military commander were clearly crossing a prohibited line by arranging for the landing of US forces in the capital city of a friendly country without a request to do so from the legal government of that country. But since the real intent of Minister Stevens was to support the insurrection against the government, the legal niceties were ignored.

At the Honolulu Rifles Armoury at 2PM the mass meeting called by the Committee of Safety drew a large crowd of settlers, and some Portuguese contract workers, as well as a smattering of *hapa-haoles*.[35] Those who attended heard the speakers denounce the Queen for attempting to overturn the Constitution and comparisons were made to the political situation that prevailed in 1887. A report from the Committee of Safety summarizing the threat to the Constitution was read aloud. Although deposing the Queen from the throne was not specifically discussed by the speakers at the mass meeting, a public resolution was passed to:

"ratify the appointment and endorse the action taken and report made by the said Committee of Safety and we do hereby further empower such committee to further consider the situation and further devise such ways and means as may be necessary to secure the permanent maintenance of law and order and the protection of life, liberty and property in Hawaii."[36]

On the slender thread of this resolution expressed at a public meeting the Committee of Safety felt itself clothed with authority to proceed to overthrow their country's government, in cooperation with the US forces.

Meanwhile, loyalists held their own mass meeting at another location in the city. The loyalist meeting was led by the stalwarts of the Liberal Party, J Nawahi, W White, R W Wilcox, J E Bush, and Antone Rosa. Suddenly, these men who had previously attacked the Queen, and the monarchy, or who had misleadingly assisted the Queen in devising a new constitution to be imposed on the

275

country by royal willpower, now realized that they had endangered the country and they tried to retrieve the situation. A mostly indigenous Hawaiian crowd of about 1000 responded listlessly to loyalist speakers as they commended the Queen and the Cabinet for avoiding the crisis. The only sign of enthusiasm from the crowd came when references were actually made to the aborted constitutional coup by the Queen on the previous Saturday.[37] A resolution was passed by the meeting thanking the Queen for not promulgating a new constitution that would have contravened the existing constitution![38]

After the conclusion of the meeting convened by the annexationists the Committee of Safety decided that they did not have enough time to mount a *coup d'état* against the government before the end of the day and they decided to ask the US Minister to defer the landing of US forces until the morrow. But when they called on Stevens to formally request that US forces be held back for a day, Stevens refused their request and told them that US forces would begin landing in Honolulu around 5PM. Nonplussed, the Committee of Safety retreated.

At the appointed hour US forces under the command of Lieutenant Commander Swinburne, the executive officer of the USS *Boston*, began landing at the foot of the harbour in Honolulu. All told, Captain Wiltse sent ashore 154 marines and sailors, with 10 officers. The US forces were equipped with two Gatling guns, and two .37 mm revolving cannon, with a caisson containing 14,000 .45 calibre bullets for the rifles and Gatlings, 1200 .38 calibre bullets for the officers' sidearms, and 174 explosive shells for the cannon. Each marine had in his knapsack 60-80 rounds for his rifle.[39] The US forces paraded up from the harbour past Iolani Palace, where they saluted Queen Liliuokalani as she watched from the palace balcony. There was some initial difficulty in finding a place for the US forces to bivouac but eventually the Arion Hall was rented and the troops marched there. Arion Hall was located behind the Aliiolani Hale, the executive building, and their location placed the US troops between the Royal Household Guard, the only professional military force available to the Hawaiian Government, and the now rapidly reforming Honolulu Rifles, the military arm of the annexationists.

Governor Cleghorn and Foreign Minister Parker immediately protested the landing of US forces on Hawaiian soil because it had taken place without the permission of the Hawaiian Government. Parker and Cleghorn called on Stevens who received them coldly and told them to put their objections in writing and if he thought they had expressed their views politely he would dignify them with a reply. By this point in time, late on Monday afternoon, Stevens was wholly in support of the annexationists who were close to forming a Provisional Government. Nevertheless, the Hawaiian Government put its objections to the American landing in writing, politely stating:

"Department of Foreign Affairs,

Honolulu, Hawaiian Islands,

January 16, 1893

Sir: I have the honor to inform your excellency that the troops from the U.S.S. Boston were landed in this port at 5 o'clock this evening without the request or knowledge of Her Majesty's Government.

As the situation is one which does not call for interference on the part of the United States Government, my colleagues and myself would most respectfully request of your excellency the authority upon which this action was taken. I would also add that any protection that may have been considered necessary for the American Legation or for American property and interests in this city would have been cheerfully furnished by Her Majesty's Government.

With the highest respect, I have the honor to remain,

Your excellency's obedient servant,

Samuel Parker

Minister of Foreign Affairs

His Excellency, John L. Stevens,

U.S. Envoy Extraordinary and Minister Plenipotentiary, Honolulu."[40]

But after the interview between Parker and Cleghorn with Stevens, Governor Cleghorn concluded that Hawaiian independence was lost.[41]

At eight o'clock in the evening the Committee of Safety met in order to put together a slate of persons to form a Provisional Government, which the Committee members intended to proclaim on the following day. Knowing that they must have as their leader a man who was instantly creditable with both indigenous Hawaiians, the settler community, and foreigners, they pressed Supreme Court Associate Justice Sandford Dole to accept the position. Despite recognizing that Queen Liliuokalani would have to go, Dole argued in favour of letting Princess Kaiulani ascend the throne.[42] But the Committee of Safety, and especially Thurston, would have none of that. Queen Kaiulani would mean the continued independence of the country, and the possibility of still greater British influence in the affairs of Hawaii. The Committee of Safety, who were the members of the Annexation Club almost to a man, were determined to hand the country over to the United States and they made their intentions plain to Dole. Dole repaired to his home to mull over his options overnight. Meanwhile, US troops were despatched to conduct fire patrols during the night in Honolulu, to protect the property of US citizens, and to prevent arson.[43]

Dawn came on January 17th and for the last time the Royal Standard of the Sovereign of the Hawaiian Islands floated over an independent kingdom from Iolani Palace. Inside the palace, the Queen now knew that she was facing the crisis of her life, with American troops positioned on Hawaiian soil without an invitation from her government and in apparent sympathy with the insurrectionists. For many old Hawaiian hands in the settler community the bonds of sentiment and attachment to the Hawaiian monarchy, and to the old Hawaii it represented, were sundered on this day. Two men who definitely experienced conflicting moral and patriotic obligations on this day were Justice Sandford Dole, and Samuel Damon.

After ruminating overnight on whether he should accept the presidency of a provisional government, Sandford Dole decided that he should accept the role, and he went to see Lorrin Thurston early in the morning to advise him of his decision. Dole then took a prepared letter to the American Legation seeking diplomatic recognition for the provisional government that would seize control of the city later that day. US Minister Stevens received Dole and told him that he had a great opportunity ahead of him.[44] Dole then sent in his resignation from the Supreme Court of Hawaii, and went to Lorrin Thurston's office where he met with the Committee of Safety, and formally accepted their offer to head a provisional government.

Samuel Damon was a loyalist who had met with the Queen's Ministers and other supporters of the monarchy as recently as the

279

preceding Sunday, when they had drafted a royal proclamation in an attempt to calm the situation. But Damon was subjected to entreaties by others in the settler community to switch sides and, after some reflection, he decided that he could no longer support the monarchy after the Queen's abortive constitutional coup. He decided to side with the annexationists. But Damon was not without a sense of personal honour, and he decided that he would not make the switch without explaining himself to his monarch. He went to Iolani Palace early on Tuesday morning and met with the Queen, advising her that he was switching his allegiance and that he could no longer support her on the throne. Damon told her that he thought her resistance to the coming rebellion would be futile. He told Liliuokalani that he had been offered a position on the Advisory Council that was being put together by the rebels but that he had not yet accepted the position. The Queen, still having some confidence in Damon, advised him to accept the position, hoping that he would be a voice of moderation among the rebels. Damon left the palace.[45]

The Hawaiian Cabinet began their final day in office disheartened. The diplomatic corps was unanimous in advising the government not to use force to suppress the rebellion. Uninvited US forces were ashore and entrenched in the capital city of the Kingdom, and in the direct face of government protests. The rebel cabal was reforming the disbanded Honolulu Rifles, and young Caucasian men of the settler community were beginning to flock to its standard. The Ministers advised Queen Liliuokalani to write to Minister Stevens and assure him that she would abide by the Constitution. Liliuokalani immediately sent a message to the US Legation stating that she would follow the "present constitution" but she received no reply from Stevens. However, Stevens did respond to the message he had received the day before, from the Cabinet, after the landing of US forces had been challenged by Foreign Minister Parker, and Governor Cleghorn. Stevens wrote to the Cabinet on January 17th stating:

> "In whatever the United States diplomatic and naval representatives have done or may do at this critical hour of Hawaiian affairs, we will be guided by the kindest views and feelings for all the parties concerned and by the warmest sentiments for the Hawaiian people."[46]

Such a message from the representative of a foreign power told the Ministers all they really needed to know. They would get no support from the United States and the implication of Steven's message was that the sympathies of the United States were wholly with the insurrectionists.

Increasingly desperate, with the government's options narrowing into a possible bloody fight against a local insurrection supported by a foreign military, the full Cabinet went to the American Legation at 2 PM to speak with Stevens and to try to convince him to support the legitimate constitutional government of the country. Stevens was ill but he agreed to receive the Foreign Minister and the Attorney General. They asked for support but Stevens refused, telling them that the US forces had been landed for peaceful purposes and he would not support the Queen's government. In Attorney General Petersen's later recollection of the interview, Stevens was asked what he would do if loyalist forces fired upon the rebels and Stevens replied that US forces would protect the insurgents if they were attacked by the Hawaiian military and police forces.[47]

The deflated Cabinet Ministers left the US Legation and went to the Police Station where Marshal Wilson had established his headquarters. Throughout the unfolding crisis Wilson had repeatedly demanded authority from the Cabinet to arrest the plotters and to use force to regain control of the situation but each time the Cabinet had refused him permission to act. The Cabinet was simply too new, and too weak, to forcefully take charge of the deteriorating situation. Now, as they convened with Wilson at police headquarters, it was too late. Ultimately, the concern of the Hawaiian Cabinet about not provoking Stevens and Captain Wiltse meant that they lost control of the tactical situation in Honolulu.[48]

While all that was happening, Lorrin Thurston, from his sickbed (influenza had struck Honolulu), drafted proclamations for the deposition of Queen Liliuokalani from the throne of Hawaii, declaring the monarchy abrogated, and establishing a Provisional Government until annexation with the United States could be consummated. Executive and Advisory Councils were established and all public officers and civil servants were directed to continue in their positions with the exception of Queen Liliuokalani, Foreign Minister Parker, Attorney General Petersen, Interior Minster Colborne, Finance Minister Cornwell, and Marshal Charles Wilson.

The Provisional Government was declared to consist of Sandford Dole as President and Foreign Minister, with Peter C Jones, late of the Wilcox Cabinet, as Minister of Finance, James A King as Minister of the Interior, and W O Smith as Attorney General. The proclamation was delivered to the Committee of Safety which now resolved itself into the Executive and Advisory Councils of Hawaii. Helped by an incident in which a member of the police was shot by an insurrectionist transporting ammunition to the rebels, thus drawing away the police who were watching the insurrectionists, the two Provisional Government councils proceeded separately on foot to the Aliiolani Hale, the government executive building and the seat of the Hawaiian Legislature. Upon arrival, they found that the Hawaiian Cabinet had negligently failed to protect the building with troops, or police, and they occupied the building with ease. From its steps an American, Henry Cooper, read the proclamation drafted by Thurston overthrowing the monarchy and establishing the Executive and Advisory Councils of the Provisional Government, which immediately began to function within the building.[49]

Outside, Colonel John Soper, the former Marshal of the Kingdom under King Kalakaua, took command of the rapidly reforming Honolulu Rifles and by 3 PM he had about 100 men under arms, with many more streaming in. Behind the Aliiolani Hale, the US forces in Arion Hall milled about watching the insurgency succeed.

Once in control of Aliiolani Hale, and despite the fact that they did not yet control any other important points, or the city as a whole, the Provisional Government immediately asked US Minister Stevens for diplomatic recognition by sending to him a message that read:

"The undersigned, members of the Executive and Advisory Councils of the Provisional Government this day established in Hawaii hereby state to you that for the reasons set forth in the Proclamation this day issued, a copy of which is herewith enclosed for your consideration, the Hawaiian Monarchy has been abrogated and a Provisional Government established in accordance with the said above mentioned Proclamation. Such Provisional Government has been proclaimed; is now in possession of the Government Departmental Buildings, the Archives and the Treasury, and is in control of the City. We hereby request that you will, on behalf of the United States of America, recognize it as the existing *de facto* Government of the Hawaiian Islands and afford it the moral support of your Government, and, if necessary, the support of American troops to assist it in preserving the public peace."[50]

At this point, the Hawaiian Cabinet made a last appeal to the US Minister to support the constitutional government of the country:

"Department of Foreign Affairs

Honolulu, January 17, 1893

His Excellency John L Stevens, Envoy Extraordinary and Minister Plenipotentiary, etc:

Sir:

Her Hawaiian Majesty's Government having been informed that certain persons to them unknown have issued proclamation declaring a Provisional Government to exist in opposition to Her Majesty's Government, and have pretended to depose the Queen, her cabinet and marshal, and that certain treasonable persons at present occupy the Government building in Honolulu with an armed force, and pretending that your excellency, in behalf of the United States of America, has recognized such Provisional Government, Her Majesty's cabinet asks respectfully: Has your excellency recognized said Provisional Government? And if not, Her Majesty's Government, under the above existing circumstances, respectfully requests the assistance of your Government in preserving the peace of the country.

We have the honor to be Your Excellency's obedient servants,

Samuel Parker, Minister of Foreign Affairs

Wm H Cornwell, Minister of Finance

John F Colburn, Minister of the Interior

A P Peterson, Attorney General."[51]

Stevens had earlier offered assurance to Thurston and his confederates that he would recognize a Provisional Government once it was declared and he was now as good as his word to the rebels, though it violated the accepted diplomatic norms towards the government to which he was officially accredited. Stevens responded to Foreign Minister Parker with a note at around 3:10 on the afternoon of January 17th in which he advised Parker that he had recognized the Provisional Government as the Government of Hawaii. He followed up with a short formal letter to the Hawaiian Ministers some time between 4 and 5 PM. He also responded formally to President Dole in a note stating:

"United States Legation,

Honolulu, Hawaiian Islands,

January 17, 1893

A Provisional Government having been duly constituted in the place of the recent Government of Queen Liliuokalani, and said Provisional Government being in full possession of the Government buildings, the archives, and the treasury, and in control of the capital of the Hawaiian Islands, I hereby recognize said Provisional Government as the *de facto* Government of the Hawaiian Islands.

John L. Stevens,

Envoy Extraordinary and Minister Plenipotentiary of the United States."[52]

The withdrawal of American recognition, the presence of US forces in the capital city, and the occupation of key government buildings by insurgents were devastating blows to the Hawaiian Government. But the Hawaiian Government had not yet surrendered and a delegation was sent to the police station from the Aliiolani Hale requesting that the Cabinet Ministers come in for a conference with the insurrectionists. The Ministers refused to go but after assurances concerning their personal safety were given Foreign Minister Parker and Finance Minister Cornwell agreed to speak with Dole and the others at the Aliiolani Hale. There, they were presented with a demand for the Hawaiian Government to surrender, and to give up the police station and barracks to the newly formed Provisional Government. The Ministers refused to do so without obtaining the agreement of the Queen and therefore it was decided that the Cabinet would go to see the Queen, accompanied by Samuel Damon who was now a member of the Provisional Government's Advisory Council, to secure her agreement.

At Iolani Palace the Hawaiian Cabinet met for the last time with their Sovereign. Also in attendance at this critical meeting were several senior loyalists including E C Macfarlane, Joseph Carter, Hermann Widemann, and Paul Neumann. Samuel Damon, lately one of the Queen's supporters but now a member of the Provisional Government's Advisory Council was also present.[53] Gone, now, were the indigenous politicians such as Joseph Nawahi, and William White, who had earlier encouraged the Queen to attempt the unilateral constitutional change that had now had such catastrophic consequences for the Kingdom. Parker, Cornwell, Petersen, and Colburn were the Queen's Cabinet Ministers, Macfarlane was a former Cabinet Minster, and Parker, Cornwell, Widemann, Neumann, Carter, and Damon were all members of the Queen's Privy Council. It was natural that she would rely on such men in a crisis, and it is unfortunate that she did not consult with them before taking the ill-advised steps that gave Lorrin Thurston and John L Stevens the opening they needed to overthrow the Hawaiian Kingdom. Both Prince David Kawananakoa, who was also a Privy

Councillor, and Prince Jonah Kuhio Kalanianaole were present at this meeting but they did not offer any advice to the Queen.

Damon told the Queen that the Provisional Government had abolished the monarchy and that her surrender was requested. He added that the US Government had recognized the Provisional Government and that the Queen could file a protest concerning her overthrow if she wished. The Queen was taken aback by the bluntness of his statement and she said nothing in reply. To fill the dead air in the conversation Privy Councillor Carter spoke by offering sympathy to the Queen but no hope. Given the circumstances, he counselled the Queen to surrender the government. He did suggest that the Queen should protest the circumstances of her overthrow. Privy Councillor Widemann concurred with the views of Carter and Damon and he drew the Queen's attention to the precedent of the British seizure of Hawaii from King Kamehameha III in 1843, which ended with the restoration of Hawaiian sovereignty. Liliuokalani's constitutional change gambit had utterly failed. Without much discussion, and faced with the unanimous view of her advisors, the Queen capitulated.

A combined surrender and protest document was carefully drafted by Privy Councillors Neumann and Carter to announce the Queen's surrender to the superior force of the United States, and to protest the same. Samuel Damon attributed to the Queen the formula for the surrender, stating later that it was the Queen's own idea that she could surrender pending a settlement to be decided in Washington, and it was on that condition that she capitulated.[54] Damon also advised the Queen to remain in Iolani Palace, and to continue to fly her royal standard, until the results of her protest to Washington became known.[55]

The Instrument of Surrender stated:

"I, Liliuokalani, by the Grace of God and under the Constitution of the Hawaiian Kingdom, Queen, do hereby solemnly protest against any and all acts done against myself and the Constitutional Government of the Hawaiian Kingdom by certain persons claiming to have established a Provisional Government for this Kingdom.

That I yield to the superior force of the United States of America whose Minister Plenipotentiary, His Excellency John L. Stevens, has caused United States troops to be landed at Honolulu and declared that he would support the said Provisional Government.

Now to avoid any collision of armed forces, and perhaps the loss of life, I do under this protest and impelled by said force yield my authority until such time as the Government of the United States shall upon the facts being presented to it undo the action of its representative and reinstate me in the authority which I claim as Constitutional Sovereign of the Hawaiian Islands.

Done at Honolulu this 17th day of January, A. D., 1893

Liliuokalani R

Samuel Parker

Minister of Foreign   Affairs

W. H. Cornwell

Minister of Finance

Jno. F. Colburn

Minister of the Interior

A. P. Petersen

Attorney General"[56]

The Instrument of Surrender was taken to the Aliiolani Hale by the Cabinet, and Damon, where President Dole received it around 7 PM and endorsed on the document the statement "Received by the hands of the late cabinet this 17th day of January A.D., 1893." Dole took no objection to the purported surrender of the Queen of Hawaii to the superior US forces as the basis for Queen Liliuokalani's submission.

Having the surrender of the constitutional government in hand Dole wrote to Stevens to say:

"Government Building,

Honolulu, January 17, 1893.

His Excellency John L. Stevens,

United States Minister Resident:

Sir: I acknowledge the receipt of your valued communication of this day, recognizing the Hawaiian Provisional Government, and express deep appreciation of the same.

We have conferred with the ministers of the late government and have made demand upon the marshal to surrender the station house. We are not actually yet in possession of the station house, but as night is approaching and our forces may be insufficient to maintain order, we request the immediate support of the United States forces, and would request that the commander of the United States forces take command of our military forces so that they may act together for the protection of the city.

Respectfully, etc.,

Sanford B. Dole,

Chairman Executive Council."[57]

Dole was concerned because Marshal Wilson still held the police station with the police forces under his command, and the Royal Guards still held the Royal Barracks. However, Stevens was wily in responding to Dole's appeal, realizing that to have agreed to provide the assistance that Dole sought would call into question the alacrity with which he had earlier granted diplomatic recognition to the Provisional Government. He deferred to Captain Wiltse but advised Dole that he did not think Wiltse would assume command of the provisional forces. However, he assured Dole that he thought the American forces would ensure that public order was maintained.[58]

Marshal Wilson, true to form as the only real force behind the royal authorities, refused to surrender the police station without a formal order from the Sovereign. The Queen and her Ministers had to draw up a written order to the Marshal, ordering Wilson to comply; "You are hereby authorized to surrender to the so-called Provisional Government this day established, headed by S.B. Dole, esq., the police station and Oahu prison and Government property in your possession or under your control."[59]

Only with a formal written order in hand was the Marshal satisfied and he yielded the police station around 7 PM in the evening. With his surrender the Hawaiian Kingdom collapsed, 98 years after King Kamehameha the Great founded the Kingdom of Hawaii in 1795.

Late on the evening of January 17th, President Dole and the members of the Executive Council took a final, fateful step. At a formal meeting of the Executive Council they decided to immediately send three commissioners (later expanded to five) to Washington to negotiate the annexation of the Hawaiian Islands by the United States. For this purpose the council appointed Lorrin Thurston, W R Castle and W C Wilder as annexation commissioners to negotiate the gift of their country to the United States of America.[60]

The diplomatic community in Honolulu extended *de facto* recognition to the new government on January 18th, with Great Britain, Japan, and China, extending *de facto* recognition a day later, on January 19th. Meanwhile, the visible symbols of the Hawaiian monarchy soon began to disappear. Queen Liliuokalani was directed to vacate Iolani Palace and to retire to her private residence at Washington Place. She was forbidden to fly the royal standard from Washington Place. The Royal Coat of Arms of Hawaii was removed from all public display and the crowns on the insignia of official uniforms were torn off. Civil servants were advised to swear an oath of allegiance to the Provisional Government within 20 days of the takeover or their employment would be terminated.[61]

Royal symbols were not the only thing that disappeared from Hawaii. The 1887 Bayonet Constitution also disappeared. That constitution was as dead under the Provisional Government as it would have been had Queen Liliuokalani succeeded in her designs to promulgate a new constitution. The new Provisional Government used General Orders to tailor the existing laws of Hawaii to fit the needs of the annexationists. The Hawaiian Legislature elected in 1892 never reconvened. By the time new elections were called the Provisional Government had converted itself into a republic, with an extremely narrow electoral franchise to ensure settler political supremacy in the country.

From its inception the Provisional Government represented only a small segment of the population and it lacked members from the indigenous Hawaiian community. It was a government that had to be prepared to sustain itself by force in the face of the population. Troops landed by the USS *Boston* remained in the city and on alert for a monarchist counterrevolution.[62] Colonel Soper's new Hawaii National Guard formed from the former membership of the Honolulu Rifles was maintained on active service until a new settler military force and a new settler police force could be created. President Sandford Dole and his wife experienced increasing anxiety for their own safety, and they were often afraid to sleep in their own house.[63] A march on Honolulu by Japanese contract workers armed with cane knives was only turned back from the city by the intervention of the Japanese consul.[64]

Finally, realizing that they governed uneasily over a country that did not support their government, or their policies, the Provisional Government bowed to the inevitable. On January 31st, the Provisional Government advised US Minister Stevens that it was "unable to satisfactorily protect life and property and to prevent civil disorders" and it asked Minister Stevens to establish a US protectorate over the country. Stevens acted immediately to support the men who were his confederates in the plan to annex Hawaii. Without any prior instructions from the State Department in Washington a US diplomat declared a formal US protectorate over a sovereign country. As the flag of the United States replaced the flag of Hawaii above the Aliiolani Hale on the morning of February 1, 1893, the USS *Boston* fired a salute to Old Glory, its national flag. Stevens reported what he had done to US Secretary of State Foster in Washington:

"Provisional Government of Hawaii is gaining power and respect. Everything is quiet. Annexation sentiment is increasing. Today at 9 AM, in accordance with the request of Provisional Government of Hawaii, I have placed Government of Hawaii under the United States protection during negotiations, not interfering with execution of public affairs."[65]

Stevens went on to tell the Secretary of State that the establishment of a US protectorate required Captain Wiltse of the Boston and himself to assume responsibility for Hawaii because the Provisional Government had no organized military and police forces to sustain itself against the possible attacks from "renegade whites," "hoodlum foreigners," and "vicious natives.""[66]

Stevens published his declaration of an American protectorate in a public notice "To the Hawaiian People" and officially informed the foreign legations and consulates of the establishment of an American Protectorate over Hawaii.

President Harrison in Washington subsequently approved everything Stevens did during the crisis.[67] However, Stevens was cautioned by Secretary Foster not interfere with the internal decision-making powers of the Provisional Government. On February 10th Rear Admiral Skerrett arrived aboard the USS *Mohican* and assumed control of the American protectorate.[68]

In Washington Secretary Foster and the Hawaiian Annexation Commissioners quickly negotiated a treaty for the annexation of Hawaii. One of the points of negotiation concerned compensation to the Royal Family of Hawaii for the loss of their Kingdom. Secretary Foster suggested $200,000 for the Queen and 100,000 for Princess Kaiulani. The Hawaiian Minister to the United States Dr.

John Mott-Smith, who had joined in the negotiations, countered with a proposal that the Queen be given $300,000 and the Princess $200,000. Lorrin Thurston said that the Queen had no claim on the United States for single cent.[69]

In the end, the United States Government agreed to pay the Queen an annuity of $20,000 per year and to make a lump sum payment to Princess Kaiulani of $150,000.[70] The Annexation Treaty was signed on February 14, 1893, and was sent to the Senate for its advice and consent under the US Constitution. In his covering letter submitted to Congress along with the treaty Secretary of State Foster said that the annexation of Hawaii was a longstanding US policy. President Harrison said that the United States had nothing to do with the overthrow of Queen Liliuokalani.[71]

In New England, the Board of Commissioners for Foreign Missions, the organization that had originally sent out the missionary contingents that had irrevocably changed Hawaiian society, and whose descendants now controlled the country, said that the United States had an obligation to ensure order and tranquillity in the islands. Whether that meant a protectorate, or outright annexation, was not for the missionaries to say.[72]

Perhaps Commissioner Blount, the emissary later sent out to Hawaii by President Grover Cleveland after Cleveland replaced President Harrison described best what actually happened on January 17, 1893:

> "The Queen finally surrendered . . . to the Provisional Government on the conviction that the American minister and the American troops were promoters and supporters of the revolution, and that she could only appeal to the Government of the United States to render justice to her.

The leaders of the revolutionary movement would not have undertaken it but for Mr. Steven's promise to protect them against any danger from the Government. But for this their mass meeting would not have been held. But for this no request to land the troops would have been made. Had the troops not been landed no measure for the organization of a new Government would have been taken.

The American minister and the revolutionary leaders had determined on annexation to the United States, and had agreed on the part each was to act to the very end."[73]

The Queen herself, in her memoir stated that her overthrow was a conspiracy to which the United States was a party and that the ". . . pitiless and tireless 'annexation policy' was effectively backed by the naval power of the United States."[74]

NOTES

[1] Alexander, 309
[2] Liliuokalani, 209
[3] Tate, 113
[4] Tate, 123
[5] Tate, 123
[6] Tate 124
[7] Morgan, 63
[8] Russ, 53
[9] Kuykendall, 528
[10] Kuykendall, 582

[11] In her memoir the Queen states that it was Marshal C B Wilson who first suggested to her that a new constitution was desirable, and two days later Captain Nowlein approached her with the same suggestion. Subsequently, she stated, Nawahi and White sought and received an audience with her at which time they formally suggested that a new constitution should be created. Until those representations were made to her the thought of promulgating a new constitution had not occurred to the Queen, or so she said. (Liliuokalani, 229)

[12] Morgan, 60

[13] The Queen states in her memoir that she received two suggested drafts, one from Wilson and another from Nawahi and Bush and that she employed a scribe, W F Kaie, to reconcile the two versions. Apparently, Kaie took copies of the drafts to Chief Justice Judd for his review, without, according to the Queen, receiving her authority to do so. In this way some knowledge of what was being contemplated began to circulate in the settler community. (Liliuokalani, 230)

[14] Under the Queen's draft the Legislature would still retain its power to force the resignation of a Cabinet by moving a vote of non-confidence against it in the Legislature. The key change in the Queen's draft was to restore to the Sovereign the same right to dismiss the Cabinet as the Legislature enjoyed. Individual Ministers would still be subject to impeachment by the Legislature for misconduct in office.

[15] Kuykendall, 586

[16] Russ, 66. The existing constitution only allowed the reigning monarch to designate a single person as their heir or heiress apparent. With this provision the Queen was carrying out the intention of King Kalakaua to establish a dynasty that would perpetuate itself.

[17] Tate, 157

[18] The Queen states in her memoir that she received petitions containing approximately 6500 signatures out of a pool of 9500 registered voters. (Liliuokalani, 231)

[19] Iaukea, 145

[20] Iaukea, 148

[21] Kuykendall, 581

[22] Robert C Lydecker, *Roster Legislatures of Hawaii 1841-1918, Constitutions of Monarchy and Republic; Speeches of Sovereigns and President*, Board of Commissioners of Public Archives, Honolulu, 1918, 183

[23] Tate, 161

[24] Kuykendall, 585

[25] For details of the national status of the committee members see Kuykendall, 587

[26] Kuykendall, 588

[27] Kuykendall, 589

[28] Russ, 75

[29] Russ, 79; The Hawaiian Gazette, January 17, 1893, Library of Congress, Chronicling America, 4

[30] Quoted in Thurston, 253

[31] Quoted in Thurston, 255

[32] Thurston, 255

[33] Quoted in *Blount Report*, 584 http://libweb.hawaii.edu/digicoll/annexation/blount/br0584.php [accessed October, 2020]

[34] Department of State, Office of the Historian, *Foreign Relations of the United States, 1894, Appendix II, Affairs in Hawaii, Stevens to Foster, No. 79*, https://history.state.gov/historicaldocuments/frus1894app2/d73 [accessed, October, 2020]

[35] The crowd was estimated at up to 1500 people.

[36] Quoted in William De Witt Alexander, *History of Later Years of*

the Hawaiian Monarchy and the Revolution of 1893, Hawaiian Gazette Co., Honolulu, 1896, 47

[37] Kuykendall, 593

[38] Tate, 173

[39] Tate, 178

[40] Department of State, *Papers Relating to the Mission of James H. Blount*, United States Government Printing Office, Washington, 1893, 337

[41] Cleghorn also went to see the British and French diplomats in Honolulu to discuss the situation.

[42] Kuykendall, 596

[43] Tate, 181

[44] Kuykendall, 597

[45] Russ, 85; Kuykendall, 598

[46] Grover Cleveland, *President's Message Relating to the Hawaiian Islands (1893)*, in H.R. Exec. Doc. No. 47, 53d Cong.,2d Sess., 592

[47] Kuykendall, 599

[48] Tate, 187

[49] Prince David Kawananakoa, was one of the clerks in the Foreign Affairs department who was put to work drafting the commissions of appointment for the new minsters of the Provisional Government.

[50] James Andrew Gillis, *The Hawaiian Incident: An Examination of Mr. Cleveland's Attitude Toward the Revolution of 1893*, Lee and Shepard, Boston, 1897, 63

[51] Gillis, 66

[52] Department of State, Office of the Historian, *Foreign Relations of the United States, 1894, Appendix II, Affairs in Hawaii, No. 11*, The Hawaiian special commissioners to Mr. Foster, Washington, February 3, 1893, Inclosure D, https://history.state.gov/historicaldocuments/frus1894app2/d73 [accessed, October, 2020]

[53] Morgan, 101.

[54] Morgan, 102

[55] Mellen, 265; Tate, 189. The very next day however, the Provisional Government ordered the Queen to lower the royal standard and to retire to her private residence, Washington Place.

[56] Department of State, Office of the Historian, *Foreign Relations of the United States, 1894, Appendix II, Affairs in Hawaii, No. 11, The Hawaiian special commissioners to Mr. Foster, Washington, February 3, 1893, Inclosure G,* https://history.state.gov/historicaldocuments/frus1894app2/d73 [accessed, October, 2020]

[57] Department of State, Office of the Historian, *Foreign Relations of the United States, 1894, Appendix II, Affairs in Hawaii, No. 14, Blount to Gresham,* Honolulu, June 28, 1893, Inclosure in No. 11, https://history.state.gov/historicaldocuments/frus1894app2/d262[accessed, October, 2020]

[58] Kuykendall, 604

[59]Grover Cleveland, *President's Message Relating to the Hawaiian Islands (1893),* in H.R. Exec. Doc. No. 47, 53d Cong.,2d Sess., 573. Later in the evening the Captain of the Royal Household Guards, Major Samuel Nowlein quietly appeared at the Aliiolani Hale and acknowledged the legitimacy of the Provisional Government as the *de facto* government of Hawaii, ending the threat of any further loyalist resistance. The Royal Household Guards were assembled and dismissed by Colonel Soper, commander of the provisional forces, on January 18th.

[60] Joseph Marsden and C L Carter were subsequently added.

[61] Kuykendall, 606

[62] Kuykendall, 607

[63] Kuykendall, 608

[64] Tate, 210

[65] Quoted in *Blount Report*, No. 8, 222 http://libweb.hawaii.edu/digicoll/annexation/blount/br0222.php [accessed October, 2020]

[66] Kuykendall, 608

[67] Tate, 196

[68] Tate, 211

[69] Tate, 201

[70] Tate, 202

[71] Tate, 204

[72] Tate, 221

[73] House Committee on Foreign Affairs, United States Congress, *Intervention of United States Government in Affairs of Foreign Friendly Governments, Part 1*, U.S. Government Printing Office, Washington, 1893, 54

[74] Liliuokalani, 250, 368

11

The Princess Beyond the Seas

Shock! Dismay! Those were the emotions that must have surged through the young Princess Kaiulani when her guardian, Theo Davies, informed her of three blunt and simply unbelievable telegrams that he had received. The three telegrams Davies received in quick succession on January 30th stated:

"Queen deposed"

"Monarchy abrogated"

"Break news to Princess"

Kaiulani knew that politics in the Kingdom were unsettled but she did not envisage this event happening. The news was more than disconcerting to Kaiulani, who would later tell *San Francisco Call* reporter Alice Rix:

> "I thought that my heart would break when I heard that the monarchy was overthrown, and I had all a girl's disappointment, and I think all a Queen's. I had wanted to be a good Queen some day. I had thought

about it and made all sorts of vows and plans you can think of. I dreamed of all that I would do for my people. I was sure that I could make them the happiest people in the world."[1]

The news of the overthrow of the monarchy, and of the request by the new Provisional Government for the annexation of Hawaii by the United States prompted Theo Davies to write immediately to Dr. John Mott-Smith, the Hawaiian Minister to the United States, to protest both the attempt by the Provisional Government to gift Hawaii to the United States, and the apparent violation of the rights of his ward in England, Princess Kaiulani:

> "I ventured to write to the Hawaiian Minister at Washington, on receipt of the news, earnestly and solemnly remonstrating against this . . . I pointed out the utter impossibility of the [Provisional Government Annexation] Commission's ever obtaining the sanction of the Hawaiian people to their proposal, and I reminded him that the Princess Kaiulani was eminently qualified for the position which, in case of the Queen's removal, would be hers by right. My efforts were in vain, for after my letter had been referred to the [Provisional Government Annexation] Commission, I merely received by cable the singular message: "Islands transferred; Princess provided for."[2]

From the first receipt of the dreadful news from Honolulu, Davies prepared to fight for Princess Kaiulani's rights to inherit the Hawaiian throne. Others were not so sure however, among them Kaiulani's own father in Honolulu, Governor Cleghorn, who wrote to his daughter in anguish shortly after the Queen was overthrown:

> "I have never given the Queen anything but good advice. If she had followed my advice, she would have been firm on the throne, and Hawaiian independence safe, but she has turned out a very stubborn woman and was not satisfied to Reign, but wanted to Rule. If she had followed in the example set by [Queen] Victoria, she would have been

302

respected by all good people. [Some] may think that it is best you should not come to the throne. You may be happier in private life and be an example to your people."[3]

Later, in the same letter, Cleghorn engaged in some wishful hindsight with his daughter, telling her that; "If the Queen had abdicated the night of the 16th or early on the 17th in your favour, the throne I think could have been saved, but she did not think they would do as they did. She still favoured the advice of [her] Ministers, wretched men, and we have all to suffer."[4]

Cleghorn wrote to her again a few days later continuing to express his bitterness at Liliuokalani's attempted constitutional coup which had precipitated the overthrow, the annexation initiative, and the loss of his daughter's prospects:

"I have only called on your aunt once since I wrote you Saturday the 4th. She was well and did not appear troubled, I cannot make her out. She has no one to blame but herself for the loss of the Monarchy. She might have been firm on her throne, if she had left a good Cabinet alone and she had a good strong one with Wilcox[,] Jones[,] Mark Robinson, & Cecil Brown.

I only hope you will not worry. You are young and have all the world before you and you are liked and respected by all the best people here. The P[rovisional] G[overment] are friendly to me, and you may be a happier woman without being a ruler."[5]

Another letter came to Kaiulani, full of sympathy and heartfelt regret from Fiona Jones in Honolulu:

"My dear Kaiulani

I cannot allow this mail to leave without sending a few words of sympathy and *aloha*. You already know of the great and sad changes

303

that have taken place here in the past few weeks, and during this time you have been often in our thoughts, and often has your name been mentioned and our hearts have gone out to you filled with sympathy and regret.

I never have known how dearly I have loved my country and my birthplace until now. Rosie[6] and I have spent hours and days talking these dreadful things all over and have shed many tears. What the result will be my dear God only knows. We do not. If this lovely land is to be always in the upset condition it has been in for some years past, I could never wish to see you subjected to the misery and unhappiness it would surely bring upon you. Would to God it could be what it has been in years gone by, and you its happy Ruler – but we cannot go backwards, we must go onward and it certainly seems as if the happy old days could never return. Keep up a good heart my dear girl, trusting all will be for the best. We are all looking forward to seeing you at no very distant day, and we pray your coming home may be brighter and happier than it seems just at this present time."[7]

The Kingdom of Hawaii was one of the smallest, and weakest independent states in the world in the late nineteenth century but it was part of the Westphalian state system, and as such Hawaii maintained a rather large diplomatic and consular service abroad. In 1890, Hawaii had stationed abroad almost one-hundred diplomatic ministers, chargés d'affaires, consul generals, consuls, vice consuls, and agents on every inhabited continent.[8] Although almost all of Hawaii's diplomats were drawn from either the settler community in Hawaii, or from among foreign residents, many of those ministerial and consular officials remained loyal to the Kingdom, and few were prepared to immediately break with the representatives of the monarchy. Among those who remained loyal to the Queen of Hawaii was the Hawaiian Chargé d'affaires in London, Abraham Hoffnung, who wrote a long letter dated February 15th to Governor

Cleghorn in Honolulu, discussing the political situation at home, and the consequences for Princess Kaiulani.

Hoffnung began by expressing his regret that the planned introduction of Princess Kaiulani at the Court of St. James prior to her anticipated return home to Hawaii had been overtaken by events. The political events in Honolulu had clearly taken Hoffnung aback when he first learned of them:

> "We were startled on the 30th ultimo to see in the cablegram from San Francisco, after the arrival of the steamship 'Claudine', the astounding intelligence that the Queen had been dethroned, a provisional government established, and the Islands practically under martial law. I need not assure you that the sympathies of myself and friends were extremely excited in favour of the Queen, and this received unanimous confirmation on the part of the British Press, which, on the same day when the news was received, and with a spontaneity which was truly remarkable, united in expressing their disapproval of the methods which appear to have been adopted by the Annexation party, and regret at the unfortunate position into which the Queen had been forced."[9]

Hoffnung declared that:

> "I called to see Lord Rosebery, at the first intimation of the revolution, [and] I was asked if I had any direct instructions, or official communication to make, and that, being without such qualification, all that I could put forward were my personal views, and these, I need not say, were entirely in Her Majesty's interest."[10]

Hoffnung was told, unofficially, by the British Foreign Office "that the change of government would not be hastily recognized, and that so far as it became the government of Great Britain, the Queen's interests would be regarded." However:

"In conversation with Sir Thomas Saunderson of the Foreign Office, I rather gathered from him that the Queen had not listened as she might have done to the advice of the British representative at Honolulu. I was not made acquainted with the details governing this remark, but no doubt it will be understood by Her Majesty. It would be a great pity if anything was neglected in respect of any friendly advice tendered by the British Government, which could only have been offered in a most disinterested form, and I still hope that the British Government will act in the spirit in which the semi-official communication was made to me in protection of Her Majesty's interests."[11]

Unfortunately, Hoffnung was left with the clear impression that although Great Britain favoured the continued independence of Hawaii, there would be no serious British opposition to American annexation if that was what the United States Government wanted, as Great Britain and its colonies had "so small an interest in the Islands." Casting about for allies for the Queen's cause, Hoffnung met with the French ambassador to Great Britain to discuss the Hawaiian situation. The French ambassador assured him that France would be unlikely to "hastily recognize what seemed to be the arbitrary action of the American Minister at Honolulu."

Hoffnung also reached out to a leading practitioner of British journalism, Sir Edwin Arnold, the recently retired editor of the *Daily Telegraph* and a well-known poet. Hoffnung met with Arnold to congratulate him on a very fine article he had recently written on Hawaii, in which he had been quite complementary to the Queen. Arnold offered his sympathies at the "painful position" in which Queen Liliuokalani had been placed by events. It was Arnold who suggested to Hoffnung that he should take "Princess Kaiulani for a personal interview with Lord Rosebery, [the British Foreign Minister] believing that this would have material effect." However, upon reflection Hoffnung decided against a meeting between the Princess and the Foreign Secretary, advising Cleghorn:

"But you are well [aw]are that since the Princess has been in England she has been altogether under the guidance and advice of Mr. Davies, and I did not feel that in so important a matter I was justified in seeking any departure from a course to which she had been accustomed, nor did I feel disposed to place myself in communication with Mr. Davies on the subject."[12]

It was probably fortunate that Chargé Hoffnung did not arrange for Princess Kaiulani to obtain an interview with the British Foreign Secretary. The Provisional Government was anxious to portray Princess Kaiulani as a pawn of the British and a meeting with the British Foreign Minister would have provided them with ammunition to use against her in the American press.

Hoffnung also considered the role that Kaiulani could play as a compromise candidate for the Hawaiian throne, stating to her father that; "it may be possible, in the event of the Queen not desiring to return to her position, that a middle course might be adopted by allowing the Princess Kaiulani to ascend the throne under the advice of a Regency. This might, and no doubt would, satisfy native sentiment . . ."[13]

Theo Davies was also thinking along similar lines. As a major actor in the Hawaiian sugar industry he understood the men who had rebelled against the Queen, and why they had felt compelled to do so when she attempted to sunder the political *status quo* under which the Kingdom had been governed since 1887. Indeed, he was quoted as saying of their overthrow of the Queen that "it was not a plot of bad men, but a blunder of good men."[14]

Davies knew that the Queen's constitutional proposals would have deprived the propertied class in the Kingdom of their control of the House of Nobles, a result that was completely unacceptable to them, and to him. The Queen's constitutional proposals would have taken away the ability of the propertied class to block legislative proposals damaging to their economic interests, potentially exposing them to significant taxation or other revenue-enhancement measures. That, coupled with the watering down of the judicial protections in her constitution by the Queen's proposed term limits on Supreme Court judicial appointments, could have placed their property interests in the Kingdom in an extremely unfavourable position.

Davies was a loyalist however, and both his duty to the Princess, and his personal sentiments for Kaiulani, strongly impelled him to seek to defend her interests. Furthermore, it is reasonable to assume that Davies had other, more practical, motivations. He had invested his time and effort in guiding the education of the heiress to the Hawaiian throne in England. Doubtless he looked forward to the day when Kaiulani would ascend the Hawaiian throne, and the influence that might then accrue both to Great Britain, and to himself, with Kaiulani on the throne. Thus, propelled by sentiment, and by imperial, as well as commercial considerations, he counselled the young Princess to take an active role in defending the rights of her country.

For the seventeen year old Princess the revolt in Honolulu brought her into the public arena in a great, painful, and unexpected rush. With the Queen deposed, her Ministers dismissed, the Legislature permanently prorogued by the *coup d'état*, and both the Hawaiian press, and the Hawaiian post, now monitored and the press intimidated by the annexationists, the legitimate officials of the

Kingdom had no public voice that was unencumbered by the fear of retribution at the hands of the Provisional Government. Only Kaiulani, Hawaii's Princess beyond the seas, was safe from the reach of the Provisional Government, and was therefore free to express her opinions, and to contradict the men who had now seized the Kingdom, and sought to extinguish its independence.

Davies presented Kaiulani with his proposal to have her speak out against the overthrow of the Hawaiian Government by proceeding to Washington to muster support for the Hawaiian loyalist cause in American society, and in the American capital city. But Kaiulani had never before assumed an overtly political role, and initially she shrank from it. Then, after reflecting on her role as the Heiress Apparent, and its responsibilities, and knowing the expectations of the Hawaiian people had for her, she realized that she was the only person resident abroad who could speak freely on behalf of the Kingdom. Although the Queen had sent agents to Washington to represent her they also had to face the fear of potential retribution when they returned home. Princess Kaiulani had no such fears because she knew that she would be safe in Europe.

Although, she regarded the situation as probably hopeless Princess Kaiulani nevertheless concluded that her position in Hawaiian society required her to try and salvage the situation. She told Davies "Perhaps if I do not go the Hawaiians will say to me hereafter, 'You might have saved us, and you did not try."[15] In the absence of the Queen, now forbidden to leave the islands, only Princess Kaiulani could speak on behalf of the Kingdom itself, with authority, a Kingdom that was now lying prostrate under an American flag, and in the hands of an oligarchy that did not represent the people of Hawaii. The Princess decided to go to America.

The relationship between Davies and his charge now began to change. No longer the overseer of her education, and of her development as a young woman, Davies now became Kaiulani's political advisor, a role that her father, Governor Cleghorn encouraged her to accept. As part of his new role, Davies drafted public statements for Princess Kaiulani, which many among the Provisional Government and its sympathizers back home in Hawaii decried as mere words put into the Princess' mouth, and unrepresentative of her true thoughts. Although Davies perfected a more florid style of writing than Kaiulani herself showed in her correspondence, Davies' drafts were intended to address an international audience that was accustomed to a more florid style, and they served their purpose.

Although the annexationists criticized the Princess as nothing more than a mouthpiece for Davies, in every constitutional monarchy royalty is advised by constitutional advisors whose ministerial or other authority entitles them to provide advice to their Sovereign, and to the Royal Family, with respect to the discharge of royalty's public role.[16] Had Princess Kaiulani returned home before the fall of the monarchy she would have been advised by Hawaiian statesmen, serving in the Hawaiian Cabinets, concerning any public statements, or activities, that she undertook.[17] Now, in the absence of any statesmen who could perform that constitutional role for her following the overthrow of the government, Theo Davies assumed the role of her constitutional advisor. While he did craft Princess Kaiulani's public statements, he doubtless took into account Princess Kaiulani's own views concerning those pronouncements. The feigned mirth of those in power in Honolulu over the Princess' public statements was largely intended to conceal a real unease at the emergence onto the world stage of the intelligent and fetching

310

young heiress, and the effect she could have on shaping American public opinion.

One who certainly did not feel anything positive about Kaiulani's addresses was the American Minister to Hawaii, John L Stevens, who was a misogynist by nature, and one who particularly despised women in public affairs. Now, however, in the shadow of the Honolulu coup that he had fostered Stevens met with a great personal loss. At the supreme moment of his success in Hawaii in fomenting the overthrow of the constitutional government, and establishing an American protectorate over the country, a great personal tragedy robbed him of the pleasure of his success. One of his daughters, who was vacationing on the island of Hawaii after Stevens had returned to Oahu on the USS *Boston* on January 17th, had subsequently decided that she should urgently return to Honolulu, perhaps at the news of the overthrow of the Queen. Friends tried to dissuade her from using a boat landing in the countryside, owing to the rough sea conditions, but the young woman insisted on using a boat landing to board an inter-island steamer. Governor Cleghorn wrote to Kaiulani concerning what happened:

> "She had been on a visit to Hawaii, and was returning to Honolulu. She was going on board on one of the back landings at Hamakua, Hawaii. She was lowered down into the boat, and had just started for the steamer when a big roller came in, and upset the boat, & she was crushed on the rocks & in spite of the Hawaiian sailor holding her & doing all in his power she and him were thrown about and she was deceased. She was a very accomplished girl, and much respected here. The funeral took place on the anniversary of your mother's death."[18]

Many of the indigenous Hawaiians who still believed ancient superstitions felt that the ancient Hawaiian gods had punished

Stevens for his role in the takeover of their country by the United States. Queen Liliuokalani was among those who thought that Stevens had received a divine retribution. Stevens and his wife would leave behind bitter memories in Hawaii when they departed the following year.

In Washington, the Provisional Government's Annexation Commissioners won the race to the American capital.[19] Actually, it was not much of a race because the steamer SS *Claudine* had been held over at the docks to take the annexationist commissioners to the United States but the Queen had been refused permission to send any representatives to Washington with the annexationists. However, the Queen was allowed to send a delegation to Washington on the next sailing to the United States, a considerable delay that worked to the advantage of the annexationists.

Arriving in Washington, the Annexation Commissioners quickly obtained approval for an annexation treaty from US Secretary of State Foster, and President Harrison. The President sent the annexation treaty to the Senate for its advice and consent on February 3rd, with earnest hopes of pushing it through the Senate before the President's term expired in early March. The Democratic Party however, was suspicious of the haste of the lame-duck Harrison Administration, and perhaps of Harrison as well, and the Democratic caucus delayed the progress of the treaty through the US Senate until Grover Cleveland returned to the presidency in March.

As Kaiulani prepared to voyage to the United States, she issued an address to the British Press, although it was really directed at the American public:

"Four years ago, at the request of [Mr.] Thurston, then Hawaiian

Cabinet Minister, I was sent away to England to be educated privately and fitted for the position which by the Constitution of Hawaii I was to inherit.

All these years I have patiently and in exile striven to fit myself for my return this year to my country. I now am told that [Mr.] Thurston is in Washington asking you to take away my flag and my throne. No one tells me even this officially. Have I done anything wrong that this wrong should be done me and my people?

I am coming to Washington to plead for my throne, my nation and my flag. Will not the great American people hear me?"[20]

That address reflected Davies view that Liliuokalani would probably never return to a restored throne, and that Kaiulani would be her natural successor. Although others had also expressed such views (Sandford Dole had even suggested it during the revolt in Honolulu) it was probably too soon for Davies to promote Kaiulani for the role of Queen. The perspective adopted by the Princess in this statement was glossed over in public accounts although not by the agents of the Queen in the United States, particularly Prince David Kawananakoa, who quickly picked up the implications of Princess Kaiulani's visit to America.

On the 22nd of February, as she prepared to sail to America Princess Kaiulani gave an interview to a special correspondent for a US newspaper. The reporter related that "she said she had no definite plans and would be guided by the advice of her guardian. She proposed to go to Boston and remain till after the inauguration of Cleveland, then go to Washington and probably make a personal appeal to the new President. She expressed the hope that she might gain the sympathy of the American people."[21]

Turning once again to a theme she had expressed in her first address that she had released in the preceding week Princess Kaiulani complained that she had not been officially notified of the deprivation of her position as the rightful heiress to the throne, and said that, "She could not see why she should be summarily deprived of her rights through no fault of her own, and without being even notified to appear in defense of them, she knew nothing of the affair except what she had read in the newspapers."[22]

Of the Harrison Administration's haste to push the Annexation Treaty through the US Senate before the President's term expired, she refused to express a public opinion, nor would she say whether she would accept financial compensation for the loss of the throne if annexation was approved. But she said that she wanted no American protectorate for Hawaii. Rather, she expressed a desire that her country should remain independent. Importantly, in relation to the Queen's attempt at forced constitutional change, Kaiulani declared herself entirely opposed to it, thus putting significant political space between the Queen's actions and Kaiulani's own position. Kaiulani, guided by Davies, was presenting herself as a reliable occupant of the Hawaiian throne in place of an unreliable Liliuokalani. Kaiulani even went so far as to commit herself to accept a regency if she ascended the throne, with Sandford Dole acting as her Regent for several years.[23] Kaiulani told the reporter that she wished for Hawaii and the United States to remain friends, and she specifically denied that she had any discussions with British officials about the current political distemper in her country, or its future. In closing the interview the Princess said "I want to do all I can for my people, and be an honest, true leader to them. I simply want to do my duty to beloved Hawaii."[24]

Perhaps more important than what she actually said was the impression that Kaiulani left with the reporter. Now, on the cusp of womanhood, Kaiulani appeared exotic and attractive, and quickly captured the hearts of the mostly male journalists that she met. Her interviewer described her as; ". . . tall and slender. With a more thoughtful and deliberate air than might be expected in a school girl. She is a brunette with eyes of hazel and features that suggest just a suspicion of Kanaka origin."[25]

Her most striking feature, often noted, was her large luminous soft brown/hazel eyes, which drew people in. Although Kaiulani was very nearsighted, she did not wear eyeglasses in public, and her resulting lack of focus gave her a faraway, dreamy look, that captured the imaginations of people, men especially.

Princess Kaiulani and her party boarded the White Star liner RMS *Teutonic* at Liverpool for the voyage to America. With the Princess was Theo Davies and his wife Mary, and their daughter Alice, as well as Mrs. Davies' maid, and Miss Whartoff, a temporary lady-in-waiting to the Princess. The *Teutonic* was the most desirable passenger liner of its day. Shortly after it was launched in 1889, *Teutonic* appeared at the Spithead Naval Review held in conjunction with Queen Victoria's Golden Jubilee. At the Spithead Naval Review the impressive new White Star liner was toured by Kaiser Wilhelm II of Germany, who was accompanied by Prince Albert Edward, the Prince of Wales. The Kaiser was so impressed with the ship that many believe it gave impetus to his subsequent decision to foster the creation of Germany's own transatlantic passenger liner services.

The *Teutonic* was over 500 feet in length and could accommodate almost 1500 passengers in three classes. The first class staterooms were designed to accommodate large family groups by providing interconnecting staterooms. The ship's twin-screw propulsion system was powered by two triple expansion engines that could deliver a speed of 20.5 knots, making the *Teutonic* one of the fastest and most desirable ships on the North Atlantic run. In fact, in the summer of 1891, the *Teutonic* would take the Blue Riband, the prize for the fastest ship on the North Atlantic passenger service, and she would retain it for almost one year, the last White Star liner ever to hold that coveted passenger liner trophy.

Phebe Rooke, Princess Kaiulani's Brighton governess, came to see her off at Liverpool and Mrs. Rooke subsequently wrote to Governor Cleghorn about Kaiulani's departure for the United States. But first Phebe Rooke gave a warning to Archibald Cleghorn, In an age when the mails were expected to be always punctual she warned Cleghorn that his letters to both her, and to Kaiulani, dated February 1st, had arrived later than other Hawaiian letters that had been dated after February 1st, suggesting to Mrs. Rooke that Cleghorn's letters were being opened and read in Honolulu by the Provisional Government, causing their delay in the mails. Turning to Kaiulani's journey, Mrs. Rooke told Cleghorn:

"You will doubtless hear from Mr. Davies and Kaiulani all the details of her proposed visit to Washington; after providing a suitable and somewhat costly outfit with the best care and economy, I took her to Southport, and saw her off, on board the *Teutonic* with Mr & Mrs & Alice Davies[,] Miss Whartoff and a maid, and I trust that they have already arrived safely. I think Kaiulani is quite right to make all the stand she can to save her flag and country in its independence but I am sure she feels strongly, as I do, that in private life with you Kaiulani would be a far happier woman than with the cares and trials of the Hawaiian throne. You will like to know that she is well and very warmly clad for the voyage, and left in very good health and spirits. She wrote from Queenstown she was well enough to dine, but that her heart sank very low on losing sight of me on the docks."[26]

After an uneventful passage, the *Teutonic* arrived at New York on March 1, 1893, where it was intercepted before docking by the revenue cutter *SS Chandler*, carrying Dr. John Mott-Smith, the Hawaiian Minister to the United States, and Edward C Macfarlane, who had been separately commissioned by both Queen Liliuokalani and by Governor Cleghorn to represent the interests of the Queen and Princess Kaiulani.[27] The Hawaiian Consul in New York, Elisha Allen, also boarded the ship after the ship docked to present himself to the Princess.

The *Teutonic* was met at the New York docks by a bevy of reporters awaiting the arrival of the Princess. Hawaii was then a remote and little-known country to the people of the eastern United States and many of the journalists were unfamiliar with the modernity of Hawaii, and the grace and refinement of its leaders. Expecting, perhaps, a semi-civilized female representative of the Hawaiian race, they were captivated upon first seeing the lithe and exotic-looking young woman who descended from the ship. Dressed in the latest Parisian fashions, she displayed every bit of the polished manners and elegant couture expected of a refined young lady of the late Victorian period. There was no hint or trace of the semi-civilized native that some naive members of the press had anticipated. Faced with the reality of Kaiulani the newspaper reports waxed poetically over "a tall, beautiful young woman of sweet face and slender figure. She has the soft brown eyes and the dark complexion that mark the Hawaiian beauty," "a charming, fascinating individual," and one possessed of the "sweet musical voice of her race." And in a country that exhibited a high degree of race-consciousness, Kaiulani's skin complexion was a notable point of interest. Although her darker skin was specifically mentioned in the press descriptions of her, it was not used as a way to differentiate, or disparage her, and one reporter even compared Kaiulani's complexion to those of American girls one could see on any day along Broadway Avenue in New York. The American press noted that she was a fine artist, a musician, and multilingual, in addition to being a delicate beauty.[28]

Kaiulani's guardian was more concerned with capturing her character for the American press so that she could be properly presented to American society. In a statement to the New York papers Theo Davies said of Kaiulani that she was "a royal lady who has with singular grace and courage endeavoured to fit herself for her high station, and shrunk from neither duty nor sacrifice in the effort."[29]

Princess Kaiulani held a press conference for the many reporters that boarded the *Teutonic*. At the beginning of the press conference Kaiulani read, in a soft voice, an address that Davies had prepared for her to the crowd of reporters:

"To the American people:

Unbidden I stand upon your shores to day where I thought so soon to receive a royal welcome on my way to my own kingdom. I come unattended, except by loving hearts that come with me over the wintry seas. I hear that commissioners from my own land have been for many days asking this great nation to take away my little vineyard. They speak no word to me and leave me to find out as I can from the rumours in the air that they would leave me without a home, or a name, or a nation.

Seventy years ago Christian America sent over Christian men and women to give religion and civilization to Hawaii. They gave us the gospel. They made us a nation and we learned to love and trust America. Today three of the sons of those missionaries are at your capital asking you to undo their fathers' work. Who sent them? Who gave them authority to break the constitution which they swore they would uphold?

To-day I, a poor, weak girl, with not one of my people near me, and with all these Hawaiian statesmen against me, have strength to stand up for the rights of my people. Even now I can hear a wail in my heart, and it gives me strength and courage and I am strong – strong in the faith of God, strong in the knowledge that I am right, strong in the strength of 70,000,000 of people, who, in this free land, will hear my cry and will refuse to let their flag cover dishonour to mine."[30]

The reporters pummelled her with questions but Theo Davies took all the questions of a political nature. Afterwards, the party left for Brevoort House, where they had booked rooms for their New York stay. A barrage of reporters continued to try and see the Princess but Davies, assisted by the Hawaiian Minster, Dr. Mott-Smith, and Edward Macfarlane, the envoy commissioned by Kaiulani's father, stayed below the Princess' rooms and handled all of the inquiries made by the press.

Kaiulani had good reason to think that her visit to America was off to an auspicious start. She had been well received and there was strong interest from the American press in what she had to say. Her first appearance before the American press had gone well and there was news that the Annexation Treaty that President Harrison was trying to force through the Senate in the last days of his administration had been stalled by the Democrats, who were now awaiting the inauguration of Grover Cleveland as President.

Nevertheless, not all voices heard upon Kaiulani's arrival in the New World were lifted in praise. Some elements of the media that strongly favoured the cause of the Hawaiian annexationists deprecated the words of the Princess. Among those was the *Sacramento Record-Union*, which gave a full display of the ugliness, and the underlying racism of the Hawaiian annexationist cause when it commented on the arrival address that Princess Kaiulani made to the American people:

> "When Princess Kaiulani tells us of 'her people' and the necessity and justness of consulting the 'pure Hawaiians' in this matter, she touches the quick. She is not herself a pure Hawaiian, but a half-breed. The intellectual capacity and physical comeliness she has comes from her educational contact with and half descent from Anglo-Saxons. Her 'pure Hawaiians' are confessedly incapable of self-government; the men who have become Hawaiians by adoption and years of devotion to Hawaiian interests are of Anglo-Saxon descent in the main. They represent advancement, progress and strength; the pure Hawaiian represents decay, retrogression and weakness. There is, after all, more of sentiment than of politics in this whole matter; for annexation is in harmony with the progressive, enlightening, uplifting sentiment of the age; 'pure' Hawaiianism is the reverse of these."[31]

In Canada, however, the Princess received some sympathetic support. In British Columbia the *Victoria Times-Colonist* stated that "the same persons and papers that make light of the claims of Princess Kaiulani . . . take the side of the robbers; and when the unfortunate victim appeals to them for justice they laugh in her face . . ."[32]

It was not only the pro-annexationist American press that criticized Kaiulani. She also received a broadside from one of the Queen's own envoys. Queen Liliuokalani was represented in Washington by one of her Privy Councillors, and a former Cabinet Minister, Paul

Neumann, who carried the Queen's brief, and who was empowered to act for her generally through a power of attorney that the Queen had granted to him before he departed Honolulu. With him had gone two other Privy Councillors, Prince David Kawananakoa and Edward C Macfarlane.

Theo Davies acted separately in advancing Princess Kaiulani's interests, and Davies and Kaiulani were compelled to execute a delicate strategy, emphasizing above all the preservation of the independence of Hawaii while at the same time asserting Kaiulani's succession rights to the Hawaiian throne without undoing the Queen's own efforts to obtain her restoration to her throne. It was a complex and overly nuanced position that drew fire from Prince David, who complained to the American press that both Kaiulani's visit, and Davies' public statements, failed to give full support to the Queen's restoration:

"I do not know why Kaiulani came over here, and I do not believe that Davies can give any reason for her coming, because I don't believe he knows himself what he brought her here for. As far as I know the Princess did not leave England with the consent of her father and if Queen Liliuokalani had wished her to come to America I certainly should have learned of it before I left Hawaii. Davies seems to be unable to explain why he came to America on such short notice, and as far as I can learn from what he says he is here for the sole purpose of working against the interests of the deposed Queen. If he has been correctly quoted in the newspapers he certainly is working in the wrong direction. What right has Davies to say that the Queen appears to have violated her oath? Davies evidently would like the Queen to step down and out. He says that the Queen should be requested to abdicate and that the Princess Kaiulani should be proclaimed with a council of regency. After hearing such views from Davies I can only imagine that he is working against the interests of the Queen, which is bad taste to say the least. Davies does not know the situation in Hawaii, nor did he know it when he left England. If he had known it perhaps he would not have left England. The fact is that Davies does not know what he is talking about."[33]

Both Neumann and Macfarlane also expressed reservations at Kaiulani's sudden appearance on the world stage with Neumann calling it a mistake, and even Macfarlane, whom Governor Cleghorn had tasked with representing the Princess' interests in Washington, telling the press that her coming was "an unfortunate thing for his side of the case." Neumann carefully monitored the activities of Princess Kaiulani in America and the Queen's team in Washington were very concerned about the ability of the winsome Princess to embarrass their own efforts in Liliuokalani's own cause.[34]

The truth was that the Queen's envoys were flummoxed by Kaiulani's sudden appearance, which upended their own strategies, of which it must be said had done little so far to advance the Queen's restoration. Paul Neumann, her chief negotiator, seemed resigned to the Queen's fall and acted more like her solicitor than as her statesman representative. Neumann held the Queen's power of attorney, which had been drafted in such broad terms that it allowed him to negotiate a financial settlement of the Queen's sovereignty claims, and that is what he appeared to be doing, with Macfarlane's support.

Neumann said he was not necessarily bound by his instructions, and although he was not personally opposed, in principle, to the American annexation of Hawaii he believed that the US Government should be negotiating its annexation with Queen Liliuokalani and her Ministers, and not with the representatives of the Provisional Government.

Davies implied suggestion of a resolution to the political crisis that involved replacing Liliuokalani with Kaiulani on the throne of Hawaii muddied the waters for the Queen's envoys with respect to the negotiation of a financial settlement because it emphasized the rights of the Heiress Apparent, Princess Kaiulani. Ultimately, however, Davies initiative in persuading Princess Kaiulani to make the trip to America worked to the advantage of the cause of Hawaiian independence because it contrasted so clearly with Neumann's strategy of exploring a financial resolution to the crisis, and effectively undermined Neumann's approach.

While Neumann's strategy was appropriate for a lawyer who was merely acting for an aggrieved client, it was perhaps not the right strategy for a statesman representative of a deposed head of state. And it was not what his client Liliuokalani really wanted either. The Queen wanted the restoration of the Kingdom and of herself as its Queen. In the result, the broad power of attorney held by Paul Neumann was withdrawn by the Queen after word reached Honolulu of the overtly financial strategy Neumann was pursuing.

Macfarlane was by far in the most difficult position because he held a potentially contradictory brief to support both the Queen and Princess Kaiulani. Macfarlane himself was personally loyal to Queen Liliuokalani, and he wrote to Governor Cleghorn to emphasize that he was following Cleghorn's instructions to promote the interests of the Queen first because he understood that it was only if the Queen's cause was clearly lost that Cleghorn had commissioned him to put forward the claims of Cleghorn's daughter.[35] Macfarlane reminded Cleghorn that Cleghorn had instructed him not to create a conflict between the Queen and the Princess, and that it was important for the Queen not to form an opinion that Princess

Kaiulani was being promoted at the Queen's expense. Macfarlane said that it had been initially difficult for him to work closely with Theo Davies because Davies came to New York with the opinion that Liliuokalani was "out of the race" as Sovereign of the Hawaiian Islands. Eventually, however, Davies and Macfarlane began to work together in harmony.[36]

Through it all Kaiulani held her head high and did not respond to any criticisms from the Queen's envoys. When Prince David called on her on the evening of her arrival in New York, she received him in the company of Mrs. Davies briefly, and perfunctorily, late at night, with the tension between them very apparent.

Unquestionably, Kaiulani supported her aunt's personal position that Liliuokalani ought to be restored to her throne but Kaiulani, advised by Davies, saw that her immediate goal must be to stop the US annexation train, and to end the American protectorate that had been declared over Hawaii by the American Minister, John L Stevens. The best way for Kaiulani to do that was to project the image of a cultured, civilized, young heiress, whose country had been seized by an illegitimate cabal. That she had accomplished that objective superbly soon became apparent. In projecting her well-mannered image of civility, intelligence, and restraint, Kaiulani stood in contrast to her aunt, whose image as Queen had been severely tarnished by her attempt to overthrow the 1887 Constitution in the days immediately before she was dethroned. Thus, unfortunately, a schism did develop in the Royal Family over Kaiulani's intervention in the political crisis but her status as a royal celebrity did give a pause to Americans who had too eagerly accepted the idea that the United States should reach out across the Pacific and swallow a small, friendly country without obtaining a deeper appreciation of the causes and circumstances that impelled such a result.

After spending a couple of days in New York City the Princess and her party decamped for Boston to spend the weekend. Davies' son Clive was a student at the Massachusetts Institute of Technology in Boston. The party arrived to find snow on the ground in Boston and on Saturday Kaiulani took her first sleigh ride through the streets of Brookline and Cambridge. The political atmosphere in Boston concerning the Hawaiian annexation question was also quite chilly for someone who was a Hawaiian loyalist, largely because both the missionary element in Hawaii's settler society, as well as the high-ranking American annexationists, such as Blaine and Stevens, were natives of New England.

Despite a political bias in New England favouring the annexationist cause Kaiulani still managed to enjoy herself. She attended the Institute of Technology on the afternoon of Monday, March 6th, where she was surrounded and attended by Clive Davies and his fellow students, American boys who were mesmerized by the presence of an attractive Princess whose origins in Hawaii may have brought to mind stories of the South Seas from Herman Melville's *Typee*, and other nineteenth century American literature. Kaiulani drew confidence from the flush of attention from the young men, teasing one young man that he 'belonged' to Kaiulani because he had been born in her country. Many of the students followed her to her hotel, where a public reception was held later during the same afternoon. The following day she visited Wellesley, a famous college for girls, where she was cheered by the students before departing for Washington, and the main purpose of her trip to America.

While Kaiulani's party was in Boston, the destinies of the United States were being committed to a man who was superbly fitted to assume the presidency of the United States from President Harrison. When Grover Cleveland took the oath of office as the 24th President of the United States on March 4, 1893, he was the most experienced man ever to begin a new presidential term simply because Cleveland had already served a full presidential term as the 22nd US president during the previous decade. Cleveland is the only US president to have been elected to non-consecutive terms of office. Thus, when he came into office a second time, and faced the Hawaiian perplexity that the Harrison Administration had bequeathed to him, he was able to quickly seize the levers of power and to deal confidently with the problem.

When Cleveland took control of US Hawaiian policy from Harrison, the new President was suspicious of the speed at which the dying Harrison Administration had tried to push the Annexation Treaty through the Senate before the Republicans vacated their executive offices. Furthermore, the presence of two delegations from the islands, the Provisional Government's Annexation Commissioners, and Queen Liliuokalani's envoys, with two competing narratives of the recent political events in Honolulu had muddied the waters. Finally, the sudden arrival from England of Princess Kaiulani, and her impact on American public opinion, gave rise to caution on the part of the President.

Meanwhile, Princess Kaiulani and her party had arrived in Washington and took rooms at the Arlington Hotel. Upon her arrival she was greeted again by Prince David Kawananakoa, who presented her with a *lei*. Still smarting from the harsh comments the Prince had made about her mission to America Kaiulani greeted him briefly, and coolly, and shortly thereafter dismissed herself from his presence and retired to her rooms.

The growing media presence surrounding Princess Kaiulani continued in Washington where the statements she uttered, the fashions she wore, and even her movements during the course of a day, were closely observed and reported on. She rapidly became a celebrity, with all the media power that comes with that status. The Princess was now in the same city as the Hawaiian Annexation Commissioners but Davies permitted no calls on her by the Provisional Government representatives. Determined to point out their abandonment of their own country he pointed to the irony of the Hawaiian flag that was raised over the hotel at which the Hawaiian Annexation Commissioners could be found while in Honolulu it was the American flag that now flew over the public buildings of the American protectorate that Stevens had declared over the Hawaiian Islands.[37]

Whether the presence of the Princess in the capital, or the press attention she garnered prompted the President to act we cannot know for certain but on March 9th, the day after Kaiulani's arrival in Washington, President Cleveland began to move decisively against the Harrison Administration's Hawaiian annexation policy. The President first withdrew the Annexation Treaty from consideration by the Senate. That was a significant development but what it portended for Hawaii was as yet unclear. The Princess and her party were jubilant at the withdrawal of the treaty, and they had high hopes that it meant that the independence of the islands would be maintained. Lorrin Thurston, the chief annexation commissioner for the Provisional Government was caught out by the new development but he put the best possible face on what was obviously a very serious reverse for the annexationists. Thurston told the *New York Tribune*; "We were not consulted in the case, and our first knowledge of what had been done was obtained through the press. Of course the President must have a reason for his action . . . We are hopeful, and will continue to look upon the bright side of the case."[38]

Republicans in Washington were appalled. The Republicans young rising star, Theodore Roosevelt, said that the withdrawal of the Annexation Treaty was a crime against both the country and against white civilization.[39] But despite those feelings, the Republican Roosevelt stayed on in Washington under the new Democratic administration as a Civil Service Commissioner.

Four days after her arrival in Washington, a formal invitation arrived for Princess Kaiulani and her party to call upon the President and the First Lady at the White House. Although the reception at the White House was framed as a social visit, an invitation by the President to the heiress of the deposed Queen to call at the White House was certainly a political act, and it was widely recognized as such.

Kaiulani dressed in her best clothes for this occasion, wearing a special outfit consisting of a long-sleeve gown, a skirt with pleats, and a fitted bodice topped by a large and elegant hat with ostrich plumes. The whole party, consisting of Princess Kaiulani, Mr. and Mrs. Davies, Miss Alice Davies, and Miss Whartoff were cordially received by the President and his wife in the Blue Room of the White House. The subject of the Hawaiian political situation was studiously avoided but the engagement was an opportunity for the Princess and her party to meet the man who would decide the fate of an independent Hawaii. It was also an opportunity to meet the young and attractive First Lady who stood by the President's side. The

President was reserved but Kaiulani apparently succeeded in making a pleasant connection with Frances Cleveland according to the press reports of the day:

> "At half-past five o'clock President and Mrs. Cleveland accorded a special reception to Princess Kaiulani, the meeting taking place in the Blue Parlour. The Princess was accompanied by Mr. and Mrs. Davies, their daughter and a lady friend. The call was entirely of a social nature, and lasted probably a quarter of an hour. The visitors were charmed with the cordiality of the reception accorded them, the ladies being captivated by the pleasing manners of the wife of the President, and the Princess said subsequently that Mrs. Cleveland was the only lady that she ever fell in love with."[40]

The visit was a great success and Kaiulani's remarks to the press about Mrs. Cleveland revealed once again her capacity to charm. Years later, Alice Davies also remembered the First Lady's "beauty and charm." While Davies made the rounds of meetings with the movers and shakers of Washington politics, Kaiulani spent the following days attending receptions and lunches where her own Hawaiian beauty and composure never failed to impress. On one occasion she was placed next to the French ambassador at a dinner and she had an opportunity to influence his view of the Hawaiian situation.[41] Perhaps the highlight of her Washington round was a reception held for her by the National Geographic Society, where she had the ability to impress many of the leading Washington luminaries, including both Republican and Democratic politicians.

President Cleveland announced that he was sending a special commissioner to Honolulu with paramount authority over all US officials in Hawaii to investigate the situation that resulted in the overthrow of the monarchy, and the request for Hawaiian annexation. Cleveland chose a prominent former Democratic congressman, James H Blount of Georgia, to be his special commissioner.[42] Blount was promptly christened 'Paramount Blount' in the media because of the plenary authority he was given to investigate the causes and circumstances of the Hawaiian situation. Blount left shortly for San Francisco, where he boarded a US government vessel for the voyage to Hawaii.

Davies and the Princess had now achieved everything that they had set out from England to accomplish. The Harrison Administration's push to approve the Annexation Treaty had been stopped and President Cleveland had withdrawn the treaty from consideration. The President had sent a special commissioner to Hawaii to make an impartial investigation of the overthrow, and of the annexation project. Kaiulani had charmed her way into American hearts and had succeeded in showing Americans that Hawaiian royalty were not backward semi-barbaric overlords, but the civilized and mannered occupants of a throne every bit as morally worthy as those of the European monarchies with which Americans maintained friendly and impartial diplomatic relations. Under such circumstances how could the loss of the Kingdom's independence possibly be justified?

Having tasted success in Washington Kaiulani and her party now prepared to return to Great Britain. They returned to New York on March 18th for a few days to prepare for their transatlantic voyage. Theo Davies booked passage for them on the Cunard liner RMS *Majestic*, the *Teutonic's* sister ship (which had also briefly held the Blue Riband for the fastest transatlantic passage during 1893). Before departing New York on March 22nd Princess Kaiulani issued a farewell statement to the people of the United States through the American Press:

"To the American People:

Before I leave this land I want to thank all those whose kindness has made my visit such a happy one. Not only the hundreds of hands I have clasped, or the smiles I have seen, but the written words of sympathy that have been sent to me from so many happy homes, have made me feel that, whatever happens to me, I shall never be a stranger to you again. It was to the American people I spoke, and they heard me, as I knew they would. And now, God bless you all for it, from the beautiful home where your fair first lady reigns, to the dear crippled boy who sent me his loving letter and his prayers.

Kaiulani."[43]

Theo Davies also spoke to the American Press. He knew that they had succeeded in deferring annexation and saved the independence of Hawaii, at least for the time being. There were also encouraging signs that the Cleveland Administration might help to arrange a monarchical restoration, and Davies still had hopes that his ward would find herself on the Hawaiian throne. Davies views were summarized in the press reports of his farewell meeting with US reporters:

"Mr. Davies, the friend and adviser of the princess, supplemented her letter with a statement, in which he said that they had no special mission to the United States, nor did they claim to have influenced in any way the status of the Hawaiian question.

A commission of gentlemen, he continued, who did not profess to represent the sovereign, the cabinet or the people of Hawaii, arrived in Washington early in February to invite the United States government to take (presumably by force) the territory of Hawaii, and to annex the same to the United States. These gentlemen were Hawaiians and were under oath to support the constitution of Hawaii. Revolution was the extreme right of every self-contained nation and sometimes the only

331

cure for misgovernment and he therefore did not protest against the right of revolution.

That the Princess Kaiulani is the legal successor of Queen Liliuokalani is a mere incident of the Hawaiian constitution, and the Hawaiians have the right by revolution to set aside the monarchical altogether. He protested, however, against the right of any committee of gentlemen without the pretence of consultation with the Hawaiian nation to attempt to transfer to any foreign government the nation and the flag that they are sworn to uphold. At first the matter was hardly appreciated in the United States, but as soon as the government realized what it was asked to do the president adopted the only proper course and dispatch to adjust this question.

The Princess Kaiulani and her friends have in no way contributed to the result, but none the less are gratified that this course has been adopted.

Concluding, Mr. Davies expressed his grateful sense of the courtesy he invariably received from the press during his visit."[44]

Kaiulani returned to England. Her father wrote to her and told her to stay there until matters at home were resolved.[45] Edward Macfarlane had wanted her to return to Hawaii immediately rather than to go back to Great Britain because he thought her continued presence in England only encouraged those who sought to block her path to the Hawaiian throne by alleging that a Queen Kaiulani would be a puppet of the British Government.

Yet there were others who favoured her candidacy precisely because of that. One prominent Hawaiian who privately expressed such views was Charles R Bishop, the spouse of the late Princess Bernice Pauahi Bishop, who had herself once rejected the throne when King Kamehameha V had offered it to her on his deathbed. Writing to Dr. John Mott-Smith, Bishop wrote that Princess Kaiulani was preferable, as the Sovereign of Hawaii, to Queen Liliuokalani because the "better class" who were British in orientation preferred Kaiulani. Such people could be relied upon to favourably influence Kaiulani, and to help her to be a good Queen.[46]

Kaiulani had been successful in presenting herself as a royal stateswoman, patriotically standing up for her country in its greatest crisis. While President Cleveland came back into office highly suspicious of the involvement of the Harrison Administration in the Hawaiian *coup d'état* that displaced Liliuokalani, Princess Kaiulani's mission likely fortified his instinct to withdraw the treaty, and to seek further information about the annexation proposal made by those who were now in charge in Honolulu. Thus Kaiulani, an attractive and polished young woman, together with her political mentor, Davies, were able to use Kaiulani's royal celebrity status to help frame the Hawaiian debate as a struggle between legitimacy and usurpation.

Serious questions now faced the US Government. Did the indigenous and other people in Hawaii truly favour annexation to the United States, or was this the project of an unrepresentative cabal? What role did the chief US diplomat, Minister John L Stevens play, and what was the role of the United States Navy and Captain Wiltse of the USS *Boston* in the January *coup d'état* that had deposed the Queen? Those were important questions that required a full investigation and that would be the purpose of the Blount mission. The same newspaper that reported on Princess Kaiulani's leave-taking of the American people also reported from San Francisco on March 21st that "Blount and party boarded the [steamship] *Rush* immediately on their arrival here yesterday afternoon. The *Rush* then started on her voyage to Honolulu."

Lorrin Thurston suspected he had been defeated in his initial attempt at annexation, and his bitterness showed in a letter that he sent back to Honolulu in which he spoke of new certainties, one being that the monarchy was gone forever from Hawaii. He said in his letter that the monarchy was *pau* (finished). Thurston accused Davies of "maundering" over the possibility of Princess Kaiulani becoming Queen but said that she had no more chance of becoming Queen of Hawaii than Dom Pedro, the recently deposed Emperor of Brazil, had of being restored to his throne.[47]

In Honolulu, there were new consequences that flowed from Kaiulani's mission, and the setback to the annexation project. The bitterness of the men who had overthrown the monarchy could now be seen in the new Provisional Government's treatment of the Queen. No longer was she to be addressed as the Queen, or even as the ex-Queen, now she was simply to be addressed as Mrs. J O Dominis, reflecting the name of her late husband. The furniture and other royal effects that belonged to the Queen were removed from Iolani Palace, and, in effect, looted, as many of the items ended up in the households of the settler community in Hawaii. Provisional Government soldiers who took possession of the palace discovered King Kalakaua's royal crown in the Palace Chamberlains office, in the basement of Iolani Palace, and the precious jewels were prised out of the King's crown and then fenced on the US mainland.[48]

Soon a short article in the New York Tribune related that; "By order of the Provisional Government, the office of Governor of the various islands in the Hawaiian group is abolished. This deprives A S Cleghorn of his place and rank. Probably he will soon be ousted from his office as Collector-General of Customs."[49]

A number of Hawaiian diplomats suffered a similar fate. For his decision to go to New York and greet Princess Kaiulani when she arrived on American shores, the Hawaiian Minister to the United States, Dr. John Mott-Smith, was removed by the Provisional Government.[50] In London, Abraham Hoffnung, the Hawaiian chargés d'affaires wrote an article about the Hawaiian revolution that supported the restoration of Queen Liliuokalani, which resulted in his ouster by the Provisional Government.[51]

For a brief period Kaiulani had to contend with suspicions from the Queen herself about Kaiulani's motives. It is possible that Prince David spoke critically to the Queen about Kaiulani's efforts when he returned from his American mission. The Prince was, of course, on the public record in the United States suggesting that Kaiulani's mission to the United States was not as supportive of the Queen's restoration as it ought to have been. The Queen also knew that Theo Davies was promoting Kaiulani's potential claim to the throne of Hawaii if, as seemed quite possible, Liliuokalani's political liabilities rendered it impossible for her return to the throne. After returning to Great Britain Davies prepared and published an article in *The North America Review* in which he stated quite plainly that, with all due respect to the Queen, if she was precluded from returning to the throne then it should go to Princess Kaiulani by right:

> "The Hawaiian statesmen . . . come as a commission to urge annexation, although the only condition by which the islands can be offered to the United States is that the United States shall first help the Commission to disfranchise three-fourths of the present Hawaiian electorate.

It was against this incredible proposal that the Princess Kaiulani came to Washington to protest, not by remonstrance, nor by argument, nor by official assertion (for all the official life of her country was ranged against her), but in the conviction that her presence would prove to the American people that all the truth had not been told to them.

Princess Kaiulani disclaims any right to interfere in Hawaiian politics so long as Queen Liliuokalani reigns; but should the throne become vacant by the death, abdication, or dethronement of the Queen, then Princess Kaiulani claims the succession as her constitutional right, of which she can only be deprived by force, fraud, or the will of the Hawaiian people constitutionally declared."[52]

Paramount Blount arrived in Honolulu on March 29th to find the American Protectorate of Hawaii still in full force with the American flag waving over the public buildings, and American troops on the streets. Immediately, Blount terminated the American Protectorate over Hawaii, giving President Dole twenty-four hours to put Provisional Government forces in place to maintain his government. April 1st was set as the date for the American withdrawal and at 11:00 A.M. on the appointed day a group of indigenous Hawaiians gathered to see the American flag lowered and their beloved national standard restored once again over the Aliiolani Hale, the Hawaiian seat of government. There was no fanfare when the American flag came down, nor while the Hawaiian flag was raised. Neither the American officials present in Hawaii, nor the members of the Provisional Government, were happy with the cessation of the American protectorate.

Unlike the disavowal of the British protectorate over Hawaii that had been established by Lord Paulet in the 1840's, which gave the Hawaiian Government of that time much cause for rejoicing, the restoration of the independent sovereignty of the Hawaiian Islands on April 1, 1893, was a defeat for the Provisional Government, and not an occasion for any public rejoicing by the settler community. As for the indigenous Hawaiians, it was dangerous to show much emotion over the restoration of sovereignty to Hawaii with *haole* settlers controlling the government, and fearful of a native uprising.

The outgoing American Minister, John L Stevens continued to defend the establishment of the American protectorate over Hawaii, reporting to the new Secretary of State, Walter Q Gresham, in Washington that under the American Protectorate 400 soldiers of the Provisional Government had been trained, and a reformed police force created.[53]

With his annexation mission completed by the *coup d'état* and the creation (and subsequent termination) of the US protectorate, Stevens had tendered his resignation to the incoming Cleveland Administration, and he soon departed the islands for the United States and retirement. However, his role in the overthrow of Queen Liliuokalani received intense scrutiny in the United States and it was apparent that he would soon be called upon to justify his actions as the US Minister in Hawaii. Captain Wiltse of the *USS Boston* was in a similar position and he was relieved of command and recalled. Wiltse died in New York on April 26, 1893, removing an important witness to the events of January, 1893.

Alarmed, perhaps, by the press attention that Kaiulani received in the United States, and worried that the men of the Provisional Government might try to drive a wedge between the Queen and her heiress, Queen Liliuokalani wrote in a direct manner to warn her niece about accepting any proposals from the annexationists:

"I would simply like to add and say that should any one write or propose or make any proposition to you in any way in regard to taking the throne I hope you will be guarded in your answer. The people all over the islands have petitioned to have me restored and it would make you appear in an awkward light to accept any overtures from any irresponsible party, and the P.G's are growing less and less and I understand they will soon 'drop to pieces as the saying is' for want of funds to carry on the Government. Mr. Spreckles will not help them or loan them any and Bishop & C would not loan them any money with out Mr. Spreckles and so we are waiting patiently till Mr. Blount the U.S. Commissioner in Mr. Steven's place, could tell us we are free."[54]

A few days later the Queen wrote again to Kaiulani, this time to tell her about a call that was made upon her by a visiting Indian Nawab, accompanied by his British aide-de-camp. The Queen was impressed by the young Nawab and since he was travelling around the world and would in due time arrive in England for a long stay she asked him to call upon Kaiulani in England, and she asked her niece to receive him when he did. Perhaps the Queen thought of him as a potential suitor for the Princess, as they were of the same age, and the Queen thought him to be good-looking. Regardless, it also gave the Queen an opening to suggest that Kaiulani, whom she still expected to return home in 1893, should travel east through Asia rather than west through the United States on her return journey. The Queen had by now heard of the rapturous American press attention that Kaiulani's visit to America had generated, and it would only have been human of the Queen to worry that the evident enthrallment of American society for her niece might build support for replacing the Queen with Kaiulani if an American restoration of the Hawaiian monarchy was in the offing. Thus, Liliuokalani suggested to her niece that:

"Since his [i.e. the Nawab's] departure I have thought that if you could on returning home take the opportunity and return by the way of China and Japan passing through France, Germany[,] Italy[,] Egypt and India, how nice it would be. Then some future day visit America again. I have my doubts as to the Chicago [Columbian] Exposition[55] and their [sic] might be another fair that would try and out do this one – but since Europe is so near you and you may not have as good a chance to go so far again I thought it well if you were to return that way."[56]

Turning to political matters, the Queen noted that the Nawab's skin colour "is that of our own race" so there was "a feeling of sympathy right away" at the Queen's current predicament. She later heard that the Nawab had wondered "why did her people permit her to be deposed?" The Queen then said to her niece in the letter "come to think of it my dear Kaiulani [I] must say it was treachery on the part of my Ministers and it helped the agitators backed by the U. S. troops[,] that was why, but don't mention this. It would not be well if it came from your lips. We have to act with [policy]."[57]

Perhaps it was sad that Liliuokalani blamed her Ministers for the great fall that she had suffered. Her Ministers had actually tried to protect her by defending the Hawaiian Constitution, which she had earlier taken an oath to sustain, and which she had subsequently tried to revoke. The Queen's real enemies were the members of the Annexation Club, supported by the local American officials, Stevens and Wiltse, who had landed US troops to support the fifth column filibusters whose *coup d'état* Liliuokalani had enabled by her ill-advised constitutional plan. Behind them were the top officials of the Harrison Administration, who had secretly abandoned friendly relations with Hawaii by abetting both the Queen's overthrow, and the annexation project. But with all that had happened to her Queen Liliuokalani seemed fatalistic, telling her niece not to be excited by what she had wrote and that she was "well and happy – it does not pay to brood."

339

Kaiulani was probably distressed at receiving letters from the Queen that might imply a suspicion on the Queen's part of disloyalty from her young heiress. Her guardian *cum* political advisor, Theo Davies, thought so too, and he recommended that Kaiulani write to her aunt, and reassure her that the Princess would neither entertain, nor accede, to any proposal to take the throne without the consent of the Queen. Kaiulani therefore wrote to her aunt and said; "I have never received any proposals from anybody to take the throne. I have not received a word of any sort from anyone except my Father. I am glad that I am able to say that I have not written to anyone about politics."[58]

Upon her return from the United States Kaiulani had not recommenced her previous studies. Her formal education was now complete, and she did not return to Mrs. Rooke in Brighton. Instead, she rented a small cottage from her former schoolmistress at Great Harrowden Hall, Mrs. Sharp, at The Yews, Burton Latimer, in Northamptonshire. There she spent a quiet few months while the drama of the annexation debate played out in Honolulu and Washington, interrupted only by a summer stay with the Davies family at their estate in Ireland, near Killiney, which was close to Dublin.

Meanwhile, in Honolulu, Paramount Blount, the special commissioner sent out by President Cleveland pursued his investigation into the causes and circumstances of the *coup d'état* against the royal government of Hawaii. Blount practised a studied neutrality between the annexationists who controlled the Provisional Government, and the loyalists who clung to the hope that President Cleveland would restore Queen Liliuokalani to her throne. Blount's neutrality caused great disquiet in both camps but more so in the annexationist camp, which had quickly become used to the overt

340

alliance of the previous Harrison Administration towards Hawaiian annexation. Slowly it dawned on them that Blount might, and indeed probably would, support the restoration of the Hawaiian monarchy. When he left Honolulu to return to Washington, Blount was already a contemptible man in the eyes of the annexationists. Upon his departure the Provisional Government's band at dockside played *Marching Through Georgia* to the former Confederate Army veteran, who had seen his native state of Georgia reduced to ashes during the US Civil War by Union General William Tecumseh Sherman's famous march to the sea.

Blount's Report was delivered to the President in July, 1893, and it condemned the *coup d'état* against the Queen as a fraudulent grab for power orchestrated by a local settler cabal that was in league with US Minister Stevens. Their assumption of power from the royal government was enforced, and subsequently sustained, by the US Navy, and the US Marine Corps.[59] The Provisional Government, according to Blount, was simply unrepresentative of the Hawaiian people and did not reflect their political views. According to Blount, there was no basis for the United States to pursue the Hawaiian annexation project.

Blount's report was received like a bombshell in Washington, and even more so in Honolulu, where annexationist hopes began to wither. Monarchists in Hawaii took renewed hope from the Blount Report that Liliuokalani would be restored to the throne, and the Queen herself retained confidence in her eventual restoration. The Blount Report had an important consequence for Princess Kaiulani as well. Blount's report framed the debate into two polar opposites, the restoration of Queen Liliuokalani to the Hawaiian throne, or the continuation of the annexation project under the direction of the men who controlled the Provisional Government. There was no consideration of a third option of placing Princess Kaiulani on a restored Hawaiian throne in place of Queen Liliuokalani. As a result Kaiulani no longer had to hold herself ready to take on the burdens of the Hawaiian throne. Now, it seemed, if restoration were to occur it would do so under the ex-Queen. The Princess could now begin to plan for a life outside the limelight, at least for the time being.

As politicians in Washington and Honolulu waited to see what actions President Cleveland would take on the Blount Report, an important milestone occurred in Kaiulani's life. On October 16, 1893, Kaiulani reached her eighteenth birthday and that was an auspicious day because under the Bayonet Constitution of 1887, and under the common law, she was now eligible to assume the Hawaiian throne without the necessity of a regency. At eighteen, an heir to the Hawaiian throne reached their constitutional majority and could, if circumstances required, ascend to the throne and reign directly rather than through a regency. The importance of this milestone prompted Theo Davies to draft an Address from Kaiulani to the Hawaiian people and in light of both her new status, and his own as her political advisor, he sent the draft address to her for her approval, and requested her authorization to release it publicly, steps that he would not have felt obliged to follow while the Princess had remained in her minority. Dutifully, Kaiulani read the draft Address and approved it for release to the Hawaiian people.

In her *Eighteenth Birthday Address*, issued on October 16, 1893, the Princess acknowledged the great "blow that had befallen the Hawaiians" and she noted "the importance that they be unified, and "that they imitate . . . my dear Aunt – our Queen" in dignity but more importantly she warned her countrymen and women to not "listen to those who would rob us of or tempt us to surrender ... our national independence." In closing she told them that at times "my heart is very sorrowful, for I want to be back in my own country. Will you pray for me?"[60]

In Honolulu the birthday of Princess Kaiulani, while no longer a state occasion under the Provisional Government, was nevertheless marked by the loyalists who crowded into a party, a combined luau and *hookupu,* that the Queen held in honour of Princess Kaiulani at Washington Place in Honolulu. Such were the numbers in the crowd that the party spilled out into the street. The crowd was serenaded by the Hawaiian National Band, which consisted of former indigenous members of the Royal Hawaiian Band who had remained loyal to the Hawaiian monarchy. After the formation of the Provisional Government, the band members, formally part of the Hawaiian military, were each required to recite an oath of allegiance to the Provisional Government, which all of the indigenous Hawaiian members of the Royal Hawaiian Band refused to do. Walking out of what was now called the Provisional Government Band, they had formed the loyalist Hawaiian National Band.[61]

In Washington, society remained all agog with whispering dreams of an American Polynesian empire. The luau was appropriated by American society and became the fashionable party of the year. The strains of the ukelele wafted through elegant parties, while American music created an ode to the fallen Queen.[62]

Far off in England, the Princess, now seemingly relieved of political aspirations for the present, began to plan for a more private life.

NOTES

[1] Rix, 17

[2] Theophilius Harris Davies, *The Hawaiian Situation* in The North American Review, vol. 156, No. 438, May, 1893, 605 at 608. The reference to the Princess being provided for was no doubt a reference to certain proposed treaty provisions concerning the payment of damages to the Princess for the loss of her hereditary rights to the throne of Hawaii.

[3] Cleghorn to Kaiulani, January 28, 1893, HSA

[4] Cleghorn to Kaiulani, January 28, 1893, HSA

[5] Cleghorn to Kaiulani, February 8, 1893, HSA

[6] An apparent reference to Rose Cleghorn Robertson, half-sister of Princess Kaiulani.

[7] Jones to Kaiulani, January 30, 1893, HSA

[8] Nicholas B Miller, *Trading Sovereignty and Labour: The Consular Network of Nineteenth-Century Hawai'i* in *The International History Review*, Routledge, Abingdon (UK), 2020, Vol 42, No. 2, 260 at 261.

[9] Hoffnung to Cleghorn, February 15, 1893, HSA

[10] Hoffnung to Cleghorn, February 15, 1893, HSA

[11] Hoffnung to Cleghorn, February 15, 1893, HSA. Sir Thomas Saunderson was at this point in time the Assistant Permanent Under-Secretary of State for Foreign Affairs. In 1894 he became the Permanent Under-Secretary of State for Foreign Affairs, the highest civil service position at the Foreign Office.

[12] Hoffnung to Cleghorn, February 15, 1893, HSA

[13] Hoffnung to Cleghorn, February 15, 1893, HSA

[14] Theo Davies, *Letters Upon the Political Crisis in Hawaii, Second Series*, Bulletin Publishing Co., Honolulu, 1894, 18

[15] Quoted in Davies, 609

[16] Thus, for example, whenever a member of the British Royal Family makes an address or a public appearance in any of the realms and territories where Queen Elizabeth II is the reigning monarch the local Prime Minister, Premier, or a Minister of the Crown always acts as the constitutional advisor to the member of the Royal Family who is making the address.

[17] This had already happened once in Princess Kaiulani's experience, when she was accompanied by Interior Minster Lorrin Thurston to a public ceremony to inaugurate the distribution of electricity in Honolulu, in 1889.

[18] Cleghorn to Kaiulani, February 8, 1893, HSA

[19] The Hawaiian Annexation Commissioners were William Richards Castle, Charles L. Carter, Joseph Marsden, William Chauncey Wilder, and Lorrin A. Thurston. All were US citizens or Hawaiian-born descendants of Americans, except Marsden, who was British descended.

[20] Princess Kaiulani, *Princess Kaiulani Protests*, The Daily Bulletin, Honolulu, Hawaii, March 02, 1893, Image 3 Chronicling America Historic American Newspapers, Library of Congress, <https://chroniclingamerica.loc.gov [accessed July 20, 2020]

[21] The Record-Union, Sacramento, Calif., 23 Feb. 1893, Chronicling America: Historic American Newspapers. Lib. of Congress <https://chroniclingamerica.loc.gov [accessed July, 2020]

[22] The Record-Union, Sacramento, Calif., 23 Feb. 1893, Chronicling America: Historic American Newspapers. Lib. of Congress <https://chroniclingamerica.loc.gov [accessed July, 2020]

[23] Under the 1887 Bayonet Constitution, Kaiulani, as Queen, would achieve her majority at eighteen so the offer of a longer regency period would have been a significant political concession.

[24] The Record-Union, Sacramento, Calif., 23 Feb. 1893, Chronicling America: Historic American Newspapers. Lib. of Congress <https://chroniclingamerica.loc.gov [accessed July, 2020]

[25] The Record-Union, Sacramento, Calif., 23 Feb. 1893, Chronicling America: Historic American Newspapers. Lib. of Congress <https://chroniclingamerica.loc.gov [accessed July, 2020]

[26] Rooke to Cleghorn, February 28, 1893, HSA

[27] Macfarlane's instructions from Governor Cleghorn were to put forward the Queen's case first but argue for the rights of Princess Kaiulani if the Queen's cause had clearly become a lost cause.

[28] Mellen, 275

[29] Theophilus H Davies, *Statement of Davies* in The Morning Call, San Francisco,Calif., 02 March 1893, Chronicling America: Historic American Newspapers. Lib. of Congress. <<https://chroniclingamerica.loc.gov/

[30] Princess Kaiulani, *Her Only Plaint*, The Morning Call, San Francisco, Calif., 02 March 1893, Chronicling America: Historic American Newspapers. Lib. of Congress. <https://chroniclingamerica.loc.gov [accessed July, 2020]

[31] *In a Nutshell*, The Sacremento Record-Union. [volume], March 03, 1893, Page 2, Image 2 Chronicling America: Historic American Newspapers. Lib. of Congress. <https://chroniclingamerica.loc.gov [accessed July, 2020]

[32] *Not Quite Consistent*, The Victoria Daily Colonist, March 8, 1893

[33] The Morning Call, March 03, 1893, Image 1, Chronicling America <https://chroniclingamerica.loc.gov [accessed July, 2020];

[34] James L Haley, *Captive Paradise, A History of Hawaii*, St. Martin's Press, New York, 2014, 302-03

[35] Apparently, there was another, albeit informal, envoy in Washington seeking to protect Princess Kaiulani's interests. Her uncle in California, John M Cleghorn, travelled there of his own volition in early February to support Kaiulani's claims to the Hawaiian throne. However, he does not appear to have made any impression on the events, and he may have returned to California before Kaiulani arrived at New York. (Russ, 123)

[36] Stassen-McLaughlin, 33

[37] Linnéa, 129

[38] New York Tribune, New York, N.Y., 10 March 1893, Chronicling America: Historic American Newspapers, Library of Congress, <https://chroniclingamerica.loc.gov/

[39] Edmund Morris, *The Rise of Theodore Roosevelt*, Ballantine Books, New York, 1979, 474

[40] Highland Recorder, Monterey, Highland County, Va., 24 March 1893, Chronicling America: Historic American Newspapers. Lib. of Congress <https://chroniclingamerica.loc.gov [accessed July, 2020]

[41] Annexation Commissioner C L Carter later found the French Ambassador to be decidedly unfriendly to the Provisional Government's annexation request. (Russ, 172)

[42] Subsequently, after the departure of Minister John L Stevens, Blount was named as Envoy Extraordinary and Minister Plenipotentiary to Hawaii.

[43] The Evening Bulletin, Maysville, Ky., 21 March 1893, Chronicling America: Historic American Newspapers. Lib. of Congress. <https://chroniclingamerica.loc.gov [accessed July, 2020]

[44] The Evening Bulletin, Maysville, Ky., 21 March 1893,

Chronicling America: Historic American Newspapers. Lib. of Congress. <https://chroniclingamerica.loc.gov [accessed July, 2020]

[45] Stassen-McLaughlin, 36

[46] Stassen-McLaughlin, 33

[47] Stassen-McLaughlin, 35. Dom Pedro was the Emperor Pedro II of Brazil, who was deposed in a *coup d'état* on November 15, 1889, despite being a popular monarch. The Imperial Family's insistence on the abolition of slavery was a contributing factor in the downfall of the Brazilian monarchy.

[48] The royal crown of the consort was saved because Queen Kapiolani took it from the palace to her private residence when she moved out of Iolani Palace following the death of the King. Today her crown is on display in the palace museum, next to the King's crown, which is now adorned with fake jewels.

[49] New York Tribune, March 9, 1893, Image 1, Chronicling America, Library of Congress, <https://chroniclingamerica.loc.gov [accessed July, 2020]. Cleghorn subsequently stepped down from his position as Collector-General of Customs in April, 1893.

[50] Russ, 171

[51] Miller, 274

[52] Theophilus Harris Davies, *The Hawaiian Situation* in The North American Review, vol. 156, No. 438 (May, 1893) 605 at 610

[53] Russ, 186

[54] Liliuokalani to Kaiulani, May 24, 1893, HSA

[55] During Kaiulani's trip to America she had received a delegation from the commissioners for the Chicago Colombian Exposition marking the 400th anniversary of the European discover of the New World by Christopher Columbus, and she had been invited to return and visit the exposition .

[56] Liliuokalani to Kaiulani, June 1, 1893, HSA

[57] Liliuokalani to Kaiulani, June 1, 1893, HSA

[58] Kaiulani to Liliuokalani June 15, 1893, HSA; quoted in Stassen-McLaughlin, 37

[59] MacDougall, 381

[60] Letterbook of T H Davies, 1893-95, BMA; quoted in Stassen-McLaughlin, 40

[61] Stone, 44

[62] Morris, 456; G P Judd, *Hawaii An Informal History*, Collier, New York, 1974, 115

12

The Islands Adrift

President Grover Cleveland was a man who believed firmly in the honour of the United States. Like many of his countrymen, Cleveland thought that the United States was fundamentally different from the autocratic or aristocratic European states. Like earlier presidents, Cleveland also believed that it was the role of the United States to shield the weaker states of the Americas from the aggrandizement of imperialistic European states. That was the underlying principle of both the Monroe Doctrine, which was applicable to Latin America, as well as the Tyler Doctrine, which was applicable to Hawaii. In 1896, Cleveland enforced the Monroe Doctrine against Great Britain when the British disputed with Venezuela over the boundaries of British Guiana. Cleveland may well have been the last US President to hold nineteenth century views about the moral purpose of the United States in its foreign relations – views that harked back to the earliest days of the republic, and to the counsel of the country's founders who advised against foreign entanglements. The Blount Report gave Cleveland confirmation of what he had already suspected. The gift of the Hawaiian Islands proffered by that country's new Provisional Government was tainted by a *coup d' état* that had been aided and abetted by State Department officials, and by the US Naval officers in Hawaii. Cleveland lamented the improper purposes of the Harrison Administration toward the Kingdom of Hawaii and he decided that the United States should seek a just result for the Hawaiian people. A new diplomatic Minister was sent to Honolulu to represent the interests of the United States and to correct the injustices that had been committed against that country by US officials. Albert S Willis was a lawyer and a former congressman who went to Honolulu with instructions to mediate the restoration of the monarchy, and to place Queen Liliuokalani back on her throne. Secretary of State Gresham, in reviewing the events that had occurred in Honolulu during the past year, told Willis that, ". . . the Queen finally, but reluctantly, surrendered to an armed force of this Government illegally quartered in Honolulu. . . ."[1] Gresham instructed Willis to obtain a restoration of the legitimate monarchical government of Hawaii with an appropriate amnesty for the members of the settler community that had participated in the coup against the Queen.

However, Queen Liliuokalani, now sensing that events were finally moving her way, became recalcitrant at the thought of granting amnesty to the men who had overthrown her in January. She called for retribution against the traitors to the Hawaiian Kingdom. Willis had an interview with her in which he thought that he heard the Queen say that she wanted to see the ringleaders beheaded, a medieval and repulsive form of execution to the mind of a North American, and a form of capital punishment that was unknown under the laws of the Kingdom of Hawaii.

Although the Queen subsequently denied that she had called for beheading as a punishment for the annexationists, she maintained that any grant of royal mercy could not be exercised until a Cabinet was once again in place that could provide her with constitutional advice on the grant of royal mercy to traitors. In any event, the Queen thought there could be no peace in Hawaii unless the perpetrators of her overthrow were banished from the Kingdom, along with their families. Stubbornly, the Queen resisted Willis' call for a general clemency.

Finally, under pressure from her own personal advisors, Liliuokalani relented, and she agreed to grant clemency but she still insisted on the deportation of the annexationists, and the forfeiture of their property, reasoning that there could be no political peace in Hawaii while they remained present in the Kingdom.[2]

Unfortunately for the Queen, her intransigence became publicly known, and the political damage that it caused could not be repaired. The Queen's desire for vengeance, while understandable, failed to take into account her own role in the *coup d'état*, which had given the annexationists their pretext for mounting the overthrow of the government. Furthermore, her express desire for retribution confirmed in the minds of the settler community in Hawaii that they would never be safe under a Hawaiian Government headed by Queen Liliuokalani. Far from leading to reconciliation, her declarations fortified the men of the Provisional Government in their intention to hang on to power no matter what the consequences. Surrendering power to the Queen, they realized, might well lead to their own demise, physically or financially.

Liliuokalani's attitude also created a quandary for the United States Government. Faced with her reluctance to grant clemency, and her unwillingness to accept the consequences of her own actions, it became apparent that the US Government would probably have to resort to the use of military force to return the Queen to her throne, and perhaps to maintain military forces in Hawaii to sustain her on her throne. In that case, American military forces would be arrayed against a substantial number of US immigrants to Hawaii, as well as US citizens, which was an appalling thought to the political and military leadership of the United States.

Surprisingly, little consideration was given at this time to the possibility of a restoration of the monarchy with Kaiulani as Queen. It was much more likely that the settler community would have accepted a monarchy under Kaiulani, rather than one under a restored Liliuokalani, but that option seems never to have been seriously considered. On December 18th, in accordance with his instructions from President Cleveland, and Secretary of State Gresham, Minister Willis demanded that President Dole surrender the Hawaiian Government to Queen Liliuokalani, a request that President Dole and his Provisional Government Cabinet refused outright.

In Washington, President Cleveland, now understanding the Queen to be unrelenting on the subject of clemency sent a message to Congress, which, coincidentally, was dated the same day as Willis' formal demand to President Dole to turn over the Hawaiian Government to the Queen. In his message to Congress President Cleveland essentially washed his hands of the entire Hawaiian fiasco and he remitted it to the consideration of Congress. In doing so the President emphasized those aspects of the Hawaiian fiasco that impelled him to resile from the annexation of the islands in order to avoid besmirching the honour of the United States. Cleveland told Congress:

"Hawaii was taken possession of by the United States forces without the consent or wish of the government of the islands, . . . the military occupation of Honolulu by the United States on the day mentioned was wholly without justification, either as an occupation by consent or as an occupation necessitated by dangers threatening American life and property

. . . if the Queen could have dealt with the insurgents alone her course would have been plain and the result unmistakable. But the United States had allied itself with her enemies, had recognized them as the true Government of Hawaii, and had put her and her adherents in the position of opposition against lawful authority. She knew that she could not withstand the power of the United States, but she believed that she might safely trust to its justice. . .

By an act of war, committed with the participation of a diplomatic representative of the United States and without authority of Congress, the Government of a feeble but friendly and confiding people has been overthrown."[3]

Cleveland said the United States had an obligation to make matters right in Hawaii, and that in the foreign relations of the United States the country had to maintain "a high standard of honor and morality." Further:

"it can not allow itself to refuse to redress an injury inflicted through an abuse of power by officers clothed with its authority and wearing its uniform; and on the same ground, if a feeble but friendly state is in danger of being robbed of its independence and its sovereignty by a misuse of the name and power of the United States, the United States can not fail to vindicate its honor and its sense of justice by an earnest effort to make all possible reparation."[4]

With that goal in mind, the President told Congress that he had instructed the American Minister in Honolulu to impress upon the parties the desire of the United States that the legitimate government of the country be restored and that those who had participated in the insurrection against it should be forgiven. But that goal had been stymied by the Queen Liliuokalani's refusal to grant clemency. Said the President to Congress:

> "In short, [the American conditions] require that the past should be buried, and that the restored Government should reassume its authority as if its continuity had not been interrupted. These conditions have not proved acceptable to the Queen, and though she has been informed that they will be insisted upon, and that, unless acceded to, the efforts of the President to aid in the restoration of her Government will cease, I have not thus far learned that she is willing to yield them her acquiescence."[5]

Accordingly, Cleveland decided to wash his hands of the entire affair and he dropped the whole issue into the lap of Congress, expressing a desire that Congress find a solution that was "consistent with American honor, integrity, and morality." Congress, of course, was a deliberative, rather than an executive body, and asking it to make a decision was tantamount to inviting interminable debate, thus deferring any action. In truth, Cleveland was repelled by what had been done to a small friendly country by American descendants, and American citizens, with the connivance of the Harrison Administration, but he doubted that he had the necessary political support from the American people to engage in a military intervention in Hawaii that would be necessary to restore the political *status quo ante*. Cleveland decided that he had done what he could, and that he could do no more.

In Honolulu, Princess Kaiulani was the heroine of the hour among the loyalists in the population. Her portrait could be seen in shop windows and songs were written about her. The annexationists in the Provisional Government continued to remain incredibly suspicious of the Hawaiian population, particularly with respect to luaus, which the Provisional Government suspected were merely fronts for loyalist meetings. Soon all large gatherings were banned by order of the government. The playing of the national anthem, *Hawaii Ponoi*, was also banned unless government permission was first obtained, and church bells that had been rung each morning to summon churchgoers for prayers for the Queen were also banned.[6]

Some who had earlier given their support to the annexationists now suffered buyers remorse when they saw how quickly the civil liberties they had enjoyed under the monarchy were curtailed, or eliminated. Robert Louis Stevenson returned for a brief visit to Hawaii from Samoa and was appalled by the usurpation of authority by the settlers, telling Archibald Cleghorn that he was prepared to help the loyalist cause in any way that he could.[7]

Kaiulani's guardian, Theo Davies, had not been idle. Davies had made a visit to Hawaii in the early part of the year to look after his business interests but he also wanted to participate in the political debate over the future of the country. Not a man to mince words he attacked the annexationists in the press by writing a series of letters to the editors of the *Daily Bulletin* and the *Pacific Advertiser*. In his first letter he discussed the three courses that had been open to the men of the settler community in responding to the Queen's attempt at unilateral constitutional change:

> "The Constitutional course would have been, to declare the Queen disqualified, by reason of her attack on the Constitution; . . . The next

possible course was the treasonable one, of violating the Constitution, by upsetting the Monarchy, in favor of a republic, or of some other form of independent government. . . . Treason, however, is a gentlemanly crime, and sometimes it is even a creditable one. . . . The third course was treachery, or betrayal of the sovereignty without the nation's consent; and treachery has never anything to recommend it, either in manners or morals. . . . There is a worldly morality, which says that 'success justifies treason.' I never heard it said that success justifies treachery, . . ."[8]

Davies attacks on the annexationists raised their ire, and the Provisional Government took advantage of political intelligence it had received, and of Davies presence in Honolulu, to summon him for an interrogation:

"ATTORNEY-GENERAL'S OFFICE, HONOLULU, H. I., February 5th, 1894

MR. T. H. DAVIES, City:

Dear Sir:-There is a matter of public interest about which I desire to speak to you.

And would ask, if convenient, you would call at my office tomorrow morning at

9 :30 O' clock.

Sincerely yours,

(Signed) WILLIAM O. SMITH,

Attorney-General."[9]

When Davies called upon the Attorney General the next day, he found himself not only in the presence of the Attorney General but also in the presence of the Marshal of the Provisional Government. They both wished to interrogate Davies about rumours of a filibuster against the Provisional Government emanating from Canada, and specifically, Vancouver, British Columbia. According to Davies:

> "Mr. Smith then politely stated that many rumours had been circulated, with regard to the enlistment of troops at Vancouver and elsewhere, and that the Hawaiian Consul at Tacoma had written officially upon the subject, and that my name had been coupled with the transaction. Mr. Smith further stated that he felt that the report was a very preposterous one, but that he believed I would be glad of an opportunity to contradict it."[10]

Davies was indignant and of course he realized that the Provisional Government was trying to intimidate him into silence or else why would they have their chief police officer, the Marshal, present at the meeting if they only wanted him to say that the report was not true? Davies told Smith; ". . . that I had no idea that my name was connected with these military reports, until I saw it in an afternoon paper; that there was not an atom of foundation for the statement; and that I knew nothing of the man who was said to be engaged in the transaction in Vancouver."[11]

Smith subsequently accepted that Davies was not involved in any mercenary activity or in any schemes concerning military intervention in Hawaii. The paranoid approach toward Davies by the Provisional Government was not necessarily an aberration however. Rear Admiral Skerrett had advised the US Secretary of the Navy in June, 1893, that the Provisional Government was kept in power by military law, and by holding people in custody without bail.[12]

Although Davies was not involved in anything nefarious in Canada, there was something happening in Canada that did concern Hawaii, and it led to one of the strangest elements of Hawaii's story during the 1890's.

The former American Minister in Honolulu, John L Stevens had perennially worried that Canada was a stalking horse for Great Britain and that it would attempt to obtain an interest in the Hawaiian Islands if the United States failed to annex them. Stevens was particularly concerned that Canada might seek a coaling or cable station. In fact, the pressing naval need for coal for the Royal Navy in the late nineteenth century had prompted the British Admiralty to reappraise Hawaii as a potential coaling station on the Panama – Japan route, and on the Vancouver – Sydney route.[13] The Colonial Secretary, Sir Henry Allard, considered that a British coaling station at Hawaii was a necessity.[14] Other pro-annexationists in the United States claimed that the fortification of the naval base at Esquimalt, on Vancouver Island, after the transcontinental Canadian Pacific Railway was completed, demanded a stronger US naval presence in the Pacific Ocean.[15]

In Canada, the main consideration in the minds of public men was to create a trans-Pacific cable to enhance communications between Canada and the South Pacific, primarily with the British territories of New Zealand and Australia. Thus, when the overthrow of the monarchy in Honolulu occurred in 1893, the Canadian Prime Minister, Sir John Thompson, assured the members of the Canadian House of Commons that Canadian concerns and interests with respect to Hawaii had been brought to the attention of the Imperial Government in London on several previous occasions, and that the Canadian Government was confident that British authorities would take Canadian views into consideration in formulating a position on the Hawaiian question.[16] But there was little that Canada could actually do about the proposed Hawaiian annexation. New Zealand also protested the possible US annexation of Hawaii to London but again without any substantial effect on British foreign policy.

The importance of Hawaii as an intermediate station on a trans-Pacific cable system had been recognized by the promoters of cable undertakings however, and from 1893 to 1894 a major effort was made by Canada to acquire one of the smaller Hawaiian Islands for use as a cable station.[17]

The island that was identified as the most suitable to support a trans-Pacific cable station under the imperial sovereignty of the British Empire was Necker Island, a small island of approximately 45 acres in size lying northwest of the main Hawaiian island chain in the North Pacific. It had first been discovered by the French explorer La Perouse, in 1786. In the 1890's it was treeless and uninhabited, and Canadian officials believed that no formal sovereignty claim to it had been made by Hawaii, or by any other country. However, an expedition under the command of Captain John Paty had been despatched in 1857, by the Kingdom of Hawaii to formally assert sovereignty over the Northwestern Hawaiian Islands. Although Captain Paty specifically claimed Laysan and Lisianski islands, he only claimed the other northwestern islands more generally for Hawaii, and uncertainty remained over the sovereignty status of Necker Island.[18]

Sandford Fleming, the leading Canadian polymath of the nineteenth century, an inventor, surveyor, and railway promoter, and the originator of standard time, envisioned the construction of a Trans-Pacific cable to connect the antipodean British colonies to

London through Canada and across the existing Trans-Atlantic cable. The vast distances of the Pacific Ocean required that re-transmitting stations be established at specific points within the Pacific Ocean. Necker Island, northwest of Hawaii, was a desirable location and, conveniently, it was thought to be unclaimed at the time that construction of the Trans-Pacific cable was being considered. For security reasons, it was desirable that the cable not be routed through a foreign country but only be routed through countries that were part of the British Empire. Although there were alternatives to Necker Island as a re-transmission station, Necker was the most cost-effective location for the location of a station on the route of the proposed Trans-Pacific cable.

In 1893, Fleming persuaded the Canadian Government to request that the British Government secure Necker Island for the purposes of the proposed cable. However, in light of the *coup d'état* of 1893, the British Government advised the Canadian Government on December 29, 1893, that; "The Secretary of State for Foreign Affairs will defer action, pending the establishment of the government of Hawaii upon a more permanent footing."[19] That was not good enough for Fleming, who was anxious to see the laying of the Trans-Pacific cable start, and he continued to press for action.

The Canadian High Commissioner in London, Sir Charles Tupper, made representations to the British Foreign Secretary, Lord Rosebery, about obtaining Necker Island and Lord Rosebery replied that nothing should be done for the time being due to the unsettled political conditions in the islands. Frustrated, Fleming consulted with the commander of the army in Canada, who suggested that a mission should be despatched from Canada to lay claim to Necker Island because "the best thing to do in a matter of that kind is

to act first and ask for leave afterwards."[20]   Fleming took his
advice and arranged for a retired officer of the Royal Navy, R E H
Gardner-Buckner to proceed to Hawaii, charter a vessel, and then
claim Necker Island for Canada and Britain. After Gardner-Buckner
was off on his mission, Fleming reported what he had done to High
Commissioner Tupper in London, who passed Fleming's report on to
the British Government, where it caused a great deal of consternation
in the British Foreign Office.

Meanwhile, in Hawaii, the Provisional Government had got wind
of what the Canadians were up to from inquiries being made about
Necker Island by the British Minister in Honolulu. The Hawaiian
Provisional Government also knew about an upcoming conference
in Canada to discuss the laying of a proposed Trans-Pacific cable. To
forestall the Canadians from creating a diplomatic incident the British
Government advised Hawaii that it would consider Necker Island to
be a part of Hawaii, and would negotiate with it on that basis.[21]

Gardner-Buckner was now in Hawaii but realized that he might
become the focal point of a diplomatic incident, and so he wisely
decided, on May 24, 1893, to drop his mission to claim Necker
Island for Canada, and on the following day one of the two ships
he had chartered for the Canadian mission to Necker Island was
taken over in charter by the Hawaiian Provisional Government,
which despatched an expedition to formally claim Necker Island for
Hawaii. A formal sovereignty claim to Necker Island by Hawaii
was made on May 27, 1893, by the representatives of the Provisional
Government. On May 31, 1894, Fleming was advised in a cable
from London that the British Government was very upset about
the mission to assert a Canadian claim to Necker Island; "[Foreign
Secretary Lord] Rosebery much annoyed at action. Will repudiate.

Fears will destroy good prospect of obtaining Necker. Prevent action becoming public if possible."[22] That was the end of the Canadian expedition to unilaterally acquire Necker Island.

Nevertheless, Canada did not entirely abandon its efforts to acquire Necker Island. The following year, after a colonial conference was held in Ottawa involving Great Britain, Canada, New Zealand, and the Australian states, and in the presence of a representative of the Board of Trade for Honolulu, it was decided that a renewed effort should be made to acquire rights to a Hawaiian island as a re-transmission site for the proposed Trans-Pacific Cable. Canada, this time with the authorization of the British Foreign Office, dispatched Sanford Fleming to negotiate directly with the government of what was now the Republic of Hawaii.

Fleming learned that the Hawaiian Government was receptive to being the host for a re-transmission station but it was felt that the Hawaiian Government would probably be unable to obtain the assent of the United States to any alienation of Hawaiian territory, due to a treaty restriction on its sovereignty that the Kingdom of Hawaii had accepted in the earlier reciprocity treaty with the United States. Nevertheless, an effort was made to secure American consent. At the request of the Republic of Hawaii, President Cleveland sent a special message to Congress on January 9, 1895, asking Congress to make an exception to the Reciprocity Treaty between the United States and Hawaii to allow Canada to lease Necker Island from Hawaii for the purpose of a cable station. The lease would have given Canada the right to occupy and use Necker but the ultimate sovereignty over the island would have remained with the Republic of Hawaii.

President Cleveland's request shocked some members of Congress, and Senator Henry Cabot Lodge complained that Canada (and Britain) had only been forestalled from taking Necker Island by the quick action of the Hawaiian Provisional Government in establishing Hawaiian sovereignty. Now, Canada was trying to obtain relief from the Reciprocity Treaty so that it could obtain a foothold in the Hawaiian Islands.[23] As the Hawaiian Government anticipated, Congress was in no mood to sanction any increase in Canadian or British influence in the islands, and influential members such as Senator Lodge continued to press for US annexation of the island chain. The Canadian effort to obtain Necker Island failed, and the island remained subject to Hawaiian sovereignty until Hawaiian annexation by the United States. Although allegations would be made in the United States during the currency of the Hawaiian annexation question that one or another country threatened Hawaii, the farcical Canadian attempt to obtain Necker Island was the only actual territorial challenge that Hawaii encountered throughout the 1890's, prior to annexation.

The Hawaiian Government may only have entered into the negotiations over Necker Island with Fleming in order to use the negotiations as leverage to pressure the US Government to lay its own cable between the Hawaiian Islands and the US west coast.[24] However, Sandford Fleming did eventually succeed in helping to create the British Empire's Trans-Pacific Cable in 1902, although, in lieu of Necker Island a more costly extension of the line had to be made to British-owned Fanning Island, 800 miles to the south of Necker Island, to host a re-transmission station.

By the spring of 1894, the Hawaiian annexation quest had been lost, at least while the Democrats controlled the presidency. The annexationists in Honolulu now had to contemplate what form a permanent Hawaiian Government should look like. Naturally, considering their objective to annex the country to the United States, they settled on a republican form of government. However, no choice could be left to the broader electorate that existed under the Kingdom, as political support for the monarchy remained strong, and an open constitutional convention could embarrassingly result in a popular expression of support for the restoration of the monarchy. Therefore, a narrow electorate of 800 was defined for elections to a constitutional convention to ensure that the result would be in favour of a republican constitution. To emphasize the policy of the annexationists, July 4, 1894, was chosen as the commencement date for the republic. Thereafter, July 4th was celebrated as the Hawaiian national holiday until annexation.

On July 4, 1894, the President of the Provisional Government, Sandford B Dole, proclaimed the Republic of Hawaii from the steps of Iolani Palace, which was now called the Executive Building. The new President of the Republic was the same as the President of the Provisional Government, Sandford B Dole. In fact, all of the former members of the Executive Council of the Provisional Government simply continued in office under the newly proclaimed Republic of Hawaii. The new constitution did provide for a bicameral legislature, and although the defined electorate was not as broad as the electorate under the Kingdom's Legislature, its 4000 electors was broader than the electorate that was created to elect the Constitutional Convention that made the republican constitution.

What sort of republic did Hawaii now have? Not a true republic, with fairness and equality among all, and public officials selected by democratic elections. Rather, this new republic was simply a political vehicle for the annexationists to continue their policy of seeking annexation by the United States. It was a white minority state of a type that became more common in the twentieth century as decolonisation threatened white rule in a number of European colonies. The Hawaiian electors were mostly property owners who all swore allegiance to the new Republic. Few indigenous Hawaiians did so, and there were no Asian residents who qualified. The new constitution formalized the rejection of the monarchy in any form in Hawaii. Other countries quickly extended formal diplomatic recognition to the new republic. Great Britain was the last foreign country to grant official recognition, which it finally did in November, 1894.

Among the general population, the loyalists still hoped for the Queen's restoration but they were disappointed that President Cleveland had not followed through on the logic of his own position concerning the 1893 *coup d'état*, and landed US troops to force a restoration of the legitimate constitutional government of Hawaii. Liliuokalani's adherents decided to send a mission to European capitals to attempt to obtain support from the broader community of nations for the restoration of their sovereign. Herman A Widemann, a former Privy Councillor under the Queen, was despatched to European capitals to drum up support for the loyalist cause. However, Widemann's mission was a failure. It was now too late for any external force to give support to the Hawaiian monarchy. The Europeans calculated that the annexationists now controlled the Hawaiian state and any attempt by a European power to intervene would prompt an American response, and probably enhance the annexation issue, and thereby ensure its ultimate success. It was better to recognize the annexationists, who were at least now able to maintain security in the new republican state.[25]

With foreign intervention to retrieve her throne now out of the question, Liliuokalani fell back on a course of action she that had followed before. She began once again to conspire with that perennial Hawaiian political agitator Robert Wilcox, to whom she had been once linked in the plots to unseat her brother from the throne, including Wilcox's ill-fated attempt in 1889. Throughout the autumn of 1894, a monarchist plot began to take shape. Officials of the Hawaiian Republic began to pick up intelligence about a forthcoming monarchist insurrection in December, leading to the arrests of John Bush, and Joseph Nawahi, but it was not until the night of January 6, 1895, that an insurrection actually broke out. Loyalist forces had planned to make their move on the morning of the January 7th but the execution of a search in Waikiki led to gunfire, resulting in the death of leading annexationist, and former Annexation Commissioner, Charles L Carter, who was a member of the Republic's Legislature at the time of his death.

The annexationists immediately called out their military forces and fighting ensued over several days on Diamond Head and in the Nuuanu, Pauoa, Manoa, and Palolo valleys around Honolulu. The government forces had the advantage in weaponry, including artillery, and the loyalist insurrectionists were short of both food and water. Cut off, and without adequate supplies, the insurrection became a loyalist fiasco and they were forced to surrender.[26]

Among the big monarchist fish that were reeled in by the victorious government forces were Wilcox, Volney Ashford (a leader of the rebels in the 1887 uprising but now a supporter of the monarchy), Clarence Ashford, Sam Nowlein, Prince David, Prince Kuhio and ultimately Queen Liliuokalani herself. At first, the settler community bayed for the blood of the loyalists and, according to the Queen, her attorney, Paul Neumann, informed her that the government planned to execute her, and several others, by firing squad.[27]

Although the Queen stated that she was prepared to face execution she decided to forestall the execution of her followers by executing an Instrument of Abdication, a document that was sought from her by the Republic. The Queen, in the presence of several of her supporters, signed the Instrument of Abdication from the Hawaiian throne that had been prepared for her by government officials. Despite her willingness to abdicate, the government nevertheless decided to try the Queen and the leading insurrectionists before a military commission, which sat for 36 days and returned death sentences for several people, including Wilcox, Henry Bertelmann, and Samuel Nowlein.

Liliuokalani went on trial before the military commission for misprision of treason, under which charge the government intended to prove that she had foreknowledge of the planned insurrection, and had aided and abetted it. She refused to admit to having prior knowledge of arms that were found stored on her property at Washington Place but it was clearly proved that she had signed commissions of appointment for new Ministers to assume office once the government of the Republic had been displaced, and that was enough to convict her.[28]

Of course, none of the major trials were fair. They were not conducted before a regular court, and were in fact political show trials, with verdicts that were a foregone conclusion. However, it is certainly true that the people put into the dock were guilty of planning, and undertaking, an uprising against the Republic of Hawaii. But sentencing left the Hawaiian Government with a dilemma. If they brought down harsh sentences, they would further alienate the substantial indigenous population, especially if the Queen were harmed. The government could then be faced with another serious security issue. Furthermore, some of the convicted people could claim foreign citizenship, and that raised the possibility of diplomatic issues.

Ultimately, none of the death sentences were carried out. President Dole, a man whom Colonel Iaukea later described as being of sterling character,[29] realized that harsh penalties would only martyr the loyalists and render it more difficult to advance the cause of annexation. Queen Liliuokalani was sentenced to five years imprisonment at hard labour, and a fine of $5000.00 but hard labour was never enforced. She remained imprisoned in Iolani Palace where she composed the *Queen's Prayer*, a hymn of forgiveness toward those who had overthrown and imprisoned her, and dedicated the hymn to her niece, Princess Kaiulani. She also composed six *mele inoa*, or name chants, for Princess Kaiulani.[30] The *Queen's Prayer* hymn is still sung in Hawaiian churches in the twenty-first century.[31]

The Republic's Government continued to keep the Queen under close watch. Even the outgoing British Minister, Wodehouse and his wife were denied permission to make a personal visit to say goodbye to her when they returned to Great Britain upon Wodehouse's retirement.[32] Finally on September 6, 1895, she was paroled to her home at Washington Place, under the care and supervision of her former Marshal, Charles B Wilson, and his wife, and they supervised the Queen on behalf of the Republic. Although the Queen had earlier been close to the Wilson's, their decision to act as the Republic's keepers, guarding her, and reporting whatever she said to the Republican government, led to a future estrangement between the couple and Liliuokalani.[33]

In November, 1896, President Dole released Liliuokalani from all legal restraints, and gave her a full pardon. All of her civil liberties were restored to her. In the meantime, all those who had been imprisoned had been released at various points in time, Liliuokalani being the last to be set free. She immediately decided to travel to Washington to see if she could retrieve her personal situation in the Hawaiian Islands before President Cleveland left office in March, and the Republican Party returned to power in the American capital. President Dole let her go, probably reasoning that after so much time had passed since the overthrow of the monarchy in 1893, there was little chance that she would find any substantive support for her personal restoration in the American capital. She found sympathy in the United States but no support for her restoration. Liliuokalani attended the inauguration of President McKinley, where her personal invitation from the American Government was addressed to "Her Majesty, Liliuokalani," a title that she was no longer addressed by in her own country by its government.[34]

For the people of Hawaii, now divided in their loyalties, and living with the bitterness of political turmoil, the future of their country continued to be obscure.

NOTES

[1] Gresham to Willis, January 12, 1894, quoted in Iaukea, 193

[2] Iaukea, 177

[3] *President Cleveland's message about Hawaii December 18 1893*; http://www.let.rug.nl/usa/documents/1876-1900/ president-clevelands-message-about-hawaii-december-18-1893.php (accessed July 26, 2020)

[4] *President Cleveland's message about Hawaii December 18 1893*; http://www.let.rug.nl/usa/documents/1876-1900/ president-clevelands-message-about-hawaii-december-18-1893.php (accessed July 26, 2020)

[5] *President Cleveland's message about Hawaii December 18 1893*; http://www.let.rug.nl/usa/documents/1876-1900/ president-clevelands-message-about-hawaii-december-18-1893.php (accessed July 26, 2020)

[6] Mellen, 272

[7] Mellen 289

[8] Theo H Davies, *Letters Upon the Political Crisis in Hawaii, January and February, 1894*, Second Series, Bulletin Publishing Co., Honolulu, 1894, 4

[9] Quoted in Davies, 9

[10] Quoted in Davies, 8

[11] Quoted in Davies, 8. The man so-named in Vancouver subsequently sent a letter to the Provisional Government absolving Theo Davies of any involvement with his alleged plans.

[12] Tate, 236

[13] Gough, 231

[14] Gough, 232

[15] Tate, 207

[16] Tate, *Canada's Interest*, 37

[17] Some of the narrative concerning Necker Island is taken from an earlier work by the author (*Canadian Boundaries: The Foreign Treaties and Other Instruments That Defined Our Realm*, Magistralis, Ottawa, 2018, 380-83)

[18] Alexander, 281

[19] Quoted in John S Ewart K.C., *The Kingdom of Canada, Imperial Federation, The Colonial Conferences, The Alaska Boundary*, Toronto, Morang & Co., 1908, 284

[20] Ewart, 284

[21] David Raymont, *Aloha, Canada* in *The Beaver*, vol. 83:3, June/July 2003, Canada's National History Society, Winnipeg (MB), 2003, 40 at 42

[22] Ewart, 285

[23] Tate, 262

[24] Ernest Andrade Jr., *Great Britain and the Hawaiian Revolution and Republic, 1893-1898* in *The Hawaiian Journal of History*, vol. 24 (1990), 91 at 103.

[25] Andrade, 104

[26] Daws, 282

[27] Liliuokalani, 273

[28] Daws, 283

[29] Iaukea, 160

[30] Williams, 110

[31] Williams, 112

[32] Mellen, 323

[33] Williams, 112

[34] Mellen, 333

13

The Wandering Exile

Back in Great Britain following her successful trip to the United States, Princess Kaiulani was excited. There was nothing more she could do for her country for the moment and Mrs. Davies was arranging for the Princess and Alice to spend the winter in Wiesbaden, in the German Grand Duchy of Hesse, to perfect their command of the German language. Kaiulani and Alice would also be accompanied by three other young women. The plan was for the young women to overwinter in Germany for five months. For Kaiulani this was a grand adventure, an alternative to her original plans for a grand European tour before her return to Hawaii — plans that had now been set aside by the overthrow of the monarchy.

Wiesbaden was a charming German city, famous for its spa, which attracted royalty and wealthy people from all across Europe. In the early 1890's, it was fast becoming a favourite summer sojourn for Kaiser Wilhelm II of Germany. Over time, the city became known for its beauty, and for its luxurious living, and many wealthy Germans settled in Wiesbaden.

In Germany, Kaiulani's social restraints were loosened. Theo Davies, Alice's father, and Kaiulani's legal guardian,[1] was far away and unable to watch the young women as closely as he could do while they were in England. Kaiulani and Alice Davies took full advantage of their new freedom to enjoy themselves to the full. Many years later, Alice Davies would claim that she had no clear memory of their sojourn in Germany, except for the fact that the Princess of Hawaii had conquered the hearts of many German officers.[2]

Kaiulani wrote home to say that she intended to perfect her command of German in Wiesbaden, and that having turned her mind to the task she would not be dissuaded from her goal. But mostly it seems that her time in Wiesbaden was about enjoying herself and developing social poise. According to Alice Davies the two young women met many young German officers who were attracted to Kaiulani's exotic looks, royal blood, and her vivacious personality. Kaiulani's friendship with a rich German count actually developed to the point where he proposed marriage to her. But Kaiulani was not in love with him and she declined his proposal. In truth, she was not yet ready for marriage, and she wanted to develop a sense of her own independence first.

Unquestionably there were young men in Germany to whom Kaiulani felt a strong attraction, and she experienced the pain of early love affairs. Kaiulani poured out the pains of unrequited love to her friend Annie Whartoff, who had accompanied Kaiulani on her trip to America. Whartoff wrote back to Kaiulani to counsel her young friend about one of Kaiulani's affairs of the heart:

> "I have thought much of you and really do hope you are not seriously feeling your friend's sudden change of manner and conduct. I cannot think he is your equal but love is love we know not how it comes or

when the little shaft enters. Anyway I know that you must love and be loved. Do not fear once to be crushed for you have pride as much as strong love in your heart . . . one can love more than once even if one feels it is not possible . . ."[3]

In Great Britain Kaiulani's guardian, Theo Davies, became concerned about the long residence of his daughter and Kaiulani in Germany. Davies began pressuring the two young women to return to Great Britain, where he could keep a closer watch on them. However, Kaiulani was having too much fun, and she balked at returning to the socially strict regimen of Great Britain. In March,1894, Davies encouraged Kaiulani's return to England so that he could brief her on political developments in Hawaii.[4] But Kaiulani refused to return, so Davies commanded his own daughter Alice to return to Great Britain without the Princess. In April, Davies tried again to persuade the Princess to return, telling Kaiulani that he could not discuss the political developments in Hawaii in correspondence. If only she would return to England he could provide her with the latest information concerning her native land.[5]

While appeals to her Hawaiian patriotism and royal responsibilities were not enough to pry Kaiulani away from the delights of Wiesbaden, Davies did have another lever to force his recalcitrant charge to return from Germany, and that was Kaiulani's finances. Now that she was emerging into adulthood Kaiulani was coming face to face with a major adult problem – how to finance one's lifestyle? Unfortunately, Kaiulani had to live in Europe under straightened circumstances following the annexationist *coup d'état*. As a former royal person (in the eyes of the annexationists) her educational allowance was an unnecessary expense and it was immediately terminated by the Provisional Government. Nor would the new Government agree to pay the $4000.00 that had been appropriated by the Hawaiian Legislature for her long-planned return to Honolulu. Kaiulani found that she must now live on $500.00 per year, which is all that her father could spare her. As a young royal personality Kaiulani had expenses related to travel, fashion, and social events, that exceeded her income. Davies admonished her for spending too much money, and he warned her that she was putting her father under financial stress. Cleghorn had admitted to Davies that he might have to mortgage his property in order to pay Kaiulani's bills. Davies appealed to Kaiulani exercise economy in her spending, but that was not necessarily advice that the eighteen-year-old Princess wanted to hear!

Eventually, however, all of Davies' pressure and cajoling worked, and Kaiulani decided to return to Great Britain. Before doing so she went to Berlin, a city that she admired, to see a grand review of the Imperial German Army by the Emperor and Empress of Germany. Some 20,000 soldiers paraded before their monarchs, and the Emperor had a hundred officers in attendance upon him. It was an impressive display of military might by the most powerful army in Europe.[6] Departing Germany at last for Great Britain the young Princess said in a letter "I was quite sorry to leave Germany, everyone had been so very kind to me there, and they have sympathized with me so much."[7] Nevertheless, despite, or rather because of her enjoyment of the country, Kaiulani was never to visit Germany again. Her father and Theo Davies afterwards kept Kaiulani's travels only within the British Isles and France, where they could keep a sharp eye on her. She would never again be captivated by the courteous young officers of the Imperial German Army.

She spent the summer of 1894 in Ireland with the Davies family at their estate at Killeny, near Dublin. Over the course of the summer there were rounds of tennis matches and parties with the young crowd that also spent their summers on the Emerald Isle. But before going over to Ireland Kaiulani faced an unpleasant task that she had been putting off for several months. Earlier in the year, Queen Liliuokalani, as the head of the Hawaiian dynastic house of Keawe-a-Heulu, had written to her niece about the subject of marriage. The Queen was responding to a direct query that Kaiulani had made concerning Prince David. Kaiulani must have heard rumours about a potential arranged match for her with Prince David, and it prompted the Princess to write home about it.

Although Liliuokalani had been free to make her own choice of a marriage partner, it quickly became apparent that she wanted her niece's match to be an arranged dynastic match, either to perpetuate the *alii* line in Hawaii, or to obtain foreign protection for the teetering Hawaiian throne:

> "You have asked me a direct question and I must be candid with you in regard to Prince David. I had not thought to mentioning to you about [your] future until the proper moment arrived but as you already mention it – it is best you should know. It is the wish of the people that you should marry one or the other of the Princes, that we may have more *aliis*. There are no other *Aliis* who they look to except Prince David or his brother, who would be eligible to the throne, or worthy of it and so they turn to these two *Aliis*, that there may be more *Aliis* to make the throne permanent, according to the Constitution. To you then depends the hope of the Nation and unfortunately we cannot always do what we like. In our position as Ruler, and which you will have to be some day, in somethings our course and actions will have to be guided by certain rules which could not be avoided."[8]

After commenting that she appreciated Kaiulani's candour and truthfulness in her letter with respect to Prince David, the Queen spoke of a potential marital match that had much more promise for Hawaii's protection from the United States:

> "I have to mention another matter, one which I think you ought to know, and I hope you will write again, at your earliest chance and inform me what your opinion is in this matter. When your Uncle the late King was living he made arrangements that you should be united to one of the Japanese Princes. He is the nephew to the Emperor of Japan. It seems that the young Prince was here on the [HIJMS] *Naniwa* on her first trip last year, but our own position was such that he could not present himself so I have not seen him. I understand now that the Prince is in England being educated, so you may meet him on your return [i.e., from Germany]. I do not know his name but should you meet him and think you could like him, I give you full leave to accept him, should he propose to you, and offer his hand and fortune.
>
> It would be a good alliance. They speak highly of his qualities, and now do not hesitate to open your heart to me. I shall be very glad if such an alliance could be consummated between you two – and I shall look forward for a letter from you with eagerness, saying it was agreeable to you & that you will encourage his suit."[9]

The Japanese Prince in question was Prince Higashifushimi Yorihito, who had earlier been known as Prince Yamashina Yorihito, when King Kalakaua met him on his world tour in 1881. Queen Liliuokalani was giving her niece two choices – marry the Japanese Prince, or marry Prince David. Of the two, the circumstances of the moment led to the Queen to press the suit of the Japanese Prince for without the strong backing of a foreign power the Queen feared the prospect of being permanently dethroned. The Queen's letter arrived in Kaiulani's hands while she was in Germany, and Kaiulani set it aside while she pursued courtship with German Army officers and aristocrats. She may have delved into flirtations in Germany precisely because of the knowledge that the head of her Royal House was pressing an arranged dynastic match upon her.

Kaiulani knew about the Japanese Prince, because the possibility of an arranged marriage for her had come up when Kaiulani was still a child, after King Kalakaua's return from his world tour. Now, as a young woman, she was just beginning to define herself as an adult, and the prospect of an arranged marriage produced anxiety in Kaiulani, and frustration that her choices in life might be so limited. Kaiulani plunged into the social whirl of the season in Wiesbaden, and deferred her response to her Queen. After returning to Great Britain from Germany, and with a new confidence in herself that was undoubtedly strengthened by her romantic conquests on the continent, she turned her mind to answering her aunt's five month old letter.

Writing from London at the end of June, Kaiulani told her aunt that she had tried to answer the Queen's letter several times but had not been able to do so until that present time. Now she answered the Queen frankly, telling her aunt:

> "I have thought over what you said in it about my marrying some Prince from Japan, unless it is absolutely necessary I would much rather not do so.

> I could have married an enormously rich German Count, but I could not care for him. I feel it would be wrong if I married a man I did not love, I should be perfectly unhappy, and we should not agree, and instead of being an example to the married women of today, I should become one like them, merely a woman of fashion and most likely a flirt."[10]

Kaiulani then sought to soften the blow she had just delivered by telling the Queen; "I hope I am not expressing myself too strongly, but I feel I must speak out to you, and there must be perfect confidence between you and me, dear Aunt."

Thus, did the young Princess declare her independence in matters of romance and marriage. She intended to marry for love, rather than for dynastic reasons. Being so far away from home and family she was able to take such a firm position with the head of her Royal House. Had she remained in Honolulu she would probably have found it much more difficult to deny the Queen's wishes.

Kaiulani spent the winter of 1894-95 on Jersey with Mrs. Rooke where she explored the Jersey landscape on a bicycle. It was while on Jersey that she learned of the abortive loyalist uprising in Hawaii and the subsequent arrest and show trials of the defeated monarchists. Both Prince David and Prince Kuhio were arrested along with about 200 other people, including the Queen herself, and Kaiulani feared for the members of her Royal House.

Prince David was quickly released but Prince Kuhio was convicted and sentenced to a term of imprisonment in the Oahu Prison, which was called *The Reef*. He was held in prison for one year before he was released. The first part of 1895 became a season of despair for Princess Kaiulani, with all of the members of the Royal Family in Hawaii held in custody by the Republic, with the exception of Dowager Queen Kapiolani, and her own father, Archibald Cleghorn.

Theo Davies kept watch on Kaiulani from afar and could not resist giving Kaiulani advice. It was good advice, particularly when he counselled her to stay away from politics and to send him any letters that raised such questions. However, Davies remained concerned that she did not share with him the identity of her friends in Great Britain, and to compensate he advised her to always use a chaperone as a form of reputation management; he thought Mrs. Rooke or Miss Whartoff would suffice in that regard.[11]

Once again, Kaiulani was invited to Ireland to summer with the Davies in 1895, and there were the usual rounds of tennis, picnics, and dances to occupy her time. She had now left Hawaiian politics and matters of state temporarily behind her. The annexationist regime in Honolulu was firmly in control, and the prospects for a restoration of the monarchy were now dimming noticeably.

On a much happier note, her father, Archibald Cleghorn, arrived in Ireland on August 10th at the Davies estate at Killaney, and father and daughter were at last reunited. They spent some time with the Davies and then Archibald Cleghorn took his daughter on a tour of his own ancestral nation of Scotland. After Scotland it was back to London briefly in November before they travelled to the French Riviera, where they would spend the winter of 1896, in the resort of Menton, not far from the Principality of Monaco.

In December, shortly before Christmas Day, Kaiulani wrote to her aunt in Honolulu. Liliuokalani had been released from her palace prison in September but she remained under house arrest at Washington Place. The Princess told her aunt that she and her father were generally enjoying good health, except that Kaiulani suffered greatly from headaches. As for the French Riviera:

"I am enjoying the change here very much, it is so very different to any place I have ever been in! We know some charming people named Kennedy, and they have been so very good to us. They have an at home every Thursday, some times they dance, but this generally depends on the set of people there, if they are young or not. The Empress of Austria is staying at the Cap Martin Hotel quite near us – She is a great walker, and goes for 5 hours at a stretch."[12]

Kaiulani and her father stayed at Menton through the winter of 1896, only departing in May for Paris. Kaiulani was now determined to stay away from Hawaii in its season of distemper. Her half-sister Rose had written to her complaining that the settler community had "defrauded and deceived" the indigenous Hawaiians. She told Kaiulani that she hated the settler community because they had stolen their country. She also warned Kaiulani that some of the once loyal settler families had now shifted their allegiance to the new republic, including the Atkinsons, the family of her childhood friend, May Atkinson.[13]

In Paris, in the spring of 1896, an unusual and fortunate bit of news reached Kaiulani. The Legislature of the Republic of Hawaii had decided to grant her the sum of $2000.00 per year, to defray her European expenses. She had not expected an olive branch from the annexationists, and coming only one year after the royalist uprising it was surprising, and suspicious, even though she sorely needed the money. Apparently, the appropriation of funds for her annuity was carried without opposition in the legislature of the Republic, and it represented a slight softening of the anti-monarchist sentiments of the annexationists.[14] Of course, the annexationists may have also calculated that it would be better if Princess Kaiulani stayed in Europe, since their annexation project continued to hang in the political balance in America, and they had seen how the Princess could influence American public opinion. In addition, the Princess continued to be very popular in Hawaii, especially among the indigenous Hawaiians, and now that Queen Liliuokalani had formally abdicated the throne following the abortive uprising of 1895, a monarchist restoration could conceivably see the popular young Princess seated on the Hawaiian throne. If the Democrats won the US presidency again in the 1896 US general election the annexationists might be compelled by the economic conditions to relinquish power to a government that could obtain a popular mandate. In that case, it was possible that the monarchy could be restored under Princess Kaiulani, and therefore it seemed prudent for the wiser among the annexationists to offer some amends to the Princess in her current exiled state.

Kaiulani and her father spent a quiet summer in 1896 at Rozel, on the island of Jersey. In the fall, Kaiulani celebrated her twenty-first birthday. She was fully an adult woman now, having surpassed the age of majority in Great Britain, the United States, and in Hawaii.[15] There was happy news of her family from Hawaii, where Prince Kuhio, now released from prison for his part in the 1895 loyalist uprising, had married Miss Elizabeth Kahanu Kaauwai, an *alii* maiden from Kauai, and Kaiulani wrote to offer her congratulations. Toward the end of the year Archibald Cleghorn and Kaiulani made plans to winter again at Menton on the French Riviera. Before going to the Riviera, they went to Scotland where they were the guests of Mr. Bailie Darsie of Fife, whose wife was descended from Tahitian royalty. There were other visits in Scotland and in England, and then they were back in London before travelling to France.

Sometime in her European sojourns, Kaiulani made a new acquaintance, the son of a British nobleman, Nevinson, de Courcy, familiarly called Toby by Kaiulani in the letters that she exchanged with him. He was several years older than Kaiulani, and the sort of man who was considered to be an ideal escort for ladies. He quickly became her friend, and her male confident. Her letters to him reflected a certain gossipy playfulness, and a freedom from social restraints that were never seen in her more formal letters to the Queen, or to her father.

In one 1896 letter, she commented on her health, saying that she has been "seedy" and her physician had diagnosed too much worry, for which he prescribed more rest. However, as she was happy to report, she was not prevented from going to dances! Nor, according to her letter, was she stopped from carrying on her flirtations! She warded off Toby's likely remonstrances by telling him "Don't be shocked and leave your lectures until we meet in Menton." She said that she and two other girlfriends were the "biggest flirts you could find" and that she had lots to confide to Toby when they next met, hinting that her father's recent trip to London allowed the young women to have "quite a time by ourselves."[16]

She wrote again to Toby from Rozel, Jersey, later in 1896, apologizing for not writing him sooner and thanking him for his birthday greetings to her, which brought to her mind another past birthday and that made her say to him that "I laughed very much when I thought of my other birthday – what fun we had that night."[17] Turning serious for a moment, she confided in Toby that:

"One of my young men came out to see me yesterday. I am supposed to be polishing him off. I can't make up my mind to do so just yet. I must have a little more fun as my flings are limited. I [want] to get as much amusement this winter as I possibly can. There is a possibility of my being married in April to a man I don't care very much for either way – rather a gloomy outlook — but "noblesse oblige". I must have been

384

born under an unlucky star, as I seem to have my life planned out for me in such a way that I cannot alter it – Do you blame me if I have my fling now – better now than afterwards. My engagement is a great secret – approved of by Mr. Davies and my Father – It is being kept secret for political reasons. Personally I think it wrong like this, as it is unfair to the men I meet now – especially if they take any interest in me."

This secret engagement has prompted much speculation in the years since Princess Kaiulani wrote to de Courcy. Her known correspondence does not contain any other references to this secret engagement, and there was certainly no subsequent public announcement of an engagement. It can be inferred that the secret engagement was afterwards broken, either by Kaiulani, or by her betrothed. Much of the speculation about her secret engagement has naturally focused on the identity of this secret fiancé, and why she would depart from her earlier insistence on marrying only for love.

Some biographers have suggested that she was secretly engaged to Prince David Kawananakoa. However, if that was true one would have expected Queen Liliuokalani to have acknowledged the engagement, at least privately, given that Liliuokalani was the head of the Hawaiian Royal House. Similarly, Dowager Queen Kapiolani might have been expected to write to her niece about it, since Queen Kapiolani was the *hanai* mother of Prince David. Furthermore, it is difficult to imagine the political reasons that would prevent such an announcement from being made. Hawaiians would have considered it quite natural for Princess Kaiulani and Prince David to wed, as that would have helped to perpetuate the royal *alii* line of descent. It seems unlikely therefore that Prince David, whom Kaiulani had not seen since her Washington trip in 1893, was the fiancé in this secret engagement.

Other candidates who have been suggested included both Clive Davies and his younger brother George Davies, both sons of Theo Davies. Princess Kaiulani undoubtedly owed a debt of gratitude to Theo Davies, who was both her legal guardian during her minority in England and afterwards her chief political advisor before, during, and subsequent to her Washington trip. If either Clive or George were put forward to her as a potential match Kaiulani might have considered that she had obligations to the Davies family, and those obligations might have outweighed the inclinations of her own heart. Her father, Archibald Cleghorn, would undoubtedly have approved a match with one of the Davies boys, as the wealth of the Davies family would have offered his daughter financial security for the rest of her life.

Furthermore, Cleghorn himself may have considered himself morally indebted to Theo Davies for guiding and protecting his daughter during her years of study and exile in Great Britain. And there would have been political reasons to delay the announcement of a match between Kaiulani and Clive, or George, Davies. The annexationists in Hawaii would have lost no time in pointing to the engagement of Princess Kaiulani and either Clive or George Davies as a further reason to suspect British intrigue, and they would have maintained that a restored monarchy would be subject to an undue degree of British influence, which would be detrimental to the American position in the islands.

But it is equally possible that the man to whom Kaiulani had become secretly engaged was someone else entirely. History has not shed any further light on this secret engagement. What is surprising is that only a few years before Kaiulani had been firm in telling Queen Liliuokalani that she would not marry for political reasons in the absence of love. Now, it seems she was prepared to do so, and perhaps also in circumstances where there were in fact political implications to a marriage. The mystery of the secret engagement revealed by her letter to Toby remains a mystery.

Throughout the winter of 1897 Kaiulani was often feeling unwell. Shortly after Kaiulani and her father arrived at Menton they learned that Queen Liliuokalani, having been freed from house arrest, and having had her civil liberties restored, was now in Washington where she was fighting for the restoration of the monarchy. The Queen sent a cable to Archibald Cleghorn requesting that Cleghorn and Kaiulani come to America and meet with her in Boston but Cleghorn demurred. Kaiulani was ill, and he wished to shield his daughter from allegations by the annexationists that the Queen and the Princess, together with Cleghorn, were engaging in new plots against the Republic.

Archibald Cleghorn's refusal to go to America with Princess Kaiulani renewed the old suspicions of the Queen about a design to supplant Liliuokalani with Kaiulani on the (now nonexistent) throne.[18] As a result, a temporary coolness arose briefly in the relations between aunt and niece. Kaiulani wrote to the Queen from Menton on March 24, 1897, complaining that she had not received any recent letters from the Queen; "I think there must really be something wrong with my letters, as I have already written to you three times during the past two months. I sent two to you in Boston and one in Washington."[19] But apparently, she had received a letter from the Queen's aide because in the same letter she said "I am so glad to hear through Capt. Palmer that you are so well and enjoying your stay abroad."[20]

The political future of the Hawaiian Islands was still unsettled. A settler-dominated government underpinned by a largely Caucasian electorate kept the annexationists in power in Honolulu while the majority of the population, indigenous as well as Asian, would almost certainly have opted for a return to the monarchy if they had been given a chance to express their political views at the ballot box. The annexationists had managed to hold on to power even in the face of a monarchist insurrection, despite a lack of support from the Cleveland Administration, which maintained a stiff correctness in US diplomatic relations with Hawaii. The coolness of the Cleveland Administration was manifested after President Dole and his government refused President Cleveland's directive to restore the constitutional government of the country in 1894. Now, however, a fresh breeze of change was blowing into Washington with the victory of the Republicans under William McKinley in the 1896 presidential election. With McKinley scheduled to move into the White House in March, 1897, there was a renewed confidence among the annexationists in Honolulu that their long-sought goal of American annexation was once more within reach.

At this time, late in the winter, a terrible family blow fell upon the Cleghorns in Europe. A letter from home told Kaiulani and her father that Kaiulani's half-sister, Annie, had died in Honolulu. It was a bitter loss for her father and for herself. Annie had travelled to Great Britain with Kaiulani in 1889, and had stayed with her for one year at Great Harrowden Hall to help Kaiulani settle into her new life at the boarding school, where they both been under the watchful eye of Mrs. Sharp. Annie, now the wife of Hay Wodehouse, the son of the longtime British Minister to Hawaii, had undergone a delicate operation but she was unable to survive it, and she had had passed away at the age of twenty-nine.[21]

In the spring Kaiulani and her father left the French Riviera for Paris. Shortly before leaving the Riviera Kaiulani wrote a brief letter to the Queen to give her the details about her forthcoming travel north to Paris, where she would stay for about three weeks if the weather held up. Kaiulani, was now quite experienced with European weather patterns, and she informed the Queen that April was generally an unfavourable month in France, owing to the strong cold winds. Unseasonable weather would be unlikely to help Kaiulani recruit her health, which she admitted to the Queen was not very good:

"I have had a touch of the grip[pe], it has left me with such a tired feeling which I don't like – One never knows what the Influenza does not leave behind it – I don't feel as strong as I ought to, and I fancy it is owing to my having had the Grip[pe] so often, 7 times since I have been abroad."[22]

While she was in Paris, Kaiulani was looking forward to attending an important annual social event in the French capital, the *Grande Bazaar de Charité*, which attracted the greater part of the fashionable set in Paris. On this occasion however, Kaiulani's uncertain health saved her life. On May 5th, the date set for the opening of the bazar, Kaiulani awoke with a severe migraine headache. A doctor was summoned and he advised that the Princess should remain in bed, and defer her trip to the *Grande Bazaar* to another date. The disappointed Princess remained in her hotel suite. Around 4 o'clock in the afternoon a great tragedy occurred when an intense fire broke out at the bazaar, trapping many people in the flames. The loss of life was appalling, and all of Paris was plunged into deep mourning. Many of the people who lost their lives were young women who were undertaking a charitable assignment, something that was expected of well-bred young women in the late nineteenth century. Kaiulani explained to the Queen:

"I have never heard of anything so fearful in my life. Nearly all the 117 victims were women, and young ones too. There is a count next door who has lost his two daughters, girls of 18 & 19. What strikes one so is its being in ones own station of life. The Smartest Society Women of Paris – The death of the Duchese d'Alencon throws the Austrian, Belgian & Bavarian Courts into mourning not counting the Orleans & King of Naples families. Just imagine all those people gone in less than half an hour, & the dreadful agony they must have suffered – I have never seen any place so overcome as the Gay City of Paris. You see all the people selling were connected with the highest aristocracy of France."[23]

Leaving tragedy behind, the Cleghorns returned to Great Britain for the summer. The early part of the summer they spent with the Davies family at their new estate, called Ravensdale, at Tunbridge Wells, in Kent County near London. There, Kaiulani wrote again to her confident, Toby de Courcy, telling him that her summer plans were to travel once again to the island of Jersey with a friend now that she was feeling much better. Her overall health continued to be delicate however, and the athletic young girl that used to surf the Hawaiian waves with abandon, and who had also been an expert equestrian, now appeared only in memory. She told Toby that on a recent day "I managed to get down for breakfast and stayed up fairly late in the evening having also played croquet during the afternoon when, on my way to bed, I again had one of my fainting fits. It showed me that I must be more careful, but all the same it is really very hard and . . . I hate posing as an invalid."[24]

Kaiulani was not looking forward to her forthcoming sojourn on Jersey. Where once she had relished with anticipation a stay in the

Channel Islands, now she now expected her visit there to be "very dull" but the reason soon became apparent. Her current young male interest was not available to her. She complained to Toby that "my particular amusement is in Woolwich for the summer . . . It is just my luck when I am well not to have anything on hand."[25]

How serious were Kaiulani's European romances? They remain a mystery. Her surviving correspondence does not contain any passionate love letters, so we cannot say whether any of her of relationships with the young men in her life went beyond an innocent friendship. In her letters, she refers to the men she socialized with as her 'young men,' or as her 'amusements.' She does seem to have preferred life on the continent however, with its more worldly perspectives, over the more strait-laced Victorian society of Great Britain. Her closest male friend, and her confident, remained Toby de Courcy who, despite their deep friendship, seems never to have been a romantic interest of Kaiulani's. As she approached her 22nd birthday in 1897, Kaiulani became more serious, and she declared to de Courcy that she was no longer a flirt: "I've quite got out of the way of flirting! I don't believe I could do it to save my skin. Now don't laugh!"[26]

Hawaiian politics continued to intrude into her life and she discussed the current political situation in her letters to Toby, suggesting that she might go over to America to call upon "my revered Aunt," but that everything was up in the air:

> "Things are extremely undecided. They talk of annexation, but whether they will get it is quite another thing. However, things are in a very bad way over there and I am now pretty certain that we shall never have back our own again.

391

I am really rather sorry the way the whole thing has finished up – much better [to] have a republic than to lose our nationality altogether – I am very sorry for my people and they will hate being taken over by another nation."[27]

Here, in a nutshell, was Kaiulani's own political analysis concerning the tragedy that had overtaken her country. While naturally she remained a committed monarchist, and she was always personally loyal to Queen Liliuokalani, her "revered Aunt," Kaiulani's own view now was that the monarchy was finished in Hawaii. "We shall never have back our own again" she wrote to Toby, but that was no longer important. What was important was the preservation of Hawaii's independence as a country. Kaiulani, as a Hawaiian patriot, might have accepted the republic if it had been committed to the continued independence of Hawaii. The indigenous Hawaiians, as she knew, would "hate being taken over by another nation," a sentiment that their young Princess fully shared.

The Republican party under President William McKinley was now in office, and the annexationist policy of the Harrison Administration was now back on the political agenda in Washington. In the American capital Queen Liliuokalani was mounting a final, futile, defence of her fallen throne. On June 16th President McKinley submitted a revised Hawaiian Annexation Treaty to the US Senate for ratification. There was immediate opposition to the treaty in the Senate however, and for the moment the future of Hawaii once again hung in the balance. For Kaiulani it was *deja vu* all over again. As in 1893, she greatly feared for the independence of Hawaii.

Theo Davies had gone out to the Hawaii to review his sugar interests in the islands, and Kaiulani was expecting a report on political affairs at home when he returned. She still relied on Davies as her principal political advisor concerning Hawaiian affairs, and she wondered, despite her own deep misgivings, whether he might advise her that now was the right time for her to return home at last. In the meantime Archibald Cleghorn and his daughter left Tunbridge Wells and wandered into Scotland, where they stayed again with Mr. and Mrs. Darsie, and afterwards visited with other Scottish friends. Then it was back once more to Jersey, where they could both retreat from the wider world.

Kaiulani despaired of Hawaii's future, especially with the country in the hands of the entrenched annexationists, and the pro-annexationist Republicans once again in power in Washington. Her love for the European lifestyle led her to imagine a life abroad, away from Hawaii, and yet Hawaii was her own country and part of her still longed to return. There was another matter as well. Archibald Cleghorn had been supporting his daughter's exile in Europe but that was costly, and the family's finances were in disorder. Archibald Cleghorn certainly felt financial pressure to return home. The fact that the Republic had finally allowed Queen Liliuokalani to leave the islands to press her case for redress in Washington in person showed that the political environment was now much less dangerous for the members of the Royal Family then it had been only a short time before. Father and daughter considered their options and decided that now was the time for the Princess to go home.

Kaiulani and her father returned to the mainland from Jersey to make a series of farewell visits with their friends in Great Britain in September, 1897. The Princess spent time with a family called the Somers, and then met up with her father to spend a few days with the Wodehouse family, the former British diplomatic representatives in Honolulu, and the parents of Hay Wodehouse, Archibald's son-in-law through his marriage to the late Annie Cleghorn. Of course there was also a farewell visit to the Davies family, Kaiulani's protectors in Europe and, in Theo Davies, her political advisor. Then her friend Lady Wiseman asked the Princess to come and spend a few days with her before leaving for home. After all the final visits were done there was still the need for Kaiulani to spend a few days on her own, packing for the long journey home.[28] Finally she was in Southampton, ready to begin her long-awaited, and long-deferred, homeward-bound journey. On October 9, 1897, Princess Kaiulani, began her journey home to Hawaii.

NOTES

[1] Although at eighteen Princess Kaiulani reached her majority for the purposes of ascending to the throne of Hawaii without a regency, as a private citizen she had remained a minor under the laws of Great Britain.

[2] McLaughlin-Stassen, 41

[3] Whartoff to Kaiulani, March 1, 1894, HSA; Stassen-McLaughlin, 47

[4] Stassen-McLaughlin, 42

[5] Davies to Kaiulani, April 30, 1894, HSA; Stassen McLaughlin, 42

[6] Zambucka, 93

[7] Kaiulani to Liliuokalani, June 22, 1894, HSA; Stassen-McLaughlin, 44

[8] Liliuokalani to Kaiulani, January 29, 1894, BMA

[9] Liliuokalani to Kaiulani, January 29, 1894, BMA

[10] Kaiunlani to Liliuokalani, June 22, 1894, BMA,

[11] Stassen-McLaughlin, 48

[12] Kaiulani to Liliuokalani, December, 1895, BMA. The Empress Elisabeth of Austria-Hungary, one of the great beauties of the age, was the consort of the Emperor Franz-Joseph. Suffering from depression following the suicide of her only son in a murder-suicide pact with his lover, the Empress spent the remainder of her life wandering aimlessly all over Europe, rarely returning to Vienna. The French Riviera was a favoured retreat for the Empress. In 1898, she was assassinated in Geneva, Switzerland, by an Italian anarchist.

[13] Stassen-McLaughlin, 48

[14] Webb & Webb, 133

[15] The traditional age of majority (i.e. adulthood) during this period was twenty-one.

[16] Kaiulani to Nevinson, de Courcy n.d. BMA

[17] Kaiulani to Nevinson, de Courcy n.d. (1896 presumed), BMA

[18] Julia Flynn Siler, *Lost Kingdom, Hawaii's Last Queen, the Sugar Kings, and America's First Imperial Adventure*, Atlantic Monthly Press, New York, 2012, 277

[19] Kaiulani to Liliuokalani, March 24, 1897, BMA

[20] Captain Palmer was Queen Liliuokalani's secretary during her 1897 mission to the United States.

[21] *Died Early This Morning, Mrs. Hay Wodehouse Passes Away After Brief Illness*, The Hawaiian Star, Honolulu, Hawaii, March 6, 1897, 1

[22] Kaiulani to Liliuokalani, March 24, 1897, BMA

[23] Kaiulani to Liliukalani, May 9, 1897, BMA

[24] Kaiulani to Nevinson, de Courcy, July 4, 1897, BMA

[25] Kaiulani to Nevinson, de Courcy, July 4, 1897, BMA

[26] Kaiulani to Nevinson, de Courcy, July 4, 1897, BMA

[27] Kaiulani to Nevinson, de Courcy, July 4, 1897, BMA

[28] Zambucka, 107

14

The Return of a Lost Princess

As Princess Kaiulani prepared to leave Europe for home word spread of the fabled Princess' forthcoming return to the United States. In September, the New York Tribune told its readers; "The Princess Kaiulani of Hawaii, who visited this country in 1893, and whose pleasing personality made a favorable impression on all who met her at that time, has been in Europe since then, and will return to this country in a week or two. In view of the fact that affairs in Hawaii are attracting much attention, and that the Queen of that country keeps herself before the public the movement of the young princess will be watched with close attention."[1]

On October 9, 1897, the American Line's fast transatlantic liner, SS *Paris*, departed Southampton, England bearing within it the young woman who was once the hope of the Hawaiian monarchy. Now she was going home to an uncertain welcome, and an unplanned life. When the ship arrived in New York she was met by reporters but she refused to be drawn into any political discussions concerning Hawaii. Later, arriving at the Albermarle Hotel with her father and her maid, she discovered Captain Julius Palmer, Queen Liliuokalani's aide-de-camp awaiting her. Palmer was a retired Massachusetts sea captain who had known Liliuokalani many years before in Honolulu, and who was now acting as her private secretary during her visit to the United States. Captain Palmer conveyed the Queen's greetings and letters, and invited Kaiulani's party to meet the Queen in Washington. After a short stay in New York, which was all agog over a young female Cuban assassin whose efforts to overthrow the rule of Spain in the Caribbean was being eagerly promoted by the American yellow press, Kaiulani and her party departed for Washington. In New York, Archibald Cleghorn and Captain Palmer had both denied that there would be any political significance in the visit of the Princess to the United States but the press nevertheless kept close tabs on the Princess throughout her American visit. The meeting of the Princess with her aunt was fraught with both family and political ramifications. Within the Royal Family of Hawaii, the dethroned monarch and her exiled Heiress Apparent would come face to face once again, and Kaiulani would have to reassure her aunt of her loyalty, despite the many things that had been said on Kaiulani's behalf concerning her suitability, or her willingness, to take her aunt's vacant place on the throne of Hawaii.

By all accounts the meeting of Queen Liliuokalani and Princess Kaiulani at Ebbitt House, in Washington, went well. The Queen was undoubtedly impressed by the graceful and mature young woman who now curtseyed before her, and whom she quickly embraced as her long-absent niece. Their meeting was friendly but there was a small degree of uncertainty. Kaiulani, in choosing to return home to Hawaii before the future of the country had been finally decided had neither sought, nor received, the blessing of her aunt as the head of the Royal House to return home. If the Queen, in some small measure, considered that to be bad form she nevertheless warmly welcomed her niece.

The Queen was in Washington making a last ditch stand against the annexation of Hawaii and the loss of her throne to the annexationists. As part of this final struggle the Queen was working on her memoirs through which she hoped to correct the aspersions against her character that several years of annexationist propaganda had striven to fix upon her public reputation.

Kaiulani did not remain long in Washington. A single meeting with the Queen would not be enough to wipe away all of the suspicions in the mind of the Queen. That would take time. Sadly, the Princess was returning home now because she believed, as she had written to tell her friend Toby de Courcy, that the Royal Family would never again sit upon the throne of the Kamehamehas. The Queen, however, had still not lost all hope for her redemption, and for the restoration of the Hawaiian world that she had known almost all of her life. Nor was this 1893, when Kaiulani had struck a blow against the annexationists in Washington simply by being, as Theo Davies had once written, "your own well-beloved self." With the Republicans in charge in Washington again there was little sympathy for the Hawaiian monarchist cause in Washington. The annexation of Hawaii was favoured by the McKinley Administration. After a brief stay of only a couple of days the Princess and her small party boarded a westbound train for their journey to San Francisco.

In San Francisco, while awaiting passage to Honolulu, the Princess gave a substantial interview to the *San Francisco Call*, and its reporter, Miriam Michelson. Ms. Michelson was quite taken by the Princess, telling her readers:

". . . she is beautiful. This royal Hawaiian girl needs not the exaggeration of newspaper gallantry. Of all her portraits there is none that does justice to her expressive, small, proud face. She is exquisitely slender and graceful, quite tall and holds herself like a – like a Princess and like a Hawaiian. I know no simile more descriptive of grace and dignity than this last. . . . She was dressed in a close-fitting black tailor-made gown, braided in black. At her throat, peeping from the top of a high collar, and at her wrist black chiffon was pleated softly. She wore but one ring, a very simple one. Her very pretty black hat flared not too much and was relieved by puffs of white chiffon. Her clothes said Paris. Her accent said London. Her figure said New York. Her heart said Hawaii."[2]

In the interview Kaiulani took interest in the fact that her interviewer had recently visited Hawaii and that led Kaiulani to speak about the beauty of her country, and her love for it. "Aren't the islands lovely?" the Princess asked Michelson. "I really ought not praise my own country,' said Kaiulani [but] 'I have never seen any place more beautiful than the islands. And aren't the people hospitable and kindly – the Hawaiians?"

"People do not know Hawaii,' said the Princess later. 'They do not realize how beautiful the islands are. You would be surprised at the ignorance of people I have met about them. Why, they would hardly believe me when I said that we had electric lights there." Perceiving, perhaps, a special future for her country, Kaiulani said "it would make a delightful pleasure place – a winter resort."[3]

Kaiulani was asked about her sojourn in Europe and she replied that she liked Germany the best, and the people there, although she said that Switzerland was the most beautiful.[4] She admitted that she was interested in the women of Russia, "The Russian women are fascinating. If I were not myself, I should choose to be a Russian woman. They are charming."

Her education in languages had helped her navigate her way around Europe. In addition to her native Hawaiian, Kaiulani spoke English, French, and German, although she admitted that her German wasn't perfect and that she had profited in her study of French by employing French maids in Europe. Although she clearly enjoyed living in Europe, Hawaii still called to her.

Asked by Michelson about her voyage home, the Princess said:

"I'm anxious to get home, to be home,' she said with a sigh. 'Of course, I've taken a house here and there,' – the 'I' sounded odd from the young girl 'but it wasn't like being in one's own place. I'm tired now. I've been living in my boxes for years past. I enjoy travelling very, very much. But I want to get unpacked now. I want to settle down and rest."

When Michelson expressed envy of Kaiulani's forthcoming passage home the Princess, with a greater understanding of what awaited her at home, replied with a sad smile; "I don't know that I am a person to be envied."

The Princess could not wholly escape the subject of politics and in her conversation with Michelson the subject turned naturally to Queen Liliuokalani, and the great blows that she had suffered since 1893. Of her aunt, Kaiulani said; "Even the enemies of my aunt, of the Queen, will tell you that all through her suffering, all through her hard treatment, she conducted herself with the utmost dignity. And she felt the indignities, she felt the insults –l know it, for I felt them for her."

Kaiulani clearly impressed Michelson, who, in summing up her interviewee told her readers that:

> "She has been made a woman of the world early by the life she has led. She is or rather she will be, a woman of strong character. She has been well fitted to play a leading role, and the knowledge of her ability and of her accomplishments makes one wish that there might be in store a future worthy of her."

The American reporter also seemed to glimpse something of what might have been – a modern queen for a precocious nation:

> "Looking at her then I thought to myself, if Kaiulani had been the aunt instead of the niece there would have been no Republic of Hawaii to ask for annexation."

At San Francisco, Princess Kaiulani and her party boarded the Ocean Company's sail-assisted steamer SS *Australia* for the final leg of her journey home. On November 9, 1897, Hawaii, her *Hawaii Nei*, came into view and, as the ship approached the dock in Honolulu, thousands of people crowded together to bear witness to the return of a much-loved daughter of the islands. For a half-hour after the ship docked, the Princess remained on board to receive special friends, including Prince David, and her friend from the Big Island, Eva Parker. Thrusting her way through the throngs of well-wishers she entered a landau bedecked with flowers for the four-mile journey to Waikiki and her Ainahau estate. Hawaiians greeted her all along the way until, at last, there it was, the entrance to her home. But what a home! Gone was the house of her childhood with both its happy and its bitter memories. In its place was a new grand home fit for a Princess of the realm. Her new house, built by her father when all had seemed as it should be, and her return from Great Britain as the heiress to the throne was expected, was a large two-storey white frame house that boasted a large lanai all the way across the front of the house, and an interior fitted with polished woods.[5] Inside there was a great room suitable for royal receptions and beyond it a screened sitting room fitted with blinds. Upstairs a suite had been built for her with both a boudoir and a dressing room off of the main chamber."[6]

The grounds of the estate were equally magnificent. A visitor to the estate in the early nineties, when the new house was almost finished gave a good description of it:

"Mr. Cleghorn's place was one of the most beautiful in the Islands. The spacious grounds were ordinarily closed to visitors, with 'Kapu' ('No Admittance') over the gate at the entrance. The new house was a white frame structure, of two storeys, with wings at either end – the favourite form of Honolulu architecture – with a wide verandah extending across the front. The shrubbery had been cut away for several yards in every direction to allow the free circulation of the air, and just beyond the main entrance stood the one incomparable banyan tree, which the owner presently informed me was the handsomest thing he had. He was not visible when we arrived, and I was helped from the carriage and sat down upon the carpenter's chest among the chips and shavings while a Chinese servant went in search of him. After a short interval he came – a tall, handsome man, erect as a field marshal, as dignified as a Spanish grandee, and altogether an impressive figure, with his keen black eyes, white beard and hair. He had been out amongst his flowers, he explained, and in proof of this he dropped a pair of pruning-shears into the pocket of his loose alpaca coat. It was not every day that one met the parent of royalty so occupied.

'The house is nearly completed,' he said, looking up at the closed windows with a wistful expression. 'I built it for the Princess, and expected to have it all in readiness, and now this overturn has come.'

403

It was a little difficult to reply to this remark. I could not assure him of any honest belief in the re-establishment of Hawaiian royalty, which I did not think would ever be accomplished. So I gently turned the conversation upon other and impersonal subjects, and told him how glad I was to see a banyan tree, and one so beautiful as the fine specimen which he had raised. This evidently gratified him, and after pointing out its various beauties he invited me to come into the house. The key was brought, and I was shown into the hall, then into the grand drawing-room, where the young heir-apparent would have held informal receptions. It was a stately apartment, probably forty feet in length and thirty feet in width, with many windows looking out upon the velvet lawn. The panelling was in beautiful native woods highly polished, and the decorative tiles in the corridor had been brought from Chicago. At one end there was a large room enclosed with Venetian blinds on two sides, the windows extending from floor to ceiling, and being provided with wire screens. This was the 'mosquito-room,' in which the Princess and the English companion whom she was to have brought back with her had expected to sit and sew, read and talk. Much was made of the screens, so universal in the United States, but which, strangely enough, were not in ordinary use in that mosquito-ridden land. On the upper floor I was shown the Princess's private suite, the bedchamber corresponding to the drawing-room below, with a boudoir at one end and a dressing-room at the other. The Hawaiian coronet, and the *kahili*, the ancient symbol of Hawaiian royalty, recurred at intervals in the decorations of the ceiling."[7]

A later portrayal of Ainahau in the magazine *Paradise of the Pacific* also gives an indication of how the estate may have appeared to Kaiulani upon her return:

"The residence faces the blue Pacific and makes a graceful setting in a spacious area of highly cultivated ground. Ten acres of land are, for the most part, covered with tropical trees, shrubs and vines, the varieties of which, almost bewildering, form a veritable botanical garden . .

. A long avenue bordered by date palms and many plants leads from the gateway to the residence . . . Directly in front of the [lanai], compelling the attention of every visitor, is a majestic banyan tree, 30 years old, and the parent of all the noted trees of its species in the city. With its great cluster of central trunks, enormous branches and abundant foliage, it is the king of trees in this park, and unless destroyed by the woodman, will long outlive every other form of vegetable growth in the demesne . . . Mr Cleghorn cultivates eight kinds of mango trees . . . The teak is an interesting tree that thrives here . . . Two or three of the spice family are represented, the important one being the cinnamon. Several Washingtonia palms are here, towering almost as high as the cocoanuts. The latter are scattered everywhere, [300] of them having been planted when Princess Kaiulani was born . . . A soap tree, indigenous to China, . . . is one of the novelties, and an Indian tree bearing red flowers like tiger claws is another. Rubber trees thrive like lantana bushes in the open waste. Camphor is also in a healthy state of development, Monterey cypresses and . . . 14 varieties of hibiscus . . . two varieties of the Hawaiian kamani tree . . . and a sago palm."[8]

In the yard peafowl still roamed, Kaiulani's much remembered birds that subsequently gave to her the sobriquet, 'The Princess of the Peacocks.' And then, farther out, her much loved and dearly missed pony, Fairy, to whom she was now reunited at last. Fairy was much older – eighteen to be precise but was still game for riding and was now suited for a less willful, less daring, and more mature mistress. But before she did anything else Kaiulani ventured out to Nuuanu Valley, the site of Mauna Ala, the Royal Mausoleum, where her beloved mother lay in her final resting place, joined now by her mother's brother and Kaiulani's dearly missed *Papa Moi,* and uncle, King Kalakaua. Then she went and visited her aunt, the Dowager Queen Kapiolani who lived in Waikiki with Prince David and Prince Kuhio, and she met Kuhio's new wife Princess Elizabeth.

A steady stream of well-wishers now made their way to Ainahau, both indigenous Hawaiians as well as *haoles*, to pay their respects to Hawaii's Princess. The throne might be gone but the high regard of the people for their *alii*, and for the Princess who was once the Hope of the Nation, remained. Kaiulani made an effort to greet everyone who came to see her and soon she entered back into the social swirl of Honolulu. Much had changed during her absence of eight years but much remained as she remembered it. And her people remembered her.

When she attended a bicycle race shortly after arriving home her appearance caused the crowd to spontaneously stand and sing *Hawaii Ponoi*, the national anthem of Hawaii. The annexationist government that ruled the Hawaiian Republic could only watch and glower at such patriotic displays. But for the most part, the officials of the Republic left her alone. She was under no restrictions, although the main proponents of the annexation movement remained unfriendly towards her. In a letter to the Queen she wrote that the only wives of government officials who were nice to her were Mrs. Dole, the wife of the President, and Mrs. Damon, the wife of Samuel Damon, the Republic's Minister of Finance:

> "The people of the Gov't. are not particularly nice to me except Mrs. Damon & Mrs. Dole – I think they are very sorry to see me here, especially as I give them so little cause to complain. Thank God, Annexation is not a fact . . ."[9]

Politics still followed Princess Kaiulani of course, although she did her best to avoid the subject. Dowager Queen Kapiolani helped Kaiulani to put the current state of affairs in Hawaii into perspective. Kapiolani told her niece that she saw little prospect for the continued independence of Hawaii, though she acknowledged that Liliuokalani still hoped for it. In Kapiolani's view, the annexationists were determined men who had risked everything to achieve their purpose and they would not let it go until their objective had been reached. The fate of the country was now a matter left in the hands of God, according to the old Queen. Kaiulani saw wisdom in that approach, as it tracked her own view of the situation. So she put the Crown behind her, and became Miss Kaiulani Cleghorn.

After Kaiulani returned to Honolulu, a letter came for her from the Queen in Washington. Disappointingly, the Queen still saw Kaiulani as a rival candidate for the Hawaiian throne, should it be restored. Liliuokalani wrote on October 26, 1897, to Kaiulani to say that she had been informed that the leaders of the Republic would offer the throne of Hawaii to Kaiulani if the annexation project failed. However, the Queen cautioned her that if she accepted the throne Kaiulani would only be a figurehead, and all power would continue to rest with those who had seized the Kingdom from Liliuokalani in 1893. While her aunt left the prospect of whether to become a figurehead monarch to Kaiulani's own good judgment, she warned her niece that accepting such a proposal would dishearten the loyal people of Hawaii, and Kaiulani would be reviled. Therefore, Liliuokalani counselled her niece not to accept the proposition that might be offered by the annexationists but rather to let the Republic fail, and then let the people decide on the question of a restoration, and on who then should sit on the throne of Hawaii.

Although some loyalist statesman had suggested to Liliuokalani that she should yield to a future candidacy by Kaiulani for the throne, the ex-Queen felt that it was a matter for the people to decide. The Queen told her niece that she thought both Theo Davies and Colonel George Macfarlane were aware of the possibility that Kaiulani would

407

be offered the throne, and that both of them were in favour of it. She also suggested that Kaiulani should discuss the Queen's letter with her father.[10]

Distress was the emotion that must have surged through Kaiulani when she read the Queen's letter, which was dated so soon after their meeting in Washington. Far from allaying the Queen's suspicions Kaiulani's meeting with the Queen in Washington had seemed only to have enhanced them when the deposed Queen saw the young and graceful woman who could have succeeded her on the throne. Kaiulani knew that those who had seized power in Honolulu with the connivance of the United States would never willingly surrender their power and there was no force in Hawaii that could compel them to surrender it. For Kaiulani, the days of the monarchy had receded into the past and she had reconciled herself to a non-royal future. It was both sad and distressing to see that her aunt still clung to forlorn hopes, and that she still saw Kaiulani as a potential rival.

Perhaps it was too much for Kaiulani to respond directly to the Queen's appeal. She asked her political mentor and advisor, Theo Davies to respond appropriately to Her Majesty on her behalf. The Queen's letter apparently came as a surprise to Theo Davies as well. In November, 1897, Davies wrote to the Queen in Washington to reassure her. Davies told her that no one associated with annexationists, or anyone else for that matter, had ever approached him with the proposition that Kaiulani should claim the throne of Hawaii. He informed the Queen that he was certain that Kaiulani would never accept the throne if it was to be offered to her unless Queen Liliuokalani granted her consent, and only if Kaiulani's assumption of the throne was endorsed by both indigenous Hawaiians, and the settler community.[11]

As for local politics, the only overt political action that Kaiulani took after returning to Honolulu was to attend a great luau where funds were raised for indigenous Hawaiian commissioners to proceed to Washington to assist the Queen and others in fighting the annexation project.[12] Otherwise she lived quietly at Ainahau, although she continued to attend some social events.

The growing Americanization in Hawaiian society, was of great concern to Kaiulani:

> "The people here are not half so happy as when I first came back. I find everything so much changed & more especially among the rising generation of Hawaiians and half Whites. I think it is a great pity as they are trying to ape the foreigners and they do not succeed."[13]

One aspect of Americanization in the islands that she definitely did not appreciate was the American tradition of the ambulance-chasing lawyer. Kaiulani complained to Liliuokalani that a *haole* solicitor had shown up at the Dowager Queen's residence and told Prince David "that he had come especially that she [Dowager Queen Kapiolani] might make her will & die comfortable." Kaiulani continued "Did you ever hear such impertinence[?] He also brought her some cake, but as he did not see her, he took it home with him! I admire the *haole* way of making a present to anyone."[14]

Princess Kaiulani was the most prominent young female in Hawaii, and that led to much popular speculation about her romantic life. When she attended social events, Kaiulani was often escorted by Prince David and rumours abounded of a romance between the royal pair. Prince David, ten years older than Kaiulani, was a handsome and debonair fixture in Honolulu society, and being also of royal blood the rumours of a match between the two of them continued unabated.

Although Queen Liliuokalani would have welcomed a match between Kaiulani and David Kawananakoa, Archibald Cleghorn voiced his disapproval. Handsome Prince David had too many female admirers, and too many romantic conquests, for Cleghorn to think that he would easily lead a settled married life with his daughter. And Kaiulani herself held fidelity in marriage to be important, telling Queen Liliuokalani of her first impression of Prince Kuhio's bride that "I find Kuhio's Wife an extremely Nice woman and am sure she will make him a good & faithful wife."[15]

Kaiulani was also romantically linked to other men in Honolulu, most prominently to an actor and journalist named Andrew Adams, who actually courted Kaiulani, and who was a particular favourite of Archibald Cleghorn. Adams seems to have been in love with Kaiulani but how deeply she felt about him is unclear. Soon he left his journalism post for a managerial job on a sugar plantation near Ewa, and he was seen less frequently with her. Another American, Captain Putnam Bradlee Strong, the son of a former Mayor of New York who passed through Honolulu was also suggested as a possible beau for Kaiulani, as was George Davies, the younger son of Theo Davies. Clive Davies, who had been once linked to Kaiulani as a prospective suitor, was now engaged to an English woman. But Kaiulani never gave her heart away to anyone, so far as is known, and those close to her denied all romantic rumours.

An important personal issue plaguing Kaiulani was her health. The years abroad had not been kind to Kaiulani's physical constitution, and she was now in delicate health. Outwardly, she appeared healthy but inside she knew she was not. When she gave an interview to the *San Francisco Call* on her journey home in 1897, she told Ms. Michelson, the reporter, much to the latter's surprise. "But I have been ill – quite ill. Even father didn't know how ill I was."[16] Anxiety over the fate of her country, and of her own fate, as well as the tolls of the vagabond existence she had lived in Europe had all conspired against the health of a delicate young woman. Returning home to Hawaii had not brought her any relief. After eight years away she found it hard to readjust to the Hawaiian climate and she wrote to Queen Liliuokalani, "I find letter writing such a tax to my head here – I wonder why that is. I don't feel the least bit settled."[17]

Kaiulani's was grateful to be home again, with the opportunity to once again enjoy the ocean, telling her aunt:

> "About ten days ago Stella Rockett, Helen Parker & I went over to your [Waikiki] place & took a bath. The water was perfectly lovely. I have had only one dip in the Sea so far, as my bathing suits have not arrived yet. We went in by moonlight in night gowns when no one was around."[18]

As she moved back into her life in Hawaii in the early part of 1898, Kaiulani began to take the reins at Ainahau as the mistress of her stately home. On February 2, 1898, Kaiulani hosted a farewell dinner at Ainahau for Clive Davies, who was returning to England to marry Edith Fox. Had there once been a secret engagement between Clive and Kaiulani? Did they share a laugh over memories of those rumours – rumours that had even found their way into the press? If there had indeed been a secret engagement between them at one time, did the knowledge of that secret add an extra layer of intimacy to the party? On yet another occasion, Kaiulani hosted a luau for

411

Prince David to celebrate his 30th birthday, with at least 200 people in attendance.

On February 15th, Theo Davies held a card party at his Honolulu residence for Kaiulani before he too sailed home with the remainder of his family for his son Clive's wedding. Davies now recognized that his efforts on Kaiulani's behalf to restore the Hawaiian monarchy and sustain Hawaiian independence had failed, and on March 1st Davies released an open letter to the people of Hawaii in which he acknowledged that his efforts to restore the monarchy had failed and that he now thought that it might be better for the indigenous Hawaiians to support US annexation because their voting rights under the laws of the United States would likely be far greater than they were under the Republic of Hawaii. Davies departed Hawaii, never to return.

Kaiulani was now a woman of stature on Oahu, a respected *alii*, a former Princess of the realm, and still a Princess in the hearts of the indigenous community. To the settler community she was a well-bred young Victorian lady. Her physical beauty, winsome personality, and evident social skills were often remarked upon, and the other women in the community took note of her. Here was a future leader of Hawaiian society, and those thoughtful women who were pillars of the settler community decided to extend an olive branch to former Hawaiian royalty. Kaiulani was invited to become the Second Vice President of the Hawaiian Red Cross Society, a position that she accepted. It was the first of what could well have become many appointments in the charitable and social fields, all of which were open to nineteenth century women of ability and social position in the Victorian age.

As Kaiulani completed her reintroduction to Hawaiian society as indigenous royalty, and as a woman of consequence, an ominous development far away portended a great change, although many in Hawaii could not then conceive how important that development would be, and how fast change would now come to their island world. On February 15, 1898, the same day that Theo Davies held his card party in honour of Kaiulani to thank her for hosting a farewell dinner for his son, a major American warship, the USS *Maine*, suddenly blew up and sank with a heavy loss of life while it lay at anchor in the harbor at Havana, in the troubled Spanish colony of Cuba.

NOTES

[1] *Princess Kaiulani Coming* New-York tribune, September 12, 1897, Page 19, Image43, https://chroniclingamerica.loc.gov/data/batches/dlc_lotus_ver01/data/sn83030214/00175039144/1897091201/0207.pdf [accessed August, 2020]

[2] Marion Michelson, *The Flower of Hawaii* in The San Francisco Call, October 31, 1897, Page 29, Image 29, https://chroniclingamerica.loc.gov/lccn/sn85066387/1897-10-31/ed-1/ [accessed August 4, 2020]

[3] During this interview both Kaiulani and an unnamed young Hawaiian woman who was attending her said that in the past they

had both been asked by Americans if they wore clothes when they were in Hawaii!

[4] It is not certain when Kaiulani visited Switzerland but it is possible that she did so during her long sojourn in Germany in 1893-94.

[5] Cohen, 18

[6] Webb & Webb, 155

[7] Mary H Krout, *Hawaii and a Revolution, The Personal Experiences of a Newspaper Correspondent in the Sandwich Islands During the Crisis of 1893 and Subsequently*, London, John Murray, 1898, 102

[8] Quoted in Woodrum, 6

[9] Kaiulani to Liliuokalani, January 5, 1898, BMA

[10] Zambucka, 113

[11] Linnéa, 182; Zambucka, 114

[12] Webb & Webb, 162

[13] Kaiulani to Liliuokalani, January 5, 1898, BMA

[14] Kaiulani to Liliuokalani, January 5, 1898, BMA

[15] Kaiulani to Liliuokalani, January 5, 1898, BMA

[16] Marion Michelson, *The Flower of Hawaii* in The San Francisco Call, October 31, 1897.

[17] Kaiulani to Liliuokalani, January 5, 1898, BMA

[18] Kaiulani to Liliuokalani, January 5, 1898, BMA

The Rent in the Fabric of the World

Grover Cleveland was the only United States president to serve two non-consecutive presidential terms. His unprecedented re-emergence in Washington in 1893, interrupted a historical transformation that had begun under President Benjamin Harrison. Cleveland represented an older tradition in American politics, one that maintained that America's republican purpose in the New World was to advance non-interference in the affairs of other countries, and to protect the independent states of the Americas from European imperialism. It was a political philosophy that could be traced back to President James Monroe and his articulation of the Monroe Doctrine to protect the new states of Latin America from European colonialism, and to the Tyler Doctrine, articulated by President John Tyler, which purported to do the same for Hawaii. Perhaps the antecedents of that philosophy can be seen in George Washington's Farewell Address to the officers and men of the Continental Army; "Give to mankind the magnanimous and too novel example of a people always guided by an exalted justice and benevolence. . ."

Of course, the United States had often fallen short of its aspirations but it had noble aspirations, unlike many of the European states whose foreign policies served only their own aggrandizement. Until the Hawaiian annexation debate the United States had maintained an exceptionalism in foreign relations that set it apart from the imperialism of the other major powers in the world. But as the country emerged into the 1890's new historical forces were working to change the underlying political philosophy of the United States, especially in regard to its attitude toward the acquisition of foreign lands.

In 1890, the US Census Bureau declared that the American western frontier was closed. That meant that the existence of wild lands west of the settled part of the United States had ceased to exist for the first time since settlers had arrived from England in the 1600's. There were no more untamed lands within the continental borders of the United States that awaited incorporation into a settled America. The declaration of the Census Bureau was a psychological challenge to a country that had always extolled the virtues of the wild frontier, and saw the tension between civilization and frontier as the mainspring in the development of the unique American character. The frontier had always loomed large in the American imagination. Now that the frontier was closed, what would replace it? Historians, such as Frederick Jackson Turner, questioned whether American dynamism, and the remarkable political culture of the United States, would now be compromised by the lack of tension between a settled America and a wilderness frontier.[1]

For some Americans, the answer was obvious. The United States, they surmised, should follow the path taken by European powers and acquire an external empire. Canada was a tempting acquisition because it bordered the United States but an earlier attempt to acquire it in the War of 1812 had failed, and Canada had remained part of the British Empire. There was also Mexico, in the south, but the United States had swallowed almost forty per cent of Mexico's territory in the 1840's, and any further encroachment would bring large numbers of Spanish-speaking Roman Catholics into the United States, which it was thought would present difficult issues of cultural absorption.

A consensus began to build that American expansion would have to occur beyond the land boundaries of North America. The Harrison Administration had already taken the first steps toward a powerful expansionist policy by embarking upon the creation of a new blue water fleet that could project American power abroad. Now, the Harrison Administration proposed the annexation of Hawaii, a policy that found favour with an expansionist lobby that brought together opinion shapers in the fields of government, the military, and journalism. Men such as Captain Alfred Thayer Mahan, the preeminent American naval strategist, and Commodore George Dewey, who would command the US Asiatic Squadron in the Spanish American War held such views, as did Commander Charles Davis, the Chief of Naval Intelligence, and politicians such as Senator Henry Cabot Lodge, Senator William E Chandler, a former Secretary of the Navy, Senator William P Frye, Senator J Donald Cameron, Judge William H. Taft, a future US President, newspaper editor Charles Dana, and John Hay, the US Ambassador to Great Britain and a future US Secretary of State. Perhaps the expansionist who loomed largest above them all was an American political force of nature, Theodore Roosevelt.

Already marked as a rising star in the Republican Party Roosevelt watched Harrison begin the laying down of a blue water fleet of battleships and cruisers and he welcomed the proposals of the Hawaiian white settler community's annexation commissioners. The return of Grover Cleveland brought new resistance to American expansionism however, and Roosevelt was appalled that Cleveland refused to annex Hawaii because of his concern for the moral dimension in the US response to the Hawaiian situation.

For Roosevelt the conceptual framework of imperialism, jingoism, nationalism, and even chauvinism merged into a philosophy that he called Americanism. In his writings he promoted the beneficial advance of the Anglo-Saxon civilization, although he acknowledged that individuals from racial minorities could rise above their station through merit. As for the foreign lands beyond the US borders Roosevelt believed that the territories inhabited by the indigenous should accrue to the dominant races of the world.[2] Roosevelt was upset by the recalcitrant spirit of American public men toward American expansion abroad, and he advocated for the annexation of the Hawaiian Islands.

Moral questions had prevented Cleveland from consummating Hawaiian annexation in 1893. President McKinley and his new Administration that entered office in 1897, came with a new American perspective, one which spoke in the diplomatic language of expansionism and was easily compatible with the imperial aggrandizement practised by the European powers.

As the new Assistant Secretary of the Navy, Theodore Roosevelt was quite certain what should be done about Hawaii. He said that he would take the islands with a naval force and leave the details for later.[3] He was among the expansionists who persuaded McKinley to send a revised Hawaiian Annexation Treaty to the US Senate for ratification on June 16, 1897.

Queen Liliuokalani had arrived in Washington in the dying days of the Cleveland Administration and she had been received by the President and the First Lady although, as a lame duck President, Cleveland no longer had the power to influence Hawaiian events in Liliuokalani's favour. Once the McKinley Administration took office Liliuokalani had no influence at all within the new Republican administration. She prepared and published her memoirs under the title *Hawaii's Story by Hawaii's Queen*. In her memoirs she presented her case to the American and Hawaiian public. Although portions of it angered her political opponents in Honolulu, her memoirs did help considerably to restore the Queen's public reputation, which had been savaged in the American press by the proponents of Hawaiian annexation.

When McKinley sent the Annexation Treaty to the Senate for ratification Queen Liliuokalani lost not time in filing a protest with the State Department. The Queen's visit to the United States had some effect on public opinion, and it bolstered the anti-expansionism cause in the United States.[4] To counter it, Lorrin Thurston, A S Hartwell, and the Hawaiian Attorney General, W O Smith, journeyed to Washington for McKinleys inauguration, and to promote their cause.[5]

The Republic of Hawaii also issued a set of six Official stamps for use in the Department of Foreign Affairs, each featuring a portrait of Lorrin Thurston, the political architect of the Hawaiian annexation project. The purpose of the stamp issuance was to reinforce the message that the Republic of Hawaii remained fully committed to

US annexation. The new, but aged, and infirm Secretary of State, John Sherman, told the Hawaiian Minister to the United States, Francis M Hatch, that he was opposed to American imperialism, and against Hawaiian annexation, but that he might favour an American protectorate over the islands.[6]

In Hawaii the American Minister, Harold Sewall, expressed concern to Washington about the continued popularity of Princess Kaiulani. All classes of Hawaiian residents held a positive view of the Princess, he reported, and even some government officials were friendly towards her. If the vote on the annexation treaty was lost in the US Senate Sewall suggested there might be a possible monarchical restoration in Hawaii under Kaiulani as Queen, although he said that the coup-makers of 1893 would undoubtedly resist the restoration of the monarchy with all their strength.[7]

The continued popularity of Princess Kaiulani was one factor that caused the Republic of Hawaii to send President Dole to Washington to lobby for the passage of the annexation treaty. Dole made the historic visit and was accorded all of the honours due to a foreign head of state. He presented himself well in American society, and he was invited to many society events but his visit did not appreciably strengthen the annexationist cause in the Senate, and the cause continued to lose overall American political support.[8]

Japan now raised concerns about the prospects of a US annexation of Hawaii and the Japanese Government approached Great Britain to suggest that a three-way protectorate be established over Hawaii by Great Britain, Japan, and the United States. However, the British had no interest in interfering with the likelihood of a US annexation of

420

Hawaii, and the government in London turned down the Japanese proposal.[9]

Relations were also strained between Honolulu and Tokyo during 1897, over immigration restrictions that were being imposed by Hawaii on Japanese immigrants. Roosevelt now took steps to ward off any possibility of a Japanese intervention in Hawaii. When the Japanese Government filed a protest over the prospect of an American annexation of the islands, Roosevelt forcefully stated that the United States did not need permission from Japan, or any other country, with respect to foreign territories that the United States chose to acquire.[10] Japan had not opposed annexation when it was first raised in 1893, but by 1898 Japan had become concerned about the status of Japanese immigrants in Hawaii and the effect that a US annexation of the islands would have on the treaty arrangements that Japan had made with Hawaii. Furthermore, Japan was now much more confident of its position in the world, having defeated Imperial China in the Sino-Japanese War of 1895. Japan's Minister to the United States, Toru Hoshi told Secretary Sherman that the US annexation of the islands would upset the Pacific *status quo*, and would present risks to the existing rights of Japanese immigrants to Hawaii under the treaties between Hawaii and Japan. He feared that the position of Japanese immigrants under Hawaiian domestic law could also be affected, and he stated that annexation would clearly jeopardize the current settlement negotiations between Japan and Hawaii over their immigration dispute.[11]

In the middle of April, 1897 the Japanese Government despatched the cruiser HIJMS *Naniwa* to Honolulu to press Hawaii to relax its opposition to further Japanese immigration. The Republic was concerned that continued Japanese immigration to Hawaii would ultimately lead to demands by the Japanese settler community for political rights that could undermine white rule.[12] The strength of the Japanese objections to Hawaiian immigration restrictions led to concerns in Washington that Japan might intervene in the islands with force to obtain redress, although the American Minister in Tokyo advised Washington that the use of force by Japan in Hawaii was unlikely.[13]

Japan continued to press Hawaii to provide Japanese settlers in the islands with appropriate civil liberties, including the rights to live, work, and travel anywhere in the country, and to engage in any occupation that they were capable of performing. Japan also desired Hawaii to grant Japanese immigrants voting rights, and the protection of their lives and property. (The regime in Honolulu had previously disenfranchised Asians in the 1894 republican constitution.[14]) These were all reasonable requests in themselves, but the question of voting rights was critical to the control of the Republic's legislature by the Caucasian settler community, and so there was considerable resistance to an expansion of voting rights in the country to include Asian settlers.

Japan advised the United States that while it had no desire to annex Hawaii for itself it was concerned that US annexation of Hawaii could impact the position of Japanese immigrants in Hawaii under US law. In fact, US annexation would result in the abrogation of the existing diplomatic agreements between Hawaii and Japan, and would result in the application of much more restrictive US immigration laws that would effectively end Japanese immigration into the islands.[15]

Roosevelt was concerned enough about the possibility of Japanese aggressive moves toward Hawaii to order that US naval forces in Hawaiian waters be maintained at full strength. At the same time US Secretary of State Sherman brushed aside Japanese objections to the Annexation Treaty by stating that American annexation of Hawaii would not affect the position of Japan in the Pacific Ocean. As for the allegation that the native population opposed US annexation Sherman simply said to the Japanese that it was a matter for the Government of Hawaii to deal with and that between the United States and Hawaii it was the Government of Hawaii that spoke for its people.[16] Nevertheless, Sherman did advise Hawaiian Minister Hatch that Hawaii should resolve its dispute with Japan over the immigration issue.

Other countries also expressed concerns about the US move to annex Hawaii. Germany tried to persuade Great Britain to join it in a protest and to insist that the United States either divide the Hawaiian Islands with Great Britain and Germany, or end US participation in the tri-country Samoan condominium as the price for acquiring Hawaii with German and British consent. Britain refused the German proposals.[17] When New Zealand, a country within the British Empire, also complained to London about the American designs on Hawaii the British Foreign Office told New Zealand that any protest against the US action would only spark an aggressive US reaction, and that would probably hasten the US annexation of the islands.

In all cases where it was approached by other states Great Britain suggested that the best political strategy was to say nothing and hope that internal American opposition in the US Senate might prevent annexation.[18] The British strategy apparently bore fruit because on March 9, 1898, the Senate Foreign Relations Committee decided that there were insufficient votes in the Senate to pass the annexation treaty.[19] As a result, the Hawaiian annexation treaty was never brought to a vote in Congress.

Events in the North Pacific now began to move toward a peaceful denouement. Hawaii eased up on the immigration restrictions that it had imposed on Japanese immigration and a change of government in Tokyo put a more conciliatory Foreign Minister into office, while the US encouraged Hawaii not to cause any further provocation to Japan.[20] The Japanese withdrew the cruiser HIJMS *Naniwa* on September 20th but Theodore Roosevelt insisted on maintaining a strong US naval presence at Honolulu and he ordered recurring ship rotations at Honolulu to maintain US naval strength in Hawaiian waters. Roosevelt even held a homeward bound US warship returning from the China Station at Honolulu to bolster the US naval presence in the country.[21] Eventually the dispute over immigration between Japan and Hawaii resolved itself into a financial question, and in the summer of 1898, Hawaii agreed to pay an indemnity of $75,000 to Japan.[22] Russia had advised the United States as early as the overthrow of the Hawaiian monarchy in 1893 that it had no concerns about the US annexation of Hawaii.[23] By 1898, Canada had also recognized that the annexation of Hawaii by the United States was inevitable, and it made no efforts to forestall the US annexation. Said the *Montreal Gazette*, "It is fate."[24]

While Hawaii was high on the agenda in Washington the most important foreign policy issue for the McKinley Administration was the Spanish remnant empire in the Caribbean, Cuba, and Puerto Rico. Cuba was enduring oppression, insurrection, and retribution, and American public opinion swung heavily against the continued Spanish colonial presence there. In Washington, plans were presented to Roosevelt on June 30, 1897, for a war of conquest in Cuba, with collateral attacks in the Philippine Islands in the Pacific, and even against Spain itself.[25]

The destruction of the USS *Maine* in February, 1898, brought imperialism, nationalism and jingoism together with American patriotism to form a poisonous brew of national aggression and expansionism against weaker countries. Although the loss of the warship was first ascribed to an accident, an irresponsible press, and a society that was searching for a new definition of national purpose created a clamour for war with Spain. Spanish repression in Cuba and the ongoing insurrection in that country against Spanish rule afforded the United States a pretext for declaring war.

On April 20th, President McKinley signed a war resolution passed by Congress demanding that Spain withdraw from Cuba, and authorizing the President to support the Cuban rebels with the armed forces of the United States. Spain severed relations with the United States the next day and war immediately broke out between the two countries. American expansionists were jubilant, and none more so than the Assistant Secretary of the Navy, Theodore Roosevelt who, in an abundance of patriotic and imperialistic enthusiasm, resigned his government post to accept a commission as a Lieutenant Colonel in a western cavalry outfit that would form part of the US invasion force for Cuba. Famously, Roosevelt would lead a charge of his unit, the Rough Riders, at the Battle of San Juan Hill that would give him all the national recognition that he craved, and would set him on a course to obtain the US presidency.

US naval power quickly gave the United States the advantage in its contest with Spain. Commodore George Dewey achieved an overwhelming victory over the Spanish Asiatic Fleet at the Battle of Manila, which destroyed the Spanish naval power in the Pacific forever, and gave the United States and Philippine rebels control over the Philippine Islands. Spanish naval forces in the Caribbean were also crushed by the US at the Battle of Santiago de Cuba. Both Cuba and Puerto Rico were taken by the US navy and army. Although Spain's North Pacific island colonies in the Caroline and Mariana chains were largely left alone, the US did seize the island of Guam in the Mariana chain because it had a good harbour.

Upon the outbreak of the war President Dole in Hawaii offered to negotiate a treaty of alliance between Hawaii and the United States, and to support the US in its war with Spain.[26] Although no formal alliance resulted, Hawaii was hardly neutral during the war. The annexationists in power in Honolulu wanted to show US officialdom the strategic value of the Hawaiian Islands. Therefore, Hawaii hosted US troops on their way to the Philippines, despite Spanish protests at this blatant violation of Hawaiian neutrality.

The strategic importance of the Hawaiian islands at the crossroads of the Pacific was not lost on Theodore Roosevelt, or on his good friends Senator Henry Cabot Lodge, and Captain Alfred Thayer Mahan. Here was a second chance to acquire the Hawaiian Islands after the abortive 1893 attempt and the American expansionists knew that another such opportunity might not come again. However, the Annexation Treaty was stalled in the US Senate, where Democratic Party opposition denied the treaty the two-thirds majority it required to be ratified.

Although the American expansionists were frustrated by their inability to secure ratification, Senator Lodge now engaged in a moment of legislative legerdemain by crafting a resolution to annex Hawaii as an amendment to a war revenue bill. Thus, rather than a treaty between sovereign nations to effect annexation, Lodge's proposal would simply amount to a joint resolution of the American Congress to take over the country. As a resolution attached to a revenue bill, such a measure avoided the two-thirds approval requirement necessary to ratify a treaty with an independent foreign state. All that would be required under a joint resolution would be a simple majority vote of the House of Representatives and of the Senate. Lodge slyly arranged for a representative from Nevada, Francis G Newlands, who was neither a Republican, nor a Democrat, but a member of the Silver Party in the US House of Representatives to propose the joint annexation resolution.

The Speaker of the House, Thomas Reed, though a Republican, and a native of Maine, as were so many who sought Hawaiian annexation, opposed imperialism and he sought to delay debate on the Newlands Resolution but ultimately he could not stop it from coming to a vote. When the joint resolution was voted on in the House of Representatives on June 15, 1898, Speaker Reed refused to preside over the House during the vote.

On both sides of the House racist arguments were made to support or oppose the annexation of Hawaii. Those in favour extolled the virtue of Caucasian rule over the indigenous population while those opposed to the annexation said it would make Americans out of people who were decidedly not American.[27] War fever, and word of the American victories over Spain in the Pacific, created a newfound appreciation of the strategic position of the Hawaiian Islands in Congress however, and a majority of the votes were cast in favour of the resolution. The Newlands Resolution passed the House by a majority of 209 to 91.[28]

Anti-annexationists were livid at the prospect of taking over another country without the consent of its people, and by the failure to follow the proper course of international law by entering into a treaty with Hawaii. Carl Schulz, a prominent anti-annexationist, wrote to President McKinley telling him that the confidence of foreign states in an unselfish American foreign policy would be destroyed if he followed through with annexation.[29]

Other prominent Americans opposed to Hawaiian annexation including the writer and humorist Mark Twain, the industrialist Andrew Carnegie, and a former Democratic candidate for President, William Jennings Bryan. One who occupied a peculiar position was former President Benjamin Harrison. He generally opposed American expansionism abroad but agreed that Hawaii should be annexed, perhaps because of the involvement of his administration in the 1893 coup, and the initial attempt to acquire the islands.

Anti-imperialists in the US thought that the American annexation of foreign countries would be a tragedy for the republic by converting it into "a vulgar, commonplace empire". But Senator Lodge retorted that if the anti-imperialists were right then all of the US expansion within North America had been a crime. To Theodore Roosevelt, the anti-imperialists were just men of "a bygone age."[30]

When the Newlands Resolution came to the Senate for debate and decision on July 6, 1898, several Senators questioned how their republic could take over another country without the consent of its inhabitants. Senator Pettigrew of South Dakota reminded his fellow senators that the current Hawaiian Government with its highly restricted franchise did not have popular support among its people.[31] But those considerations no longer mattered.

After defeating a Democratic amendment to allow universal male Hawaiian suffrage, the vote was held. The final tally in the US Senate was 42 for annexation, 21 opposed, and 26 not voting, enough support to pass the resolution as part of the War Revenue Bill. A few minutes later the entire War Revenue Bill was adopted by the Senate with Hawaiian annexation buried within it. The very next day, July 7, 1898, President McKinley signed the bill, and with it the death warrant for the independence of the Hawaiian Islands. President McKinley claimed that the annexation of the islands was a military necessity for the United States, and that Hawaii would be an essential American military bastion in the Pacific.[32] It has been treated as such by the United States ever since the vote in the Senate in 1898.

The Spanish-American War ended favourably for the United States, as the American expansionists knew it would. During a fifty-five-day period in the middle of 1898, the United States seized, or annexed, the Republic of Hawaii[33], Guam, Wake Island, the Philippine Islands, Puerto Rico, and Cuba.[34] Virtually overnight, the United States became a prominent imperial power. The following year the US extended its overseas expansion by partitioning the Samoan Islands with Germany. The McKinley Administration retained the eastern half of the Samoan island chain for the United States.

The anti-imperialists of America, steeped in the lore of the American revolution, and anxious to preserve their country's traditional insular focus, had been defeated. The new, thrusting men of the imperialist faction, enthralled by American hard power, men such as Roosevelt, Lodge, and Mahan, had seized the republic's foreign policy tiller and now they charted a new aggressive course for the United States that would ultimately make it the world's dominant power in the twentieth century. The world at large was surprised, even shocked, by the sudden change that seemed to have come over the people of the United States of America. In Great Britain, the *Times* called the change wrought by the creation of the American Empire "a break in the history of the world."[35]

In Hawaii, those who loved their country, and cherished its independence, Princess Kaiulani prominent among them, wept at these developments. When the latest Annexation Treaty was stalled in the US Senate Hawaiian loyalists had hoped that the independence of their country could be saved, even if its historic monarchy could not be saved. Now, that hope too, was lost.

As fateful days approached in the spring of 1898, tragedy once more enveloped Kaiulani. Word came from Great Britain that Theo Davies, her guardian and political mentor, had died on June 2nd. The death of the man who had guided her through the labyrinth of so many political challenges, and who had watched over her personal welfare (even when she mischievously did not want him to) was now gone from her life. Kaiulani was shocked, stunned, saddened, and depressed by his passing.

Worst of all was the news that came on July 13th, when a steamer arrived in Honolulu carrying the news of the US annexation. It was a day of mad rejoicing, and overwhelming relief for the annexationists but a day of mourning for Hawaiian patriots. The annexationist's goal of gifting the country to the United States of America had been achieved.

In Washington, all of Queen Liliuokalani's hopes were now destroyed. There would be no restoration to the throne of the Kamehameha's. It was over. The Queen decided to return home, leaving Washington for San Francisco where she spent a few days before boarding the steamer SS *Gaelic*, which brought her home to Honolulu. On the night of August 1st the *Gaelic* arrived at midnight. The docks were crowded with indigenous Hawaiians. Here and there a few loyal *haoles* could also be seen. Kaiulani had come down to the docks to greet her aunt at this sad homecoming. When the *Gaelic* docked, Prince David boarded the ship and a little while later the Queen disembarked from the vessel on his arm, softly calling *aloha* to the crowd of loyal subjects who stood watch at her homecoming. At the Queen's carriage she came face to face with Kaiulani, and the two women embraced. Then with Prince David, and the Queen, Kaiulani went into the carriage, which was pulled by two white horses that belonged to Kaiulani, and the horses silently carried the Queen and her party home to Washington Place in the wee hours of the morning.[36]

How to sum up the political legacy of Queen Liliuokalani? She was born a high *alii* in an era when indigenous Hawaiians remained numerous enough to dominate the state and she imbibed the culture of the old Hawaii with its class distinctions, and its reverence for the *alii*. She grew up to adulthood in an era of powerful Kings, none more so than King Kamehameha V, who enforced his will upon the country extra-constitutionally. He took the throne without acknowledging the existing Constitution, and refused to take the constitutional oath of office. He then convened a constitutional

431

convention to create a new, more powerful kingship and finally he dismissed the constitutional convention when it did not suit his purposes. Thereafter, he imposed his own constitution on the country, vesting more power in the monarch, and abolishing the office of *Kuhina Nui*, which might have been a check on the exercise of kingly powers.

With Kamehameha V as a powerful example in Liliuokalani's young adulthood she saw her brother obtain the throne but only by creating a deep division amongst indigenous Hawaiians, a schism between the Kalakaua line and the remaining Kamehameha's that was never healed until death took Emma, Ruth, and Bernice, the last of the original royal line. Always, the thought that the new royal line had to prove its worthiness to occupy the throne of the Kamehameha's lurked in the back of her mind as Queen Liliuokalani struggled to maintain indigenous control over the Hawaiian Government. She considered the reformist constitution of 1887 as a stain on the rights of the Hawaiian *alii*, and her brother's weakness in accepting it as potentially raising questions about the fitness of their family to reign. She aided those who sought to destabilize the country with insurrections during the final years of her brother's reign. When she eventually came to the throne after the death of her brother she determined at all hazards to restore the monarchical authority that her brother had surrendered to the *haole* business community. However, Liliuokalani's ill-judged efforts at constitutional change brought the Kingdom to ruin.

Had she been willing to reign rather than to rule, and had she focused her efforts on preserving the monarchy as a symbol of national unity she might well have preserved the independence of the country. But Liliuokalani does not bear sole responsibility for the political disaster that overtook the Hawaiian people. Indigenous politicians such as Wilcox, Bush, Nawahi, and White must also bear a share of that responsibility for undermining the political unity of the indigenous population, and for allying with the Reform Party in the Legislature to defeat the Queen's appointed Cabinets. Nawahi and White were responsible for encouraging the Queen to embark upon unilateral constitutional change. But of course, nothing could justify the betrayal of the country by the Hawaiian-born subjects amongst the settler community, who collaborated with US officials, and with Republican administrations in Washington, to bring about the overthrow of the monarchy and the annexation of the country by the United States.

Ironically, if Liliuokalani had come to the throne ten years earlier, in 1881 instead of 1891, she might have proven to be a widely respected monarch because she lacked the personal character flaws of King Kalakaua. Liliuokalani's strong Christian faith, which was acknowledged in her lifetime (though not necessarily during the political upheavals of the 1890's) gave her a moral authority that was absent in her brother, and that might have helped her to bridge the divide between the settler community and the indigenous Hawaiian monarchy. As it was, Liliuokalani's education, and her life experiences, worked against her when she rose to the throne in the aftermath of the 1887 revolt, and the adoption of the Bayonet Constitution. The political instabilities of the last years of her brother's reign, compounded by the cultural dislocations of a declining indigenous Hawaiian population, mass immigration from Asia, and the virtually complete capture of the Hawaiian economy by western settlers, all proved overwhelming to a monarch born into a different era.

Dawn broke in Honolulu on August 12, 1898. It was a day that broke many hearts in the breasts of loyalist patriots in the capital city of the Hawaiian Islands. That morning US sailors and marines were landed from the US warships in Honolulu harbour, and were escorted by the Hawaiian National Guard to Iolani Palace for the formal ceremony that would extinguish the sovereignty of the country.

A crowd of Caucasian settlers congregated on the lawn before the entrance to the palace. A few Asians and Portuguese immigrants also attended but almost no indigenous Hawaiians could be seen at the ceremony. Invitations had been extended to the Royal Family as a courtesy, as well as to other prominent indigenous Hawaiians but none would accept to attend this tragic event in the life of their country.

Princess Kaiulani's own formal invitation from the Republic read:

> "The Minister of Foreign Affairs invites the Princess Kaiulani to be present at the Ceremony attending the Transfer of the Sovereignty of the Republic of Hawaii to the United States of America, at the Executive Building at half after eleven, Friday morning, August 12th 1898.
>
> R.S.V.P."[37]

One indigenous Hawaiian who did attend, the wife of a settler official in the Hawaiian Government, wept for her country through the entire ceremony. Her tears were matched by a soft rain from the heavens.[38]

Queen Liliuokalani, whose invitation from the Republic to attend the annexation ceremony had been simply (and rudely) addressed to Mrs. J O Dominis, gathered together the members of the Royal Family, and her retainers, at Washington Place in a funereal atmosphere. A famous photograph exists of the high *alii* at Washington Place on the day of annexation. The Queen and Princess Kaiulani are wearing black. Kaiulani's black gown is long and embroidered. She wears a *lei* reflective of her rank as an *alii*. Her black hair is pulled back and tied. Her hands are held quietly in front of her as she stands to the side of the Queen. The expression on her face is vacant, and lost. How keenly she must have felt the loss of Hawaii's sovereignty on that day.

The Queen sits in the middle of the photograph, with the mass of her retainers and supporters standing behind her. Almost all appear to be indigenous Hawaiians. The Queen's expression reflects her loss but there is also a strength shown in her gaze that portends her future battles. The Queen is not yet done fighting for her own personal justice.

Across the street the Hawaiian Band[39] under Bandmaster Henry Berger prepared for a moment filled with poignancy, the final playing of *Hawaii Ponoi* as the national anthem of an independent country. At Iolani Palace, now called the Executive Building, the American Minister, Harold Sewall stood and faced the President of Hawaii, Sandford Dole, at noon, as the invited guests assembled for the occasion watched.

Sewall said to Dole:

> "Mr. President, I present you a certified copy of a joint resolution of the Congress of the United States, approved by the President on July 7th, 1898, entitled 'Joint Resolution to provide for annexing the Hawaiian Islands to the United States.'
>
> This joint resolution accepts, ratifies and confirms, on the part of the

United States, the cession formally consented to and approved by the Republic of Hawaii."[40]

Then President Dole said to the American Minister:

"A treaty of political union having been made, and the cession formally consented to and approved by the Republic of Hawaii, having been accepted by the United States of America, I now, in the interest of the Hawaiian body politic, and with full confidence in the honor, justice and friendship of the American people yield up to you as the representative of the Government of the United States, the sovereignty and public property of the Hawaiian Islands."[41]

Sewall replied:

"Mr. President: In the name of the United States, I accept the transfer of the sovereignty and property of the Hawaiian Government."[42]

Henry Berger then raised his baton and with tear-filled eyes he led the Hawaiian Band in the soft strains of *Hawaii Ponoi*. The music was not up to the Band's usual standards. Many of the indigenous musicians could not bring themselves to perform it and Berger quietly excused them, telling them to go around the corner of the palace until it was all over.[43] As the band played *Hawaii Ponoi*, the national flag of Hawaii was lowered from its place of honour atop Iolani Palace.

Then the US Admiral commanding the US forces gave a signal and a huge American flag was raised atop the palace while buglers played the martial strains of the American anthem, the *Star-Spangled Banner*. The flag caught the breeze and spread itself wide over the ground below. Hawaii was American.[44] President Dole and his Ministers were re-sworn to office under the constitution of the Republic, which continued to govern Hawaii pending the passage of new legislation from Congress for the governance of Hawaii.

Annexation day was a day filled with celebrations for the settler community, and for those few indigenous Hawaiians, and other ethnicities, that supported them. The annexation of Hawaii suited the founders of the new imperialist version of the United States. Soon there would be an American-controlled isthmus canal, and later would come the military bases in Hawaii and a large navy to wield American power in all corners of the globe. In Hawaii on annexation day there were parades and new oaths, and at night Iolani Palace was illuminated, and a fireworks display lit the sky. The self-congratulatory celebrations continued far into the evening with a formal reception at Iolani Palace and an Annexation Ball in the former throne room of the palace, where few indigenous Hawaiians could be seen.[45]

After the ceremony transferring sovereignty, President Dole met briefly with the troops of the Hawaiian National Guard to commend them for their service and to express the thanks of the Republic of Hawaii. Well might he do so for the settler military forces of the Provisional Government, and then of the Republic of Hawaii, had sustained the settler minority in political office. Now, the responsibility for keeping the settlers in power would be the responsibility of the United States armed forces, and of the United States executive branch, which would appoint their governors.

NOTES

[1] Despite the view of the Census Bureau there was still an American frontier but it was in remote and cold Alaska where the harsh climate and living conditions attracted few settlers.

[2] Morris, 464

[3] Morris, 573

[4] Tate, 270

[5] Tate, 267

[6] Tate 271

[7] Tate 287

[8] Tate, 288

[9] Merze Tate, *Great Britain and the Sovereignty of Hawaii*, Pacific Historical Review , Vol. 31, No. 4 Nov., 1962, University of California Press, Berkeley (Cal.) 327 at 346

[10] Morris, 579

[11] Tate, 282

[12] Morgan, 205

[13] Morgan, 203

[14] Morgan, 207

[15] Morgan 209

[16] Morgan, 215

[17] Tate, *Great Britain*, 347

[18] Morgan, 215

[19] Tate, 293

[20] Morgan, 216

[21] Morgan, 214

[22] Tate, 299-300

[23] Tate, *Great Britain*, 343

[24] Tate, *Canada's Interest*, 41

[25] Morris, 577

[26] Tate, 296

[27] Stephen Kinzer, *The True Flag, Theodore Roosevelt, Mark Twain, and the Birth of American Empire*, Henry Holt and Company, New York, 2017, 10

[28] Kinzer, *The True Flag*, 17

[29] Kinzer, *The True Flag*, 46

[30] Steven Hahn, *A Nation Without Borders, The United States and Its World in an age of Civil Wars, 1830-1910*, Penguin Books, New York, 2016, 496

[31] Kinzer, *The True Flag*, 59

[32] Hahn, 493

[33] The Hawaiian claims to Johnston atoll and Palmyra atoll also passed to the United States with the annexation of the Republic of Hawaii.

[34] Cuba received its independence from the United States in 1902, but it remained under the indirect control of the United States, essentially until 1959. Several periods of US military intervention in Cuba occurred in the pre-World War One era.

[35] Kinzer, *Overthrow*, 81

[36] Williams, 123

[37] Cohen, 33

[38] Siler, 286

[39] After the 1893 coup the celebrated Royal Hawaiian Band was first renamed the Provisional Government Band and then under the Republic it became The Hawaiian Band. Subsequently, it was renamed The Territorial Band after 1900, when Hawaii became a territory. Finally, in 1909, its original name, The Royal Hawaiian Band, was restored, and it continues to be known by that name to

the present day. Today it is under the jurisdiction of the City of Honolulu.

[40] Robert C Lydecker, *Roster Legislatures of Hawaii 1841-1918*, Published under Authority, Hawaiian Gazette Co, Honolulu, 1918, 252

[41] Lydecker, 252. However, the treaty mentioned by President Dole was never ratified in Washington, and so there was no treaty between the two countries within the comprehension of American law.

[42] Lydecker, 252

[43] Stone, 46

[44] Siler, 286

[45] Mrantz, 35; Mellen, 350

16

The Mistress of Ainahau

Although annexation was now complete, the separate country of
Hawaii had not yet passed into history. A kind of shadow country
continued to exist for the next twenty-two months. Although the
United States had assumed the sovereignty of Hawaii, it had done
so by means of a congressional resolution, rather than by the normal
procedures of international law. The annexation should have
involved the ratification of a treaty between two sovereign states
but it had proved impossible to obtain the two-thirds majority of
the US Senate that was required for approval of a treaty under the
Constitution of the United States. As a result, upon annexation
there were no treaty provisions establishing a future government for
the islands. The United States decided to establish a Commission
to determine the future political structure of Hawaii, and the laws
necessary to support that new political structure.

In the interim, the American Minister informed Hawaiians at the
annexation ceremony, "the President . . . directs that the civil,
judicial, and military powers . . . exercised by the Officers of

the Republic of Hawaii, as it existed just prior to the transfer of sovereignty," should continue.[1] Thus, the Republic of Hawaii would continue to exist in shadow form. Nor did Hawaiians now become American citizens. They remained Hawaiian citizens until the future constitutional structure of this newest American possession was determined. As a result, Hawaiians continued to travel abroad on Hawaiian, not American passports, and the Hawaiian consular service of the Hawaiian Department of Foreign Affairs continued to provide services to Hawaiian citizens abroad. A much relieved Sandford Dole and his confederates continued to hold the offices they had seized in 1893, but with annexation achieved domestic political tensions relaxed, and the former oppressiveness of the Republican government disappeared.

Kaiulani was now free of the burdens of the monarchy. It was certain now that the monarchy was *pau*. But what of Hawaii's future? And what of her own future? What was she now, a Hawaiian, a *hapa haole*, Scottish, American? Alice Rix, a reporter with the *San Francisco Call* came to Ainahau to interview her, and to define the former Hawaiian royal for the American public. Rix found Ainahau to be not quite what she expected. She felt that it lacked a certain exotic quality that she prized:

"The stairs of Aina Hau are broad and one sees them from the rooms below and I waited in the drawing-room, a big cool, modern affair, in pale terra-cotta, its ceilings panelled in red and gold. Its walls yawning into rooms beyond, after the hospitable Hawaiian fashion which makes the rooms of each floor one vast suite. The furniture is quite conventional, the usual jumble from all places and most periods. A superb table of the coca wood, carved and inlaid with other native woods, has the center of the room, and two *Kahilis*, the exaggerated feather duster with its ivory or carved wood stick, which is the emblem of the dead monarchy, fully eighteen feet high, nodded from opposite corners. Otherwise there is no native touch to distinguish this drawing-room of a daughter of the Kamehamehas from that of any other young woman in comfortable circumstances. I found this disappointing. The place is historic. It has been the demesne of royalty since the coming of Kamehameha, the Conqueror. Its vista of the Diamond Head is known as the Queen's View. There are King's Walks and Prince's Ways all through its labyrinth of tropic growth. When Governor Cleghorn planted three hundred palms in honor of his daughter's birth his gardener disturbed the bones of the slumbering chieftains of his daughter's race. The grass houses of her forbears are still preserved upon the grounds. The big two-story house in which she lives has sheltered crowns in family intimacy. By all the laws of poetry and romance this room should be other than it is. But poetry and romance were first to yield to the civilizing touch which has crept upward to the native's throat. The decorative arts of the Hawaiians are no more."[2]

But the appearance of the Princess herself did not disappoint Rix. Waxing poetic at the sight of Kaiulani, Rix said of her:

"The Princess stopped upon the landing three steps above the base and shook out a tail of yellow chiffon, the sweeping skirt of a glorified *holoku*. The royal yellow floated from the shoulders clung to her youthful bust and arms, cast its glow upward over her face and throat, fell in waves about her feet. She looked like some dark, soft-petaled, slim-stalked lily growing in a patch of sun. . .

The Princess carried an ancient native fan, a matter of braided palm, of length and subtle grace, and she fanned herself slowly with that long, majestic outward, upward sweep which is the grace of the higher Honolulu as it is that of all Spain. She walked admirably, holding her supple body with fine reserve moving with a sort of indolent dignity, very foreign, very fetching, and I should say, out of a slender knowledge

443

of kingly things, very regal, and it occurred to me that this girl who has just lost a Throne would have graced it well.

There is much in heredity and more in education. The Princess Kaiulani was reared to be a queen. She has the grand air, a small, proud head fine, direct eyes under sensitive, snaky, brilliantly black brows, a little haughty nose a little bitter-sweet mouth, a crisp English accent, a manner distantly gracious, the bearing of a woman born and educated to a sense of superiority."[3]

Alice Rix had come to see how Kaiulani would adapt to the prospect of the US annexation and Kaiulani left Rix in no doubt that she deplored the fate of the indigenous Hawaiians in their own country:

"Oh they have been too kind, too simple, too trusting. They have listened and believed until they have been betrayed. Do you know what one of them, one of our old chiefs said to me? He came to me over miles and miles of country on horseback to know if the news was true. He would not take the word of any one except my father or myself. 'And we will have no country of our own now?' he said. You know the *Aloha Aina*, the love of country is very strong in our hearts. My father told him 'No.' 'And no flag?' 'No' my father said, 'and no flag.' And then he asked about me. Some of my people are very fond of me. 'And the Princess?' he asked. My father said, 'The Princess will be Miss Cleghorn.' 'No flag' he said 'no country? Is that what Christianity has done for us? The missionaries came here to us and taught us to look to heaven for happiness, and while our eyes were on the skies they have taken our land from under our feet . . .' 'Could you feel anything but bitterness? There is nothing in our philosophy more than in yours to reconcile us to the extinction of our race."[4]

Kaiulani declared that she remained wholly Hawaiian, despite the long exile that she had endured from Hawaiian shores, and despite the loss of her country so soon after her return:

444

"I am all Hawaiian. I love this country of mine. Its sky its trees, its people. Its food. I went to school in England, you know, and after the first excitement I began to long for the island food – a longing which never passed away. When I came home at last I ran about like a thing mad. I looked for all the hiding places, I climbed to the roof of the house where I used to climb to get away from my governess. I cried because my palms had grown beyond me. I asked for all native things – poi, taro, even the raw fish we eat. You would think that a girl educated in England would shrink from that at least."[5]

Her patriotism was undoubtedly stimulated by her return to Hawaii, and by her assessment of the challenges that had to be faced by the indigenous community. Now, there was one more political challenge that had to be faced. The victorious settlers were determined to deny indigenous Hawaiians a political voice in whatever new political structure was created for American Hawaii. The political commission that President McKinley sent to the islands would hear submissions from both sides and make recommendations to Congress that would subsequently be embodied in the legislation to establish a new government for American Hawaii. The annexationists had been successful in removing the indigenous Hawaiian monarchy from the apex of the Hawaiian state, and of minimizing their representation in the Republic of Hawaii's Legislature. Now the settlers shuddered at the prospect of readmitting indigenous Hawaiians into a new Territorial Legislature. Most Hawaiian annexationists were essentially white supremacists in their political outlook, and they thought that political power should be concentrated in their own hands for the welfare of the public, meaning themselves.

The President's Commission assembled in Honolulu and consisted of President Sanford Dole and Associate Supreme Court Justice Walter

445

Frear representing Hawaii, with Iowa Senator Shelby Collum, Alabama Senator John Morgan, and Illinois Representative Robert Hitt, the Chairman of the House Committee on Foreign Affairs, as the representatives of the United States. Senator Morgan, a southerner, and a well-known American white supremacist, was a longtime proponent of Hawaiian annexation who had chaired an 1894 investigation of the Hawaiian revolution by the Republican Senate, which had refuted the Blount Report. The Morgan Report had sought to protect the reputations of all of the American officials implicated in the 1893 *coup d'état*, laying responsibility for it on Queen Liliuokalani, for the most part.

As the highest state officials in the defunct Kingdom of Hawaii, Queen Liliuokalani and Princess Kaiulani took up the cause of universal male suffrage for indigenous Hawaiians.[6] Queen Liliuokalani adopted the strategy of following the Presidential Commission around the Hawaiian Islands to make the support of the population for the deposed monarch obvious to the American commissioners. The Queen was accorded the precedence that her rank deserved by all indigenous Hawaiians wherever she went, and that no doubt helped to impress upon the commissioners of the need to act fairly toward the indigenous population.

The American commissioners knew that the United States was unacquainted with the practices of governing an empire, and there was already serious trouble brewing in the Philippine Islands, where the indigenous population wanted their independence but President McKinley had resolved to deny it to them. Early moves in a prolonged guerilla war in the Philippines were already underway by the time the American commissioners came to Hawaii. Both the American and the Hawaiian members of the Presidential Commission were anxious to avoid serious trouble in Hawaii.

Kaiulani took a different approach than the Queen. She remained in Honolulu to interact with the American commissioners, and their wives. While she was bitter at the loss of her country, she understood that vast geopolitical forces had ultimately driven Hawaii into the embrace of the United States, telling Alice Rix:

> "I think this is a hasty move forced on the American Government; a scheme which the war with Spain has helped. And I cannot but think it is a very great mistake. We would have given everything we had to give – we always had given every thing, haven't we?"[7]

When Mrs. W C Wilder gave a reception for the wives of the commissioners at the Wilder estate of Eastbank, Kaiulani made a point of attending it to ensure that the wives of the American commissioners formed a good impression of the cultured and sophisticated indigenous Hawaiians.

Kaiulani's most important effort came on the evening of September 7th, when she hosted a grand luau at Ainahau for the members of the commission and officials. For that event, Kaiulani went all-out as a hostess. Ainahau was decorated for the occasion with lit Japanese lanterns placed along the pathways of the estate, and a martial band was provided to serenade the Americans and the settler community with favourite American tunes, such as *Sweet Adeline* and *There'll Be a Hot Time in the Old Town Tonight*, a tune that was popularized by Theodore Roosevelt, and his Rough Rider cavalry regiment in the Spanish-American War.

In the Great Room at Ainahau, three long tables were set up to accommodate forty guests at each table. Each table was laden with Hawaiian foods and at each place-sitting there was either a *lei* of pink carnations, or a *lei* of fragrant green *maile*, for each guest. When the supper was ready, the guests proceeded into the Great Room by two's, integrating a local settler, or American, with an indigenous Hawaiian. Kaiulani herself entered on the arm of Senator Collum. For this occasion the indigenous Hawaiians dressed in their best apparel, and Kaiulani was stunning in a brocaded imperial yellow *holoku* with a brilliant yellow *lei* of *O'o* feathers surrounding her neck.

As the guests took their places at their tables, they found a Hawaiian royal presiding at each of the three tables, Queen Liliuokalani, Prince David, and Princess Kaiulani. As it was her home, Kaiulani was seated at the centre table, and a famous photograph of the event shows her looking up at the camera with an expression of satisfaction at the results of her efforts to impress the visiting Americans. At that moment, she was every inch the Mistress of Ainahau, secure in her stately home, and a woman of polished and easy manners.

For the American guests, the luau was a new experience, and they had to be taught to eat *poi* with their fingers from a calabash, the same as indigenous Hawaiians did. Some were initially reluctant but most of the guests quickly followed the examples set by their royal hosts and tried the different, and to American minds, exotic cuisine of the Hawaiian Islands. *Kahili* bearers standing behind the three royal persons who were present also gave an exotic feel to the meal, and the large Hawaiian flags decorating the walls of Ainahau led no one astray as to where the patriotic heart of their hostess lay.

After the luau the guests were invited to wander through the lit gardens at Ainahau while the remainders of the meal were cleared away and the Great Room converted into a ballroom for a night of dancing to the tunes of the martial band. By all accounts it was a fabulous evening and it certainly contributed to a very favourable opinion that formed amongst the American commissioners toward the Hawaiian population. This was what the American commission had hoped to see – an exotic but civilized people who might easily adapt themselves to an American form of government.

In the end, the indigenous Hawaiians got what they wished for. Universal male suffrage was granted by the United States for both indigenous Hawaiians and settlers thus guaranteeing that indigenous Hawaiians would be able to control the Territorial Legislature, or at least ensure that the concerns of the indigenous Hawaiians would receive the same respect that they received under the monarchy's legislature. While the efforts of the former Royal Family, and especially Kaiulani's grand luau at Ainahau, helped smooth the way for the enfranchisement of male indigenous Hawaiians there were also stronger currents that helped to ensure that Hawaiians received the political rights of American citizenship.

The Commission accepted that elections to the new House of Representatives of the Territory of Hawaii should be open to male citizens of the United States of the age of 21 who could speak, read, or write in English or Hawaiian, provided that they had resided in Hawaii for one year, and had resided in their own electoral district for three months. They also had to ensure that they were not behind in the payment of their taxes. Such enfranchisement rules were similar to other US incorporated territories. The literacy requirement was not a barrier because all of the people of Hawaii, both the indigenous and the settler communities, exhibited a high degree of literacy. However, in the case of the territorial Senate the Presidential

Commission proposed an electoral restriction. In addition to the franchise requirements for voting for Representatives, Senatorial electors would also have to possess property worth at least 1000 dollars, or an annual income of 600 dollars.[8]

As a result of the Great *Mahele* instituted by King Kamehameha III there was property ownership by indigenous Hawaiians, and their land titles were protected under the same land title laws that protected the property rights of the settler community in Hawaii. Indeed, as late as the 1930's there were still indigenous Hawaiians who owned thousands of acres of land under registered fee simple titles.[9] However, some Hawaiians did not own land equal to the value of 1000 dollars, or did not own any land at all. In Hawaii, the white settlers knew that they could claim control of the territorial Senate only if a property requirement was set too high for large numbers of indigenous Hawaiians to qualify.

By this point in time most American legislatures had abolished property qualifications for electors, and the proposal for a property qualification for the electors of the Hawaiian Senate was viewed as a retrograde step in a democracy when the Hawaiian Report filed by the Presidential Commission was considered by Congress. It was a principle of American democracy that citizen landowners ought to be able to elect the people that could make rules concerning their property. As a result, the property qualifications were removed by Congress from the bill to establish the new Territorial Government. The settler community had to be content with a denial of American citizenship to the Asian residents of Hawaii, who did not become American citizens (although any of their children subsequently born in the Territory of Hawaii would automatically become American citizens).

450

President Dole filed a minority opinion to the Presidential Commission's Report of 1898, in which he dissented from the majority recommendations because of the powers that it recommended should be given to the territorial governor. In Dole's opinion, "The [territorial] governor, under the provisions of the act recommended by the commission, will have less check to his administration of affairs than was the case with the sovereigns under the monarchy."[10] There was a delicious irony in Dole's objections.

Basking in her success as a political hostess, but saddened by the losses of Theo Davies, and of her beloved country, Princess Kaiulani fled Honolulu for the countryside. She went to her sister Helen's home deep in the Manoa Valley, in mid-September. There, in secluded nature, she could finally relax and seek to restore her own sense of well-being. Kaiulani felt depressed at the events of the past year and she was still struggling with her future role. Her stay in the Manoa Valley undoubtedly helped, but it did not wholly dispel her heartsickness at the losses she had endured.

Other family matters also contributed to her sense of malaise. There had been a serious dispute within the Royal Family. Dowager Queen Kapiolani, had decided, or been persuaded, to transfer her landed property to her *hanai* sons Prince David, and Prince Kuhio, as part of an estate planning scheme. However, after the Dowager Queen had deposited a title deed of transfer in escrow with the land titles registry, a dispute arose between the old Queen and her nephews, and the Honolulu papers reported that she had filed an application with the Supreme Court to annul the deed of transfer.[11] Such a dispute did the reputation of the Royal Family no good, and doubtless some *haoles* with annexationist sentiments secretly smiled over the travail in the former reigning family. Happily, a resolution was ultimately achieved, and the dispute went away through a settlement out of court, which avoided any laundering of the Royal Family's private issues in public.[12]

Her kingdom was gone but Princess Kaiulani continued to be treated as royalty by the Hawaiian people. Much speculation continued about her romantic life. After her return to Hawaii the foreign press continued to run stories about the men to whom the Princess was linked with romantically. The most important and well-known of her putative suitors continued to be her cousin, Prince David Kawananakoa, who was a frequent visitor to Ainahau. Rumours of a romance between Kaiulani and Prince David had come into sharp focus when the *New York Times* published an article on February 12, 1898, which stated that a marriage had been arranged between Prince David and Princess Kaiulani, and that a formal betrothal would occur after the execution of deeds in a family settlement concerning dowager Queen Kapiolani. But no formal betrothal occurred, and the *New York Times* article was merely another example of rumour and conjecture, about Kaiulani's romantic affairs. Princess Kaiulani had known Prince David since she was a child, and she had always enjoyed her visits with him, and with his two brothers, but it seems that her affection for her attractive cousin was essentially platonic. Kaiulani's niece later said that David and Kaiulani enjoyed a relationship similar to that of a brother and a sister.[13] Although Kaiulani was popular with men, and certainly loved by some of them, rumours of marriage remained just that – rumours.[14]

After a refreshing stay in the Manoa Valley with her sister, Kaiulani returned home to Ainahau on October 12th. She celebrated her twenty-third birthday – her last, quietly at home on October 16th. Then it was back into a whirlwind of social engagements starting with a reception for 200 guests at Ainahau on October 19th. A few days later she convened a dancing party which the local press predicted would be very enjoyable for her guests, owing to Kaiulani's notable abilities as a hostess. She held her last house party a few days later. At the beginning of November she attended a diplomatic reception at the Japanese consulate, and her final public appearance in Honolulu that autumn was at the departure of Queen Liliuokalani, who had decided to proceed once again to Washington to fight for her ownership of the Crown Lands, which she held was hers by right.[15]

In November, the Queen boarded the SS *Coptic* for the voyage to San Francisco. To see her off, Princess Kaiulani, Prince David, and Archibald Cleghorn were all present. The sailing of the *Coptic* was delayed but Kaiulani remained on board the ship to give moral support to her aunt as she embarked upon her journey to Washington. A number of other retainers were also present, including Colonel George Macfarlane, the brother of E C Macfarlane, and a former member of the Queen's military staff. He felt the poignancy of the parting of the two royal ladies, recalling later that:

"They little, thought it was a final parting, but it was none the less! Pathetic. The boat was delayed, and though the hour was late – and Kaiulani delicate, she refused to leave, and stayed on board some five hours to see the last of her aunt. Any heart must have been touched at [the] sight of those two royal women clinging together in their fallen dignity."[16]

Colonel Macfarlane engaged Kaiulani in conversation, and noted the wistfulness of her demeanor:

"I was trying to console Kaiulani with some cheerful prospects. 'All has not been taken from you,' I said. 'The American Government respects your position and will help you to keep it up. Your aunt will receive an income that will still enable her to live as an ex-Queen. You will still be able to live as a Princess; your birth and antecedents will never be forgotten, and you will remain, leader of society here, the first lady in the land.' 'Yes,' she answered me, with a tired smile, 'but I shan't be much of a real Princess, shall I? They haven't left me much to live for!' And as she spoke she caught her hand to her side and I could see the rapid beating of her heart. 'I don't talk about it,' she went on; 'I try not to grieve my father, who watches over me so devotedly and seeks to make up to me with his love for all I have lost. For his sake I try not to mind – to appear bright and happy; but I think my heart is broken."[17]

After the Queen's departure Kaiulani stayed quietly at home. Apparently, she still found time and satisfaction in horse riding, although Fairy was retired from carrying her. Much later a resident of Honolulu would recall that in his childhood a beautiful, slim, but saddened Princess who rode on horseback near his home, wearing black riding clothes accented by *ilima leis that* adorned her neck.[18] She also fed her little flock of peacocks that were called *pikake* in Hawaiian. Because she loved peacocks, and the scent of jasmine, today in Hawaii flowering jasmine is also called *pikake,* in memory of her.[19]

Her sadness at the annexation of her country by the United States had been revealed in her interview with Alice Rix, where she had quoted her father with sentiments that she herself endorsed:

"My father says it is as though a dear friend had come to us for hospitality and we had gladly offered our best in his entertainment and loved to show him every courtesy and honor and then he had said to us, 'Go

454

now, out of your house. I have been so well treated in it that I have learned to like it and want it for myself."[20]

The rapid collapse of an independent Hawaii in the months after her return was forcing Kaiulani to make uncomfortable personal adjustments. In Europe she had been treated as royalty. In the United States, she was a media celebrity. Back home in Honolulu however, she was treated by the white minority that still held power as a mere ornament of the fallen regime. She lacked influence and power to affect the course of events and, as one raised in Hawaii to understand the full social significance of her position as an *alii*, Kaiulani was frustrated. She wrote to her aunt, Liliuokalani to say that she now lived in a "semi-retired" way, and she thought that people must wonder what had happened to Hawaiian royalty. Kaiulani herself now questioned what would be the continuing purpose of Hawaiian royalty under the new American regime.[21]

The weeks passed and the holiday season approached. Kaiulani received pleasant visits from Andrew Adams, on leave from his position as a manager of a sugar plantation at Ewa. However, Kaiulani's mind was turned to a forthcoming visit to Hawaii Island. Her good friend, Eva Parker, was getting married and Kaiulani was excited to attend the wedding, and to help her friend celebrate her nuptials. It would be Kaiulanis first visit off of Oahu since she returned from Europe and she held many happy childhood memories of her vacations on Hawaii Island with her mother, who had once been the Governor of the island. Thus, it was with a light heart that she and her maid boarded the inter-island steamer SS *Kinau* on December 7th for her trip to the Big Island, and to the Parker Ranch at Mana.

NOTES

[1] Lydecker, 253

[2] Alice Rix, *The San Francisco Call* [volume] (San Francisco [Calif.]) 1895-1913, August 07, 1898, Image 17, LOC, Chronicling America, 17

[3] Rix, *The San Francisco Call*, 17

[4] Rix, *The San Francisco Call*, 17

[5] Rix, *The San Francisco Call*, 17

[6] Although female *alii* had served in the House of Nobles under the Kingdom, and several had held political appointments, such as Kaiulani's mother, Princess Likelike, who had served as Governor of Hawaii Island, female suffrage was not yet accepted by most western societies, including the United States. In the United States by 1900 only one territory, Wyoming, had enacted female suffrage (in 1869) and it had seen its statehood application resisted by Congress for some years afterwards because of that decision. Wyoming was finally approved for admission to the union only in 1890, and then only by a narrow vote of 139 to 127 that was in part due to its enfranchisement of women. Indigenous Hawaiians therefore had to focus on obtaining universal male suffrage to avoid political marginalisation. Female suffrage had to wait.

[7] Rix, *The San Francisco Call*, 17

[8] S M Collum, *Message from the President of the United States transmitting the Report of the Hawaiian Commission Appointed in Pursuance of the 'Joint Resolution' to Provide for Annexing the Hawaiian*

Islands to the United States, etc., Washington, Government Printing Office, 1898, 15

[9] Banner, 157

[10] Collum, 20

[11] Webb & Webb, 172

[12] Webb & Webb, 175

[13] Zambucka, 154

[14] Zambucka, 116

[15] The Supreme Court of the United States would eventually find against the Queen, based on Hawaiian jurisprudence developed through earlier litigation between King Kamehameha V and Dowager Queen Emma. The title to the Crown lands passed to the United States.

[16] *The Princess Died of a Broken Heart, Says Colonel Macfarlane*, in the *San Francisco Call*, Volume 85, Number 130, 9 April 1899, 17

[17] Macfarlane, *The San Francisco Call*, 17

[18] John W Perry, *The Island Rose*, in *Hana Hou magazine*, Hawaiian Airlines, Issue 6.5: October/November 2003, https://hanahou.com/6.5 [accessed August, 2020]

[19] Perry, *The Island Rose*

[20] Rix, *The San Francisco Call*, 17

[21] Zambucka, 133

A Ride in the Mountains

The Parker Ranch on Hawaii Island was a vast historic ranch that traced its beginnings back to the reign of King Kamehameha the Great. The wealthy Parker family were staunch loyalists, and their patriarch, Samuel Parker, had served as the head of the last royal cabinet before the overthrow of the monarchy. The Parker girls, Helen and Eva, had grown up in a life of splendour that rivalled, and possibly exceeded, the life of a Hawaiian princess. Kaiulani had known the Parker girls since she was a child in Waikiki, and she had renewed her acquaintance with them in London after she went to Great Britain for her education. At the time, the Parker girls had seemed older and more sophisticated to the ingenue Kaiulani but now, in adulthood, Kaiulani was their equal as a woman. She had remained friends with both of them after her return home to Hawaii.

The wedding of Eva Parker and Eva's cousin, Frank Woods, was the social event of the Christmas Season in Hawaii in 1898, and Kaiulani entered into the social swirl of house parties, picnics, and dances, culminating in the wedding on December 14th. At many of these events Kaiulani was escorted by another Parker cousin, the handsome Sam Woods, although Prince David was also a wedding guest.

After the wedding the guests were invited to stay over for the Christmas holidays. Kaiulani was enjoying her escape from Oahu so much that she took up the offer of her hosts and she spent a splendid Christmas holiday at the Parker Ranch, along with many of the other guests. The days drifted by and 1898 turned into 1899 before Kaiulani wrote to her father to wish him a belated Christmas greeting. She told her father that she had attended a ball, and that she had been out riding and jumping over obstacles. She asked him to have a maid send over some *holokus*, and she also requested some minor medications, headache powders and quinine pills. Kaiulani and her friends visited Waipo, where she was serenaded by the indigenous Hawaiians, and she also went to see the famous volcanoes, the abode of the goddess Pele.

In mid-January, after many of the guests had already departed, Kaiulani lingered on in the Big Island with a few of the remaining guests. One January day she and some others went horseback riding up into the mountains of Hawaii. While they were out a cold rain came upon them, what the locals called the Waimea spear of the wind, a sharp cold blustery rain that the mountain winds drove horizontally into unwary travellers caught within its embrace.

Kaiulani's party had protective rain gear with them but Kaiulani declined to put hers on. Accounts of the horseback ride vary but some accounts say that Kaiulani spied an old *kahuna* on the trail and she spurred her horse to pass by him without speaking, thus preventing her from taking out her rain gear. Other accounts suggest that she was in a fey mood, and that she spurred her horse into the driving rain without a care for the consequences. Whatever the motivation, the fact was that Kaiulani became drenched to the skin, and she arrived back at the Parker Ranch at Mana cold and wet. The following day, Kaiulani awoke feeling out of sorts and in the ensuing days she developed a cold, and a fever that worsened. Her health then rapidly declined. By January 24th, the Honolulu newspapers were reporting that she was ill and that her father, together with her family physician, had hastened to Hawaii Island to see her. They found Kaiulani quite ill at the Parker Ranch and it was decided that she should return home to Waikiki. In her weakened condition her father and her doctor decided to have Kaiulani borne to the coast in a litter. On February 9th, she was taken down to the coast at Kawaihae, and from there she was taken out to the steamer SS *Mauna Loa*. On the sailing day her symptoms were lessened, and they were mostly confined to a pain on the left side of her head, and in her left forearm. At her home at Ainahau she rested in her darkened bedchamber while her family physician, Dr. Walters, became increasingly concerned about the decline in her health. He called in another physician, Dr. Miner, for a second opinion. As their patient struggled, the doctors diagnosed her with inflammatory rheumatism complicated by an exophthalmic goiter, which was an eye issue. Her delicate health in her past may have been a symptom of a thyroid disease, which may have weakened her heart.

Archibald Cleghorn spent time with his bedridden daughter and brought her the news that the chief annexationists had all signed a petition to the US Congress calling on the United States to continue to pay to Kaiulani the pension that the Republic had previously granted to her. To explain to the settler community why the Princess was worthy of a public pension, the annexationist media foghorn, the *Pacific Commercial Advertiser*, declaimed:

"The plan of sending a petition to, Congress asking that Princess Kaiulani be suitably provided for by law is most timely and just. The fact that so many who were actively engaged in the overthrow of the Monarchy unite in this request, shows a disposition to act generously toward a young woman who was the victim of a stupid blunder that irretrievably ruined the Monarchy. Since the overthrow, the Princess has behaved with excellent judgment in most embarrassing circumstances. Although the late Mr. T. H. Davies, in his singular regard for the native race, made her unduly prominent after the overthrow, it must not be forgotten that she was a young person who naturally yielded to older advisers. Mr. Davies himself, educated by the course of events, finally accepted, and advised her to accept the situation. The Princess did not manifest disloyalty to the Republic, and at no time suggested or encouraged an attempt to restore the old order of things. Her self respect, her love of country, and of her race, her own high prospects, prevented her from looking upon the Overthrow with any pleasure. If she had accepted it with any alacrity, it would have been contrary to human experience, and so unprecedented as to have raised doubts about her capacity to feel or think . . .

Aside from her relations to the Monarchy, the Princess, by her behavior, her disposition to make of herself a good example of the educated Hawaiian woman, swings us around into the ranks of those who feel that when she ceases to be the ward of the little Republic, she should become, so long as she lives, the ward of the Territory. Those of us, who were born here, those of us who by long residence take a kindly interest in the natives, desire that this representative of the little Hawaiian Monarchy should always live in dignity and comfort with us."[1]

It was another measure of recognition from the settler community, and an indication that despite the political divide between annexationists and loyalists, a broad measure of respect existed among

461

the settler community for Kaiulani, as well as perhaps some regret over her circumstances following the collapse of the monarchy.[2]

Press bulletins were issued to advise the public of the progress that Princess Kaiulani was making in her recovery, and for much of the time that she was ill her doctors expected her to make a full recovery. She was young, they thought, and she should be able to pull through. As the days passed however, her condition grew more ominous, and the inflammatory rheumatism began to affect her heart. By the beginning of March the doctors were alarmed that she was not recovering from her illness. Her life was now truly endangered. Kaiulani herself did not seem to realize how grim her illness was and she only expressed a concern that she would not be able to attend a forthcoming fundraising function for the Hawaiian Relief Society.[3] The worry and the hope of her physicians were reflected in a press bulletin they issued on Sunday, March 5th, in which they told Hawaiians that Princess Kaiulani was resting better and was able to obtain a little sleep on the previous Saturday night. Her condition took a "bad turn" on Sunday morning but the doctors felt that she was improving throughout the day on Sunday, and they advised that she was "slightly better," although not yet out of danger.[4] It was all wishful thinking.

Later, as the Sunday night wore on, Kaiulani's condition suddenly took a worse turn and as the crisis grew her immediate family members were called to her bedside. Her health totally collapsed in the early hours of Monday morning. Archibald Cleghorn was joined at the vigil over his dying daughter by Kaiulani's sisters Helen, and Rose, and by Kaiulani's friends Kate de Vida, and Helen Parker. Word was sent to the residence of the Dowager Queen, where Prince David lived, and soon he was at his dying cousin's bedside as well.

462

From 1:30 A.M. on March 6th Kaiulani's breathing became irregular and those around her knew the end was coming. At precisely 2 AM Kaiulani moved slightly and then cried out with an indecipherable cry, which some thought was 'Mama,' or 'Papa,' or even 'Koa,' a nickname for Prince David. With her final cry, Kaiulani passed beyond the realm of the living. She was 23.

Immediately, her beloved peacocks outside began to screech loudly, and they could not be quieted. Many in Waikiki, and some who lived up to half the distance to Honolulu from Waikiki later said that they knew the Princess had died when her peacocks began their cries. Honolulu society was stunned. People had forgotten that Kaiulani had a delicate constitution. Dr. Walters, her physician later said that he thought she could have surmounted one of her two health challenges but not both.

By morning the government of the Republic had met and decided to offer a state funeral for the Princess. The Cabinet realized that the reconciliation of the indigenous and settler communities following annexation demanded that royal honours be accorded to the departed Princess. Archibald Cleghorn accepted their offer but he refused to allow a formal lying-in-state inside the former Iolani Palace, now called the Executive Building. Memories of the overthrow, and of the imprisonment of his sister-in-law, the former Queen, in Iolani Palace were still fresh. The *Independent* reported on the Hawaiian Cabinet's decision:

> "The flag over the Executive Building was hoisted at half mast when Colonel Boyd this morning officially notified the Government of the death of Princess Kaiulani.
>
> The Secretary of the Foreign Office was instructed by President Dole

this morning to notify the Consular Corps of the demise of Kaiulani, and the upper courts adjourned their sessions out of respect to the late chiefess.

Minister Damon, on behalf of the Government, has tendered a State funeral, which, it is understood, has been accepted by the bereaved father of the Princess. It is stated that the present arrangements provide that the funeral shall take place from the Kawaiahao Church on Sunday next with the Bishop of Honolulu as the chief officiant, and that the body will be in State at Ainahau, the late residence of the Princess, on Wednesday next, between the hours of 10 a.m and 4 p.m. The funeral will be conducted on the rules observed at Royal functions of like mournful character."[5]

The departed Princess was laid out at Ainahau on the Wednesday after her death, dressed in a white robe, and placed in a white casket carved from Koa wood. She faced the Pacific Ocean, where she had once swam and surfed as a little girl. Her casket rested on a bier covered in a purple pall lined with yellow silk and embroidered with her personal coat of arms. White orchids and orange flowers were scattered about, and the scent of flowers pervaded the whole house, while outside Henry Berger and The Hawaiian Band played dirges. Ainahau was opened for mourners and among the very first that morning was the Dowager Queen Kapiolani, who came with her whole retinue to mourn her niece. People came from the city and the countryside all day long to pay their respects to the lost Princess. When the time came to close the house to the public, the Cleghorn family retainers were permitted to pay their final respects to the mistress of Ainahau. Some of them had known Kaiulani since she was a little girl. Finally, her bereaved father went in to take his final leave of his daughter, and everyone, even the faithful *kahili* bearers, who had stood their mournful watch all that day while mourners

464

passed the bier, were excluded from the room. A quarter of an hour later, a shattered Archibald Cleghorn emerged. In Washington, Queen Liliuokalani was informed by a letter of sorrow, dated March 9th, from her attorney J O Carter that her niece had passed away after "much suffering."[6]

At midnight Kaiulani's remains were taken into the city to lie in state at the Kawaiahao Church, the Royal Church of Hawaii, although Kaiulani herself was actually a member of the Anglican denomination at St. Andrew's Cathedral, rather than the Congregationalist Kawaiahao Church. A large crowd followed the hearse to the church, where it arrived at 2:00 A.M., and where it was received by Bishop Willis of St. Andrews, who conducted a brief service upon the arrival of the casket. The church had been decorated for a royal funeral with fragrant *maile* tied around the pillars of the church, exuding their scent throughout the building. In the centre of the square where her bier lay an arch had been created that was topped by a white dove with outstretched wings. The bier was surrounded by 20 large *kahilis*, and the casket was covered with a yellow feather pall of Hawaiian royalty. At both the head and the foot of the bier were floral crowns. Above, the royal standards granted by King Kalakaua to Princess Likelike, and to her daughter, Princess Kaiulani, were raised. On each side of the casket were four *kahili* bearers who, at roughly three-minute intervals, lowered their *kahilis* toward their opposite number, pausing, and then returning their *kahili* back to its erect position.[7] At St. Andrew's cathedral the royal pew was draped in black.[8] Chants and *meles* continued through that first night that Kaiulani rested at Kawaiahao Church. For the following three days she lay in state in the church.

Saturday, the day before Kaiulani's funeral, it had rained but on

Sunday the sun emerged in time for the funeral service at 2 P.M.. With Bishop Willis officiating, and Reverend Parker of the Kawaiahao Church present to assist him, the service began with the organ playing *In Memoriam*, which had been composed for Princess Likelike's funeral, and never played afterwards until Kaiulani's funeral. Bishop Willis read the solemn readings, and the 23rd Psalm was chanted, while the St. Andrew's Choir sang the 39th Psalm. The Kawaiahao Church's Choir sang *Brief Life is Here Our Portion* in Hawaiian, and Reverend Parker adjured those who were present to "follow her example" of a life well-lived. The recessional hymn was *Angels Ever Bright and Fair*.[9]

Outside minute guns boomed, and church bells tolled, as the funeral procession formed to take Princess Kaiulani on her last journey to the Royal Mausoleum at Nuuanu. A select group of 250 Hawaiian men, uniformly dressed in white pants, white hats, blue jerseys, and yellow cloaks took up black and white ropes to draw the catafalque bearing the remains of the Princess through the streets of Honolulu. Her casket was topped by a white veiled crown, and a pall of woven gold *ilima* flowers, while burning *kukui* torches lined the road, as the rains stopped and the procession got underway.[10] Perhaps twenty-five thousand people lined the streets of Honolulu to watch Kaiulani's passing, as mournful wailing pierced the air, competing with the sound of the guns. From the church, the procession moved along King Street to Alakea Street, then up Emma Street, and along Vineyard Street to Nuuanu Avenue, and from there it turned onto Mauna Ala to reach the Royal Mausoleum. The Order of the Funeral Procession was as follows:

The Marshal of the Republic and Officers

The Company of Police

The Hawaiian Band

St. Louis College Students

Oahu College Students

Kamehameha School Students

St. Andrew's Priory Students

Band

Fraternal Societies

St. Antonio Beneficente Society

Sociedade Lusitania Beneficente

Aha Hui Kalaiaina

Aha Hui Aloha Aina

Aha Hui Aloha Aina O na Wahine

Grand Marshal and Aides

Band

Second Battalion US Volunteer Engineers

Detachment of Blue Jackets from *USS Seindia* and *USS Iroquois*

Band

First Regiment National Guard of Hawaii

Protestant Clergy

Clergy of the Roman Catholic Church

The Right Reverend the Bishop of Panopolis

Choir

Officiating Clergy

The Right Reverend the Bishop of Honolulu

THE CATAFALQUE

and

Pall Bearers

Carriage of Hon. A S Cleghorn with Mrs. J W Robertson and Mrs. J H Boyd

Carriage of the Ex-Queen, Liliuokalani

Carriage of Her Majesty the Queen Dowager with Prince Kawananakoa, and Prince Kalanianaole and his wife

The President and Staff

The Cabinet Ministers

The Justices of the Supreme Court

The Special Agent of the United States

Officers US Army and Navy

President of the Senate

Speaker of the House

Consular Corps

Circuit Judges

Government Officials[11]

The public was invited to follow the procession after the Government Officials. It took a full two hours for the funeral procession to reach the Royal Mausoleum. Among the pall bearers were two of the men that had been romantically linked to Kaiulani, Prince David Kawananakoa, and Andrew Adams. At the Royal Mausoleum Kaiulani's white casket was carried inside and laid to rest beside that of her mother, Princess Likelike.[12] A shaft of sunlight lit the casket as it moved into the mausoleum and a rainbow appeared in the distant mountains.[13] Bishop Willis read the Anglican Order for the Burial of the Dead. And then it was over.

Afterwards rumours would fly among the superstitious in Hawaii that Kaiulani had been prayed to death by a sorcerer *kahuna*. Perhaps those rumours were sparked by the knowledge that Kaiulani may have encountered a *kahuna* on the road on that fateful day when, possessed of high spirits, she refused her rain gear in the cold Waimea rain.[14] To quell such rumours Colonel George Macfarlane, who both knew and cherished Kaiulani, refuted the allegations in an interview with the press, in which he said:

"The Princess Kaiulani prayed to death? Nonsense' hotly asserts Colonel

Macfarlane, 'the kind of exaggerated rumour, based on native tradition, that always gets afloat when a royal personage dies. Yes, I know the things that were whispered when her mother Princess Likelike, died, and though there was probably no truth in current reports they undoubtedly had some justification in the doings of older days. Many a great chief has been prayed to death by witch *kahunas*, with the aid of certain subtle poisons of which they knew the secret; a decoction of dried fern tips, for instance, is supposed to have deadly effect without leaving any trace. At any rate there was no medical analysis in those times.

'But Kaiulani . . .' The colonel suddenly breaks off with a quiver in his voice. 'Kaiulani' he continues, impressively, after a moment's silence, 'was adored by her people; her death is the greatest blow that could have befallen them; with her their last hopes are buried. There is not a native in the islands who could have wished to compass that sweet girl's death.' 'Then it is not true that some of them resented her attitude toward annexation?' The colonel sits up energetically: 'Every one admired her attitude; they could not do otherwise. Her dignity, her pathetic resignation, her silent sorrow, appealed to all. The natives loved her for her quiet, steadfast sympathy with their woe, her uncomplaining endurance of her own; the whites admired her for her stately reserve, her queenly display of all necessary courtesy, while holding herself aloof from all undue intimacy. All were attracted by her sweetness and grace; it was impossible not to love her."[15]

In truth, Kaiulani was widely loved in Hawaii, and there was no one who would have wished to harm her, either physically or supernaturally. Her sudden passing was one of those unexpected tragedies of life, and one that added a special poignancy to the passing into history of the sovereign realm of Hawaii. Letters of condolence began to flood into Ainahau from all parts of the United States, as well as from Europe, and they continued for some time afterwards, illustrating that the young Princess had touched the hearts of the world.

NOTES

[1] *Pacific Commercial Advertiser*, Honolulu, HI, February 3, 1899, https://chroniclingamerica.loc.gov, 4

[2] Linnéa, 212

[3] Webb and Webb, 197

[4] Linnéa, 213

[5] *To Honour the Dead*, in *The Independent*, Honolulu, Hawaii, March 6, 1899, 2

[6] Williams, 133

[7] Zambucka, 146

[8] Webb & Webb, 202

[9] Webb & Webb, 203; Zambucka, 147

[10] Mellen, 361

[11] Cohen, 35. The catafalque was accompanied by small kahilis on the inward side, and large kahilis on the outward side, of the procession.

[12] In 1907 the mausoleum was converted into a chapel and the caskets were removed and re-interred in the present Kalakaua Crypt on the grounds of the Royal Mausoleum.

[13] Mellen, 361

[14] In his *A Brief History of the Hawaiian People*, Professor W D

Alexander recounted two methods that sorcerer *kahunas* used against wayward travellers. The first was *hoopiopio*, in which a *kahuna* entered a road over which a victim was to pass "and made a magic mark across the road, at the same time muttering an imprecation to Uli (i.e. the chief god of sorcery). When the traveller crossed the magic line the spell was activated. A second variation was called *pahiuhiu*, in which a square was drawn by the *kahuna's* finger in the road, and then divided into four equal parts surmounted by a stone over which a prayer was uttered to secure the demise of the victim. If the victim stepped on the stone the spell would be activated. (Alexander, 70)

[15] *San Francisco Call*, Volume 85, Number 130, 9 April 1899, 17

Epilogue

The country that Princess Kaiulani was born into, and died in, outlived her by only 15 months. On June 14, 1900, the Hawaiian Organic Act came into force and the Republic of Hawaii disappeared, taking with it the separate citizenship of Hawaiians together with their foreign consular service, passports, currency, postage stamps, and all the other accoutrements of a separate country. Hawaiians became American citizens and the laws and symbols of the United States became the laws and symbols of Hawaii. Hawaii became an incorporated territory of the United States of America, with an expectation that eventual statehood would follow. But statehood would be long delayed. The islands were too far away, and too exotic, for mainland Americans of the early twentieth century to agree to add Hawaii's star to their flag, and it was not until 1959 that Hawaii became the 50th state of the United States, after a plebiscite approved integration into the Union. Only the people of the small island of Niihau, where the Hawaiian language continued to be spoken as the common language of the community, voted against statehood.

Queen Liliuokalani carried on after the annexation, fighting in the courts to obtain control of the Crown Lands, which she felt, in justice, belonged to her. The Supreme Court of the United States disagreed and held that the Crown lands were now the property of the United States. Liliuokalani however, remained the sovereign in the hearts of the indigenous Hawaiian people. The Hawaiian flag continued to defiantly float over Washington Place. At St. Andrew's Cathedral Liliuokalani sat in one of the front pews, and Sandford Dole sat in another front pew, on the other side of the Cathedral, symbolizing in stark terms the division of 1893. Although the Queen remained bitter at the fate destiny had dealt her, the passage of the years mellowed her bitterness, as it did of those who had opposed her, and eventually she became a living symbol for all the people of Hawaii. She remained the honoured, titular, monarch of the Hawaiian Islands. Her presence often marked major public events, where she was invariably treated with dignity and respect. Every second year Liliuokalani hosted a reception at Washington Place for the members of the Territorial Legislature.[1] However, she appeared only once in public with Sanford Dole — on the occasion of the 75th birthday of Royal Hawaiian Bandmaster Henry Berger.

On February 15, 1901, the *Hawaiian Star*, reported that the Territorial Government had decided to restore the title of 'Her Majesty' to Liliuokalani, and that henceforth she would be referred to as 'Her Majesty, Liliuokalani', in all official and judicial documents in Hawaii.[2] In 1917, in the throes of the World War, the Queen raised the American Flag over Washington Place to support the American troops fighting in Europe, and the American sailors on the high seas. It completed the old Queen's reconciliation with the past. On November 11, 1917, Queen Liliuokalani died at Washington Place at the age of 79. She was given a Royal State funeral, as befitted the former head of state of the Hawaiian Islands, and she was interred in the Royal Mausoleum.

Dowager Queen Kapiolani survived her niece Princess Kaiulani by little more than three months. Queen Kapiolani died at Pualeilani, her estate in Waikiki, on June 24, 1899, at the age of 64. Like her niece before her, the government of the Republic of Hawaii accorded the Dowager Queen a Royal State funeral, following which she was interred in the Royal Mausoleum.

Prince David Kawananakoa became politically active in the Democratic Party of the United States. He was one of the original five founders of the Democratic Party in the Territory of Hawaii, and he was also a delegate to the 1900 Democratic National Convention in Kansas City, Missouri, where the territorial Hawaiian Democratic Party was recognized by the national party. Kawananakoa ran unsuccessfully for the Hawaiian Congressional Delegate seat in Washington in 1900, losing to Robert Wilcox of the Home Rule Party. Once romantically linked to Kaiulani, he married Abigail Campbell in 1902, and had three children with her. He died in San Francisco on June 2, 1908, at the age of 40. He was given a Royal State funeral by the Territorial Government, following which he was interred in the Royal Mausoleum

Prince Jonah Kuhio Kalanianaole and his wife left Hawaii in 1899, to travel abroad, primarily in Africa. While in Africa, Prince Kuhio joined the British Army in its fight and eventual suppression of the Boer Republics during the Boer War. After the Boer War Prince Kuhio returned to Hawaii where he joined the Home Rule Party but in 1902 he split from that party, taking a large number of his supporters with him to establish his own political party, the *Hui Kuokoa*. Afterwards, he was persuaded to join forces with the Republican Party, despite it being the political bastion of the sugar interests, and of the Hawaiian settler elites that had overthrown the monarchy.

The Republicans nominated Prince Kuhio as their candidate for the Hawaiian Congressional Delegate seat in 1902, pitting him against Robert Wilcox. Prince Kuhio won that election and served as Hawaii's delegate to Congress for the remainder of his life, being reelected in ten subsequent congressional elections. He died in Washington on January 7, 1922, at the age of 50. He was given a Royal State funeral by the Territorial Government, the last such honours granted to the former Royal Family, and he was interred in the Royal Mausoleum. Kuhio is well-remembered today in Hawaii, and a state holiday is devoted to his memory.

Archibald Cleghorn continued to live quietly at Ainahau, following the death of Kaiulani. Now regarded as a distinguished elder statesman of Hawaii, he served as the first Parks Commissioner for the City of Honolulu where his knowledge and skill of plants served him well. In 1907, his name was proposed as the next Governor of Hawaii but he asked that his name be withdrawn from consideration. On June 24, 1910, he was present when the remains of the members of the Kalakaua dynasty, including those of his wife and daughter, were removed from the Royal Mausoleum and re-interred in a new crypt hewn from rock on the Royal Mausoleum grounds, an occasion which caused him much personal distress. He died at Ainahau on November 1, 1910, at the age of 74.

Of Kaiulani's supposed suitors Clive Davies assumed a board directorship of T H Davies and Co. after the death of his father. He married and had five children, one of whom later also became the Chairman of T H Davies and Co. Clive Davies died in England, on November 16, 1952. Clive's brother George, also linked romantically to Kaiulani, became for a brief time the British Vice-Consul in Honolulu. He served with the British army in World War One, and then later served in Parliament. He was knighted by King Edward VIII in 1936. George Davies died on June 21, 1950.

Prince Higashifushimi Yorihito, whom King Kalakaua and Queen Liliuokalani both saw as a potential future husband for Kaiulani in an arranged dynastic marriage continued his career in the Imperial Japanese Navy throughout World War One. He reached the rank of Admiral during his lifetime and he was made a Marshal-Admiral posthumously. He married Iwakura Kaneko, a daughter of Prince Iwakura Tomomi, but they had no descendants. He died on June 22, 1922, in Tokyo, at the age of 54.

Andrew Adams carried a torch for Kaiulani for many years after her death, annually bringing flowers to her tomb, even as an elderly man. He did not marry until 1934, some 35 years after he served as a pallbearer at the funeral of his beloved Kaiulani. Adams held territorial appointments as a sugar expert, and as a member of the Territorial Tax Appeal Board. He died in Honolulu on April 26, 1949, at the age of 82.

Of Kaiulani's European friends Nevinson William de Courcy, whom she called Toby, and whom she looked upon as her male confident, subsequently married Matilda H Grace Russell in England. Toby died on November 4, 1919, at the age of 50.

Alice Davies, the daughter of Theo Davies, and Kaiulani's close companion on her trip to the United States in 1893, when Kaiulani went to Washington to plead the cause of Hawaiian independence to President Cleveland, and who also accompanied Kaiulani to

Germany in 1893-94, married an American, Hiram Warner. She died in England in 1962, at the age of 88.

Eva Parker, the friend whose fateful wedding Kaiulani attended in December, 1898, lived with her husband Frank Woods on Kahua Ranch, where they later entertained the famous American author Jack London, and his wife. Eva died in Hawaii in 1922, at the age of 50. Today, a cottage built by her husband, and named for her, perpetuates her memory on the grounds of the elegant Mauna Lani resort.

Of Kaiulani's political opponents the most prominent was Sandford B Dole who took the helm of the uprising when it was offered to him by Lorrin Thurston, and tenaciously held it through annexation. After the Organic Act came into force Dole was appointed the first Territorial Governor of Hawaii by President McKinley. Dole resigned as Governor on November 23, 1903, to accept the post of Judge of the US District Court of Hawaii that was offered to him by President Theodore Roosevelt. Dole remained a Judge until 1915, when he retired. He died in Honolulu on June 9, 1926, at the age of 82.

Lorrin Thurston resigned his government posts after annexation was achieved and went into the newspaper business by purchasing the *Pacific Commercial Advertiser* where he could guide and shape Hawaiian public opinion. The newspaper he purchased continued to promote the sugar interests in the Hawaiian Islands. Thurston had no regrets about the overthrow of the monarchy, or the annexation of his country by the United States. When nostalgia for the old days of the monarchy began to grow in the second decade of the new century Thurston worked on the preparation of his memoirs to defend the overthrow. Thurston remains a polarizing figure in Hawaiian history. He died in Honolulu on May 11, 1931, at the age of 72.

John L Stevens, the American Minister who called for US troops to be landed to intimidate the royal government of Hawaii as the insurrection got underway in January, 1893, and who recognized the Provisional Government even before it was in control of the capital city, was replaced by President Cleveland and he never held another US diplomatic appointment. Stevens defended his actions in Hawaii, both in print, and in testimony before Congress, but his reputation suffered under the attacks of the anti-imperialists. Suffering from poor health, and bereaved by the loss of a daughter that occurred shortly after the *coup d'état* in Hawaii, Stevens died at his home in Maine on February 8, 1895, at the age of 74.

James G Blaine, the friend and boss of John L Stevens, was forced to leave the State Department before the end of the Harrison Administration due to his failing health. Blaine partisans nevertheless put his name forward as a prospective candidate for President in 1892, in place of President Harrison but Blaine did not go the Convention and he maintained that he was not seeking the nomination. Nonetheless, he earned 182 votes, which was good enough for second place behind Harrison. Blaine's health declined rapidly, and he died at his home in Washington on January 27, 1893, three days before his 63rd birthday, and just as the United States was learning of the overthrow of Queen Liliuokalani in Honolulu.

Captain Gilbert C Wiltse of the *USS Boston*, the military commander of the US forces that were landed in Honolulu in January, 1893, was recalled under a cloud of suspicion by President Cleveland. In late

April 1893, he became ill at his home in New York City, and he died there on April 26, 1893, after a short illness. He was 54.

President Benjamin Harrison returned to the practice of law after his presidency and he took up the case of the border dispute between Great Britain and Venezuela in 1898, a dispute which had almost led President Cleveland into a war with Great Britain. However, Venezuela was unsuccessful in the arbitration and the disputed territory was given to British Guiana by an international arbitration panel. The following year, Harrison was a delegate to the 1899 Hague Peace Conference. In his post-presidential years Harrison voiced disapproval of the policies of the American expansionists, which put Harrison at odds with the McKinley Administration. But Harrison never resiled from his position that the United States was right to annex Hawaii, and he lived long enough to see his policy brought to fruition. Harrison died in Indianapolis on March 13, 1901, at the age of 67.

Theodore Roosevelt, a veritable political force of nature in American history, returned from the Spanish-American War, the one indisputably imperialist war waged by the United States, as a genuine hero for his actions at the Battle of San Juan Hill. Roosevelt was subsequently elected Vice President of the United States on the Republican ticket in 1900, and when President McKinley was assassinated a few months after his inauguration Roosevelt succeeded to the highest office in the Republic. He thrust America forward onto the international stage, beginning the American reach across the globe that would reach its zenith in the late twentieth century. He served as President until March 1909 and he died in 1919, at the age of 60. His visage is sculpted into the Rushmore National Monument in South Dakota.

Of the men who encouraged Queen Liliuokalani in her fateful decision to attempt to impose a new constitution on Hawaii in January, 1893, none remained prominent in Hawaiian society for very long after annexation.

Joseph Nawahi did not live to see the death of his country. A Hawaiian patriot he remained loyal to Hawaii, and a monarchist. Anticipating the 1895 revolt, the Republic arrested Nawahi on charges of treason in December, 1894, but there was insufficient evidence to convict him, and he was acquitted and released in the spring of 1895. Unfortunately, he contracted tuberculosis while in Oahu Prison, and his health rapidly declined following his release. He died in San Francisco on September 14, 1896, at the age of 54. There was huge outpouring of public honour and remembrance during his funeral on Hawaii Island, the most significant display of public grief for a non-royal Hawaiian in living memory up to that point in time.[3]

William White ran for Senator in the inaugural Territorial Legislature and won but he was defeated for reelection in 1902. He ran successfully for election as the Sheriff of Maui in 1903 but the Supreme Court of Hawaii voided the elections, declaring the enabling legislation to be unconstitutional. Thereafter White ran unsuccessfully for the territorial Senate six times and once for Deputy Sheriff but he never held public office again after 1903. White died in Honolulu on November 2, 1925, at the age of 74.

Major Samuel Nowlein, the commander of Queen Liliuokalani's Royal Guard, one of those who had counselled her to adopt a new constitution by royal fiat, and who had also been an insurrectionist against the Republic in 1895, later moved to Maui where he died on December 5, 1905, at the age of 54.

Charles B Wilson, the former Marshal of the Kingdom of Hawaii and the Queen's guardian under the Republic, joined the Hawaiian Republican Party after annexation but never rose to prominence within it. He subsequently worked for the roads department. He died in Honolulu in 1926 at the age of 76. His role in guarding the ex-Queen during the time that she was placed under arrest and house arrest led to a coolness between the former monarch and her former Marshal that the passage of time did not wholly mend.

Robert Wilcox, the perennial insurrectionist won election as the Hawaiian non-voting Delegate to Congress in the 1900 territorial elections, and served for two years in Washington as Hawaii's representative under the Home Rule Party banner. In 1902, he was defeated for reelection by Prince Kuhio. Wilcox sought election in 1903, as the Sheriff of Honolulu but he became ill while campaigning, and he passed away a few days later, at the age of 48.

Of the Americans who supported the right of Hawaii to continue to exist as an independent nation, none was more important to that cause than President Grover Cleveland. After leaving the White House Cleveland settled in Princeton, New Jersey, and became a trustee of the renowned university located there. His health declined over the winter of 1907-08, and he died on June 24, 1908. His final words were "I have tried so hard to do right." Cleveland was 71.

Jame H Blount, or Paramount Blount, as he was called in the American press, retired from public life after completing his assignment in Honolulu for President Cleveland, and filing his famous report which blamed US officials for their part in the overthrow of the monarchy in Hawaii. He returned to his home state of Georgia where he died at Macon, Georgia, in 1903, at the age of 65.

And what of Hawaii today, the beloved country that Princess Kaiulani left before her time? It has survived, though it has changed beyond all recognition from the time of the Princess. It became the military bastion that Captain Mahan, Theodore Roosevelt, and Henry Cabot Lodge said it would. Today, from its mighty Hawaiian fortress the United States can dominate half of the world from Pearl Harbour. The US Pacific Command located in Oahu encompasses responsibilities from the US west coast all the way to the coast of India, and from the North Pole to the South Pole.

For the people of Hawaii, and especially those of indigenous descent, the years since the overthrow of the monarchy, and the annexation of the country, have brought positive as well as negative consequences. The past has now receded beyond living memory and although there has been a Hawaiian cultural renaissance in recent decades what has been wrought cannot now be undone.

And yet for many Hawaiians, and those of many diverse racial and ethnic backgrounds who have made their home in Hawaii, there is still much to admire in a young Hawaiian Princess who stood forth on the world stage when the fate of her country hung in the balance, and who provided it with a symbol of personal courage, fortitude, and civility. Hers was a patriotic love of her wondrous islands, and of the peoples whose lives strengthened them. As a woman who was both Hawaiian and European, she crossed the cultural divide that existed in her country, and she was able to appreciate the strengths of each community. If there had been no overthrow of the monarchy, and if she had lived, and succeeded to the Hawaiian throne, she might have ushered in a period of cultural harmony, as a living national symbol of her increasingly cosmopolitan country. We will never know.

Kaiulani's aspiration was for the harmony and success of a country, and of a people, that were small by comparison to other countries, and other peoples, but with a spirit large enough to embrace not only those who were born to the islands but also those who had willingly chosen it to be their home.

That is a still an aspiration that is worthy of remembrance.

NOTES

[1] Williams, 125
[2] However, the Territorial Government still refused to call her "Queen" in official correspondence.
[3] Liliuokalani, 300

Sources

Primary Sources

The primary sources I have relied on consist of the letters to and from Princess Kaiulani lodged in the Hawaiian State Archives, primarily in the Cleghorn Collection, and in the Bishop Museum Archives, primarily in the Kaiulani Collection (MS Gen. Letters 4.40, 4.41, 4.42) and the Kalanianole Collection (MS Gen Letters I-K 3.12).

In the footnotes, the acronym BMA is a reference to the Bishop Museum Archives, and the acronym HSA is a reference to the Hawaiian State Archives.

I am grateful for the assistance of professional archivists at both institutions for assisting me in locating relevant materials.

Secondary Sources

Newspapers and Magazines

The Daily Bulletin, Honolulu, Hawaii

The Evening Bulletin, Maysville, Kentucky

The Hawaiian Gazette, Honolulu, Hawaii

The Hawaiian Star, Honolulu, Hawaii

The Honolulu Advertiser, Honolulu, Hawaii

The Highland Recorder, Monterey, Highland County, Virginia

The Independent, Honolulu, Hawaii

The Morning Call, San Francisco, California

The New York Tribune, New York, New York

The Pacific Commercial Advertiser, Honolulu, Hawaii

The Sacramento Record-Union, Sacramento, California

The San Francisco Call, San Francisco, California

The Times, London, England

The Victoria Daily Colonist, Victoria, British Columbia

Theophilius Harris Davies, *The Hawaiian Situation, The North American Review,* vol. 156, No. 438, May, 1893

Theo H Davies, *Letters Upon the Political Crisis in Hawaii, January and February, 1894, Second Series*, Bulletin Publishing Co., Honolulu, 1894

Doug Herman, *Shutting Down Hawai'i: A Historical Perspective on*

Epidemics in the Islands, March 25, 2020, Smithsonianmag.com, Washington

L T Meade, *Girl's Schools of Today II, St. Leonard's and Great Harrowden Hall*, The Strand Magazine, London, 1895

John W Perry, *The Island Rose, Hana Hou magazine*, Hawaiian Airlines, Issue 6.5: October/November 2003

David Raymont, *Aloha, Canada, The Beaver*, vol. 83:3, June/July 2003, Canada's National History Society, Winnipeg (MB), 2003

Joseph Theroux, *Kamehameha IV and the Shooting of Henry Neilson*, *Honolulu Magazine*, Honolulu Magazine.com

Books and Pamphlets

William De Witt Alexander, *A Brief History of the Hawaiian People*, Published by Authority of the Board of Education of the Hawaiian Kingdom, American Book Company, New York, 1891

William De Witt Alexander, *History of Later Years of the Hawaiian Monarchy and the Revolution of 1893*, Hawaiian Gazette Co., Honolulu, 1896

Author unknown, *Coronation of Their Majesties the King and Queen of Hawaiian Islands, at Honolulu February 12, 1883*, Advertiser Steam Printing House, Honolulu, 1883

Stuart Banner, *Possessing the Pacific, Land, Settlers and Indigenous People from Australia to Alaska*, Harvard University Press, Cambridge (MA) 2007

Glen Barclay, *A History of the Pacific, From the Stone Age to the Present Day*, Sidgwick & Jackson, London, 1978

Harold Whitman Bradley, *The American Frontier in Hawaii*, Peter Smith, Gloucester (MA), 1968

I C Campbell, *A History of the Pacific Islands*, University of California Press, Berkeley, 1996

Stan Cohen, *Princess Victoria Kaiulani, and the Princess Kaiulani Hotel in Waikiki*, Pictorial Histories Publishing Co., 1997, Missoula (MO)

Theo Davies, *Letters Upon the Political Crisis in Hawaii, Second Series*, Bulletin Publishing Co., Honolulu, 1894

Gavan Daws, *Shoal of Time, A History of the Hawaiian Islands*, University of Hawaii Press, Honolulu, 1968 (1974)

Arthur Power Dudden, *The American Pacific, From the Old China Trade to the Present*, Oxford University Press, New York, 1992

John S Ewart K.C., *The Kingdom of Canada, Imperial Federation, The Colonial Conferences, The Alaska Boundary*, Toronto, Morang & Co., 1908

Frank Freidel, *The Presidents of the United States of America*, White House Historical Association/National Geographic Society, Washington, 1964

Walter Murray Gibson, Jacob Adler and Gwynn Barrett ed., *The Diaries of Walter Murray Gibson 1886, 1887*, University Press of Hawaii, Honolulu, 1973

James Andrew Gillis, *The Hawaiian Incident: An Examination of Mr. Cleveland's Attitude Toward the Revolution of 1893*, Lee and Shepard, Boston, 1897

Barry Gough, *The Royal Navy and the Northwest Coast of North America 1810 – 1914*, University of British Columbia Press, Vancouver, 1971

William Graves, *Hawaii*, National Geographic Society, Washington, 1970

Rhoda E A Hackler, *Iolani Palace*, Friends of Iolani Palace, Honolulu, 2016

Steven Hahn, *A Nation Without Borders, The United States and Its World in an age of Civil Wars, 1830-1910*, Penguin Books, New York, 2016

James L Haley, *Captive Paradise, A History of Hawaii*, St. Martin's Press, New York, 2014

A G Hopkins, *American Empire*, Princeton University Press, Princeton, 2018

Curtis Piehu Iaukea and Lorna Kahilipuaokalani Iaukea Watson, Niklaus R Schweizer (ed.), *By Royal Command, The Official Life and Personal Reminiscences of Colonel Curtis Pi'ehu Iaukea at the Court of Hawaii's Rulers*, Angel Inc., Honolulu, 1988

Donald D Johnson with Gary Dean Best, *The United States in the Pacific, Private Interests and Public Policies, 1784-1899*, Praeger, Westport (CT), 1995

G P Judd, *Hawaii An Informal History*, Collier, New York, 1974

Stacey L Kamehiro, *The Arts of Kinship: Hawaiian Art and National Culture of the Kalakaua Era*, University of Hawaii Press, Honolulu, 2009

Elizabeth Kieszkowski (ed.), *Na Hale Ho'ike'ike o Na Mikanele*, Mission Houses Museum, Honolulu, 2001

Stephen Kinzer, *Overthrow, America's Century of Regime Change From Hawaii to Iraq*, Times Books, Henry Holt and Company, New York, 2006

Stephen Kinzer, *The True Flag, Theodore Roosevelt, Mark Twain, and the Birth of American Empire*, Henry Holt and Company, New York, 2017

Mary H Krout, *Hawaii and a Revolution, The Personal Experiences of a Newspaper Correspondent in the Sandwich Islands During the Crisis of 1893 and Subsequently*, London, John Murray, 1898

Ralph S Kuykendall, *The Hawaiian Kingdom, Volume III, 1874 – 1893, The Kalakaua Dynasty*, University of Hawaii Press, Honolulu, 1967

Liliuokalani, *Hawaii's Story by Hawaii's Queen*, Lothrop, Lee & Shephard Co., Boston, 1898

Liliuokalani, *Hawaii's Story by Hawaii's Queen*, Mutual Publishing, Honolulu, 1990

Sharon Linnéa, *Princess Kaiulani, Hope of a Nation, Heart of a People*, Eerdmans Books for Young Readers, Grand Rapids (MI), 1999

Christopher Lloyd, *Pacific Horizons: The Exploration of the Pacific Before Captain Cook*, George Allen & Unwin Ltd., London, 1946

Captain A T Mahan, USN, *The Influence of Sea Power Upon History 1660 – 1783*, London, Sampson Low, Marston, Searle & Rivington, 1890

Robert Massie, *Nicholas and Alexandra*, Dell Publishing, New York, 1967

Matt K Matsuda, *Empire of Love, Histories of France and the Pacific*, Oxford University Press, Oxford, 2005

W David McIntyre, *Winding Up The British Empire In The Pacific Islands*, Oxford University Press, Oxford, 2014

Gordon Medcalf, *Hawaiian Royal Orders*, Oceania Coin Co., Honolulu, 1963

Gordon Medcalf and Ronald Russell, *Hawaiian Money, Standard Catalogue, 2nd ed.*, Ronald Russell, Honolulu/Washington, 1991

Kathleen Dickenson Mellen, *An Island Kingdom Passes, Hawaii Becomes American*, Hasting House, New York, 1958

William Michael Morgan, *Pacific Gibralter, U.S. – Japanese Rivalry Over the Annexation of Hawai'i, 1885 – 1898*, Naval Institute Press, Annapolis (MD), 2011

Edmund Morris, *The Rise of Theodore Roosevelt*, Ballantine Books, New York, 1979

Maxine Mrantz, *Hawaii's Tragic Princess, Kaiulani, The Girl who Never Got to Rule*, Aloha Publishing, Honolulu, 1980

Peter C Newman, *Caesars of the Wilderness, Company of Adventurers Volume II*, Viking, Toronto, 1987

William Adam Russ, Jr., *The Hawaiian Revolution (1893 – 94)* Susquehanna University Press, Selinsgrove (PA), 1959

Allan Seiden, *The Hawaiian Monarchy*, Mutual Publishing, Honolulu, 2014

Julia Flynn Siler, *Lost Kingdom, Hawaii's Last Queen, the Sugar Kings, and America's First Imperial Adventure*, Atlantic Monthly Press, New York, 2012

Scott C. S. Stone, *The Royal Hawaiian Band, Its Legacy*, Island Heritage Publishing, Waipahu (HI), 2004

J Patricia Morgan Swenson, *Treasures of the Hawaiian Kingdom*, Daughters of Hawai'i, Honolulu, 2007

Merze Tate, *The United States and the Hawaiian Kingdom: A Political History*, Yale University Press, New Haven (CT), 1965

Lorrin A Thurston, Andrew Farrell (ed.), *Memoirs of the Hawaiian Revolution*, Advertiser Publishing Company, Honolulu, 1936

Sarah Vowel, *Unfamiliar Fishes*, Riverhead Books, New York, 2011

Nancy Webb & Jean France Webb, *Kaiulani, Crown Princess of Hawai'i*, Mutual Publishing, Honolulu, 1998

Riánna Williams, *Queen Lili'uokalani, the Dominis Family, and Washington Place, their home*, Ka Mea Kakau Press, Honolulu, 2015

Richard A Wisniewski, *The Rise and Fall of the Hawaiian Kingdom, A Pictorial History*, Pacific Basin Enterprises, Honolulu, 1979

Dorthea Woodrun, *Governor Cleghorn, Princess Kaiulani and Ainahau; Recollections of a Gracious Era in Hawaii's History*, Island Development Corp., 1964, Honolulu

Kristen Zambucka, *Princess Kaiulani, The Last Hope of Hawaii's Monarchy*, 1976, Mana Publishing Co., Honolulu

Academic Papers

Ernest Andrade Jr., *Great Britain and the Hawaiian Revolution and Republic, 1893-1898*, The Hawaiian Journal of History, vol. 24 (1990)

Douglas V Askman, *Royal Standards of the Kingdom of Hawai'i, 1837-1893*, The Hawaiian Journal of History, vol. 47 (2013)

Ralph Thomas Kam, *The Legacy of Ainahau, The Geneology of Ka'iulani's Banyan*, The Hawaiian Journal of History, vol 45 (2011)

Marilyn Stassen-McLaughlin, *Unlucky Star: Princess Kaiulani*, The Hawaiian Journal of History, vol.33 (1999)

David A. Swanson, University of Washington, *The Number of Native*

Hawaiians and Part-Hawaiians in Hawaii, 1778 to 1900: Demographic Estimates by Age, With Discussion, Paper Presented at a Conference of the Canadian Population Society, Calgary, Alberta, June 2016

Merze Tate, *Canada's Interest in the Trade and the Sovereignty of Hawaii*, Canadian Historical Review, vol. XLIV, No. 1, March, (1963)

Merze Tate, *Great Britain and the Sovereignty of Hawaii, Pacific Historical Review* , Vol. 31, No. 4 Nov., 1962, University of California Press, Berkeley (CA) (1962)

Nicholas B Miller, *Trading Sovereignty and Labour: The Consular Network of Nineteenth-Century Hawai'i, The International History Review*, 2020, Vol 42, No. 2, (2020)

Internet Materials

Blount Report, 584 http://libweb.hawaii.edu/digicoll/annexation/blount/br0584.php

Library of Congress, *Commercial Reciprocity Treaty between the United States of America and the Kingdom of Hawaii*, loc.gov/law/help/us-treaties/bevans/b-hawaii-ust000008-0874.pdf

Metropolitan Museum of Art, *Necklace (lei niho palaoa)* early 19th century, accession of the Metropolitan Museum of Art, New York, https://www.metmuseum.org/art/collection/search/313842

Mindi Reid, Princess *Ka'iulani, Rose of Two Worlds*, Electric Scotland, https://electricscotland.com/history/women/wh36.htm

President John Tyler, *Special Message*, The American Presidency

494

Project   https://www.presidency.ucsb.edu/documents/
special-message-4235

Government Papers

Grover Cleveland, *President's Message Relating to the Hawaiian Islands (1893)*, in H.R. Exec. Doc. No. 47, 53d Cong.,2d Sess.

S M Collum, *Message from the President of the United States transmitting the Report of the Hawaiian Commission Appointed in Pursuance of the 'Joint Resolution' to Provide for Annexing the Hawaiian Islands to the United States, etc.*, Washington, Government Printing Office, 1898

Congress of the United States, House Committee on Foreign Affairs, United States Congress, *Intervention of United States Government in Affairs of Foreign Friendly Governments, Part 1*, U.S. Government Printing Office, Washington, 1893

Department of State, *Papers Relating to the Mission of James H. Blount*, United States Government Printing Office, Washington, 1893

Department of State, *Papers Relating to the Foreign Relations of the United States*, Transmitted to Congress With the Annual Message of the President, December 4, 1883, No. 329, Washington, 1883

Department of State, Office of the Historian, *Foreign Relations of the United States, 1894, Appendix II, Affairs in Hawaii,*

Robert C Lydecker, *Roster Legislatures of Hawaii 1841-1918, Constitutions of Monarchy and Republic; Speeches of Sovereigns and*

President, Board of Commissioners of Public Archives, Honolulu, 1918

Henry A Pierce, *An Argument before the Committee on Foreign Relations of the Senate of the United States, with regard to a treaty of reciprocity between the United States and the Hawaiian Islands*, Proceedings of the Senate Committee on Foreign Relations, Washington, January, 1875

Senate of the United States, *Report of the Committee on Foreign Relations, The United States and the Hawaiian Islands*, Senate of the United States, Washington, February 24, 1888

Joseph P Smith, Director, *Hawaii*, Bureau of the American Republics, Document 178, Part 14, Senate, 55th Congress, 2nd Sess. Washington, 1897

Audio-Visual Resources

Tom Coffman (originator) and Joy Chong-Stannard (director), *Nation Within, The Story of America's Annexation of the Nation of Hawaii*, Hawaii Public Television, Kaneohe, (HI.), 1998 (VHS Tape)

Vivian Ducat (originator) and Susan Fanshel (editor), *Hawaii's Last Queen*, Ducat Segal Productions (for The American Experience), WGBH (PBS), Boston, 1997 (VHS Tape)

Kristin Zambucka; Heather Kuupuaohelomakamae Marsh; Bill Ogilvie; John Lim; Leo Anderson Akana (originators), *A Cry of Peacocks*, Green Glass Productions, 1993 (VHS Tape)

CPSIA information can be obtained
at www.ICGtesting.com
Printed in the USA
BVHW031846310321
603864BV00001B/6